TWITCH
UPON A
STAR

The Bewitched
Life and Career of
ELIZABETH
MONTGOMERY

TWITCH
UPON A
STAR

HERBIE J PILATO

TAYLOR TRADE PUBLISHING
LANHAM • NEW YORK • BOULDER • LONDON

Published by Taylor Trade Publishing
An imprint of The Rowman & Littlefield Publishing Group, Inc.
4501 Forbes Boulevard, Suite 200, Lanham, Maryland 20706
www.rowman.com

16 Carlisle Street, London W1D 3BT, United Kingdom

Distributed by National Book Network

British Library Cataloguing in Publication Information Available

The hardback edition of this book was previously cataloged
by the Library of Congress as follows:

Pilato, Herbie J.
Twitch upon a star : the bewitched life and career of
Elizabeth Montgomery / Herbie J Pilato.
p.   cm.
Includes bibliographical references and index.
1. Montgomery, Elizabeth, 1933-1995.   2. Actresses—United States—Biography.
I. Title.
PN2287.M69335P55   2012
791.4302'8092—dc23
[B]
2012017147

ISBN 978-1-58979-749-9 (hardback)
ISBN 978-1-63076-025-0 (pbk : alk. paper)
ISBN 978-1-58979-750-5 (electronic)

∞ ™ The paper used in this publication meets the minimum requirements of American
National Standard for Information Sciences—Permanence of Paper for Printed Library
Materials, ANSI/NISO Z39.48-1992.

Printed in the United States of America

For the highest good of all those concerned . . .

Also by Herbie J Pilato:

Glamour, Gidgets, and the Girl Next Door:
Television's Iconic Women from the 50s, 60s, and 70s

The Essential Elizabeth Montgomery:
A Guide to Her Magical Performances

Retro Active Television:
An In-Depth History of Classic TV's Social Circuitry

The *Bewitched* Book

Bewitched Forever

The *Kung Fu* Book of Caine

The *Kung Fu* Book of Wisdom

The *Bionic* Book

Life Story: The Book of *Life Goes On*

NBC and Me: My Life as a Page in a Book

"Win, lose, or draw, I'm going to keep
on being Elizabeth Montgomery."

—Elizabeth Montgomery, 1965

"Lizzie didn't want to walk around for the
rest of her life being *Samantha*."

—Ronny Cox, friend and co-star of Elizabeth Montgomery's

"I ain't never met another woman I wanted to be like."

—*Belle Starr*, as played by Elizabeth Montgomery in the
1980 TV-movie of the same name

CONTENTS

PREFACE

In 1979, Elizabeth Montgomery appeared in the NBC TV-movie *Jennifer: A Woman's Story*, in which she played *Jennifer Prince*, the widow of a wealthy shipbuilding executive. In this backdoor pilot for a new series (that Montgomery chose not to pursue), *Jennifer* battled the highbrow board members of her late husband's company that she struggled to control.

On *Bewitched*, which originally aired on ABC from 1964 to 1972, Elizabeth portrayed the beloved nose-wriggling house-witch *Samantha Stephens*. In an episode from 1969, "The Battle of Burning Oak," *Samantha* and her feisty mother *Endora* (Agnes Moorehead) forged one of their rare but sturdy alliances, and set out to discredit the braggart members of a private mortal club. With this and every segment of *Bewitched*, Elizabeth played *Samantha* not so much as a *witch-with-a-twitch*, but as a woman who *just so happens* to be a witch who just so happens to twitch. How she machinated the magic was secondary to the sorcery itself; the supernatural acts were not nearly as pertinent as the distinguishing and ironic essence of *Samantha*: her humanity.

In like manner, Elizabeth eagerly utilized her benevolence with an extraordinary life and career, relinquishing an arrogance that could have easily evolved by way of her prestigious upbringing. As the liberal daughter of film and television legend Robert Montgomery, a staunch Republican, and Broadway actress Elizabeth Allen, an elegant Southern belle, she became disillusioned with the loftiness of Hollywood. She retained an unaffected demeanor on the set of any one of her nearly 500 individual television and film performances, or when approached on the street by some random fan. In either scenario, she relished the simple treasures of life, just as *Samantha* embraced the "everyday, mortal way."

Elizabeth, however, was not immortal in real life. Her light was dimmed too soon. On May 18, 1995, she died a victim of colon cancer—only two months after completing production of *Deadline For Murder*, her second CBS TV-movie as true-life Miami crime reporter Edna Buchanan (her first, *The Corpse Had a Familiar Face*, aired in 1994).

The shining star, the iconic actress, the outspoken political activist, the kind and loving mother to three children (with *Bewitched* producer/director William Asher: William, Jr., Robert, and Rebecca), and the very private and all-too-human woman was gone. It was devastating news for those within her intimate circle and to the millions of fans who continue to worship her from afar.

More than fifteen years after her painful demise, countless Facebook pages are adorned with her name; over 800,000 readers of *TV Guide* once voted her more popular than Barbara Eden, the star of classic TV's other supernatural blonde-led sitcom, *I Dream of Jeannie* (a blatant replica of *Bewitched* that infuriated Elizabeth); and her TV-movies remain classics.

In 1974, she received an Emmy nomination for *A Case of Rape*, which originally aired on NBC (a decade before the network aired the similarly themed film, *The Burning Bed* starring Farrah Fawcett). *Case* became the first issue-oriented TV-movie of its time, helped to change human rights and legislation for rape victims, and registered itself as one of the highest rated TV-movies in history.

In 1975, Elizabeth received another Emmy nomination for ABC's *The Legend of Lizzie Borden* (a namesake and alleged distant sixth cousin that she took a particular delight in portraying), which will soon be remade for the big screen.

Her feature films remain revered as well: 1955's *The Court-Martial of Billy Mitchell;* 1963's *Who's Been Sleeping in My Bed?* (in which she co-starred with Dean Martin and good friend Carol Burnett); and *Johnny Cool,* also released in 1963, directed by William Asher (who died in Palm Desert, California, on July 16, 2012, at age 90, due to complications from Alzheimer's disease), whom she met and fell in love with on the set.

Approximately one year later, on September 17, 1964, *Bewitched* debuted and was party to the escapist entertainment that America sorely needed amidst the upheaval of the era. Elizabeth, like her contemporary, actress Jane Fonda (to whom she was frequently compared in appearance and talent), protested the country's involvement with Vietnam. Her father was none-too-pleased with his daughter's political views. Such opposition was an earmark for their entire relationship until the day he died, in 1981, succumbing to cancer, like Elizabeth.

A few years later, she delivered the chilling narration for two controversial feature film documentaries: *Cover Up* (1988), which detailed the murky circumstances surrounding the Iran-Contra affair, and *The Panama Deception* (1992), about the American invasion of Panama (which won the Oscar that year for Best Feature-Length Documentary). Into this mix she, along with Elizabeth Taylor, another legendary actress and good friend, became one of the first courageous few to lend support in the mid-1980s to those suffering from AIDS, then a widespread and misunderstood disease affecting mostly homosexual men.

Subsequently, among her multitude of enthusiasts are those within the gay community. Her appeal and notoriety with this portion of the population is unparalleled thanks in part to her humanitarian efforts for research into AIDS (no longer just a "gay disease"). In 1992, she sealed that acclaim when she served as Co-Grand Marshall for the Los Angeles Gay Pride Parade with former *Bewitched* star Dick Sargent (who had recently exited the closet).

Through it all, the central message of *Bewitched*, as she suggested, believed, and trumpeted, was prejudice. *Samantha* was a sorceress isolated in a mortal world, a *witch out of water*, a repressed housewife instructed by an overbearing human husband (*Darrin*, played by Dick York, later replaced by Sargent) to never reveal her true identity.

Despite what critics perceived as confinement, *Samantha* was a free spirit, an independent soul. It was her choice to live the mortal life, and Elizabeth sought to convey the significance of that directive. Liberated women embraced her contributions with *Bewitched* and beyond, and *Samantha* became the first independent and *powerful* woman of the television age. She reflected the progress womanhood had made in the eyes of the public at large. This on the heels of Betty Friedan's blockbuster book, *The Feminine Mystique* which, when released in 1963 (one year before *Bewitched* debuted), documented more than any other single factor the launch of women's lib.

Like many raised in the glare of Hollywood, Elizabeth lived a life that was sprinkled with stardust and littered with trauma. She had loving but disparate relationships, including a core-shaping and life-shifting association with her father, who objected to her liberal views and her initial decision to become an actress.

She loved life and life loved her back, although not always as evenly, particularly in the form of marriages to first husband New York blue-blood Fred Cammann, and her second husband, the troubled and alcoholic actor Gig Young. Her third and fourth husbands, William Asher and actor Robert Foxworth (best known as *Chase Gioberti* on CBS-TV's *Falcon Crest*), were equal lights in her life, but like all true love affairs, even these relationships proved uneven.

Eight years after her divorce from Asher, she appeared in the 1982 TV mini-series *The Rules of Marriage*, which co-starred Elliot Gould. They played *Joan* and *Michael Hagen*, a successful suburban couple who found new partners after separating on their fifteenth wedding anniversary. Like much of Elizabeth's work, *Rules* broke the rules, when its characters "broke the fourth wall" and periodically talked to the camera, documentary style, as on contemporary shows *The Office* and *Modern Family*. But *The Rules of Marriage* was not a comedy, and no one was laughing on stage or off.

Joan Hagen was a seemingly happy affluent wife, and so was Elizabeth when wedded to Asher during the original reign of *Bewitched*. *Marriage* showcased the disintegration of a seemingly perfect marriage, as both husband and wife became involved in a series of affairs. Asher strayed from Elizabeth throughout their marriage and into the final years of *Bewitched*, which ultimately led to her two-year affair with *Bewitched* producer/director Richard Michaels and to their subsequent divorce and business dissolve. *Bewitched* was cancelled in 1972 and the Asher marriage ended in 1974, around the time she met and fell in love with Foxworth on the set of her TV-movie *Mrs. Sundance*. She didn't leave Asher for Foxworth; she fell in love with Foxworth after her marriage ended.

Foxworth was to have played *Michael Hagen* in *The Rules of Marriage*, but when cast as *Chase* on *Crest* he was replaced by Gould (formerly married to Barbra Streisand, another high-powered, strong-willed independent female force in the entertainment industry).

Elizabeth now sought work diametrically opposed to *Bewitched*, but periodically opted to play characters that represented her role in real life. She gave 100% to each character she portrayed, but savored parts that were leaps and bounds from *Samantha*. Unsuppressed ambitions may have taxed at least her first marriage (to Fred Cammann), but beyond that her career took a backseat to family. There was no stopping her always forthright but elegant manner; while the parallels between her and twitch-witch *Samantha*—her most famous role (for which she was Emmy-nominated five times)—were undeniable:

Elizabeth was born to two actors not of the ordinary (screen idol Robert Montgomery and Broadway thespian Elizabeth Allen). *Samantha* was born to two extraordinary beings (*Endora* and *Maurice*, played by acting legends Agnes Moorehead and Maurice Evans).

Elizabeth was raised in privilege with mansions, movie stars (like Bette Davis and James Cagney) as good friends, the best schools to attend (including Harvard-Westlake School in Los Angeles and the Spence School for Girls in New York), and traveled the world. *Samantha* was raised in opulence, had the best teachers the witch world had to offer, and enjoyed otherworldly travels.

Elizabeth shunned the arrogance of her elitist background and retained an approachable demeanor. *Samantha* rejected the arrogance of her supernatural heritage and remained down-to-earth.

Elizabeth's first upper crust New York husband (Cammann) was thrown out of the social register because he married an actress, a profession frowned upon by his aristocratic family. *Samantha's* clan believed her mortal husband *Darrin* disgraced their aristocratic family heritage, and just as Cammann wanted Elizabeth to give up her craft of acting, *Darrin* wanted *Samantha* to give up witchcraft.

Elizabeth made frequent attempts to stop acting but failed. Her talent was her destiny. Despite *Samantha's* earnest attempts to embrace the mortal life, she never quite stopped using her powers to assist *Darrin* and friends. Her magic was her birthright.

Elizabeth deeply loved each of her four husbands. *Samantha* deeply loved her two *Darrins*.

Elizabeth embraced her theatrical gifts and challenging marriages. *Samantha* embraced her special powers and mixed marriage.

Elizabeth raised her family in the traditional manner. *Samantha* raised her children in again—the "everyday mortal way."

Elizabeth played childhood games with her look-alike cousin Amanda

Panda Cushman. *Samantha's* adult life was challenged by her fun-loving look-alike cousin *Serena* (played by Elizabeth, but billed as *Pandora Spocks*).

Elizabeth became a beloved celebrity worldwide and *Queen of the TV-movies*. *Samantha* was elected *Queen of the Witches*.

Elizabeth was a political activist who defended her rights and the rights of others, from Vietnam to the Reagan era and beyond. *Samantha* fought city hall in the mortal world, defended her rights to the *Witches Council*, and decried arrogance in both realms.

Elizabeth represented the grassroots movement of the day: women's liberation. *Samantha* defended her personal *witch's honor*.

Elizabeth cherished her family and home life beyond Hollywood, and ultimately accepted her immortal legacy as *Samantha*. *Samantha* treasured her family and human life, and ultimately accepted her mortal existence.

This book is about Elizabeth's mortal existence. From the day she was born, she had a nervous facial tic that was destined to inspire *Samantha's* magical mugging twitch. It was a mere spec in a vast list of traits and characteristics, characters, and performances that appealed to a mass group of people; that's also what this book is about . . . and everything else in between.

INTRODUCTION

Elizabeth Montgomery welcomed me into her hushed world.

I was enamored with the rise, demise, and rebirth of *Bewitched*, and she was intrigued. She marveled in my appreciation of not only her most famous show, but her varied accomplishments, talents, and charitable ways. Initially reticent then unrestrained she, for the first time in twenty years, offered in-depth conversations about her life and career. She explained during the first of what would become four interviews in the spring and summer of 1989:

> It's a strange thing . . . I loathe to chat away about me. I've never liked it. I
> always hate interviews. I just want to act, and do the best job I can. Hopefully people will appreciate it. That's what my job is. It isn't sitting down
> and talking about me. If I were a gardener (which she fancied herself as
> around her home in Beverly Hills), I would be out there trying to make
> gardens as pretty as I could, and not expect people to come up to me and
> ask a lot of questions. What it boils down to is this: It's always easier for me
> to talk about other things than it is to talk about me.

She described our conversations as "cathartic." She spoke about her famous father, film and TV idol Robert Montgomery; her childhood; years of education; early motion pictures, stage, and television appearances. She addressed what it means to be an actress; her friendships with President John F. Kennedy (assassinated on November 22, 1963—the day rehearsals began for *Bewitched*), Carol Burnett, and her *Bewitched* co-stars, including Agnes Moorehead and Paul Lynde; her TV-movies and feature films and, of course, *Bewitched* itself. She discussed all she did and didn't understand about

I

herself and her massive following; all she gave, all she became, all she hoped to be, all she was: a wife, a mother, a friend, a TV legend, a pop-culture icon, a courageously bold endorser of human rights.

My *Bewitched* books concentrated on her most renowned performance, but a more expansive magical story was yet to be told. *Twitch Upon a Star: The Bewitched Life and Career of Elizabeth Montgomery* tells that story. The unpublished memories she shared with me in 1989 are now interspersed with her commentary from other interviews, before and after we met. Only following our chats did she allow for lengthier conversations with regard to *Bewitched* after she ended the show in 1972. She then seemed more comfortable discussing her career, specifically her days on *Bewitched* from which she had long kept safe distance. She later gave interviews to *One on One with John Tesh*, *The Dennis Miller Show*, *CBS This Morning*, and *The Advocate* magazine as well as to acclaimed film historian, preservationist, and author Ronald Haver, who for twenty years (he died in 1993) served as the curator and director for the Los Angeles County Museum of Art's film center. The latter interview transpired for a commentary track accompanying the fiftieth anniversary documentary 1991 laserdisc release of *Here Comes Mr. Jordan*, the 1941 film classic starring her father, Robert Montgomery.

Elizabeth and I also talked about her dad; as well as her mother, former Broadway actress Elizabeth Allen; and her maternal grandmother Rebecca Allen; all of whom played substantial roles in the development of her life and work; a career that she sometimes felt was overshadowed by *Bewitched*.

Yet she had little choice but to address her immortal link to *Samantha*. By the time we met in 1989, twenty-five years after *Bewitched's* debut, she and the show's popularity reined steady, expanded by way of nostalgic-oriented networks like Nick at Nite, TBS, and WGN. The series flooded the airwaves, she was finding a new audience, and original and novice fans were falling in love with her all over again. When I asked if she understood just how happy she makes viewers, how classic and contemporary fans adore her just as much, if not more as when the show premiered in 1964, she replied:

> Well, I do now. I mean, you've pointed it out to me certainly. I know they like the show and everything. But it's never been anything that's kind of been bounced in my face as much as it has now with your focus on it. And

I tell you something if only one person feels as you do then that's fine with me. Something was accomplished, because your dedication to this has been absolutely extraordinary. It's the work that is to me its kind of own reward. I know that sounds terribly Pollyanna, but I don't care because that's true for me. And it's the same with you. To put that much energy into what you have done and for us to be sitting here is very good for both of us. It's good for you on every level that you have explained to me, and it's fun for me to sit down and talk about it with somebody who enjoys it that much because I've done so much since *Bewitched*. While doing something you're so concentrated on it, you don't get a chance to sit back and say, *Wasn't that or isn't that fun?* I'd like to think that the stuff that I've done since has meant something to somebody on various different levels. Because I've tried to be real diverse in the work that I've done since I left *Bewitched*.

Her post-1989 interviews with others proved insightful from a personal standpoint; one in particular stands out from the pack. In 1990, veteran television journalist Ann Hodges, mother to a dear friend, talked with Elizabeth for *The Houston Chronicle* about her CBS Hallmark Hall of Fame TV-film *Face to Face*. After the interview, Ann put down her pen and paper and said, "I just have to tell you. My daughter is very good friends with one of your biggest fans." Before Ann had a chance to finish her sentence, Elizabeth blurted out the name, "Herbie!"

There are countless individuals and fan-based groups who assuredly know the more minute trivia related to Elizabeth's entire body of work, but that she would think of me amidst a random reference remains a cherished memory and not insignificant praise. I was honored to hear of that interchange which I will forever humbly embrace. I can do nothing less. Elizabeth was one of the kindest people I ever met, and one of the least arrogant in or outside of Hollywood. I admired her lack of pretension and strive to meet that standard every day.

That said, she was also one of the most complicated individuals on the planet—a conundrum that makes her story so compelling—and one in turn that I felt driven, dare I say, *bewitched*, to explore and share within these pages. This book is also filled with collected reflections from her family members and friends, and coworkers from her TV-movies, feature films, TV guest-star appearances, and other performances and, of course, *Bewitched*. Thoughts from interviews that she and others granted to me appear alongside selected commentary previously published in studio bios, press releases, newspaper and magazine articles, books, TV talk shows and news programs, and online sources.

There are new memories from my exclusive interviews with her friend and fellow actress Sally Kemp (whom Elizabeth met while attending the New York American Academy of Dramatic Arts and who offers some of the most profound insight into Elizabeth's young life); Florence *The Brady Bunch* Henderson (also from the Academy); her TV-movie co-stars and friends, including David Knell (who played her son on *Belle Starr*); Ronny Cox (from *A Case of Rape* and *With Murder in Mind*); the Oscar-winning actor Cliff Robertson (who died only two weeks after granting his interview); *Bewitched* guest star Eric Scott (who would later be cast in *The Waltons*); Peter Ackerman—son of *Bewitched* executive producer Harry Ackerman; *Bewitched* writer Doug Tibbles; Emmy-winning actor and Elizabeth's fellow political advocate Ed Asner (*The Mary Tyler Moore Show*); actress, comedienne, women and children's advocate, and political blogger Lydia Cornell (*Too Close For Comfort*), among many others.

Also included are never-before-published commentary from my original *Bewitched* interviews in 1988 and 1989 with Harry Ackerman, William Asher, Dick York, and Dick Sargent (the two *Darrins*); David *Larry Tate* White, and others associated with the series, including *Bewitched* director Richard Michaels who, in 2006, went on *Entertainment Tonight* and admitted to his affair with Elizabeth. It was an affair that contributed not only to the demise of *Bewitched* and the Asher marriage, but to the end of Michaels' nuptials to Kristina Hansen.

When I interviewed Michaels in 1988, I was not aware of his liaison with Elizabeth, but you'd think I'd have had a clue.

We met in Santa Monica for lunch at The Crest, then a new, but very regular eatery, along the lines of Perkins or Denny's, if maybe just slightly upscale. Michaels was cordial, informative, intelligent, and his memories of *Bewitched* and all that it entailed were astounding. But as we finished our interview, he started to tear up. "When you talk with Elizabeth," he instructed me, "you be sure to tell her that I said there will never be anyone else like her in the world. Never!"

Originally taken aback by the statement, especially when he made me vow to relay it, I ultimately agreed, and upon meeting Elizabeth, kept my promise.

After hearing Michaels' message, she looked at me and said, "That's very sweet." And that was that. With hindsight being 20/20, it appeared that Michaels was still in love with Elizabeth, and most likely remains so. (Who wouldn't be?)

Another unexpected event occurred when, upon my second interview with Elizabeth, she surprised me by having invited *Bewitched* actor David White to join us. He and Elizabeth had not seen one another since the series ended in 1972. At the time, that was approximately eighteen years. Portions of their individual and interlocking commentary from that day, all never before published, now appear in this book.

Who would have thought that Elizabeth and David, along with so many other *Bewitched* luminaries, Dick York, Dick Sargent, Harry Ackerman, Alice Ghostley (who portrayed *Samantha's* bubbling witch maid *Esmeralda*), et al. would be gone only a few years later? White died in 1990; York in 1992; Sargent in 1994; and Elizabeth in 1995; the latter three of which while only in their sixties.

Unfortunately, I was unable to attend Elizabeth's memorial service at the Canon Theatre in Beverly Hills on June 18, 1995. I was also unable to attend a ceremony in her name, when finally, if posthumously, she received her designated star on the Hollywood Walk of Fame, January 4, 2008.

Fortunately, my good friend and radio journalist Jone Devlin managed to at least attend the *star* ceremony, and shared with me what transpired at the event. In addition to what was reported in the press, and from further research, I learned that it was an illustrious event.

Unfortunately, Sally Kemp, Lizzie's best friend from their youth, was also unable to be present at the *star* ceremony, at which the name *Elizabeth Montgomery* was so elegantly chiseled in glittering stone on that famous walkway. While pleased that her friend was immortalized in exactly that manner, Sally was puzzled as to why her friend would later answer to anything but her formal birth name.

"It's strange for me to hear Elizabeth referred to as *Lizzie*," Kemp told me in 2012. "Never while I knew her was she called that. She didn't like *Liz* either . . . only *Elizabeth*. *Lizzie* must have been born after she and Gig (Young) decamped to L.A. I just wonder where it came from."

At the Walk of Fame ceremony the answer was provided by Liz Sheridan, best known as *Helen Seinfeld*, Jerry's mother on NBC's iconic 1990s non-sitcom *Seinfeld*. Sheridan is also known as *Mrs. Ochmonek*, a *Mrs. Kravitz*-type neighbor on NBC's 1980s alien-com *Alf* which like *Bewitched* was an otherworldly, fish-out-of-water sitcom (*Samantha* was a witch in a mortal world; *Alf* was an alien in a human world).

Best friends in their later years Sheridan was introduced to Elizabeth through writer William Blast, who in 1974 penned *The Legend of Lizzie Borden*. From what I learned Sheridan explained at the ceremony, Elizabeth wanted to be called *Lizzie* from the moment she played *Borden*. It was a nice play on a name, especially when Sheridan was around, because Sheridan's younger sister could never quite pronounce the name *Elizabeth*, the formal first name she and Lizzie shared. According to what Sheridan explained, it always came out *Dizabeth*.

In the event, Sheridan became Dizzie and Montgomery became Lizzie, and there they were . . . *Lizzie* and *Dizzie*.

So, however serious Elizabeth was about her life and career she knew when not to take herself seriously. She imbued a playful spirit towards *Borden* that stemmed from her childhood. "I used to get teased all the time about the childhood rhyme, *Lizzie Borden took an ax*, etc," she said in 1989.

Robert Foxworth and I were apparently then slated to reap the brunt of that teasing, so to speak, as when Elizabeth revealed to me a memory she had of the two vacationing at her summer home shortly after the *Lizzie Borden* movie aired. At one point during the getaway, it was raining, and he was kneeling in front of the fireplace, attempting to ignite a flame. "And I had an ax in my hand," she remembered, "because we had just chopped some wood."

Foxworth had then turned toward her, pointed to the ax, and made a request: "Would you please put that thing down?"

The ax was making him nervous and she knew it, but with a devilish smile belying what she recognized as the truth, Elizabeth asked, ever so innocently, "What?"

He reiterated: "Would you please put that thing down?!"

She finally complied, and once they cozied up to the fire, he made an admission: "I have to tell you. That ax really gives me the creeps."

She told me this story in 1989 at her Beverly Hills home, while holding the prop ax from the *Borden* film, and standing next to another fireplace. So I knew exactly how he felt. "You see," she said with utter delight, as I sat squirming. "This is the actual ax. It used to have hairs on it, and I keep telling people not to dust it, but they do. And they've taken some of the blood off it. It's not very sharp. But it would do the job."

She had a wicked sense of humor, a measure of which I had already experienced.

In the early part of 1989, and upon her permission, Bill Asher had given me her phone number. I called her, and did not hear back from her until four months later. Or at least that's how long it seemed.

This occurred about ten years before cell and smart phones hit the mainstream market. At best I stayed close to my old-fangled answering machine, but I still missed her call—on several occasions; although she later confessed to hanging up many times without leaving a message.

Why? She didn't know how to respond to the *Bewitched* theme and "twitching" sound effects from the show's opening credits that I had taken great pains to strategically record on my machine (again, in a pre-high-tech-phone-apps-ring-tone era).

We finally did connect while I was living in Santa Monica and had one day temporarily stepped away from the phone to place a load of towels in the wash. I later noticed the flashing message light on my machine; pressed *play*, and heard: "Hi! It's Lizzie Montgomery. I keep missing you, you keep missing me. This is crazy!"

Like Sally Kemp, not only was I surprised to hear the nickname *Lizzie* being voiced by the actress herself, but I was somewhat frazzled in general that *Elizabeth Montgomery* had just telephoned my house and left a message on my machine. In any event, I collected my thoughts, waited a few moments and then called her back. She picked up the phone, we exchanged *hellos*, and I apologized for missing her call.

"I was doing my laundry," I said, as if talking with an old friend, which in a way I was. I had been watching *Bewitched* nearly my entire life and easily recognized Elizabeth's voice and mannerisms.

Upon hearing of such a humble task, she responded with her trademark giggle and said, "And so you should."

It was so typically Elizabeth to put me or anyone else at ease. Our conversations continued and she was nothing less than charming and disarming with each subsequent visit, either by phone or in person.

At our first meeting, we were both nervous. I tripped over her coffee table, and she carefully weighed her words. During our second meeting, we considered the signatory roles she played in my life, and she was slightly more relaxed and free with her phrasing. At one point, we took our conversation from her living room to the kitchen so she could feed her dog Zuelika. A small countertop TV was blaring in the background, set on a PBS cooking show.

I picked up our conversation: "You know . . . whatever critic has reviewed you in the past . . ."

"I know," she interrupted, "because forget it . . . *you're worse than my father*, right?"

I smiled, but at the time, did not fully grasp the assumption. Only later did I comprehend what she meant. In researching this book, I realized just how muddled her relationship was with her father. As individuals, they were each complicated. In combination, they were confounding.

But whenever she spoke of him, in our conversations or with others, there was an underlined air of respect. He and her mother, actress Elizabeth Allen, had raised her well, in tandem with Allen's mother, Elizabeth's beloved grandmother, Rebecca "Becca" Allen.

Becca also had a positive influence on Elizabeth's brother, Robert "Skip" Montgomery, Jr., whom I had the privilege of speaking with shortly after she passed away in 1995.

A few years later, I was saddened to learn of Skip's own passing in 2000. When Bill Asher told me, I wanted to call Skip's wife Melanie, but never did. I regret that, and not speaking with Skip more often. But I'll never forget our first conversation. He was so cordial and down to earth, just like Elizabeth. As much as they were blessed in life, neither possessed an ounce of arrogance.

He called to inquire what I wanted to do with the crystal unicorn I had given to Elizabeth upon our first meeting. *Samantha* liked unicorns; and so did Elizabeth; and she loved presents and appreciated gifts, even in the most token form.

Yet the crystal unicorn was no small token. At the time, I had little extra cash to spend on so extravagant a gift. Elizabeth, of course, was worth it, but she was stunned when she saw it. She turned toward me, gave me a big hug, and said in that lyrical voice of hers, "Oh my . . . you know, don't you? You know!"

Skip had the same kind of upbeat, chipper, affable voice.

"Hey, Herbie!" he said that day when I picked up the phone. "How ya' doin'? This is Skip Montgomery. . . . Listen, I have the unicorn that you gave Elizabeth. Do you want it back?"

"No, no, no," I replied. "You keep it. I wanted her to have it—and I want you to keep it in her memory."

We talked a little more, exchanged addresses, and the following December, I received a Christmas card from him and Melanie, a special memento I cherish to this day more than I could have ever treasured the return of that unicorn.

The entire Montgomery family has always been kind to me, including Elizabeth's children, as well as Robert Foxworth, who I had profiled for *Sci-Fi Entertainment* magazine in 1996. And certainly, too, Bill Asher.

One day, in between interviews with Elizabeth, she telephoned me out of the blue, just to see how I was. That morning, I was upset. The strings were broken on the guitar my father had purchased for me when I was a young boy. I was desperate to fix them, not because I played the guitar so well—which I never properly learned to do—but because the instrument held sentimental value. (Like that Christmas card from Skip would years later.)

For some reason, I explained all of this to Elizabeth and to my surprise she in turn told me that Billy Asher, Jr. would fix my weeping guitar.

"Why don't you bring it to my son?"

"Uh? What do you mean?"

"That's what he does. He owns a music shop in Santa Monica."

"You're kidding? I live in Santa Monica."

"Where?"

"On 17th and Santa Monica Blvd."

"I'm going to make this real simple for you. His shop is at 17th and Wilshire Blvd."

"That's just up the street."

"Then you better get going."

We said goodbye, I hung up, packed my guitar and was out the door.

By the time I reached Wilshire, Elizabeth had already called Billy to tell him I was on my way. When I arrived at his shop, he was standing at the counter. I shook his hand, explained about the guitar, and a few days later, it was like new again.

We chatted about his Mom, and I immediately noticed he had inherited her down-to-earth demeanor. When I told him so, he shared a few stories of what it was like growing up as not only her son, but the son of the legendary director Bill Asher.

He recalled a time in 1968, when he was just four years old, and a certain bewitching "screen transfer" proved somewhat confusing for him.

One Thursday night at around eight o'clock, he was at home watching his Mom on TV. It just so happened that Thursday night was the one day a week when the *Bewitched* cast and crew worked later than usual. Elizabeth did not usually arrive home until about 8:15 or 8:30 PM, but this one night she walked in the Asher's front door, just as *Samantha* popped out on *Bewitched*. Eight-year-old Billy was startled. "Geez, Mommy," he said, ". . . you really *are* a witch."

Elizabeth offered a careful explanation: "No, Honey . . . I just play one on TV."

Another time, when Billy was a teenager, circa 1977, he was again in the Asher living room but this time with a friend who was unaware of his heritage. At one point, Elizabeth walked in the room to get a magazine off the coffee table.

His friend screamed, "Oh, my gosh! It's Elizabeth Montgomery!"

"Naw," Billy said, ever carefree. "That's just my mom."

Not one to boast about position or social status, Billy, along with his brother Robert (named for Elizabeth's father) and sister Rebecca (named for her grandmother Becca) always chose to walk with dignity and integrity, as they do to this day.

Rebecca has always been cordial in the few phone conversations we've shared, displaying her mother's sense of humor each time. When I first talked with her, it took her a few weeks to call me back—just as it had been with Elizabeth. When I mentioned this to Rebecca, she laughed and said, "It must be genetic."

Genes had everything to do with it, especially when it came to Elizabeth's grandmother Becca, for whom her daughter was named—and whom she brought up at the close of our third interview in 1989—following my confession.

"You know who I really am, don't you?" I posed, if somewhat cryptically.

"No," she said, followed by a cautious pause, ". . . who?"

"I'm your guardian angel."

Surprised and relieved, she smiled sweetly and said, "The last person who referred to themselves that way was my Grandmother Becca. And if it's true—that you are indeed my guardian angel sent to replace her—well, then you better do one hell of a good job."

More than twenty years after that exchange, I make an earnest attempt to do just that with this book, which could be described as part biography, part media history guide, part psychology book, part mystic primer, part political dossier, all trustingly compelling.

But Lizzie placed high expectations on biographies, in particular, referring here to the one-page actor profiles that publicists for the studios and networks put together to promote the TV show or film in which a given actor is currently starring:

> I've always found them very self-conscious and they've always bothered me. I've never found one that somebody's written that I've liked. I always think they are dry and stupid, and don't really mean much to anybody.

Hopefully, *Twitch Upon a Star: The Bewitched Life and Career of Elizabeth Montgomery*, will mean something to someone—be it a member of Elizabeth's family, a friend, a fan—because it's a real story, a human story, an honest story—because sincerity was one of the many virtues which Elizabeth held dear. It's a profile in humility and generosity because such traits shaped who she was, strived to be, and became, and who she remains in the hearts and minds of millions. It's a portrait painted with reminiscences of her playful spirit, intelligent mind, and expansive resume; it's the sum of her intricacies and complexities.

I agonized over whether or not to present particular passages in this book; some may be disturbing to read; they certainly proved challenging for me to report. I'd type in specific paragraphs and then delete them; I'd paste them back in and then cut them out again. Finally, I decided to buckle down and include them because it was time to address the elephants in the room. The previous books were fan letters about a fantasy TV show, written as though seen through rose-colored glasses. With this book, I had a job to do. This time, it's not a fairytale, but a true love story, and all true love stories are earmarked with happy and sad elements. As a human being, I was forced to ponder those elements; as a journalist, I couldn't ignore what I heard, some statements of which were glaring. In previous books, as Elizabeth's "angel," confident, friend, or fan, I regret ignoring those statements; had I found the courage to reveal them, *this* story may have had a different ending.

I also sensed that if I had not elected to write an honest biography about Elizabeth, eventually someone else might do so and not as delicately as I believe the material is presented within these pages.

In either case, it was clear to me that Elizabeth was multitalented, multi-faceted and multi-complex; reclusive and protective; generous to a fault but private. She was anything but easy to figure out, certainly more challenging to analyze than any of her performances, and she delivered diverse interpretations of a myriad of characters with what appeared to be total ease.

One of her more off-beat roles was that of private detective *Sara Scott* in the 1983 CBS TV-movie *Missing Pieces*, a mystery story that was adapted from Karl Alexander's novel *A Private Investigation*. Similarly, this book detects and connects the missing pieces of a clandestine and extraordinary existence as it expounds on the amazing journey of a public figure who employed her widespread image for a better world. It's for the multitudes who remain charmed by the contrasting work of an actress before, during, and after her superstar-making twitch as a witch named *Samantha*, a beloved character who retained a fiercely independent spirit amidst other unique roles that were brought to life by a majestic, courageous, and real-life heroine named Elizabeth Montgomery.

At its core, *Twitch Upon a Star: The Bewitched Life and Career of Elizabeth Montgomery,* is about a celebrated individual who, for the sake of clarity, simplicity, and intimacy, and in tribute to her unaffected demeanor, will from here on be mostly referred to as either "Elizabeth" or "Lizzie," both which she so modestly and endearingly insisted on being known as at different times throughout her life and career.

PART I

Prewitched

"I just never had the desire to be a star."

—Elizabeth Montgomery, *Look Magazine*, January 26, 1965

$\mathcal{O}$ne

~

Once Upon a Time

"I like to grow naturally instead of being pruned into formality."
—Elizabeth Montgomery, *TV Radio Mirror
Magazine*, November 1969

Elizabeth Montgomery literally grew up on television, making her small screen debut on December 3, 1951 in "Top Secret," an episode of her father's heralded anthology series, *Robert Montgomery Presents*, which aired on NBC between 1950 and 1957. She'd appear in a total of twenty-eight episodes, but it was in "Secret" that she played none other than the apple of her father's eye. Written by Thomas W. Phipps and directed by Norman Felton, this episode also featured Margaret Phillips (as *Maria Dorne*), James Van Dyk (*Edmund Gerry*), John D. Seymour (*Dawson*), and Patrick O'Neal (*Brooks*):

> Foreign service agent *Mr. Ward* (Robert Montgomery) brings his daughter *Susan* (Lizzie) on a mission to a country on the brink of revolution with spies on all sides complicating the matter at hand.

The "Secret" title may have represented Elizabeth's off-screen desire for privacy, while other *Presents* headings also proved significant, such as "Once Upon a Time," written by Theodore and Mathilda Ferro; airing May 31,

1954. This time, Elizabeth played a newlywed who contemplates how different life might have been had she married someone else.

In real life, Lizzie didn't just contemplate that notion, she lived it . . . four times, with Fred Cammann, Gig Young, Bill Asher, and Robert Foxworth.

Ten years after the "Time" episode of *Presents* aired, *Bewitched* debuted with the Sol Saks pilot, "I *Darrin*, Take This Witch, *Samantha*," narrated by Jose Ferrer. The show opened with his first line, "Once upon a time . . ."

Whether represented on *Robert Montgomery Presents* or recited on *Bewitched*, it was a fairytale phrase that Lizzie adored and which ignited her interest in both projects, especially *Bewitched*. As she recalled in 1989, Bill Asher was in the room when she first read that term in the initial *Samantha* script.

"Okay, I love it!" she said.

"That's it?" Bill wondered. "*Once upon a time*, and you love it?"

"Yeah!" she mused. "Anything that starts out that way can't be all that bad."

It was a spontaneous decision that intrinsically represented the essence of her carefree spirit which, in turn, contributed in no small measure to the show's enormous success.

In fact, before Jose Ferrer got the job, she had asked her father if he would narrate the *Bewitched* pilot. In the interview she granted to Ronald Haven for the *Jordan* laserdisc, she referenced her dad's decline to speak life into *Bewitched*, calling his response, "very strange":

"No . . . I don't think so."

"Why not?"

"It's your show."

"Ah, ok. All right."

Elizabeth was disappointed, and she later told him so. She would have enjoyed him kicking off *Bewitched*, her new series in 1964, just as he had given a jumpstart to her TV career when she made her small-screen debut on *Robert Montgomery Presents* in 1951.

For Lizzie, success was at times a burden, especially when it came to public revelations. For one, her age was a sensitive issue, cloaked in a chicane. But as author and genealogist James Pylant explains, "Celebrity genealogies are always hard to trace." In 2004, Pylant authored *The Bewitching Family Tree of Elizabeth Montgomery* for genealogymagazine.com. "Biographical data abounds," he said, "yet there's no guarantee of accuracy."

Elizabeth played into such wriggle room. Various studio and network press bios document her birth year as 1936 and 1938. In reality, it was 1933, as recorded in the State of California, California Birth Index, 1905–1995, published in Sacramento by the State of California Department of Public Health, Center for Health Statistics.

When she died in 1995, a few obituaries listed her age as fifty-seven, trimming five years off her birth date. Others offered conflicting details about her marital status: some said she was single at the time of her demise; some said she was survived by her fourth husband, Robert Foxworth.

But the "marital mystery," as Pylant put it, was orchestrated by the self-protective Lizzie, who kept a step ahead of the press. She viewed her relationship with Foxworth as confidential. Even their marriage in 1993 was shrouded from the media. The event took place at the Los Angeles apartment of her manager Barry Krost and not a soul knew about it until after the fact.

Nevertheless, she appears on the Social Security Death Index as "Elizabeth Asher," the surname of her third ex-husband, *Bewitched* producer/director William Asher. There, at least, her birth date is correct—April 15, 1933—although "Elizabeth A. Montgomery" is the name listed on her death certificate. The "A" is either for "Asher" or "Allen," the maiden name of her mother, actress Elizabeth Allen.

According to A&E's *Biography, Elizabeth Montgomery: A Touch of Magic* (which originally aired on February 15, 1999), Lizzie's middle name was "Victoria," a moniker sometimes linked with royalty, as is the name "Elizabeth" itself.

But that fits. From the mid-1970s until her demise in 1995, she was known as *Queen of the TV-Movies*. On *Bewitched*, *Samantha* was crowned *Queen of the Witches* (in the episode, "Long Live the Queen," September 7, 1967); before that *Aunt Clara*'s (Marion Lorne) bumbling magic mishaps forced Sam's introduction to *Queen Victoria* (Jane Connell in "Aunt Clara's Queen Victoria Victory," March 9, 1967).

Before Lizzie basked in the sparkle of stardom as *Samantha*, she was born in the shadow of Robert Montgomery's fame. The story of who she was begins with him; the seeds of who she became were indelibly planted by this versatile actor and political idealist—a father who was just as complex as his daughter; a daughter who had a father complex.

Five years after his marriage to Broadway actress Elizabeth Allen on April 24, 1928, Lizzie was born into her privileged childhood, at the peak of his film popularity.

Talented, handsome, athletic, rich, and famous, Robert had the right social credentials, coupled with a solid intellect. Before his stable career on the small screen of the 1950s, he was a feature film legend of the 1930s and 1940s.

Although he was a Republican, and she a Democrat, Lizzie followed in his social advocacy. It was difficult for her to fathom and accept the scope of his notoriety before she ever began to question her own. She would later ponder the harvested influence over a legion of *Bewitched* buffs, because she had seen the role celebrity played in her father's life. Once she glittered with fame, it was hard for her to embrace praise even from those whose lives she helped improve.

A political promoter rooted with a conservative outlook, her father held a stoic position in moderate contrast to her liberal stance; but both believed in the American dream (and the freedom that goes along with it).

In 1935, he was elected to the first of four terms as president of S.A.G., the Screen Actors Guild. It was here his political agenda began to take shape. In this capacity, he gained publicity in 1939 when he helped expose labor racketeering in the film industry. He went on to become a lieutenant in the U.S. Navy Reserve, an assistant naval attaché at the American Embassy in London, an attendant at a naval operations room in the White House, a commander over a PT boat in the Pacific, and an operations officer during the D-Day invasion of France. He was awarded the Bronze Star and later decorated as Chevalier of the French Legion of Honor.

In 1947, he headed the Hollywood Republican Committee to elect
Thomas E. Dewey as President. That same year he testified as a *friendly
witness* in the first round of the House Un-American Activities Committee,
denouncing communist infiltration in Hollywood. Following President
Eisenhower's 1952 campaign, he was called on by the Principal Head of
State to serve as a special staff consultant to television and public communications—the first individual to hold such a media post for the White House.

Robert came to Eisenhower's attention because of his affiliation with
Robert Montgomery Presents. During the 1960s he was engaged in a futile
campaign against the practices of commercial TV, which he summarized in
the book *An Open Letter from a Television Viewer* (J. H. Heineman, 1968).
Also in the 1960s, the decade in which his daughter would begin to turn the
world on with her twitch, Robert served as a communications consultant to
John D. Rockefeller III and a director of R. H. Macy, the Milwaukee
Telephone Company, and the Lincoln Center for the Performing Arts.
From 1969 to 1970 he was president of Lincoln Center's Repertory Theatre.

Steven J. Ross is the author of *Hollywood Left And Right: How Movie
Stars Shaped American Politics* (Oxford University Press, 2011). On April 22,
2012, Ross appeared on C-SPAN at the Los Angeles Festival of Books.
When asked what role Robert Montgomery played in the Hollywood/
political game, he replied:

> Robert Montgomery actually had gone to prep school with George Mur-
> phy and the two of them were very close friends and Murphy . . . during
> the late '40s and '50s was a very prominent Republican activist. In fact, he
> was Louis B. Mayer's [MGM executive] point man going around the coun-
> try and when in 1952 Eisenhower wanted some help from Hollywood, or
> should I say the GOP got Eisenhower help, the two people who advised
> him on media strategy were Montgomery and Murphy. And Eisenhower
> liked the two of them so much that he basically told his Madison Avenue
> firm that had been hired to do the TV, "You can keep writing the ads, but
> they're going to show me how to appear on TV." Afterwards, Eisenhower
> asked both men to come to Washington with him. Murphy kindly deferred
> and Montgomery still kept his career but he actually had an office in Wash-
> ington to help Eisenhower for eight years with sort of media appearances
> and helping him stage his presence. Remember . . . this is a period when
> TV is just really emerging as a national phenomenon and politicians don't

really know how to deal with television. They were teaching them things like how to use makeup, what color glasses to use, how to face a camera . . . how to do sound bites . . . how to hold your body, camera angles . . . everything that a sophisticated actor would learn, they taught to Eisenhower.

As recorded in James Pylant's expertly researched *Bewitching* article Robert Montgomery was born Henry Montgomery, Jr. on May 21, 1904 in Duchess County, New York.

Beacon is commonly given as his birthplace, though he was actually born in Fishkill Landing. (Beacon was formed from the adjoining towns of Fishkill Landing and Matteawan in 1913.) Metro-Goldwyn-Mayer (MGM) promoted Robert Montgomery's movie persona as a sophisticated, well-bred socialite by embellishing the elite family background of its handsome star. And while the actor was *born in a large house on the banks of the Hudson River*, and his father served as an executive of a rubber company, the 1920 Federal Census leaves a somewhat different impression. Fifty-two-year-old Henry Montgomery, the vice president of a rubber factory, and Mary W., age forty-seven, with sons Henry, Jr., age sixteen, and Donald, age fourteen (all New Yorkers by birth), boarded in a Beacon hotel kept by William Gordon. Henry, Sr., was a first generation American, his father being Irish and his mother was Scottish. Mary W.'s father was a Pennsylvanian, while her mother was from the West Indies. Twenty years earlier, the 1900 Federal Census shows the newly wedded Montgomerys ("years married: 0") boarded in William Gordon's hotel, then in Fishkill. Private secretary Henry Montgomery (Sr.), age 32 (born in May of 1868) and 'Mai W.,' age 24 (born in March of 1876) were among the hotel's many boarders. Mrs. Montgomery's birthplace is listed as New Jersey and her mother's birthplace is Jamaica. Robert Montgomery's mother is named in biographies of her son as Mary Weed Barnard, but her maiden name was actually *Barney*. At the time of the 1900 federal census, the Montgomerys had been married a little over six months, their marriage date being 14 December 1899. Mrs. Montgomery appears twice on the federal census in 1900, the second instance being as 'May W. Barney,' age twenty-five, born in March of 1875 in New Jersey. Her marital status was indicated as single, then written over to read *married*. She is named as a daughter of eighty-one-year-old Nathan Barney, who rented a Third Street home in Brooklyn, wife Mary A., age fifty-six (born in October 1843), sons George D., age thirty-four (born in October 1865 in Connecticut), Nathan C., age twenty-seven (born in June 1873 in New Jersey), and Walter S., age eighteen (born October 1882 in New Jersey). A twenty-three-year-old Irish servant also made her home with the family. Mr. Barney was born in Pennsylvania, and Mrs. Barney was born in 'Jamaica, W. I.,' a fact consistent with what May W. Montgomery supplied in 1900. According to *Genealogy of the Barney Family in America*, Mary Weed Barney was born on 30 March 1875 in Bayonne, Hudson County, New Jersey, to Nathan Barney, Jr. and his second wife, the former Mary A. Deverell. The Barney genealogy identifies the parents of Henry Montgomery, Sr., as Archibald Montgomery and the former Margaret Edminston of Brooklyn. Henry Montgomery, a one-year-old, is found in the household of Irish-born Archibald Montgomery—a prosperous shipping merchant—and Margaret (born in Scotland) on the rolls of the 1870 Federal Census in Brooklyn.

In 1970, Robert Montgomery gave an interview to Richard Lamparski for his book, *Whatever Became Of . . . ? Volume III* (Ace Books, 1970). He explained how he had to support himself after his father, "an executive with a rubber company," died and left the family without an income.

As Lizzie expressed to Ronald Haver in 1991, "Daddy had to quit school and go to work, to help support the family; and his father just kind of fell apart."

That's putting it lightly. According to Pylant, Henry, Sr. was depressed, suffered a nervous breakdown, and subsequently committed suicide:

Not only did Robert Montgomery have to cope with the tragedy of his father's death, he had to face a financial crisis as well as the social stigma of having a suicide in the family. Henry Montgomery's nervous breakdown was also a public reminder of the scandal that unfolded in newspapers a generation earlier when Archibald Montgomery, Robert's grandfather, was accused of being an insane alcoholic. The charges against Robert's grandfather were dismissed, yet the damage had been done to the family name. Whispers of a nervous breakdown, insanity, alcoholism and suicide were devastating to a prominent family's social standing. Wire reports of Henry Montgomery's suicide caused the story to be spread in newspapers across the country.

On October 25 and 28, 1884, respectively, *The Brooklyn Eagle* published the articles, "Is He Insane? The Predicament of a Well-Known South Brooklyn Man" and "The Montgomery Suit: Withdrawal of the Suit at the Insistence of the Family," both about Archibald.

On June 25, 1922, *The Philadelpia Inquirer* published the item below titled "Man Jumps To Death From Brooklyn Bridge: Hundreds See Suicide From Trolley To Rail":

> A man believed to be Henry Montgomery, of Brooklyn, leaped to his death from the Brooklyn Bridge this evening, in the view of hundreds of pedestrians and surface car and elevated train passengers. He leaped from a passing car to the bridge roadway, stepped to the rail without looking back and jumped.

On June 26, 1922, *The Denver Post* published the following item under the heading "Wealthy N.Y. Rubber Firm Head Drowns Himself In River":

> Henry Montgomery, 45 years old, of Brooklyn, wealthy retired president of the New York Rubber company, committed suicide late Sunday afternoon by jumping into the East River. Montgomery, who had been suffering from a nervous breakdown which forced his retirement ten months before, had apparently planned to take his own life, and left instructions for notifying his relatives.

Either way, Henry (Sr.) left his family penniless, and his son Robert (Henry, Jr.) was forced to pick up the slack—as a railroad mechanic and oil tanker deckhand—and he was none too pleased about it. Fortunately, by the late 1920s, and following ineffectual attempts to become a writer, he became an established Broadway actor, joining his stage peers in the mass migration into film as *talkies* came into play.

But his subsequent tumultuous relationship with Lizzie may have been ignited by the resentment and the frustration he experienced in his pre-acting days. No doubt those years helped to foster a strong work ethic that he would later instill in Lizzie. But initially, it was no pleasant experience. What's more, a future family tragedy would further loosen and then only entangle the father-daughter link between Elizabeth and Robert Montgomery.

Elizabeth and her father did not always see eye to eye, and they were defi-nitely on opposite ends of the political spectrum, but their lives were in many ways similar. He was educated at exclusive private schools, as she would be later (at his instruction). She made her theatrical stage debut at six years old in *Red Riding Hood's World* (a French language stage production at the aristocratic Westlake School for Girls in Los Angeles); his theatrical film premiere occurred much later in life (with the comedy, *Three Live Ghosts*, in 1929); but they both loved acting (after his initial objection to her vocational choice).

Contracted with MGM, Robert would later be pigeonholed as that carefree leading man; just as Lizzie would later be typecast as a lighthearted leading witch. And just as she would later distance herself from *Samantha* (with a list of edgy TV and motion picture roles), Robert tried to break the happy-go-lucky mold and waxed *psychotic* in several feature films, including: *The Big House* (a prison movie released in 1930 that set the pattern for similar future films) and *Night Must Fall* (a 1937 thriller in which he played a mysterious brutal killer who terrorized the countryside).

The latter earned him an Academy Award nomination. He received a second Oscar nod in 1941 for *Here Comes Mr. Jordan*.

On a flight to his next fight, boxer *Joe Pendleton's* (Robert) soul is prema-turely snatched from his body by the newly deemed *Heavenly Messenger 7013* (Edward Everett Horton) when his plane crashes. Before the matter can be rectified by *7013's* supervisor, the celestial *Mr. Jordan* (Claude Raines), *Joe's* body is cremated; so *Jordan* grants him the use of the body of wealthy *Bruce Farnsworth* (original character unseen), who's just been murdered by his wife (Rita Johnson). As *Joe* attempts to remake *Farnsworth's* unworthy life in his own clean-cut image, he falls for *Betty Logan* (Evelyn Keyes).

Lizzie failed to win an Emmy for playing a witch on *Bewitched* (for which she was nominated five times, with a total of nine nominations throughout her career); her father failed to ace any formal acting award for playing a seraph (or a psycho).

In 1945, legendary film director John Ford became ill on the set of *They*

Were Expendable, and Robert stepped in as his replacement, making his first mark as a director. After receiving this initial tech credit, he turned out an unusual, controversial production titled *Lady in the Lake* (1947), a Raymond Chandler mystery thriller told in the first person through tricky subjective camera angles (much like Lizzie's *Missing Pieces* 1983 TV-movie). Playing the hero (private eye *Philip Marlowe*), he was seen on the screen only twice—once in the prologue, then within the body of the film, when he briefly crossed in front of a mirror. All other scenes were shown from his point of view, as if seen though his eyes. Robert went on to direct and star in several other films that received varied response before retiring from the big screen, and turned his attention to politics, TV, and the stage.

On Broadway in 1955, he won a Tony Award for best director for the play *The Desperate Hours*. He later formed Cagney-Montgomery Productions with early screen idol James Cagney to produce *The Gallant Hours* (1960), his final effort as a film director. Cagney was fond of Lizzie, and later became a mentor of sorts, maybe something even closer.

As she told Ronald Haver for the 1991 laserdisc release of *Here Comes Mr. Jordan*, Cagney was one of her dad's closest friends who was like a second father to her, and it never occurred to her that Cagney was a big star.

Another larger-than-life celebrity who both Elizabeth and Robert Montgomery befriended was film legend Bette Davis. Lizzie would later take the lead in the 1976 TV-movie, *Dark Victory*, a remake of Davis' 1939 motion picture; Bette had co-starred with Robert in 1948's *June Bride* (directed by Bretaigne Windust). In time, Lizzie and Bette became closer friends than Bette and Robert, and he became jealous; not so much of Bette, but of Lizzie. But as Bette recalled to author Charlotte Chandler in *Bette Davis: A Personal Biography—The Girl Who Walked Home Alone* (Simon and Schuster, 2006), Robert left little to be desired or envied. She even went as far as to describe him as "a male Miriam Hopkins," a reference to her arch rival on the big screen.

Actress Hopkins had well-publicized arguments with Davis (who reportedly had an affair with Hopkins' then-husband, Anatole Litvak) when they co-starred in the films *The Old Maid* (1939) and *Old Acquaintance* (1943). Davis admitted to very much enjoying a scene in the latter movie in which her character forcefully shakes Hopkins' character. There were even press photos taken with both divas in boxing rings with gloves up and *Old Acquaintance's* director Vincent Sherman standing between the two.

Davis never came to such blows with Robert Montgomery on the set of *June Bride*, but she came close. She explained in Chandler's book:

> He was an excellent actor, but addicted to scene stealing. He would add business in his close-ups which didn't match mine, so that there would only be one way to cut the film—his way. Mr. Montgomery understood films. (Director) Windust, who was not a film man at all, never noticed, and I couldn't have cared less. Montgomery was welcome to all the close-ups he wanted. I act with my whole body.

In 1991, Elizabeth told Ronald Haver that her father and Davis didn't get along. After Lizzie had moved out of the Montgomery homestead, Robert would call and invite her to dinner.

"I can't," she'd reply. "I'm going over to Bette's."

"Oh," he'd say, and hang up.

After meeting at various social events in New York, Davis became somewhat of a mentor for the young ingénue. In fact, while only in her late teens, Lizzie was invited by Davis to her home in Maine on a street named, "appropriately enough," Elizabeth said, "Witch Way." That name represented Davis' reputation and not *Bewitched*, which was years from creation. But for the moment, the *witch* reference seemed to fit Davis and, as Lizzie told Haver, "She knew that."

One weekend on Witch Way, Lizzie and Bette picked beans from Davis' garden and later strung them inside the house, while sitting in front of her fireplace. Shortly after, an argument ensued between the two, Davis stalked out of the room, and then stopped in her tracks. She turned to face Lizzie and said, "*Betty*—when they do the story of my life, you should play me, and I'm not sure that's a compliment." Lizzie thought that was funny; Bette Davis was the only person Elizabeth Montgomery ever allowed to call her "Betty."

According to James Pylant's *Bewitching Family Tree*:

> Elizabeth Montgomery's death certificate gives her mother's maiden name as Elizabeth Allen, a Kentucky native. The 1930 federal census of Los Angeles County, California, shows Robert Montgomery, age twenty-five, born in New York, *Actor, Motion Pictures*, and wife Elizabeth A., also twenty-five, born in Kentucky, and a fifty-year-old servant lived on Blackwood Drive in Los Angeles. The *age at first married* for both was twenty-three. The couple had married on 14 April 1928 in New York, and the following year they moved to Hollywood when Robert signed a contract with M-G-M. Elizabeth was the couple's second child. Tragically, their first born, Martha Bryan Montgomery, died at age fourteen months in 1931.

In May 1965, *Movie TV Secrets* magazine published the article, "Witches Are People Too," by Jackie Thomas. It explained how Robert was devastated by the loss; how tiny Martha's death left him in a state of severe depression that immobilized him for months. A friend who knew the Montgomerys described his condition:

> I don't think I've ever seen anyone as shaken as Bob. All his life seemed to be invested in that child; when she died something in him died with her. I don't think he has ever really recovered. Something inside him was twisted and destroyed by Martha's death.

Lizzie was interviewed for that same article. She addressed her father's strict reign over her youth, one that seemingly increased with time, as if in gradual reaction and retaliation to her infant sister's death, a young sibling she never knew. Little by little, her father's stern rule nibbled away at her self-esteem until the day she died in 1995. But thirty years before in May 1965, it was a different story.

She said she was too sure of a great many things. Being the daughter of a star had its effect on her. Not that her father went out of his way to make things easier for her, because he didn't. In fact, she said, at times he bent over backwards to go in the opposite direction. "Maybe that was his problem," she thought. "He gave me the best of everything—clothes, education, things like that, but he demanded a lot, too. Dad is a very complex man. I don't think I've ever been able to come up to Martha in his eyes."

However, five months prior to that she told *TV Radio Mirror:*

I never replaced Martha in his heart, but I did help to soothe his grief.

As was explained in Richard Lamparski's book, *Whatever Became Of . . . ? Volume III*, between 1928 and 1950, Robert Montgomery was married to "actress Elizabeth Allan" (with an "a"), an actress best known for her pairing with Ronald Coleman in the 1935 film, *A Tale of Two Cities*. But this Elizabeth Allan, born British in Skegness, England, in 1908, was not Lizzie's mother, nor was she ever married to Robert.

A little over two decades later, the American actress Elizabeth Allen (with an "e") was born "Elizabeth Ellen Gillease" on January 25, 1929 in Jersey City, New Jersey. In 1972, she co-starred on ABC's *The Paul Lynde Show*, playing Lynde's on-screen wife in this series that was executive produced by *Bewitched's* Harry Ackerman, and William Asher and Elizabeth Montgomery under their banner production company, Ashmont Productions. But this Elizabeth Allen was not Lizzie's mother either, nor was she ever married or related to Robert Montgomery.

However, a second American actress named Elizabeth Allen (with an "e") arrived on the scene before Gillease. James Pylant provides the details in his *Bewitching* article:

Elizabeth Daniel Allen was born on 26 December 1904 in Louisville, Jefferson County, Kentucky, to Bryan Hunt Allen and the former Rebecca Lowry Daniel. Elizabeth Montgomery's maternal grandparents—like her paternal grandparents—were newlyweds at the time of the 1900 federal census enumeration. Fifty-seven-year-old widow Ellen W. Daniel, born in Indiana in February of 1843, owned a house on Brook Street in Louisville, Kentucky, which she shared with daughter Lizzie W., age twenty-five; son William A., age thirty-five, daughter-in-law Mollie, age thirty-six, and daughter Rebecca Allen, age twenty. Except for Ellen Daniel, all were born in Kentucky. Rebecca Allen's marital status is given as married, with *o* given for the number of years married. Bryan H. Allen is listed elsewhere in Louisville, although his marital status is recorded as single. An inspector for a gas company, he was born in November of 1877 in Kentucky to a Missouri father and a Kentucky mother. Rebecca Lowry Daniel Allen—Elizabeth Montgomery's beloved *Becca*—was born in June of 1879 in Kentucky (as per the 1900 census), but her death certificate gives 5 June 1886 as her birth date. Her death certificate also identifies her mother's maiden name as Wright. Daniel family genealogists show that Ellen Wright was the wife of Coleman Spencer Daniel, who died in Louisville on 8 June 1898, two years before Mrs. Ellen W. Daniel is shown on the rolls of the twelfth federal census as a widow. Daniel family records show Ellen Wright Daniel died two years later on 7 June 1902. The same record gives 16 February 1843 as her birth date, which agrees with what is found on the 1900 census. Coleman S. Daniel and Ellen Wright wedded in the bride's native Switzerland County, Indiana, on 20 May 1864. The daughter of John W. Wright, who represented Switzerland County in the state legislature, Ellen Wright was only six months old when her mother, Ellen (Lowry) Wright, died at age 36. Her father remarried the following year to Rebecca D. Saunders. Clearly, when Ellen (Wright) Daniel named her daughter Rebecca Lowry Daniel, she did so in honor of her mother and stepmother.

It was Lizzie's grandmother Becca with whom she formed a special bond (and who eventually introduced her to the potentially lighter side of life, like horse racing and gambling.)

Becca moved with her daughters Elizabeth Allen and Martha-Bryan to New York City in the early 1920s where Martha-Bryan had a role in the Broadway play, *He Who Gets Slapped*, which played at the Garrick Theater. In all, Martha-Bryan, mother to Lizzie's first cousin, Amanda (a.k.a. "Panda," a childhood playmate), was in two dozen plays at one point before she met her husband-to-be Arthur Cushman.

Into this mix, Elizabeth Allen also performed in several live stage productions until she married Robert Montgomery on April 14, 1928. She received superb reviews for many of these plays, such as with *Revolt*, of which *The New York Times* said, "The lovely Miss Allen is poised for leading lady status anytime soon. She always brings freshness to her roles."

Allen and Robert were married at the Episcopal Church of the Transfiguration also known as "The Little Church Around the Corner" on 29th Street between Fifth Avenue and Madison Avenue. The church was also the home of the Episcopal Actors' Guild, of which she and Robert were members.

She retired almost immediately at Robert's request for her to concentrate only on being his wife. Lizzie chatted about Elizabeth Allen to *Modern Screen* in May 1965:

> Mother is a marvelous person. Just great. It's her attitude toward people that's so marvelous. She's a very warm, outgoing, generous human being. She'd acted on Broadway (that's where she met Dad); so did her sister, Martha-Bryan Allen. Both of them got reviews that are so extraordinarily good, they make you sort of proud. Mother did light comedy; she co-starred with Lee Tracy and Elizabeth Patterson. But she gave up her career when she married Dad and I don't believe ever regretted it for a moment. She loves her house and she and Dad gave my brother and me a wonderful childhood. It just couldn't have been happier, healthier or more fun.

When Lizzie was a stage-struck teen, Robert tried to sway her decision from acting by using his wife a prime example. According to the August 1967 edition of *Screen Stars* magazine, Robert told Lizzie that her mother was wise to forfeit her career to marry him and raise a family. He went on to tout his wife as the toast of Broadway, but that she knew her career would be detrimental to raising children. "It's difficult to know who your real friends are," Robert added. "Worst of all, acting requires the constant rejection of your real self. Sometimes you don't even know who you are anymore. Imagine what that does to a family!"

Lizzie wouldn't have to wonder about the consequences; she'd experience them first hand.

Two

~

Grim

"There's a little bit of a displaced person in everybody, and it's
nothing to be ashamed of."

—Elizabeth to Ronald Haver, 1991

Elizabeth's young life was divided between her parents' massive estate in
Patterson, New York, and their elegant home in Beverly Hills. It was there
they hosted various dinner parties and Sunday brunches that were attended
by the conservative likes of James Cagney, Bette Davis, Rosalind Russell,
Irene Dunne, Frank Morgan, and George Arliss. Her parents moved in
A-list circles, and were considered Hollywood royalty. They were well-
groomed, poised, and intelligent leaders of the community. They were
quiet, private, and peaceful in their everyday lives and, like many of their
friends (and later, Lizzie), rejected exhibitionism and screwball conduct.

On October 13, 1930, Robert Montgomery and Elizabeth Allen gave
birth to the little girl they named after Allen's sister Martha-Bryan, the
infant-child whose subsequent tragic death in December 1931 at only fourteen months (due to spinal meningitis) would forever change the Montgomery family dynamic.

Elizabeth's parents resided in a small house in Los Angeles until 1932,
when they moved to Beverly Hills. Approximately one year later, little
Lizzie arrived at 4:30 AM on April 15, 1933 (and not 1936 or 1938). However, after her brother Skip was born on February 15, 1936, the family

moved to Holmby Hills, an affluent neighborhood in West Los Angeles just north of Sunset and east of Beverly Glen, in a custom-built sixteen-room mansion with an Olympic-sized swimming pool. They lived there until they all moved to New York.

Franchot Tone, a substantial star in Robert Montgomery's league at the time, then purchased the Beverly Hills home. Elizabeth later attempted to buy it back when she married Bill Asher, but Tone wouldn't budge. Subsequently, the Ashers purchased their Beverly Hills estate on Laurel Canyon Drive from Howard Hawks (the legendary director of westerns, along the lines of John Ford), where Lizzie remained after her divorce from Bill, through her marriage to Bob Foxworth, and until her demise.

Elizabeth told Ronald Haver in 1991 that her childhood was "all very kind of abnormally normal." As Foxworth explained on A&E's *Biography* in 1999, the upscale world that she grew up in did not contribute to a regular childhood. She was expected to dress properly and to have good manners and behave in a certain way. She took that as an act, Foxworth believed, because it failed to mirror her own true feelings. So, in a sense, he said, "she was always an actress."

In March of 1939, Robert Montgomery told *Collier's Magazine* that his farm in the Towners section of Patterson, New York, near Brewster was his refuge from acting. He lived there three months a year and any visitor to the farm who mentioned the entertainment industry in any way was reportedly "apt to be slugged."

Robert Montgomery's love-hate partnership with Hollywood would mirror his personal relationship with Lizzie. She didn't get along with her father because, as Foxworth also surmised on A&E's *Biography*, to some extent her father was envious of Elizabeth's popularity.

Billy Asher, Jr., the first of Lizzie's three children with William Asher, blamed the ongoing rift between his mother and grandfather on their opposing political views. He, too, appeared on *Biography*, and said, "They just didn't see eye to eye."

In later years, she and her dad seldom spoke. But if she phoned him, at least he'd answer, as he did when Hollywood called him abroad in May of 1939.

It was then he traveled to England to make *The Earl of Chicago*, which would become Lizzie's favorite of his films:

A Chicago gangster (Montgomery) learns he has inherited an earldom in England, and he travels to London in order to claim it; he does so, even though he remains involved with mobsters back in the States. Ultimately, he transforms from a two-bit gangster and ends up living in an English castle with this wonderful old valet (Edmund Gwenn) who proceeds to tutor him in the ways of being an earl. Unfortunately, his previous life continues to haunt him; he commits murder, is tried by a jury of his peers in Parliament, and ends up in prison. In the end, his valet brings his best clothes, knickers, silk stockings, and patent leather shoes, coat with lace collar, ultimately dressing him for his execution.

In 1991, Elizabeth expressed to Ronald Haver just how impressed she was with this movie:

> It's just a gem, and it's not because he's in it. I could see anybody in it, as long as they were as good as he was in it. It is imaginative, it's beautifully directed, it's cleverly acted. Edmund Gwenn is so fabulous. It builds to such a point where they had the courage to do what they did at the end, instead of somebody saying, *You're kidding, you can't do that. How can you possibly end it this way?* I was just flabbergasted the first time I saw this. (You think) *Superman will swoop down and take this man away.* But he doesn't, and by God, the guy walks out of the prison, down to the guillotine, starts to walk up the steps and there's a wonderful cut of Edmund Gwenn in the window, looking down, where *The Earl of Chicago* is totally panic-stricken at this point. The look on his face is just the most horrendous thing. I mean, he's just scared to death, and quite rightly, when he realizes (that) nothing (is) going to save him. And he turns around and he looks as if he's about [to be] ready to run, and looks up at the window, and sees the valet at the window, and the valet bows to him, and he realizes, *Oh, God, it's just a killer.* He realizes he's gotta go through with this. Oh, I was in tears. I almost am now thinking about it. It was just extraordinary.

Lizzie then elaborated on the scene during which the Earl was tried in front of Parliament, how her father decided not to see the set before filming, or that scene's dialog. He knew his character was on trial; he had a vague concept of the questions and answers; but he had no idea about protocol:

> He just didn't want to make himself familiar with the script at all. And I think when you watch the movie, you can tell, because when those doors

open onto that room, it's like (he thinks), *My God, this sure isn't like any little courtroom in Chicago that I've ever seen before.* It's just this kind of awestruck kind of almost childish thing that happens to this man. I love that movie. Can you tell?

Although Elizabeth's adult relationship with her father was strained, she never stopped loving him, and he never stopped loving her or her brother Skip. Family-oriented, Robert, unlike *The Earl of Chicago*, refused to go to Britain unless his wife and children accompanied him, and they did.

But while the Montgomerys journeyed to the United Kingdom, the Nazis invaded Norway, World War II began, and Robert promptly joined the American Field Service Ambulance Corps and was attached to the French army as an ambulance driver. A young Lizzie and her even younger brother Skip were then shipped back to the United States on an Arandora Star steamship bound for New York City.

Due to the radio silence of the time, it was eight days before their parents learned of their safe arrival under the care of Lizzie's grandmother Becca, who was there to greet and take them back to California.

In 1991, Elizabeth offered a concise description of her father to Ronald Haver for the fiftieth anniversary laserdisc release of *Here Comes Mr. Jordan*:

> . . . primarily self-educated . . . well, brilliantly . . . with a very kind of quirky sense of humor, very stubborn . . . arrogant . . . pompous to a point where I wanted to slap him sometimes . . . could be extremely understanding one minute and just irrational the next . . . I don't mean irrational, I mean to someone that disagreed with him, irrational, obviously . . . very obviously right-wing, politically . . . but . . . he was terrific with little children, and they seemed to adore him, which is always a good sign [she laughed], and he loved animals . . . he adored my mother . . . he adored my stepmother . . . he was very hard on my brother, much more so on him than me . . . he loved pretty things, like antique stuff, or modern even. He loved Andrew Wyeth, who was also a friend of his . . . he loved Daumie, Max Beerbohm. I loved the way he dressed . . . There were times when he'd be kind of tweedy . . . Maybe that was his pompous wanting to be

King of England department . . . I always remembered too, when I was little, how handsome he looked in a dinner jacket. He always seemed very at home when he was dressed up a lot. Very relaxed; so it just suited him very well; as did . . . riding a horse. He had his own kind of style . . . and he had a great voice, really nice voice. He used to read Dickens' *A Christmas Carol* every Christmas and I used to love that. It was wonderful.

Robert Montgomery was clearly a larger-than-life figure in Lizzie's eyes, but she still referred to him as just plain "Daddy" in much the same way that *Samantha* called to her warlock father named *Maurice* (pronounced as *More-eese*) played by the late Maurice (pronounced *More-iss*) Evans.

In fact, before Evans was cast as *Maurice*, Lizzie asked Robert to play the role. "Unfortunately," she recalled in 1989, "he said no. But I would have loved him to do it. He would have been divine in the role."

She couldn't help but feel despondent about the ordeal. She was already disappointed that Robert had declined to narrate the *Bewitched* pilot in 1964; now he rejected the chance to play his daughter's father on-screen, as she had played her father's daughter on that "Top Secret" episode of *Robert Montgomery Presents* in 1951.

Robert, however, had been ill when she asked him to portray *Maurice*, so he may not have been able to do the role even had he so desired. And while Lizzie believed Evans was "perfect" for the part of her majestic TV father, that's how she also had described her real "Daddy."

As a child, Elizabeth had not realized her father was a star. He just worked for a living, like everyone else's dad; he just so happened to be an actor and worked at a movie studio. That didn't seem out of the ordinary. As she explained to *Photoplay Magazine* in 1968, his work never entered their home and she rarely saw him on the job. She visited one of his sets once, maybe twice, when she was growing up, but she didn't discover his occupation until someone told her at Westlake.

As she lamented in 1992 to John Tesh on his short-lived TV show, *One on One*, it was kind of like finding out there was no Santa Claus. It never occurred to her that he was "doing something odd . . . or wonderful . . . or not so wonderful" with his career.

However, in August 1967, Jacqueline Starr wrote in *Screen Stars* magazine:

Robert Montgomery tried everything in his power to keep his daughter from confusing the Robert Montgomery—suave movie hero—with Daddy, the loving gentle man who was, nevertheless, human and capable of error. But Liz saw only a bigger-than-life father, the one on the screen. And when he tried to tell her about all the everyday problems of being an actor she just wouldn't listen. She was convinced that everything Daddy did was perfect and she intended to follow suit herself. That's when she ran into genuine trouble.

However wonderful or not so wonderful Robert Montgomery was, he could not prevent his legal detachment from Lizzie's mother Elizabeth Allen. In turn Lizzie, like other children of dysfunctional households from any era, was forced to become what was then referred to as a "product of a broken home."

Her parents divorced on December 5, 1950 after Robert had an affair with yet another Elizabeth in the fray, this one Elizabeth "Buffy" Grant Harkness, who was married to William Harkness, one of the wealthiest socialites in New York City. Buffy was also heiress to the Standard Oil fortune and she married Robert on December 9, 1950, a mere four days after his divorce from Elizabeth Allen.

At the time, it was noted that not only did the second Mrs. Montgomery have the same first name as her predecessor but she bore a striking resemblance to her as well. But according to the January 1965 edition of *TV Radio Mirror*, the first Mrs. Montgomery's only comment about her former husband's new marriage was:

Moving East wasn't the best. Usually, Hollywood gets the blame for divorces, but in this case, it was the reverse. I had hoped we could work out our differences, but now I realize it can't be.

In the same article, Lizzie insisted:

I felt no bitterness when my parents parted. There was no spite or name-calling. There was no open quarreling that I knew of. They separated with the same dignity and mutual respect I had come to expect from them.

Yet, how could she feel anything but devastated by her parents' dissolve? At this early stage in their relationship, she had worshipped her father and the divorce most probably contributed to the wedge between them; and feeling worse for her mother didn't much help matters. She and her brother Skip may have moved to Manhattan with Mrs. Montgomery to help ease the traumatic transition, but Lizzie continued to put up a less traumatized front to cover her disillusionment.

"When you think everything's fine, this comes as a blow," Elizabeth admitted to *Modern Screen* in May 1965. "But we saw Dad all the time."

She was proud that her parents had remained together for so long. Childhood friend Billie Banks explained as much to MSNBC's *Headliners & Legends* in 2001. The sense of united family was "extremely important" to her, Banks said.

As Lizzie herself told *TV Guide* in 1961, her "wonderful feeling of security" had stemmed from her mother and father. In describing her and Skip's relationship with them, she unabashedly added: "Our parents protected us from too much Hollywood stuff, but it seeped through."

How could it not? Robert Montgomery expected a great deal from those in his inner personal and professional circles and, as time marched on, Lizzie fit into both those categories. On a subconscious level, she may not have even allowed herself to fully grieve her parents' divorce, which could have added to the emotional burden of it all, further widening the already significant gap between them.

As Liz "Dizzie" Sheridan revealed to *Headliners & Legends* in 2001, Elizabeth once told her, "I don't think my father liked me very much." On that same program, *Bewitched* director Richard Michaels claimed Elizabeth wanted praise from her father more than anyone else in the world, but it wasn't as forthcoming as she desired, at any stage of the game.

Five years later, Michaels appeared on *Entertainment Tonight* and dropped a bombshell: he and Elizabeth had an affair, one that ultimately contributed to the end of *Bewitched* in 1972 and, in 1974, the end of her marriage to Bill Asher, Michaels' mentor.

For Lizzie three times was not the charm in the marriage department, at least not as she had once hoped. Although her nuptials with Asher at first seemed ideal, she disengaged from him, sadly, just as she had from Fred Cammann and Gig Young. But she remained loyal to Asher, partially in respect of his talent, but mostly because of their three children.

It was the same sense of loyalty she retained for her parents when *they* divorced, despite her distress at the disintegration of what she viewed as the perfect family. She still kept a stoic upper lip during their separation proceedings and decades later mourned their demise. When Robert Montgomery passed away at age seventy-seven in 1981 in Manhattan, she refused to speak with the press, especially the tabloid press.

"I hate those magazines," she said in 1989, one of which contacted her not more than two days after her father died, asking, "How does it feel, now that your father's dead? You never agreed with him anyway. We'd like your comments because we know you never got along with him politically."

She hung up without dignifying the call with a response. "And that was the last time I spoke to that magazine," she acknowledged, "and haven't since."

In the long term, Lizzie was proud of her ancestry, as was evidenced by the names she and Bill Asher would later bestow upon their children. As *Bewitching* genealogist James Pylant chronicled:

> Their third child was named Rebecca Elizabeth Asher. *I knew . . . another Becca had arrived*, the actress said when she gave birth to her daughter. Rebecca Lowry Daniel Allen died in 1964, just as her actress-granddaughter launched the first season of (*Bewitched*). Elizabeth Montgomery and husband William Asher had given family names to their two older children, with William Allen Asher bearing his father's first name and his maternal grandmother's maiden name, while Robert Deverell Asher carries the first name of his maternal grandfather and the middle name of his great-great-grandmother, Mary A. (Deverell) Barney.

As Lizzie explained to *TV Radio Mirror* magazine in November 1969, she named her daughter in tribute to her grandmother as well as a childhood friend:

> With Rebecca Elizabeth, it's been legitimate to call her *Rebel*. I sort of hope that happens. I went to school with a hellion named Rebecca whose nickname was *Reb*—not *Becky*. If the baby had been a boy he'd have been called *John*. I kind of like Adam—but *Adam Asher*?! That's too *cutesy pooh*.

The latter distinction never came to fruition, except partially.

On *Bewitched*, *Darrin* and *Samantha* named their son *Adam* who was born in the sixth season of *Bewitched* (and played by David and Greg Lawrence, who were fathered by Tony Curtis in real life); but Lizzie and Bill Asher never had another child after Rebecca.

Then, after Elizabeth ended *Bewitched*, there was another relative, if distant, who played into the fold: an accused ax murderess whom she portrayed in the 1975 TV-movie *The Legend of Lizzie Borden*, based on the real-life woman who was accused of murdering her father and stepmother in 1893. James Pylant's research revealed that Elizabeth and Borden were sixth cousins once removed, both descending from seventeenth-century Massachusetts resident John Luther.

Author Rhonda R. McClure originally documented the relative connection in her book, *Finding Your Famous (And Infamous) Ancestors* (Cincinnati: Betterway Books: 2003); in which she asked, "I wonder how Elizabeth would have felt if she knew she was playing her own cousin?"

Retro curator Ed Robertson is the host of *TV Confidential*, one of radio's most renowned showcases of nostalgic television talent and discussions. He's also the author of a number of acclaimed classic TV literary companions, including guides to *The Rockford Files* and *The Fugitive*. He weighs in on the Lizzie/Borden relative link: "Whether that's true or not, I don't know. But I'm not sure whether Elizabeth would have taken on the role, or at least allowed Borden to be characterized the way she was in the role, had she known she was in fact playing one of her cousins."

Years after playing *Borden*, Elizabeth finally learned of her lineage with the character. Entertainment historian Thomas McCartney, who has archived Elizabeth's career since 1994, puts it all in perspective: "She was bemused by the idea, but never said anything else."

That sounds about right; *no response* was a typical Lizzie response.

Several decades before Elizabeth played *Borden*, her grandmother Becca was born "Rebecca Lowry Daniel Allen" in 1886. Seventy-eight years later, Becca succumbed to cancer in Los Angeles, approximately ten days before *Bewitched* debuted on September 17, 1964.

Lizzie's mother Elizabeth Allen passed away at age eighty-seven on the Montgomery farm in New York, June 28, 1992, the same day Lizzie served as Co-Grand Marshall with her former *Bewitched* co-star Dick Sargent in the Los Angeles Gay and Lesbian Pride Parade.

Elizabeth Allen's cause of death was never documented, but she had been in poor health for quite some time, then died suddenly and quite unexpectedly. Shortly thereafter, Lizzie's childhood landscape was sold.

In the short period between that time and her own passing in 1995, Elizabeth continued to view the big picture of her parents' influence as she always had, especially the impact made upon her by her father. She followed his pathway to a successful and prestigious career and, in the process, learned to handle the good with the bad, the advantages and the obstacles that went along with being born the child of a star.

Three

~

Elizabeth Montgomery Presents

"Our hope was that she would turn out to be a good actress and
not just the daughter of Montgomery."

—Robert Montgomery, *TV Radio Mirror Magazine*, January 1965

Rebecca Allen wasn't an actress, but Elizabeth thought she should have
been. Next to her parents, Becca was the greatest influence in Lizzie's life;
she provided a sense of safety and comfort in her youth. As Lizzie recalled
to *Modern Screen* magazine in 1965, "It was a feeling only grandmothers
know how to give."

Whenever Robert Montgomery and Elizabeth Allen were away on
business or vacation, Lizzie and her brother Skip never felt rejected. Becca
was always there, Lizzie said, to offer encouraging words, to make sure she
and Skip held their parents close at heart, and "prayed every night."

"It was really too bad," she told *TeleVision Life* magazine in January
1954. "I mean, Mother and Dad being on the road so much and missing
my birthdays. But it didn't bother me too much . . . I wasn't a neglected
child."

Little Elizabeth didn't see as much of her father as she would have liked,
but she and Skip had a nurse for years. She claimed to have "had a wonderful childhood," but at school, she'd have to watch her words. When classmates mentioned a dinner out with their parents, Lizzie would join in with,

"Daddy took me to Romanoff's." But they'd offer blank stares and, suddenly, she said, "I'd be all alone."

But Becca was waiting in the wings, ready to pick up the pieces, particularly when it came to her granddaughter's "play-acting." According to the article, "The Girl Behind the Twitch," published in *Modern Screen* magazine, May 1965, Becca watched everything performed by Lizzie, who described her grandmother this way:

> . . . such a lovely lady . . . a small woman with enormous brown eyes and a lovely kind of auburn hair. Up until the day she died she was the youngest looking thing, terribly young and vital. She adored California and was a one-woman Chamber of Commerce . . . She had such a love of life . . . an extraordinary imagination . . . and . . . such warmth. There wasn't a soul she ever met who didn't adore her. She loved children and was so good with us. She wrote a lot of songs and poems I would love to see published. Maybe someday I'll illustrate them and send them off to a publisher.

That never happened. But Lizzie was busy with other endeavors, namely, Billy Asher, Jr., whom she had just given birth to and who she said was "one of the biggest thrills" of Becca's life. "I'm just sorry he's going to miss having her for his audience. She was only the greatest audience I ever had." And she wasn't kidding.

When she was about eight years old, Lizzie's flair for the dramatic was already in bloom. She and her cousin Amanda "Panda" Cushman would play detective, foreshadowing characters Lizzie would depict in TV-movies like 1983's *Missing Pieces* and the Edna Buchanan films from the mid-1990s (including her final performance in *Deadline for Murder*).

When Panda wasn't available, Lizzie's little brother Skip would pinch-hit. Although his chances for getting the juicy roles were slim to none because his older sister would always win out—even if she was not right for the part.

According to what Elizabeth told *Modern Screen* in 1965, she and Skip once performed in their own edition of Walt Disney's classic animated feature, *Snow White and the Seven Dwarfs*, released in 1937. The pre-production dialogue went something like this:

"I'll play the king," Skip would say.

"No," Lizzie countered. "I'm going to play the king."

"Then can I be the princess?"

"No, you're a boy. You can't be the princess."

"Then, I'll be the prince."

"No, I'm going to be the prince, too."

"But how can you be the prince, when you're a girl?"

"Well, just because . . . I'm the director."

Lizzie ultimately cast Skip as the announcer, hidden *off-stage* in a closeted area, from where he spoke into a wastebasket, which added a grand reverberation to his voice.

Before their first performance, for which Lizzie naturally tapped herself as the lead, she'd tell Skip, "Go out and announce me."

Ever the loyal young sibling, Skip walked into the middle of the Montgomery living room, their stage, and declared to the audience, only Becca, "I am presenting . . . Elizabeth Montgomery!"

But Lizzie protested from behind the invisible curtain.

"No, no, Skip," she interrupted, "the *great* Elizabeth Montgomery."

"I am presenting the *great* Elizabeth Montgomery," he then said, adding, "but I don't know what she's going to do!"

"*Don't know what she's going to do?!*" Lizzie yelped from the sidelines. "Of *course* you know what I'm going to do!" Turning to her grandmother, she said, "Clap, Becca, clap!"

Becca consented, and then sat patiently and watched whatever production Lizzie presented (and she'd keep watching through the years).

Elizabeth's creative control of this pubescent *Snow White* production offered telling signs of her early confidence and ambition which diminished over time, while the "presenting" part of Skip's intro foreshadowed the title of their father's TV series, *Robert Montgomery Presents*, on which Lizzie would make her professional debut playing her father's daughter.

According to *Cosmopolitan Magazine*, July 1954, Mr. Montgomery was there, beside Becca, for Lizzie's *Snow White* re-do, somewhere in the proverbial bleachers, cheering her on, at least during the *wishing-well* moment that transpired in Disney's original *White* film. As Robert recalled, his daughter's rendition was somewhat scaled down:

If you remember the scene, *Snow White* would sing a line of that song, "I'm Wishing," and then an echo would sing it back to her. Well, Elizabeth was apparently all by herself in her room, singing the song in front of (that) wastebasket, which she was using as a wishing well. And sure enough, an echo was coming from somewhere in the room.

Further investigation identified the echo as Skip's voice, but the father Montgomery was impressed nonetheless:

How hammy can you get? Anybody who at the age of five would go to all that trouble to set up a scene could never be anything but an actress in later life. So I wasn't surprised when Elizabeth came to me a few years later, when she was around fourteen, and announced she was planning to go on the stage. I never discouraged her, because I think being an actress is as good a life as any if you really work hard at it, and Elizabeth is a hard worker. She asked me if I would appear with her in her first play, and I said I would.

In 1951, Lizzie made her social debut at New York's Debutante Cotillion and Christmas Ball, and her father kept his promise: that same year, she made her TV acting debut on his show. But she never doubted his word; she believed her parents empathized with aspirations of all shape and color, specifically theatrical endeavors. As she told *Modern Screen* in May 1965, "They certainly understood Skip and me and never ever discouraged either one of us about the theater."

But her acting bug stung deeper than Skip's. She'd go on to perform in a variety of roles and mediums for fifty years; he appeared in TV westerns for about four years. Then he retired from the entertainment industry, and began working at the Hayden Stone brokerage firm.

Elizabeth was terribly proud of him. As she explained to Ronald Haver in 1991, her father was "very hard on my brother, much more so on him than on me. But I think Skip turned out to be a much better person, maybe in spite of it, I think, because he's a terrific guy. My brother's really neat."

"There's only a two-year gap between my brother and me," she said in 1965, this time, in August to *TV Radio Mirror* magazine. "I can't recall an instance of jealousy between us as we grew up. Oh, I guess there were occasions when kid brother got in big sister's way. But jealousy? Not a bit of it."

"Well," as *Samantha* might have said, except maybe only once, although the incident had more to do with sexual discrimination than sibling rivalry.

"A Second Baby, A Special Problem" was published by *TV Radio Mirror* in November 1966 which profiled the birth of Lizzie's second son, Robert, named for her father—and her brother. In the article, Lizzie recalled a childhood moment when Skip was allowed to cross the street by himself whereas she wasn't.

"Why can't I do that?" she asked her mother.

"Don't forget," she replied. "Skip is a boy."

That seemed most discriminatory to Lizzie, but she kept her mouth shut:

> I knew Mom did not make her decisions lightly and, once made, she stuck to them, without discussion. Of course, once I reached my teens, she'd sit down and talk such things over, explaining why she had come to certain judgments, and she would listen carefully to my arguments on why I deserved fewer restraints.

Certain restrictions may have inhibited Skip's career in acting aspirations, but not his life in general. Lizzie was right. He was a "neat" person.

According to Montgomery archivist Tom McCartney, www.bobsbe witchingdaughter.com, and www.earlofhollywood.com, Skip was born Robert Montgomery, Jr., in Los Angeles on February 15, 1936. Although his birth year has been incorrectly reported as 1930, Skip was actually three years younger than Elizabeth and six years younger than their late sister Martha Bryan.

Though Lizzie and Skip were raised in Hollywood, they enjoyed their summers at the Montgomery country estate in Patterson, New York or in the U.K. where their father worked in films.

In 1939, Skip became the youngest Lifetime Honorary Member of the Screen Actors Guild, over which his dad presided as president. In 1945 he attended school in Arizona. Five years later, when their parents divorced, Skip remained with Lizzie in the family's Upstate New York home with their mother and attended St. Mark's School in Southborough, Massachusetts in 1952. In 1958, Skip, then twenty-two, formally joined the family business by becoming a working actor. That same year, he also became a father when his wife, socialite Deborah Chase, gave birth to a son, Robert Montgomery, III.

The following year, he won small roles in movies such as *Say One for Me* and *A Private's Affair* as well as on TV shows such as *The Loretta Young Show* (NBC, 1953–1961), in which his sister performed, and *Gunsmoke* (CBS, 1955–1975), the latter in which he made his TV acting debut. Here, he appeared in the macabre episode "Lynching Man" which originally aired November 15, 1958.

Directed by Richard Whorf and written by John Meston, this segment also featured an overacted performance by guest star George Macready (who had played Elizabeth's father in NBC's *Kraft Television Theatre* production of "The Diamond as Big as the Ritz" in 1955):

> A mild-mannered *Hank Blenis* (O. Z. Whitehead) doesn't stand a chance in the Old West. He owned an apple farm back in Ohio, but now he's not even sure how to ride a horse. Unfortunately, he won't soon have to worry about learning to do so; when his healthy stallion is stolen, and he's left for dead, hung by a tree. Meanwhile, one man vigilante *Charlie Drain* (Macready), whose father was lynched when he was a child, sets out to find *Hank's* killer. This infuriates *Marshall Matt Dillon* (star James Arness), who along with his sidekick *Chester* (Dennis Weaver), sets out to find the real culprit. They soon meet the kindly farm hand *Billy Drico* (Skip), shortly before uncovering the mystery, while losing *Charlie* in the process.

While Macready over-projected his part, Skip appeared to underact. Although his was a minor role, Skip could have made the part of *Billy Drico* something more. It was his TV acting debut. Understandably nervous, he made every attempt to live up to his father's great expectations. But his anxiety appears to have got the best of him. Skip did not give the role his all; he appeared awkward and uncomfortable on camera. Unlike Lizzie, unfortunately, his performances were not given a chance to be properly modulated; he never quite attained the opportunity to hone his craft under his father's watchful eye. By the time Skip started to legitimately pursue acting, *Robert Montgomery Presents* had completed its run.

But, happily, Robert Montgomery, Jr. had other things on his mind.

Nine months after *Gunsmoke*, on July 10, 1959, he and his wife welcomed a daughter into the family when Deborah Elizabeth Montgomery was born.

He continued acting on television with minor roles in such popular fare as *Sea Hunt* (in two episodes, one in 1959, the other in 1961), the anthology show *Death Valley Days* (hosted by future president Ronald Reagan), and a series called *The Tall Man*, which was created by Samuel Peeples (of *Star Trek* fame), in which he played a character named *Jimmy Carter* (precursing at least the name of yet another future president).

Skip also acted on the big screen with in 1960: a small part in *The Gallant Hours*, a feature his father both produced and directed, and enjoyed a larger role in the science fiction film, *12 to the Moon*.

But correctly sensing that his career was going nowhere fast, in 1962, he left the world of acting and became a Wall Street stockbroker with Hayden Stone & Co. where he enjoyed a lucrative career for the next two decades.

He spent his golden years in Tallahassee, Florida, where he became the community liaison for Florida State University's Graduate Film Conservatory. He also established the Sleepy Actors Group, which provided housing for students working on their thesis films and hosted a database listing production related services and locations.

In 1998, he served as executive producer on the independent film, *Roses*.

On February 7, 2000, he underwent surgery for lung cancer and the outlook seemed positive. But on April 28, that prognosis turned grim, and he died suddenly at the age of sixty-four, leaving behind his third wife, Melanie, son Adam, and daughter Meghann.

Years before, "kid brothers" was one of the many commonalities Elizabeth shared with her friend Sally Kemp, whom she met while attending the New York American Academy of Dramatic Arts. Kemp had few memories of Skip when they were all young and didn't recall much of Skip's relationship with his father. But what she did recall is noteworthy:

> I too had a brother Skip's age, two years younger than I. Elizabeth and I were starting our adult lives and careers; our brothers were still in school when we first knew each other and I seldom saw them together. She seemed fond of him; he was cute, blond, curly haired, choirboy face but our paths at that age didn't meet very often. Little brothers weren't foremost in our minds. Whenever I was with Bob (Sr.) and Elizabeth it was in a more

adult situation. Skip would be doing whatever it is young boys do. Bob seemed very proud of Elizabeth when I was with them and Buffy (Harkness, Bob's second wife), too, was proud of her. It was all, from my point of view, very warm, funny, and delightful. Bob often made Elizabeth and I sing Broadway songs for him and any guests around. I saw only a privileged, affectionate family. One I envied at times. Buffy was always gentle, gracious, and perfectly lovely to everyone. If there was any trouble underneath I never saw it.

After Robert Montgomery passed away in 1981, Kemp on several occasions spent time with Skip and his family and found him to be "a charming man, very like his father." She was sad when he died "far too young," succumbing to lung cancer in 2000, and she still has infrequent contact with his family.

Bicoastal from birth, in their youth, Lizzie and Skip were at home among Hollywood stars and the East Coast upper crust. They both attended elite private educational facilities that provided solid preparation for their adulthood. But while Skip left Hollywood behind, Lizzie delved right into the mix of it, helped along by that refined academic background.

From September of 1939 to June of 1950, she attended the Westlake School for Girls, an exclusive elementary academic hall in Beverly Hills. From September 1950 to June of 1951, she was enrolled at the aristocratic Spence School for Girls (where she played field hockey) in New York City.

The following information for both facilities was gathered from their respective websites:

In October 1989, the Boards of Trustees of both the Westlake School for Girls and the Harvard School, a military school for boys that was established in 1900, agreed to merge the facilities. Today, Harvard-Westlake School is an independent coeducational college preparatory day school, grades 7–12, that ultimately commenced in September of 1991. In 2010, 566 of its students took 1,736 A.P. tests in 30 different subjects, and 90% scored 3 or higher. The school ranks among the top high schools in the country in number of National Merit Semifinalists. In the class of 2011, there were 90 students who received National Merit Recognition, with 28 students as National Merit Semifinalists.

Clara Spence, a visionary educator, founded her Spence School for Girls in 1892, welcoming ten students to a brownstone on West 48th Street in New York City. The outside world of politics, the arts, and the community was embraced in her school and from the beginning Spence girls developed a keen sense of self-confidence and assumed their roles as significant members of the community. The facilities motto, "Not for school but for life we learn," has defined a Spence education throughout its long history. Or as Spence herself once said of her renowned facility it was "a place not of mechanical instruction, but a school of character where the common requisites for all have been human feeling, a sense of humor, and the spirit of intellectual and moral adventure.

All of which describes Lizzie in spades.

Actress June Lockhart, best known for her iconic roles as the intergalactic mother *Maureen Robinson* on TV's *Lost in Space* (CBS, 1965–1968) and the kindly country physician, *Dr. Janet Craig* on *Petticoat Junction* (CBS, 1963–1970), played an integral role in Lizzie's life.

Before her stops in *Space* and at *Junction*, she was guest-star on *Bewitched* in a first-season episode called "Little Pitchers Have Big Fears" which co-starred Jimmy Mathers, brother to Jerry Mathers, better known as *The Beaver* on *Leave It to Beaver* (CBS/ABC, 1957–1963).

Years before her *Bewitched* guest-spot, Lockhart made nine appearances on *Robert Montgomery Presents*. She is the daughter of actors Gene and Kathleen Lockhart who portrayed *Mr.* and *Mrs. Bob Cratchit* in the 1938 film edition of *A Christmas Carol*, in which June played one of the *Cratchit* children. Reginald Owen who, decades later guest starred on *Bewitched* as *Ockie*, boyfriend to Marion Lorne's *Aunt Clara* (and *Admiral Boom* in 1964's *Mary Poppins* movie), played *Scrooge*.

What's more, June's father Gene was good friends with Lizzie's father Robert, both of whom were instrumental in the founding of the Screen

Actors Guild (S.A.G.). Gene also made four appearances on *Robert Mont-gomery Presents*, of which three were with June (and directed by Grey Lock-wood). Meanwhile, Kathleen Lockhart had a small role in Robert Montgomery's 1946 film, *The Lady in the Lake*.

Although June did not appear with Lizzie in any episodes of *Presents*, she recalls:

> I used to watch her work. And I remember seeing her once in rehearsal. She was very professional, and her reputation for always doing live TV was legendary. And the directors that I worked with, who had also worked with her, said she was just a joy and lots of fun. And that was my experience with her when I did *Bewitched*. Both she and Bill Asher were fun to work with. We shot the episode at the Rancho Golf Course on Pico Blvd. and Motor Avenue [in West Los Angeles]. There wasn't a dressing room for Elizabeth or me. So I joked with her and asked, *What are we supposed to do? Change in the front seat of the car?* But then a short time later, the crew brought in a few portable dressing rooms. I was just glad I didn't have to change outside on Motor Avenue.

However, June's stint on *Bewitched* is not her most vivid recollection of Elizabeth. That part of her memory is savored from another time, decades before, when they both attended the Westlake School for Girls in Beverly Hills. Although June was a senior and Lizzie was just in kindergarten, the two crossed paths one very special morning when only four people in the world—June, Elizabeth, Miss Carol Mills, the Westlake principal, and a very uniformed Robert Montgomery—were there to experience what June now reveals for the first time anywhere:

> In the middle of World War II, Robert Montgomery was in the South Pacific, I believe as Lt. Commander or higher. So, one day, there we were, Elizabeth and I, both at Westlake. I was coming back from the Borders wing on campus, back over to the classrooms and Miss Mills was standing next to Elizabeth, outside where the circle driveway was. I greeted them both and Ms. Mills said, *Wait here a minute, June.* So I stood with them and asked, *What's going on?* And she said, *You'll see.* And within a few moments a car pulled up and out got Robert Montgomery in full uniform, back from a very long trip overseas in the South Pacific. Upon seeing her father get

out of the car Elizabeth, with screams of delight, ran towards him. And he picked her up in his arms and hugged her so tight. He then came over to Miss Mills and I, greeted us, and then got back in the car with Elizabeth and drove away. Of course there were tears on our cheeks after seeing this great reunion between Elizabeth and her father. And he came to pick her up in the middle of the school day . . . and there was nobody else around . . . there were no other students milling about; no one. Just Miss Mills, me, and Elizabeth. And I remember that day clearly, even so vividly I can remember where the sun was at the time. It must have been maybe 11:30 or 12 noon. And of course no one was let out of school in the middle of the day unless it was really very important. So Miss Mills and I just looked at each other and it was a sweet wonderful warm moment that we had just witnessed. A very exciting moment, too, because we later learned that Robert Montgomery had just returned not only from the South Pacific but [that] it was a very important business. He did not just come back on leave, where he would be home for a month or so, and then have to go back. It wasn't like that. He was back for good. And whatever work he was involved with in the South Pacific was very top secret.

After revealing this story, June laughs in irony upon learning that Lizzie's first episode of *Robert Montgomery Presents* was titled "Top Secret," in which she played none other than the daughter to her father's character, a spy, who teamed together for a covert adventure in a foreign land.

In January 1965, Elizabeth talked to reporter Eunice Field and *TV Radio Mirror* magazine for the article, "Elizabeth Montgomery: You Know Her as a Witch, Now Meet Her as a Woman." "I'm afraid I gave my teachers gray hair," she said, "because all I could think of was *Dramatics*."

But it was her mother who saved her from getting Ds in every subject; she'd permit little Lizzie to take part in school plays only if her daughter maintained a B average. Miss Mills, Lizzie's headmistress at Westlake, would call the Montgomery child into her office and say, "You're not stupid. You need to apply yourself and you can get all A's." Lizzie would curtsy and reply, "Yes, Ma'am," and then go to the drama department instead of the library as she had promised, all of which became a weekly ritual.

"I spent half my time in the headmistress's office," she admitted to *TV Guide* in 1961, "and the other half," she said, in the drama department. Her classmates included the distinguished daughters of actors Spencer Tracy, Herbert Marshall, and Alan Mowbray, and classical pianist Arthur Rubenstein (father to actor John Rubenstein, who later co-starred with *Bewitched* guest-star Jack Warden on the 1980s CBS series, *Crazy Like a Fox*).

But Lizzie was unimpressed. She was bored with school, and always knew that *she* "wanted to be actress."

Beyond her homebound performance as *Snow White*, her first public theatrical performance would be at Westlake, when she was just 6, in that French language production of *Little Red Riding Hood*. "Naturally," she had said of this early endeavor, "I already knew enough to go to Daddy for professional advice."

According to *TV Radio Mirror* in January 1965, he told her, "Forget about acting, Honey. Just think you really are the wolf and act the way you think a wolf would act." It was her introduction to *method acting*.

Slightly less appreciative may have been the faculty of Westlake. Miss Mills may have been correct. Lizzie was a good student but she didn't always work as hard as she could have. It didn't help that she had a penchant for bringing unusual pets to class. According to *Modern Screen* magazine in 1965, one Easter she received a pig which, "horribly enough," she called *Pork Chop*. Her instructor was not too sure how to cope with that and was even more perturbed when Lizzie arrived in class with Chinese hooded rats.

The rodent business began when her mother once traveled east by train to see her husband, Robert Montgomery. Lizzie accompanied Mrs. Montgomery to the station, where she noticed a little boy walking around the station with one of the Chinese hooded rats on his shoulder. Lizzie announced that it was just the thing to have as her mother boarded the train. But Elizabeth Allen's last and very definite word was *no* . . . until, of course, the following Christmas when her daughter received two tiny animals as gifts she named Connie and Otis.

From there, *the things* just multiplied like crazy, she said, and at one point she owned approximately fifteen rats at once. "They used to get out of their cages and we were always counting noses, tails, and whiskers to be sure we had them all."

On one of those days when Connie and Otis were let lose in the Montgomery abode, Allen asked Lizzie to place her new playthings back in their cage. To which Lizzie replied, "But I want one to sleep on my bed."

"You can't sleep with the rat, Elizabeth."

"The dog sleeps on the bed."

"That's different."

"Why?"

"Well, you might roll over on it."

The wise Lizzie child was finally convinced to place her pet rat, be it Connie or Otis, back in its gilded environment, although not for long.

One evening the Montgomery family was entertaining guests, as they were prone to do, and little Elizabeth came down from her room for a meet and greet. She did everything expected of a young lady of her stature: curtsied and politely introduced herself, saying, "How do you do?"

Then the unexpected happened, causing one unsuspecting female guest to let out a shriek and drop her martini. Two little rat heads peeked out from behind Lizzie's hair bows and two skinny rat tails were protruding on either side.

"Elizabeth, try to keep the rats upstairs," murmured Mrs. Montgomery.

Her poor mother! At one point they had three dogs, two cats, a white duck called "Pittosporum," some alligators, and a cockatiel named "Nankypoo." The problem was Nankypoo, which her parents had given her. As Lizzie remembered in *Modern Screen*, 1965, her mother was always saying, "Will you please make sure the bird stays upstairs?" If that sounds like a wild thing to say about a bird, it's because Nankypoo was never in his cage. He was always walking around, following some unsuspecting individual. In fact, he never flew; he walked. "He'd get up on top of doors but he wouldn't fly," Lizzie said.

If that wasn't enough, another time, Nankypoo walked into the living room, walked up to the coffee table, hopped up on the edge of the table, and then onto a certain female visitor's glass and proceeded to drink it nearly dry. Lizzie always thought it might have been the same woman who dropped her martini over her rats, because this time she and all the other women in the room screamed loudly. Nankypoo had walked across the table, hopped to the floor, walked two feet and fell flat. "He must have had a dreadful hangover next day," she mused.

A few years after those early spirited days at Westlake, Lizzie, at 17, embarked on her final semester with the school and faced a tough decision. Her family was leaving Los Angeles, and she could either remain at Westlake or enroll for a year at the Spence School for Girls in New York. The thought of being separated from her family was one she could not imagine. So she left Westlake and went to Spence where, she said, they were "very dear" to her, and where she enrolled in various courses in French and architecture that she called "interesting."

After attending the Spence School, she spent two years studying acting at that same city's renowned American Academy of Dramatic Arts. Her charismatic charms were surely visible to audiences at this early stage, but her student performances drew the most stringent commentary from her father. He would send her curt, disapproving notes for performances that he deemed less than worthy. "Not good enough," he would scribble. "Try again."

"Daddy listens to my ideas, and then criticizes," she told *TV People and Pictures Magazine* in October 1953. "It's all impersonal and constructive."

According to *People Magazine* in 1995, Lizzie once said, "Like Daddy, I try to be neat, concise in my work, and in anything else for that matter."

In 1989, however, she laughed and said her father's response to her chosen profession was, "Oh, shit!"

"That was the first time I had ever heard that word. And I was no more than six years old."

But they were still chums, at least from when she was a child until she became a star on her own and of her own show. As she conveyed to *TV People and Pictures* in 1953, "We're terrific companions and are so much alike. We love to Charleston together. And Daddy is the only one who can tire me out. Usually, I sit out the Charleston at a dance. It's too strenuous for my dates."

According to "Our Name Is Montgomery," published in *TeleVision Life Magazine*, January 1954, Elizabeth dated her first boy at fourteen, when she and her family lived in an elegant white home in the Bel Air district of Beverly Hills. "Dad sort of scrutinized each young man when he came to call for me," she said. "It was really sort of sad; they were all terrified of him. Sometimes he was a little cold, when he really disliked the boy, but most times he tried to make them feel at home."

By the time she was twenty, she was on her own. Sometimes her mother asked her about the boys she dated, sometimes she didn't. "I was brought up to be trusted," Lizzie said.

In either case, Mrs. Montgomery didn't wait up for her daughter to arrive home from a night out on the town. And as for marriage, it was far from Lizzie's mind at the time. She wanted to first start her career. As if mimicking the plot of *Bewitched* that would debut ten years later, she added, "I really don't think it's fair to the man if he doesn't know what he's getting—an actress or a housewife."

As played out in the pilot of *Bewitched*, *Samantha* didn't reveal to *Darrin* that she was a witch until after they married.

Lizzie's relationship with her parents, specifically, her father, was passive-aggressive, to say the least. Robert and his friends, like James Cagney, eventually assisted with her theatrical pursuits, but also became her toughest critics, even when it came to how she dressed and carried herself. According to the Ronald Haver interview in 1991, Robert's primary acting advice to Lizzie was to listen to the other actors in a scene, while Cagney cautioned her about the way she walked. "Be sure you're listening to what the other person is saying to you," her father would tell her. Cagney advised, "Just learn your lines and just don't bump into anything."

Cagney once went as far as to say, "Elizabeth, you are the clumsiest person for a graceful person I've ever met in my life." And she agreed. "I could ride (horses) like the wind," she said. "I was very athletic. But trust me, to walk from here to that door I'd probably fall down three times. It was awful."

But at least she'd fall gracefully, and looked good on her descent.

In 1988, Byron Munson, *Bewitched's* costume designer, always said Lizzie had "horrible taste in clothes." Maybe that's because her father was never around. He had only visited the *Samantha* set a few times, and it was only once documented with a photo-op.

Ten years before *Bewitched*, however, he was there to adjust her sense of fashion. According to *TV People and Pictures*, October 1953, he'd tell her, "Never get flamboyant and always dress well."

But at the end of that same month in 1953, she told *TV Guide*, "I like to fuss and primp before (a) party. Clothes have to fit right and be right so that I can concentrate on my date and not what I'm wearing."

"Some parties are just impossible to figure out in advance," she added. "Whenever I show up with shoulders bared, someone else is covered up to the neck. And then, when I cover up, no one else does."

It all sounded like a plot on *Bewitched*. In fact, it was. Namely, the pilot episode in which *Darrin's* former girlfriend *Sheila Summers* (Nancy Kovack) invites him and his new bride *Samantha* to a party *Sheila* claims would be "casual." It ends up being nothing of the sort, and Sam is embarrassed in her less-than-formal wear. Then, in "Snob in the Grass," from the fourth season, *Sheila* tricks her again. This time inviting the *Stephenses* to a formal party, but upon arrival in their finest duds, they see the other attendees in casual wear.

In both episodes, *Samantha* lets *Sheila* "have it." She twitches to her heart's content, at one point twirling *Sheila* into a frenzy of wardrobe malfunctions, leaving her emotions frazzled and her clothes unraveled, while *Darrin* stands by in amusement and somewhat guarded approval.

But Lizzie's wardrobe approval rating with her father wasn't as flexible as *Sam's* nose wriggle. So she'd keep things simple. He liked her in suits and thought blue jeans were acceptable only in the summer, as long as they were clean. She wore little makeup, liked pearl chokers, face veils, and poodle haircuts. Her father also insisted that she watch her posture. "I get a slap on the back if I don't stand up straight," she told *TV People and Pictures*.

Unphased, Lizzie would merely get annoyed when in her youth her schoolmates and her dad called her "Betta," just as when Bette Davis called her "Betty." More than anything, her ambition, at least at this acting stage of the game, was her true calling—to become as accomplished and respected a performer as either Davis or her father, despite her wardrobe or lack thereof.

Bill Asher directed her third feature film, Paramount's 1963 release *Johnny Cool*, the year before they combined their powers to be on *Bewitched*. As author Ronald L. Smith observed in his book, *Sweethearts of '60s TV* (S.P.I. Books, 1993), the studio had been grooming Lizzie as a "sultry, super bewitching sex symbol, five foot eight in heels." *The New York Times* deplored the "flaccid direction of William Asher," but not the scenes featuring Lizzie, especially when she does her soul searching wearing nothing but a lap robe. "Miss Montgomery, without the benefit of wardrobe, attracts more attention then the entire uncomfortable cast," all of whom remained clothed.

$\mathcal{F}our$

~

Brush with Fame

"My art belongs to Daddy."

—Elizabeth, to *Screen Stars* magazine, August 1967

Both of Lizzie's parents were very talented and artistic individuals. They were also wise in other ways of the world, and she trusted them for counsel in all areas, specifically when it came to her choosing a vocation.

According to *TV Radio Mirror*, April 1970, her mother once told her not to be "foolhardy" or "back away from obstacles . . . enjoy everything you do to the fullest or don't do it. There's nothing worse for the people around you than if you're doing something which makes you miserable."

And in Lizzie's jubilant and advantaged youth, acting made her the happiest, although it was merely first on her list of four main potential career choices. The remaining three were: a jockey, a criminal lawyer, or an artist for Walt Disney. Of the last, she mused in 1989, "For some reason he never asked me. Can you imagine? The poor thing . . . certainly ruined his career."

As *Modern Screen* magazine pointed out in May 1965, the walls of Lizzie's dressing room were lined with some quick sketches of a child named Annabelle about whom Elizabeth was writing a book. Annabelle had pigtails with polka dot bows but she also had ragamuffin eyes, "round, listening eyes, full of warmth and love like Elizabeth's."

Today, her friend Sally Kemp says Elizabeth was very serious about her artistic endeavor:

> She always wanted to draw for Disney. She drew all the time. We would get in trouble in class at the Academy because she was always drawing little creatures and caricatures, and she'd sometimes get caught. I knew she was talented, but I didn't know how seriously she thought about it. We never talked about it. That was just one of the things that Elizabeth did . . . was draw charming pictures. I pretended to be a ballerina. And Elizabeth would draw pictures.

Soon, Elizabeth would be *starring* in *moving* pictures, including *Bewitched*, the opening animated credit sequence of which featured the cartooned caricatures of her first with Dick York and then later with Dick Sargent. But she wasn't impressed. As she explained in 1989:

> I didn't like *those things*. They were real *stick-figury*. They didn't look right to me. It was a cute idea. If that had been a basic storyboard, I would have said, "Great! Now, where can we go from here to make it a little more *snappier* and sophisticated" because I thought (the way it was) was too simple.

She said the *Bewitched* animation didn't have to be as elaborate as in the 1988 animated feature film *Who Framed Roger Rabbit* but, in another nod to Walt Disney, she smiled and suggested, "I'm talking *Bambi*, maybe." Meanwhile, her own artwork looked right to *Bewitched* director R. Robert Rosenbaum, who was later crowned Head of Production for Lorimar Television (which produced shows like *Falcon Crest*, starring Lizzie's future husband, Robert Foxworth). But while still guiding *Samantha's* live-action adventures, Rosenbaum praised not only Lizzie's on-screen abilities but her off-screen artistic talents. "One gift I'll always treasure," he said in 1988, "is the painting of a man in a director's chair that Elizabeth created for me."

As was detailed in *TV Guide*, May 13, 1967, Lizzie had dabbled in watercolors and in quite effective pen-and-ink sketches. Her art had a fetching quality. "I'd love to do watercolors like Andrew Wyeth," she said, but added firmly, "I know I never can." A friend then theorized, "Liz is not sure of herself artistically. She is not willing to put herself on the line until she is damn sure she is the best artist in the whole world." The friend likened all this to *Bewitched*. "The show is fun, but no challenge. Liz is too happy being *Samantha* to try anything truly difficult."

All of that would later change with her post-*Bewitched* TV-movies like 1972's *The Victim* and 1974's *A Case of Rape*, both of which explored the darker themes that Lizzie had experimented with in pre-*Samantha* TV guest appearances like *Kraft's Theatre '62* rendition of "The Spiral Staircase" (NBC, October 4, 1961) and the *Alcoa Premiere* episode, "Mr. Lucifer" (ABC, November 1, 1962).

According to the August 1967 edition of *Screen Stars* magazine, Lizzie once said, "My art belongs to Daddy." And although she was an artist of many colors, she wasn't referring here to her painting and drawing ability, but to her talent as an actress. In her heart, she knew she inherited her theatrical abilities from her father. She appreciated that talent and she ultimately credited him for helping her to hone it, whether that guidance took the form of general advice over the years, for example, by his insistence that she attend the New York American Academy of Dramatic Arts, or actual hands-on experience during early TV performances on *Robert Montgomery Presents*. Either way, Lizzie received formal dramatic training, although sometimes *melodramatic* training by way of *Presents*. As she told Ronald Haver in 1991, that show became an outlet for her dad's need for "control . . . the desire to thin-line." She wasn't sure how well-liked her father was as a person, but *Robert Montgomery Presents* was liked by the audience. It became one of television's pioneering live dramas.

Her initial performances on *Presents* elicited excited responses from various producers. So much so, she eventually made her Broadway debut as the ingénue in *Late Love*, which ran from October 13, 1953 through November 7, 1953 at the National Theatre (today known as the Nederlander), and from November 9, 1953 to January 2, 1954, at the Booth Theatre, for a total of 95 performances.

Love also starred Arlene Francis, and Cliff Robertson who, after prolonged failing health, died at age eighty-eight on September 10, 2011 (the day after his birthday and two weeks following his interview for this book).

In his prime, Robertson was a handsome actor with a stellar resume and even more fascinating life, one worth noting if only because it peaked and somewhat mirrored Lizzie's life.

Born on September 9, 1923, in La Jolla, California, he was two years old when he was adopted by wealthy parents who named him Clifford Parker Robertson III. After his parents divorced and his mother passed away, he was reared by his maternal grandmother, whom he adored. He later gained attention for his second marriage to actress and heiress Dina Merrill, daughter of financier E. F. Hutton and Marjorie Merriweather Post, heiress to the Post Cereal fortune and one of the world's wealthiest women. (The two would periodically work together, notably in a two-part episode of the ABC/Screen Gems 1960s camp series, *Batman*, in which he played a villain named "Shame" to her "Calamity Jan.")

In 1963, he portrayed John F. Kennedy (who was good friends with Lizzie via Bill Asher) in the feature film *PT-109*, and would go on to win an Oscar for his lead performance in *Charly*, the 1968 feature film in which he played a mentally challenged man who undergoes an experiment that temporarily transforms him into a genius. Although never elevated to the top ranks of leading men, Cliff remained popular from the 1950s into the twenty-first century with roles such as the kindly "Uncle Ben" in the first *Spider-Man* feature film (released in 2001).

Like Elizabeth, he did not shun controversy or tolerate injustice. In 1977, he blew the whistle on a Hollywood financial scandal. He discovered that David Begelman, president of Columbia Pictures, had forged his signature on a $10,000 salary check, and contacted the FBI and the Burbank and Beverly Hills police. Hollywood insiders were none too pleased with the unattractive publicity and Robertson said that neither the studios nor the networks would hire him for four years.

But decades before, in 1953, he worked with Lizzie in *Late Love*, an experience he recalled in 2011 if only for the appreciation she had for their co-star Arlene Francis:

> Arlene was a big TV star at the time, and she had been in the theatre in her earlier days. She brought a humanistic element to the play. She was also a very down-to-earth person, who was bright, quick, and witty. And Elizabeth admired and respected that. Liz was very young and, therefore, not too experienced. But she was quite ambitious and very professional. She had that respect for her craft that she garnered from her father, I'm sure. He was from Brooklyn, but as he got older he went into theatre and then on

to Hollywood, where he became quite a successful film star. From there, he went into television.

Cliff's relationship with Lizzie never waxed romantic, but as he said, they became those "good pals." Meanwhile, her sophisticated family, particularly on her mother's side, took a shine to him, partially due to his Southern roots and possibly due to his cosmopolitan upbringing.

"Her family was very nice to me," Robertson said. "They used to invite me up to their place in New York. She had an elderly aunt, a wonderful lady who lived in Beverly Hills. And I used to see (Becca) for a number of years, and then she passed away."

But her maternal relatives were not particularly fond of her father or his profession. "I don't think the Southern tier of her family was completely impressed by Robert Montgomery, or any actor." As Robertson acknowledged, Lizzie still became enamored with acting, but with provisions.

> She was determined not to be thought of as just a social actress, and she was also determined to be recognized as a professional. She knew she had to work hard to earn that respect. She was well aware that her father was a fine and respected actor, and a well-known producer. And she knew and respected that difference as well. She in no way ever wanted to be treated special because she was his daughter. She was very democratic that way, and I don't mean (just) politically.

The "political" relationship between the liberal Lizzie and her Republican father may have at times proved a challenge, but Robertson described the association as "very good," with reservations:

"I would say Elizabeth was always politically aware, not oriented. And I suspect her marriage to Bill Asher had something to do with that, at least later on. I don't know that for certain, but I suspect that." When reminded that it was Asher who directed President Kennedy's birthday celebration at which Marilyn Monroe sang a breathy "Happy Birthday, Mr. President," the near-ninety-year-old Robertson exclaimed, "Yes, of course. Because he knew JFK. That fits!"

Equally surprised to learn that *Bewitched* began rehearsals on November 22, 1963, the day President Kennedy was assassinated, Cliff went on to explain how much Lizzie's particularly bright appeal contributed to the success of that series during what became a very tumultuous and dark time in American history. "She was most certainly the main ingredient that was brought to that show. What you saw on the screen was pretty much who she was . . . that was her personality. She was delightfully up. She was smart. But she wasn't smart-ass."

In the *TV Guide* article, "Like Dad, Like Daughter," published July 24, 1953, Lizzie expressed hopes of one day finding fame by way of her famous father. Although she refused to ride that road on his name only, he sought to simplify her path as much as possible. That summer she became a member of his select acting company and, despite the nepotistic boost, they both insisted that she, then only twenty, would ultimately have to make it on her own.

"I have a standing offer with Liz," Robert Montgomery said. "Any time she wants to discuss her career with me, I'm available. But the decisions are hers."

"I grew up with Dad's acting, which probably raised my hopes of becoming an actress," she added. "But I think I'd have wanted that even if Dad had never acted."

She had looked forward to winning a role in *Eye Witness*, a 1950 film her father was making in England. She asked for a screen test and Robert consented. "The only trouble with that," she said dolefully, "was that another actress (Ann Stephens) got the part."

The following year, she finally won her father's approval for that now famous *Montgomery Presents* episode, "Top Secret," the last line of which Robert called "the best one in the script. It was originally to have been mine," he said. "But Liz wanted it, so I had to give in. What else could I do?" Fall prey to her charms, it would seem; just as her mother did on many an occasion. As Lizzie explained in 1965:

> They were both sweet enough to point out some of the difficulties of a show business life, especially for a girl. The difficulty is actually the matter of exposing yourself to a series of rejections. It isn't like any other business. You're selling yourself, offering yourself, and if you don't get a part, it's you

who are being rejected. It's something you have to learn to live with if you're really serious about acting.

She was clearly very serious about her theatrical pursuits and her parents, specifically her father, were willing to support the task at hand. He promised her when she was fourteen years old that she could make her professional debut with him, and with the "Secret" episode on *Presents*, he kept that promise. "He knew me well enough to know that being an actress would never interfere with me," she said in 1953. "Actually working with him gave me an enormous respect for the business."

But in July 1954, she told *Cosmopolitan* writer Joe McCarthy a different story. According to the article, "The Montgomery Girl," she wasn't at all happy with working in her father's summer stock TV theatre:

What will people think? People will say I'm working on this show because I'm Daddy's daughter. That bothers me. I don't want anyone to think I'm not standing on my own two feet. Golly, at times like this I wish Daddy were a laundry truck driver or a certified public accountant.

Then for *TV Guide*, August 7, 1954, she added:

The trouble is that if Daddy were driving a laundry truck, I'd probably be washing shirts in his laundry instead of acting on Summer Theatre.

Meanwhile, her father, interviewed for the *Cosmopolitan* piece, had a less intense view of the scenario:

I'm sure the only person who is sensitive about our father-daughter relationship is Elizabeth herself. Actually, I've gone out of my way not to push her along. Partly because nobody helped me when I was young and I think it's better that way, and partly because Elizabeth is a strong-willed girl with a mind of her own and she doesn't need help.

Robert claimed Lizzie didn't ask him to make even a phone call on her behalf when she was trying to land the ingénue role in *Late Love*, the live stage production in which she made her Broadway debut in the fall of 1953. "She never discussed the play with me before she took the role," he relayed to *TV Guide*, "and she never talked with me about how she should handle her part while she was in rehearsal. As a matter of fact, she didn't show me the script of *Late Love* until a few days before the played opened."

She may have simply wanted to wing it alone this time. As she told *TeleVision Life Magazine* the following January, 1954:

> You have two strikes against you when you're a movie star's child. There are some people who are waiting for you to do something wrong. If a director tells you to do something you really don't agree with, you're not in a position to object. The extras would just love it if Montgomery's daughter argued with the director.

But no one showed her any animosity. "Everybody's been just so wonderful and kind," she said. Her father's company excluded.

According to *TV Radio Mirror* in January 1965, when a preparatory edition of *Late Love* was performed in Hartford, Connecticut, a proud if judgmental papa was in the audience. He went backstage after the curtain fell and said, as she hung on his every word, "Well, my girl, naturally, I hope you'll improve before you get to Broadway."

To which she dutifully responded, "You're right, Daddy. I'll try harder." And she did. *Late Love* hit Broadway on October 13, 1953, and before its season (of 95 performances) was up on January 2, 1954, Lizzie had won the coveted Daniel Blum Theatre World Award. A note of congratulation arrived from her dad. It said simply, "Good."

Upon receiving it, she sighed and said, "That one word from my father was equal to a volume of praise from anyone else."

Later on *Bewitched*, an affirmative "Good!"—with an exclamation point—became one of the popular one-word catch phrases that Lizzie incorporated into *Samantha's* speech pattern whenever she approved of some random magic or mortal occurrence on *Bewitched*.

As opposed to when *Sam* would squeal "Well?!" whenever she was unable to answer one of *Darrin's* spastic queries of "What's going on?!"

On August 7, 1954, *TV Guide* published the article, "Biggest 'Barn' On Earth: Summer Stock Was Never Like This"; it profiled *Robert Montgomery's*

Summer Theatre (also known as *Robert Montgomery's Playhouse*), which was a summer replacement series for *Robert Montgomery Presents*. At the time the show was in its third hit season. Robert Montgomery was proud of the series, which he conceived in 1952 as what *TV Guide* called, "a sound way to hold onto his network spot during the dog days of July, August, and early September." Or as he further explained, the program gave "a group of young actors a chance to put on a show of their own, undominated by big names and formidable reputations . . . this week's star may be next week's butler." *Presents* always aired live (only Robert's intros and farewells were on film), and the scripts had "nearly always been reasonably lively," *TV Guide* said.

After her affair with *Late Love* ended, Lizzie was seduced by a role in *A Summer Love*, which aired as a critically praised episode of her father's summer series on July 20, 1953:

> An egotistical actor many times married (John Newland), falls hopelessly in love with a young ingénue (Lizzie) in his theatre troupe. But upon meeting her family, he enlists the assistance of a former wife (Margaret Hayes) to help him secure happiness with his new love.

She also received high marks from her co-star, the reputable John Newland who, according to *TV Radio Mirror*, said, "Elizabeth is one of the most flexible actresses I've ever known."

Robert, meanwhile, was more subdued with his review. "Elizabeth," he remarked, "always remember that, if you achieve success, you will get applause; and, if you get applause, you will hear it. But my advice to you concerning applause is this: Enjoy it, but never quite believe it."

The following May, Lizzie continued to address whether or not her prestigious lineage helped or hindered her career. In the article, "The Girl Behind the Twitch," published by *Modern Screen*, she said, "Celebrity off-spring or no celebrity offspring, it's one thing (to have a name) to open doors and another to keep them open. Nobody will take a second chance on you unless you're good, no matter who you are."

Or as she reiterated to John Tesh in 1992, "A name will open doors."

But when she wed senior actor Gig Young in 1956, Elizabeth Montgomery considered changing her name to "Elizabeth Young," if only out of respect to her new husband, and maybe as a tiny jab to her dad. "I gave it to him good," she mused to *TV Guide* in 1961.

Robert, however, recoiled at the notion and responded with a "real pathetic look," she recalled. He was unhappy with her choice to marry a "father-figure" of a man more than twice her age. What's more, he was concerned that the public would think she was the daughter of rival actor Robert Young who, during the reign of *Robert Montgomery Presents*, was the star of the hit family show, *Father Knows Best* (CBS/NBC, 1954–1960). Not only would Robert Young have another hit series (*Marcus Welby, M.D.* on ABC, 1969–1975, debuting in *Bewitched's* sixth season); but like Lizzie's father, he had been a film star of the 1930s and 1940s at the same studio, MGM.

In effect, Mr. Montgomery wondered if Lizzie was "ashamed" of him and their family name. And even though she at times enjoyed confounding him, a brief press item about actress Lee Remick's wedding may have offered at least a measure of relief.

Lizzie was a dear friend of Remick's and served as matron of honor at her marital ceremony, held at the Church of St. Vincent Ferrer in New York. As archived in the Thomas Crane Public Library, the wedding announcement/press release, dated August 3, 1957, was titled: "Lee Remick, Quincy Star of TV and Movies, Bride of William A. Colleran in New York City." It described Lizzie as:

> Mrs. Elizabeth Montgomery Young of New York City, daughter of Robert Montgomery, film star, TV actor, and producer. Mrs. Young will wear a ballerina gown of pastel mint green chiffon with a harem skirt, matching accessories, velvet coronet, and will carry a nosegay of white carnations and pink sweetheart roses.

Despite such intermittent clarifications, Lizzie's lineage was always in question, as when George Montgomery, another contemporary of her father's with whom she shared no relation, was added to the name game. (Additionally, George, Lizzie, and Robert were no relation to actor Earl Montgomery—born 1894, died 1966—who is periodically albeit inaccurately linked to Robert Montgomery's film, and Lizzie's favorite of her father's movies, *The Earl of Chicago*.)

Film historian Rob Ray co-hosts the esteemed weekly Friday Film Forum at Long Beach School for Adults in Long Beach, California. As he sees it, George Montgomery was more of a common man who came to prominence in the early 1940s as the more established stars like Robert went off to war. George was a Twentieth Century Fox contract player who made minor hits like 1942's *Roxie Hart* (*Chicago* without the music), "but he never really became a star. He usually supported the female star in a list of films and had the lead in B movies."

George also went on to support and marry TV legend Dinah Shore, and lived somewhat in her shadow when she became a hugely popular star of her own show. While she devoted all her time to a successful television career and entertained millions, he became a talented carpenter and wood-worker (a role he later popularized in Pledge TV commercials of the 1970s).

Eventually, he became bored and "started dallying with the hired help and other available women," Ray says. "She caught him and divorced him in 1963, but they remained friends and had children together; and he was at her side when she died, long after her very public relationship with Burt Reynolds. He died sometime later in the nineties. But he was always just another average vendor selling his wood pieces at those home craft festivals around the country back in the '80s and '90s. You'd never guess he had been a star, except that he still had the star charisma.

Robert Montgomery's life was quite a different story. He came from money and entered films around 1930 at MGM as what Ray calls "a suave, Cary Grant–type in the days before Archie Leach (Grant's real name) became Cary Grant." He worked largely at MGM, which is now owned by Ted Turner, and remained a star into the forties. But as they aged, Grant garnered the suave roles and Robert moved into films noir and war movies in the 1940s and went behind the cameras directing and producing especially on television in the 1950s. During the Red Scare of the late 1940s and early 1950s, he was considered a loyal, conservative old-money establishment Republican, which Ray says, "Elizabeth rebelled against."

Just as her career took off with *Bewitched*, Robert's started slowing down. He largely stayed out of the limelight for the rest of his life until his death in 1981. "I never, ever saw him appear with Elizabeth anywhere after she became a star," Ray intones. "I suspect she always feared being known as 'Robert Montgomery's daughter' and did everything she could to downplay that relationship, including not casting him as her father in *Bewitched*."

Actually, she did cast him, but he said no. By the time *Bewitched* became a hit—which was immediately after it debuted in 1964—it was Robert Montgomery who became known as "Elizabeth Montgomery's father." Fact is, she became a bigger star than he ever was. As Lizzie's friend Sally Kemp revealed on MSNBC's *Headliners & Legends* in 2001, she encountered people who knew of Elizabeth, but were unfamiliar with who her father was.

In 1999, Billy Asher, Jr. told A&E's *Biography* that post-*Bewitched*, people would approach Robert Montgomery and identify him as Elizabeth Montgomery's father. That just tickled Lizzie to no end. At such times she responded with a triumphant "Yes!" because as Billy saw it, she had a very strong sense of who she was as a person.

The label, "Robert Montgomery's daughter," was an albatross around her neck. "And boy, did she want to get past *that*," Billy added. Indeed. As reported in Elizabeth's interview with *TV Radio Mirror* in January 1965,

> "After ten years as an actress, you'd think people would have stopped asking me how it feels to be Bob Montgomery's daughter," she grumbles, but without losing the twinkle in her eyes. "How the devil do people think it feels? I'm deeply fond of my father, he feels the same about me. Just like any father and daughter. What else is there to be said about it?"

With that in mind, and although a reserved actress, Lizzie did not shy away from the public life created first by her father's name and then her own. In the end, her charismatic father trusted his dynamic daughter to follow her own career path. In the early days, pre-*Bewitched*, and upon her request, he remained accessible to her, but was sure not to play favorites. She would still have to "prove herself," he said, which she certainly would do, time and again.

Elizabeth's relationship with Robert Montgomery, however, also helped to build her character and strengthen her spine in an industry that many times takes no prisoners. As Bill Asher, Sr. told *Screen Stars* in August 1965, "She is perhaps a little overly conscientious, in short, a worrier. But that's a good way to be in a demanding profession."

However, he concluded, "I think she gets her professional attitudes, her capacity for taking infinite pains, from her father."

Bottom line: Elizabeth wasn't all that interested in following her father onto the big screen. She felt more comfortable on TV and the Broadway stage, venues that for her boded well. By the time "Top Secret" aired, she had just graduated from the American Academy of Dramatic Arts (with Sally Kemp, and June Lockhart of *Lost in Space* fame, herself the daughter of esteemed actors Gene and Kathleen Lockhart). Lizzie had also served a summer internship at the John Drew Memorial Theater, in Easthampton, Long Island. Because of her youthful appearance, she was placed in ingénue roles at this theatre and was already concerned about being typecast, some thirteen years before immortalizing *Samantha* on *Bewitched*. "Even though I'm twenty now," she bemoaned to *TV Guide* in 1953, "everybody thinks I'm about fifteen. If this keeps up, I'll probably be playing ingénues until I'm forty."

Of a liberal mindset with no interest in making a mark in feature films, Lizzie preferred to play comedic parts, which were at the very least a staple of her dad's career. She was also interested in pursuing musical comedy but confessed, "I can't sing." Or at least she believed she couldn't carry a tune, which she would later disprove as *Serena* in a few peppy musical episodes of *Bewitched* and as the guest-hostess in 1966 on ABC's *The Hollywood Palace* variety show. For the moment, however, she only danced, with training in ballet, in case a Broadway musical ever materialized. But that opportunity never presented itself.

Except for her initial "Top Secret" segment of *Robert Montgomery Presents*, she had not yet even acted on TV, mostly because the American Academy of Dramatic Arts frowned upon students performing in any manner outside its walls. But she held no ill will against the school. In fact, she was grateful to it for teaching her how to read lines, something her father had prodded her to do for years. As she continued to tell *TV Guide* in 1953, "Dad taught me to read everything since I was a little girl."

Despite and during her privileged upbringing, she developed a daring sense of humor, which later contributed to an approachable persona that was unaffected by the various Hollywood machinations. As she explained to *TV Radio Mirror* in 1965:

The parents of Hollywood children really do try to protect them from acquiring too much of the glamour stuff too soon. But, of course, some of it is bound to seep through. Still, it was only in rare cases that the kids got a lopsided view of their position in life. Take me, for instance. I never felt special because my father was a star. Most of the people who came to our house were important in one phase of the industry or another. Many of the kids I went around with at school came from richer or more renowned families than the Montgomerys. I'd say my environment was more likely to teach me humility than the feeling of arrogance.

In 1989, she once more attributed her kind demeanor to her family's guidance. Had she behaved with even the slightest trace of pretention, she said her father would have "picked me up by the feet and slammed me against the wall. And I probably would have deserved it. So, it's no credit to me how I was raised. But it's an enormous credit to my Mom and Dad."

As previously noted, when Robert Montgomery served in the Navy from 1940–1945 during World War II, Lizzie's maternal grandmother Becca Allen became a member of the Montgomery household, contributing a great deal to both Lizzie and her brother's Skip's non-pretentious character.

Out of all the adults who supervised Lizzie as a child, her grandmother Becca certainly seemed to be the one who, more than the others, had it all together. She was young at heart, carefree, and knew how to enjoy life beyond the rigid underpinning of her conservative Southern upbringing. She was supportive of Lizzie's life and career, encouraging, worldly, but unaffected and open-minded. In short, she was *hip*, long before that word was introduced into the vernacular. No wonder Lizzie loved her so much. They bonded on so many levels and were on much more common ground than Lizzie ever shared with her parents.

As Lizzie acknowledged in 1989, had she behaved insolently, Becca would have objected with a sardonic "Oh, please!"

But still, Lizzie looked back and pondered, "Who knows what a *value* is? When you're a tiny child, you really don't know."

To her credit, she admitted to not being "the easiest child to get along with. I was stubborn. I had a very bad temper that I have since learned to control because Daddy had a worse one." But her mother used a different strategy in reprimanding her. "Mom had a habit of becoming very quiet," she recalled. "She would let Dad do the heavy-duty, very articulate disciplining. And I tell you, it was better to raise a hand than an adjective, a verb, or a noun."

"Boy," she added of what could be her father's periodic stern ways, "he could really give it to you." Yet she took it all in stride. In the era in which she was raised, the 1930s–1940s, parents were taught not to spare the rod, or they would spoil the child. "I can barely think of a time when I resented getting in trouble," she said in 1989.

Not one to shirk responsibility, she kept herself in check. If she fell from any particular grace under her parents' close watch, then she stepped up to the plate and took the blame. "If it was my fault, it was my fault," she intoned with unabashed honesty. But she resented getting punished, as much as getting caught. "Because that just meant that I wasn't as clever as I thought I was."

Lizzie believed her parents were rarely incorrect in the way they raised her and she had no complaints. Although she admitted her parents and Becca were "very strict," they made certain she retained her own sense of values. Homework had to be done. Grades were expected to be good. "There were always choices within choices," she explained. "It wasn't just totally regulated. They gave me a lot of freedom to a point."

Despite that latitude, there were specific restrictions that she termed "weird." For one, her parents forbade her from going to the movies, which was unfortunate because for her so simple an excursion was "an amazing treat." That isn't to say her parents denied their daughter the joyful pastime that millions around the world continue to embrace unto this day. They did not put their collective foot down and demand that she never step foot in a movie theatre. "It was much subtler than that," she said.

"Oh, now, Elizabeth," she recalled her father saying, "you have something a hell of a lot better to do than on a Saturday afternoon than sitting in a movie theatre."

"But everybody else gets to go," she would protest.

"We don't care what everybody else is doing," would be the response. "This is what *you* are going to do." She said such exchanges were "fairly regular," and in time, she became intrigued with not attending the cinema, a media-sensitive prohibition that may have seemed odd, particularly due to her father's movie stardom. But she didn't think they were trying to *protect* her. "That might not be the right word," she said. Instead, she viewed the prevention measure as a modus by her parents to steer her from temptation. "I was a mad enough child that I would want to jump into it immediately," she concluded in 1989 of the movie-going experience.

However, in 1991, during her conversation with Ronald Haver, she explained how her father's film *Here Comes Mr. Jordan* played into the game of her non-movie-going experience when she was as a child. She began by explaining an early scene in the movie in which the plane carrying her father's character, *Joe Pendleton*, was falling apart. It became a particularly traumatic sequence for her to watch as a child:

> When I saw that strut, or whatever that's called, on the plane snap, and plane suddenly started to go, I was just a mess. I hated that. I hated it when I was little. That's probably why they never let me see movies because I just reacted so badly to everything. I didn't see (Disney's) *Snow White* (*and the Seven Dwarfs*) until it was like rereleased for the fortieth time or something because I swear I was like fifteen or sixteen . . . They would never let me see it because of the witch.

Sally Kemp recalls things differently. "We'd go to the movies all the time." But this was in their teen years, when they met as students at the prestigious American Academy of the Dramatic Arts in New York. Somewhat more independent by then, it was Lizzie who now set the rules, if only to confuse Sally with the provisions. Lizzie would take her cousin Panda to Walt Disney pictures, but Sally was only allowed to see horror movies, and she never understood why. "It was like she had some kind of catalogue," Sally says, mimicking her friend's logic in the situation: "*Sally goes to horror movies and my cousin goes to Disney films.*"

Sally found the cinema segregation particularly puzzling, mostly because Panda, with whom she remains good friends today, seemed better suited for viewing horror films. "She had more of a macabre streak than I did."

Ever unpredictable, Lizzie surprised Sally one day, inviting her to see the classic 1953 feature film, *Lili*, starring Leslie Caron, Mel Ferrer, Jean-Pierre Aumont, and Zsa Zsa Gabor. Though a few of the characters may not always be on their best behavior, this delightful romantic comedy with a dash of fancy could hardly be classified as a monster movie:

A circus troupe in France takes under their wing a poor 16-year-old girl named *Lili Daurier* (Caron). After her father dies only a month before, *Lili* finds herself stranded in a strange town. *Marc the Magnificent* (Aumont), a magician in a local circus, takes a particular interest in *Lili*, though not romantically, for he views her only as a troubled child. Rejected, *Lili* turns to the circus puppets with whom she sings away her troubles, oblivious to the puppeteers behind the curtains. Upon her initial chorus with the puppets, a crowd gathers. The circus almost immediately has a new act, and the little girl lost is found, even though she's not at all fond of the angry *Paul* (Ferrer), the carnival's owner, who is also the main puppeteer. In time, *Lili* realizes *Marc* the magician is married (to his assistant, Gabor), and that her feelings for him were mere fancy, for it is *Paul* who she truly loves. It's a fact she learns almost too late if not for the indelible mark *Paul* makes by infusing his heart and soul into the beloved puppets, which at the film's conclusion, have seemingly come to life.

Upon close inspection of the film, it may be clear as to why Lizzie held it so dear—and why she chose to share it with a good friend like Sally.

Lili had lost her father when she was only sixteen. Sally's father had died when she was young. *Lili* tells a joke early on in the film that references horses, which both Lizzie and Sally adored.

Lili to Marc: When is a singer not a singer?
Marc: When?
Lili: When he is a little horse.

Other quotes from the film are more reflective: "A little of what you want is better than large quantities" and "Refusal to compromise is a sign of immaturity."

On screen, *Lili* was seeking answers to life's biggest questions. Off screen, in the 1953 reality of her youth, and with an adventurous, if short, life ahead of her, so was Lizzie. With her good and generous heart, she may have then felt Sally was also seeking the same answers. Instead of viewing the beastly images of the horror movies they all too frequently attended, Lizzie may have wanted her good friend to gaze upon the simple beauty of *Lili*—a film that Sally would later view sixteen times. "I love it," she says.

"And I think of Elizabeth each time I see it" (as will probably anyone who reads this passage).

The similarities are significant between *Lili* and Lizzie's return to comedy with the CBS TV-movie, *When the Circus Came to Town*, which originally aired on January 20, 1981.

> *Mary Flynn* (Lizzie) lives a middle-aged existence that is tedious and empty. When the circus arrives in her small town, she decides to leave home and join its ranks. In the process, *Mary Flynn* is rejuvenated with a new life purpose. She ultimately finds happiness and love with circus ring leader *Duke* (Christopher Plummer), if fleeting.

A tender and happy story, filled with hope and promise for change, the movie (which was filmed at the Coastal Empire Fairgrounds near Savannah, Georgia) might have been equally pleasing to *Bewitched* fans, providing them with an opportunity to see their beloved Elizabeth Montgomery in a lighter role that most would find fitting to her comedic forte. What's more, *Circus*, like much of Lizzie's work, was filled with lines that could have easily been pulled from the dialogue of her real life. At various points in the film, her character, *Mary Flynn* said:

> "I don't believe in age discrimination."
> "My father just passed away." (The movie aired in 1981—the year Robert Montgomery died.)
> "I have often been complimented on my appearance."
> "I'm deathly afraid of heights" (which Lizzie was in real life).
> "I could never do anything in front of a crowd."
> "I read a lot of Shakespeare myself" (which Robert Montgomery instructed Lizzie to do as a child).
> "Southerners have a long tradition of taking care of their own."
> "Maybe I'll bleach my hair. I used to see all the blond ladies walking around like someone told them it was all right to be sexy. But not me."
> "I always wanted to marry the man I felt close to in bed."
> "I always wanted for somebody else to tell me that things were okay."

Although a few other lines weren't entirely true to Lizzie's form, they came close. At one point in the movie, Lizzie's *Mary* tells Plummer's *Duke*,

"I have guts," which was true of Lizzie. But then *Mary* added, "I also have bad posture," which was not true of Lizzie. Her father wouldn't have allowed it.

In another partially true-to-life moment, *Duke* quizzes *Mary*:

Duke: So you were a *Daddy's girl*?
Mary: I was a Momma's girl until she died. *Then* I was a Daddy's girl.

Off-screen, Lizzie's mother died in 1992, approximately eleven years after her father.

In general, however, *When the Circus Came to Town* still spoke to Lizzie's reality, as did many of her performances through the years, including *The Awakening Land*, which, like *Circus*, was also directed by Boris Sagal. More significantly, *Land* was filmed on vast country landscapes in Illinois, many of which played into Lizzie's memory of her youth growing up on the expansive Montgomery homestead in Patterson, New York. In *Land*, Lizzie portrayed a pioneer woman named *Sayward Luckett Wheeler*, and she was surrounded by a plethora of animals for which she had a great affection, especially horses.

Five

~

The Equestrians

"I have a pair of jodhpurs that look like they belong on a Madame
Alexander Barbie doll."

—Elizabeth Montgomery to Ronald Haver, 1991

Lizzie's early life was a relative age of innocence, one in which she strived
to appreciate the simple pleasures, significantly helped along by her love for
animals. As she explained in 1989, "I've had dogs, cats, crickets, crocodiles,
alligators, deer, goats, pigs, horses, chickens, and anything else you could
name."

Consequently, she frequently performed on screen with nonhumans
such as a chimpanzee in the 1963 feature film *Johnny Cool*, a seeing-eye dog
in the 1984 CBS TV-movie, *Second Sight: A Love Story*, and any number of
minions from the animal kingdom on *Bewitched*. Due to her realistic theatrics, the audience was made to believe that she was bonding with the given
goose or frog, etc. As *Bewitched* writer Richard Baer asserted in 1988, "This,
I believe, is a very difficult thing to do. Yet, there wasn't any question as to
whether she could pull it off."

In fact, according to the March 1965 issue of *TV Picture Life* magazine
and the January 1965 edition of *The Saturday Evening Post*, a special cat
named "Zip Zip" later played into Bill Asher's direction of Lizzie on
Bewitched. Whenever he was looking to pull a particular emotion for her to
utilize as *Samantha*, he would say, from the sidelines, "Zip Zip!"

But all other creatures aside, it was Lizzie's particular affection for horses that stood out, a bond which her son, Billy Asher, Jr. said was influenced by her dad. "My grandfather was an equestrian," the young Asher relayed in 2001 on the televised *Headliners & Legends* profile of his mom. "When she was very young he had her on a horse and she was drawn right to it."

When she was three years old, Lizzie's father sat her on a pony and said, "Ride!" and so she did; whether around the Montgomery homes in Beverly Hills/Bel Air and Patterson, New York, or in Britain, where she spent school vacations while her father produced films there. To help pass the time, she took horse-jumping lessons and frequently rode with him in the English countryside and London's Hyde Park. She even won a number of ribbons for horsemanship.

As she told Ronald Haver in 1991, "I'll always remember him on horse-back . . . and teaching me to ride. I remember him being very athletic . . . on horseback is how I . . . immediately think of him. That and like polo, and jumping."

Their shared love for mares was one of the non-Hollywood pastimes that contributed to their strong bond in Lizzie's youth. Although Robert at first objected to his daughter's chosen profession, investigative journalist and best-selling author Dominick Dunne told A&E's *Biography* in 1999 that Lizzie and her father thought very highly of one another. According to Dunne, Robert embraced the idea of Lizzie as an actress. "She was a thor-oughbred," Dunne assessed with no intended comparison to horses, which Sally Kemp confirms both she and Lizzie "adored. I think she even had a pet llama. And if she didn't, then she always wanted one."

In time, her art once more would imitate her life—in fact, a few times more. Lizzie rode a variety of mares in her twin TV-movie westerns, *Mrs. Sundance* (1974) and *Belle Starr* (1980), while horses came into play on two episodes of *Bewitched*.

As she explained to *TV Radio Mirror* magazine in November 1969:

> Lord, I *adore* horses. We go to the track every Saturday. I even named a character in *Bewitched* after a horse. There's a horse named John Van Mill-wood, a great big thing that can't get his legs straightened out until he's halfway around the track. And once when a script had a character—I think it was an old boyfriend of *Endora's*—he had some plain old name so I asked if we could call him *John Van Millwood*.

In 1989, she correlated working on *Bewitched* to playing the horses:

There wasn't a moment when I thought, *Oh, I'd rather be someplace else.* First of all, the only other place I'd probably have rather been was the race track and there was always that on the weekends . . . or the tennis courts, right? So that was cool. It's ever so amazing to be paid for something you really enjoy doing," she went on to say. "I still feel that way about acting. I mean, in general, it's a grind. I think physically you pace yourself and that's the way it goes. Horses do that . . . so can people . . . well, jockeys kind of help.

The two *Bewitched* episodes that showcased her love for horses—as well as the race track—were "The Horse's Mouth," a black and white segment from the second season with Dick York that aired March 3, 1966, and "Three Men and a Witch on a Horse," a color episode from the last season with Dick Sargent, airing December 15, 1971.

In "Mouth": A race horse named *Dolly* feels neglected and flees from her owner and into *Samantha's* backyard, while her sister *Adorable Diane* keeps winning races *Dolly* helps to set up. To fully understand her quandary, *Sam* transforms *Dolly* into a woman. When *Darrin* objects to the magic manifestation, *Samantha* says it's a special opportunity to fully understand a horse's day at the races.

In "Three Men": *Endora* transforms *Darrin* into a gambler, after which *Sam* insists the spell be broken. Ignoring her daughter's plea, *Endora* has *Darrin* bet on a horse named *Fancy Dancer* who is bound to lose—and on which he convinces *Larry* and a client to place all bets. As a result, *Sam* pops over to the stables to have a motivating chat with *Dancer*, who ultimately wins the race for fear of ending up at the glue factory.

In 1968, writer Rick Byron interviewed Lizzie for a *Photoplay* magazine article called "The Lady Gambles." Here, she expressed her fondness for horse racing by comparing two views from abroad, most assuredly influenced by her periodic summer vacations in England with her father. "I'm about as thoroughly American as anyone can be," she said, and yet she felt that the United States was missing some of the ceremonial aspects of the

British who, she believed, knew how to "do things in a beautiful, pageant-like manner. "That's one of the reasons I love the races. They're so ceremonious, so steeped in tradition." Whenever she heard the song "My Old Kentucky Home" at the famed Derby, she was driven to tears. "That is how wonderful I think the tradition is," she decided.

At one point in the interview, Lizzie apologized for what she considered to be a boring life, but in the process revealed more insight into her personality than she have may realized or intended. "I'm sorry that I haven't given you much," she said. "I'm afraid I'm a pretty dull interview. The fact of the matter is that I'm not really wild about talking about myself (which is also what she had said in 1989). I'd much rather talk about books or movies or . . . horses."

Her love of horses may have been ignited by her father, but her penchant for the real life race track was instilled in her by her grandmother Becca. According to what Robert Foxworth said on A&E's *Biography*, it was Becca who introduced Lizzie to horse racing. When Lizzie was a little girl, Becca one day walked into her room and said she would not be attending school that morning. Instead, little Lizzie would be accompanying Becca to the races. "You'll learn much more about math at the track than you ever will in class," Becca said.

In a 1993 interview with magazine journalist Bart Mills, Lizzie professed, "I love the track." She didn't own any race horses herself because, "I can lose money perfectly well on other people's horses." Although, she wasn't doing too badly at the time; the Santa Anita Race Track had been "very good to her." "I go as often as I can," she explained, "and when I can't go, I send my bets with my friends . . . There's nothing like a day at the races. There are no phones and if you're lucky, you come back richer."

However, Lizzie's mother was reportedly not at all fond of the equestrian creatures and vice versa. According to Montgomery archivist Tom McCartney, Robert Montgomery had named his polo pony after his wife. Lizzie once recalled the day the two *Bettys* met for the first time. Apparently, they both took a strong dislike to one another. As Elizabeth recalled at the time, her mother was the only person she knew who could fall off of a polo pony that was "standing perfectly still."

☆

Next to her affection for horses, Lizzie's second favorite member of the animal kingdom had to be dogs, various breeds of which she owned through the years.

In 1989, it was the beautiful female canine, Zuleika, named after the heroine *Zuleika Dobson* from the book of the same title written by Max Beerbohm whose entire literary collection Lizzie inherited from her father.

As she explained to Ronald Haver in 1991, Robert Montgomery had instructed her to read Beerbohm, Dickens, Thackeray, and Shakespeare since she was six years old.

> I was really weird as far as that was concerned. (If) you saw a funny little boney-kneed scrawny kid sitting down with Hamlet, at the age of about six, wouldn't you think she was kind of odd? Yes. It's true. It's absolutely true. I was very peculiar. And I guess nothing changes. And I am so really grateful to him for all that and forcing me . . . certainly not against my will . . . to be an avid reader when I was little, so of course I still am. But I think that's why he was so hell-bent on wanting to read everything and (owning) collections of authors . . . because (learning) meant a great deal to him.

Originally published in 1911, *Zuleika Dobson* was a shameless parody about what happens when an enticing young woman enrolls at the elite all-male Judas College, Oxford. A conjurer by trade, *Zuleika Dobson* can only love a man who is immune to her allure: a circumstance that proves ruinous, as many of her love-sick beaus lose the will to live due to her cold-shoulder. Filled with notable catch-phrases ("Death cancels all engagements," utters the first casualty) and inspired throughout by Beerbohm's robust creativity, this rhapsodic take on Edwardian undergraduate life at Oxford has, according to literary great E. M. Forster, "a beauty unattainable by serious literature."

"*Zuleika Dobson*," Forster had also said, "is a highly accomplished and superbly written book whose spirit is farcical. It is a great work—the most consistent achievement of fantasy in our time."

Beerbohm, who lived between 1872 and 1956, and whom George Bernard Shaw once dubbed "the incomparable Max," was an essayist, caricaturist, critic, and short story writer who endures today as one of Edwardian England's leading satirists. *Zuleika Dobson* was Beerbohm's only novel, but a particular favorite of Robert Montgomery's.

Upon subsequently reading the adventures of *Dobson*, Lizzie so loved the character's first name that she gave it to what would become one of her many household pets. As she explained in 1989, the *Zuleika* character in Beerbohm's book was "so beautiful that the statues that she drove by in her carriage broke into cold sweats when she went by. So I thought, 'Well, if I ever get a real pretty dog, I'm going to give her that name.'"

Approximately five years before Zuleika came into Lizzie's life, there was "Emma," a Labrador retriever and her co-worker, as it were, on the TV-movie, *Second Sight: A Love Story*, which originally aired on CBS, March 13, 1984. Here, Lizzie portrayed *Alaxandra McKay*, a stoic, reclusive blind woman who must come to terms with her disability and the subsequent need to utilize the services of a seeing-eye dog. Lizzie in 1989:

> I became very attached to that dog. I always get very attached to every pet I work with. But there was something special about Emma. I think it's because I worked with her for such an extended amount of time (three weeks) before I even started shooting the film. Her trainer, Lee Mitchell, is the most wonderful, gentle person for seeing-eye dogs, and he worked so hard with me with this dog. So I got attached to her, and she got attached to me. And that was it, and the way it should be.

Lizzie and Emma shared nearly every scene together in *Sight* and, at the film's wrap party, found it difficult to detach from one another, so much so, Mitchell at one point turned to Lizzie and asked, "Would you like to have Emma?"

Lizzie was shocked. "It never occurred to me that they would want me to keep her."

She tried to talk herself out of it, if only because she thought the gifted canine would be better placed with someone who was visually impaired. "Emma was totally trained as a seeing-eye dog and I thought she could at least be used as a companion for someone who really needed her," Lizzie said.

But Mitchell was persistent. Emma was too strong for any disabled candidate. His remaining list of specially trained dogs had already been paired with clients and continuing sessions with Emma would not have been a practical business decision. "Aside from that," he said to Lizzie, "she's attached to you."

"Oh, no—she's not!" Lizzie protested, hoping to convince herself of what she knew in her heart was simply not true. She also found it especially hard to dissuade Mitchell, because during their conversation, Emma remained right by her side, panting, with an eager joyful gleam in her eyes.

Lizzie melted. "Oh, shit!" she thought. "I don't believe this!"

Although she still needed time to decide, Mitchell would not take *no* for answer, and pressed her further. "You know you want that dog!"

In the end, Elizabeth finally consented to keep Emma, but unfortunately this story does not have a happy ending. The dog later developed tumors and died.

"It was just the most heartbreaking thing," Lizzie said. "I was just a wreck. It took forever for me to get over losing her."

Long after Emma was gone, the pang of her loss certainly haunted Lizzie with each viewing of *Second Sight*, once even while working on another of her movies, *Face to Face*, which aired on CBS in 1990, but which she filmed with Bob Foxworth in Africa in 1989. For some reason, *Sight* was being screened on the closed circuit monitors on the *Face* set. For those who have not seen the film, be warned, here is a spoiler alert:

At the end of *Sight*, Elizabeth's character, *Alexandra*, no longer requires Emma's assistance and the two are forced to part ways. Consequently, *Alexandra's* heartbreak became Lizzie's heartbreak in reality, and she was reminded of it every time *Sight* was seen, particularly on the set of *Face to Face*. It didn't much help matters that *Alaxandra* cried in those last aired moments in the movie.

When reminded of that scene in 1989, Lizzie explained how that moment between *Alaxandra* and Emma became intolerable for her to watch and experience, even in rehearsals:

I don't like to cry. In fact, I hate it. I mean, I really hate it. So for me, having to cry when I'm working in a scene, well . . . I really have to *do a number on myself*. It's just not a pleasant thing to go through. It's a lot of hard work for me to get to that point. Yet, when an actor performs in certain scenes, you have to do it, and it's yucky. After going over it the first time, I turned around to say something to the director, and noticed that half the crew had disappeared. They each went off to their own little corners and cried, including the cinematographer, Frances Hayes, my wardrobe assistant, and Adele Taylor, the hairdresser. No one stuck around. They were all sobbing and they just left. They couldn't handle it.

It was the kind of emotional effect Lizzie's performances would have on fans and friends alike. Her talent and persuasive personality was evident from a very early age. According to what her former schoolmate Billie Banks revealed on MSNBC's *Headliners & Legends*, even as a child Elizabeth commanded a star-like charisma and respect, and that she at times would wriggle her nose for "good luck" during school exams.

Another childhood friend, Deborah Jowitt, appeared on *Legends* and said Lizzie had a "mischievous . . . happy-go-lucky nature" and was known for her humorous comments and "funny faces."

Sally Kemp today recalls the particular facial expression—an animal imitation—that would later prove quite fortuitous. "We called it her 'bunny nose,'" she explains in reference to Elizabeth's inevitably famous proboscis wriggle. "And we all tried to do it, but nobody could."

By *we*, Sally means herself and cousin Panda, who were both Elizabeth's inseparable sidekicks in their youth. A good portion of that friendship was spent riding horses and roaming the endless acres of the Montgomery homestead in Towners, New York—a sprawling landscape located within Patterson, New York, and near Brewster, a place Sally remembers as a "Kennedy-like compound."

At the turn of the twentieth century, Towners was one of Patterson's major population centers, particularly while it was a junction of the New York Central's Harlem Division and the New Haven's Maybrook Line. The commercial vicinity included a blacksmith shop, a meat market, hotel, grocery store, and hardware store. There were rumors of a reservoir project and cessation of passenger rail stops that contributed to the decline of the community as a vital commercial spot.

In short, and at least geographically speaking, Towners was to Patterson what Beverly Hills is to Los Angeles County. Elizabeth talked about the area to *Modern Screen* in May 1965.

Every summer she and her entire family, including her various aunts, uncles, and cousins, would travel back East to stay. There were three lakes in the area and, as she said, "We swam like crazy." With rowboats and horses, "It really was the most wonderful life a child could have. We had such freedom, and such good discipline. We were taught never to go off on our own. We were taught to have respect for horses and guns (her family enjoyed shot-putting and hunting, the latter of which she later deplored). The older kids looked after the smaller kids and it was just a great big happy sort of world with no such thing as competition or any feeling of being left out. My whole life we went there, every summer. I loved the place so."

The "left out" line was an omen of sorts. At the time of that interview, Lizzie had received her first Emmy nomination for her 1960 performance in *The Untouchables*, and would later garner a total of eight more nominations, collectively, for *Bewitched*, *A Case of Rape*, *The Legend of Lizzie Borden*, and *The Awakening Land*. But she never won.

Also, too, as will later be delineated, she loved to play games, whether it was with friends at home or behind the scenes, or on camera for game shows like *Password* or *The Hollywood Squares*. And although she later claimed indifference to her lack of Emmy victories, it was clear that, in some venues, she retained a competitive spirit throughout her life, sometimes less productively than others.

By the time Lizzie and Sally Kemp were playing with horses in Patterson, New York, Robert Montgomery and Elizabeth Allen had divorced, and he was living with his second wife, Buffy, in what Sally describes as "a beautiful home," which was located near an equally attractive home owned by Lizzie's Aunt Martha-Bryan, sister to Elizabeth Allen, and mother to Panda.

A little more background on Martha-Bryan Allen proves bewitching:

She was born on April 30, 1903. In 1925, she met her future husband Arthur Cushman. The couple had two children: Arthur, Jr., born in 1927, and Amanda, born in 1932.

Rebecca raised her two daughters, Elizabeth Allen and Martha-Bryan, with the help of her brother William, as father John Allen was not a consistent presence in their lives.

In the meantime, the affluent Cushman family also lived in Patterson, close to the Montgomery brood in Duchess County, where their ancestors had dwelled over several generations. Arthur Cushman owned a large farmhouse in which their daughter, Elizabeth's cousin Panda, resides to this day.

The Cushmans were so affluent, they lived on Cushman Road, which was named for Lizzie's Uncle Arthur—a moniker that she would later bestow upon the beloved *Bewitched* character played by Paul Lynde.

In fact, the crossroads between Patterson and *Bewitched* were manifold. Lizzie exhibited a special love for the area that was later reflected in the characters and places mentioned on the show. But most probably only viewers from the Patterson area would understand the various references to Towners and Patterson that would appear in the show's scripts. For a 1968 interview with the New York *TV Time* magazine, Lizzie revealed, "Our life in Patterson was a paradise for us. That's why I placed *Darrin* and *Samantha* in the town. If I can't be there year-round, than at least *Samantha* can."

In the intervening time, *Samantha* and *Darrin's* last name of *Stephens* may have served as a nod to the members of the Stephens family who have represented Patterson in the New York State Assembly for several decades. The TV couple's daughter, *Tabitha*, attended the *Towners Elementary School*. Flowers within the premise of the series were delivered by *Patterson Florist* and *Mrs. Phyllis Stephens* (*Darrin's* mother played by Mabel Albertson, sister to Jack *Chico and the Man* Albertson) shopped at the *Patterson Department Store*.

Further still, real-life Towners/Patterson street names were often utilized on *Bewitched*. In the *Bewitched* episode "Sam in the Moon," *Samantha's* pharmacist was named *Max Grand* (played by Joseph Mell), after a long time Patterson resident.

The Grands and the Montgomerys were close friends and neighbors. The Montgomery home was the second house on the left on Cushman Road off NYS Route 311. The Grands lived on the first house on the right on NYS Route 164, off Route 311. For many years, the only house in between was the Ludkin residence, which was at the start of Cushman Road at Route 311. The Ludkins operated a turkey farm and factory for many years, while most of the property in the area was owned by members of the Montgomery and Cushman families.

As the years passed, and as both of her daughters grew into adulthood, Lizzie's grandmother Becca would later divide her time every year between the homes of Elizabeth Allen and Martha-Bryan, and her own abode three thousand miles away in Malibu, California.

Six

Training Days

"School bored me and I always knew I wanted to be an actress."
—Elizabeth in *TV Guide*, August 19, 1961

In the core of her *Bewitched* years, Lizzie shared a home in Malibu with her husband Bill Asher and their three children. Years before that business and family foundation was developed and secured, she paved the groundwork for her career. After graduating from finishing school, otherwise known as high school, she attended the American Academy of Dramatic Arts in New York.

According to the October 1953 edition of *People and Pictures* magazine, Robert Montgomery had instructed Lizzie to attend the Academy, and to play summer stock in preparation for a professional career:

> Last summer she was an apprentice in summer stock. She graduates from the academy this summer. This doesn't make her a finished actress, of course, but it does give her preparation. Actually, there's no school that can imbue anyone with talent, but a school can give technique and knowledge of the job to be done. My advice to all young people [who are interested in acting] is not to quit school. Finish college if possible and major in dramatics.

Either way, Lizzie attended the Academy, where she befriended Sally Kemp. Like Lizzie, Sally did not attend college, but was a good student. So her mother gave her a choice. She could rise to her debutante ovation, receive an education in Paris, attend Sarah Lawrence College in the States, or enroll at any other upper-crust educational facility that would accept her. She also had the option of attending the Academy in New York. "And as soon as that became a possibility," Kemp says, "that's where I was going."

As fate would have it, Sally had already bonded with Panda Cushman, Lizzie's first cousin by way of her Aunt Martha-Bryan. The two had been acquainted in boarding school, and to this day, Sally says Panda remains one of her "closest friends."

But years before today, near the end of their shared educational tenure, there was Sally's enrollment at the Academy, and Panda was delighted. Lizzie would attend the same school, and Panda encouraged Sally to make the new connection. Shortly thereafter, Sally says she and Elizabeth became instant friends, and sat next to each other in every class.

Once in the fold, certain traditional and universal school laws did not escape the halls of the strict Academy. "We weren't allowed to chew gum or anything like that," Sally recalls. However, such classic constraints did not prevent her new best friend from playfully breaking the rules. Ever of the avant-garde mindset, Lizzie soon discovered what Sally recalls as "little violet candy, which you can still buy today. They're similar to little lifesavers, but they smelled like perfume."

While in class at the Academy, the then teen girls would keep that smelly candy moist in their mouths, and not in their hands. "We figured nobody would know it was candy," Sally intones.

At the time, the Academy was still located at Carnegie Hall. Classes were held in different studios, and large portraits of great actors and opera singers, who were either alumni or present teachers, donned the walls of each studio, which they rented to teach classes.

"Elizabeth was always a bit more rebellious," Sally admits. When it came to rambunctious scheming to while away the hours, Lizzie would take the lead. "This is what we have to do," she'd tell Sally, and they would commence one exciting endeavor after another.

One especially adventurous day, Lizzie had a particular plan in mind. "As soon as we break for lunch," she told Sally, "I have found a way to get into the balcony of Carnegie Hall through a special door."

Sure enough, when the clock struck twelve, the two brave young souls journeyed through that secret passageway and, once on the other side, they came across none other than the one and only musical maestro, Arturo Toscanini, rehearsing with his famous orchestra.

In time, the two young women would sit mesmerized before the music master on a near-daily basis. "And of course, we would also be late for class," muses Sally, the daughter of the famous bandleader Hal Kemp who, in 1940, was voted along with Glenn Miller and Tommy Dorsey as one of the top three dance bands in America (although, tragically, Hal was killed that year by a drunk driver on his way to play an engagement at the Coconut Grove).

So, whenever the opportunity arose, the daring duo of Lizzie and Sally would sneak away through that secret door to that hall of Toscanini, whom Sally says they perceived as "a very little man."

One afternoon, however, a sour note was heard in the massive musical camp of the tiny Toscanini who became displeased with an orchestra member's performance. As Lizzie and Sally stared from the dark trenches, Toscanini halted his ensemble, pointed to the unfortunate musician in question, shouted in Italian something they assumed was quite derogatory, took his baton, broke it in two, tossed it across the room, and marched off the stage. As Sally remembers it, the mischievous Lizzie then whispered to her asking, "Ok, what's gonna happen now?"

Finally, one of the violinists in the orchestra deadpanned, "I think we're breaking for lunch."

"It was all such fun to watch," Sally chortles. "And Elizabeth and I would do things like that all the time."

A kinder, gentler *Thelma and Louise* of their day, the dynamic twosome of Lizzie and Sally would later become a daring trio, when they befriended yet another young classmate at the Academy named Jarmila Daubek. Jarmila was the daughter of Czech baron George Daubek and Jarmila Novotna, the celebrated Czech soprano and actress who, from 1945 to 1956, was a star of the Metropolitan Opera. According to Sally, both Jarmilas were extremely attractive, but the younger Jarmila, the close chum to both girls, "was even more beautiful."

"She arrived at the Academy a few days after Elizabeth and I did," Sally explains. "But as soon as we caught sight of her, well, we both shrank. She was taller than we were. She had stunning chestnut hair, and the most beautiful skin we had ever seen, along with these huge brown eyes. She was just exquisite."

"We have to make friends with her," Sally remembers Lizzie saying.

When Sally wondered why, Lizzie mused, "Because she's prettier than we are, and we have to keep her on our side."

But according to Sally, Jarmila had a gentle disposition, and was embarrassed when people found out that she was a baroness.

Just as when a shy Lizzie during these Academy days never touted herself as the daughter of a famous movie star, or as when years later on the *Bewitched* set, she remained accessible to the cast and production team. As the show's star, she could have easily adopted a condescending approach, but instead took the high road, discouraging brass and presumption. She may have lacked confidence at times, but she was replete with courage and conviction. She was equally cool and self-reliant. She embraced every opportunity to shock with subtlety those who may have felt even the slightest intimidation by her heritage or very presence.

Case in point: a certain fellow classmate at the Academy named Florence Henderson who would also later become a classic TV icon by way of an ABC sitcom. Henderson played mom *Carol Brady* on *The Brady Bunch*, which debuted in the Fall of 1969, *Bewitched's* sixth season (the year Dick Sargent replaced Dick York as *Darrin*).

When I first met Elizabeth at the American Academy of Dramatic Arts, I thought she was so beautiful and elegant. But she was also always sweet and friendly. And Sally Kemp was also so nice and friendly with a great smile. I thought they were the best dressed and most sophisticated girls in the school.

"She had a beautiful singing voice," Sally says of the multitalented and ever-youthful Henderson who, when Lizzie and Sally knew her, was set to audition for the 1952 Broadway musical, *Wish You Were Here*, which was an adaptation of *Having Wonderful Time* (both of which were directed by Josh Logan). "But the show's producers needed to see how she would look in a bathing suit."

So, their fellow classmate Candi Parsons lent Florence swimwear from her wardrobe. Now outfitted with the perfect look, the future *Mrs. Brady* went on to win the part. Billed as "the new girl" in *Wish You Were Here* (which also featured Jack Cassidy, Tom Tryon, Phyllis Newman, Reid Shelton, and Frank Aletter, Lizzie's co-star from *Mr. Lucifer*), Florence enjoyed a healthy run of 598 performances in the show.

Years after they graduated from the Academy Florence, as opposed to Lizzie, seemed more at peace with the sitcom character that brought her fame. While Florence would continue the role of *Carol Brady* in countless *Bunch* sequels, Lizzie literally began to fight her way out of her most recognizable TV persona with very non-*Samantha* roles, post-*Bewitched*, in TV-movies like *A Case of Rape*, (NBC, 1974), *A Killing Affair* (CBS, 1977; with O. J. Simpson), or *Act of Violence* (CBS, 1979). She'd come to terms with playing *Samantha* only decades after she first played the role. "But she was a terrific actress and a fascinating person," Henderson intones.

The *Brady* TV parent also thought the *Bewitched* star must have been "a wonderful mom" in real life, which she decided after meeting Rebecca Asher, Lizzie's daughter. Though Florence never appeared on *Bewitched*, she did a guest spot on another high-concept ABC comedy titled *Samantha Who?* on which Rebecca was hired as script supervisor. "She was lovely, and we had some wonderful talks," she concludes.

When Lizzie attended New York's American Academy of Dramatic Arts it was a breeding ground for future stars-in-the-making. Past graduates included the likes of Grace Kelly (who would ultimately leave Hollywood and become Princess Grace of Monaco) and Anne Baxter (who played royalty of a whole other kind in 1965's classic film *The Ten Commandments*).

There were additional students of the Academy and other similar institutions who paid tuition with funding from, for example, their G.I. Bill, namely actor James Arness. A contemporary of Lizzie's, Arness would later become a legendary TV star in his own right, taking the lead in *Gunsmoke* (CBS, 1955–1975) on which Lizzie's brother Skip ultimately made his TV debut. Meanwhile, too, Arness was brother to another soon-to-be-popular actor, Peter Graves, future star of *Mission: Impossible* on CBS, 1966–1973/ ABC, 1989–1990. In either case, Arness utilized his military assistance to join an acting program at the Bliss-Hayden Theatre, a small established theatre school in Lizzie's future city of Beverly Hills (where he was ultimately discovered by an agent).

Other Academy graduates would periodically assemble for training or observation purposes, sometimes even after they graduated. As Sally Kemp recalls, one day in the green room there prowled a certain young charismatic man who left a year or so before she, Lizzie, and Jarmila. "But he was always lurking around there."

Many of the thespian alumni would "make the rounds" following graduation, she says. "In those days, you could do that." It was one of many traditions that allowed for aspiring actors to pay random first visits to producers' offices. "I never had the courage to do that. But it was possible."

"We were more privileged than many of the other students," Sally says of the fortunate young life she shared with Lizzie and Jarmila. "There were those who had worked for years as waiters and waitresses to make money in order to attend the Academy."

In any case, the newfound male dramatic arts alumnus who frequently concealed himself and his perceptions in the distance was just about to spark Sally Kemp's interest.

During his periodic peeks from inside the Academy green room, the relatively new graduate remained clandestine and silent until one day, when he stopped Sally and said, quite unabatedly, "You're one of the three graces, aren't you?"

Sally was flustered and a little annoyed.

"Yeah," the young man affirmed. "You, Montgomery, and the baroness—we call you the three graces."

Now flattered and somewhat embarrassed at how she and her dear friends were perceived by a few of their former, present, and maybe even some future schoolmates, Sally said, "Oh . . . well, that's lovely. Thank you so much." Then added, "But who are you?"

"My name is John Cassavetes," the young man answered.

"How do you do," she replied in turn. "I'm Sally Kemp."

Almost urgently, she then walked away, and thought sadly, "That boy's just never going to amount to anything. He's always in the green room."

She was dead wrong, of course, as the young Cassavetes would go on to become one of the greatest actors and directors of their generation. In the article, "A Second Look: John Cassavetes' Touch is Clear in 'Too Late Blues'" by Dennis Lim, Special to the *Los Angeles Times*, May 27, 2012, Cassavetes was dubbed "the original Method actor turned DIY [do-it-yourself] filmmaker." As Lim went on to explain, "For that reason his early forays into studio directing . . . 1961's *Too Late Blues* for Paramount and 1963's Stanley Kramer-produced *A Child Is Waiting* for United Artists—are usually thought of as footnotes at best, or compromised failures at worst (a view that has been ascribed to Cassavetes himself)."

Before dying too young at fifty-nine in 1989, he was featured in a list of celebrated big and small screen appearances. Those included the occult theatrical film, *Rosemary's Baby*, about an evil coven of witches, which was released in 1968. The latter part of that year also marked the fifth hit season of *Bewitched*, two episodes of which ("The Battle of Burning Oak" and "*Samantha's* Shopping Spree") made a reference to *Rosemary's Baby*, which also happened to feature Maurice Evans.

As fate would have it, Cassavetes was linked to Lizzie via a few TV appearances. First, in 1954, for an episode of *Robert Montgomery Presents* titled "Diary," and then on his own show, *Johnny Staccato*, for an episode called "Tempted" (which aired November 19, 1959):

> *Faye Lynn* (Lizzie) literally runs into *Johnny* (Cassavetes), seeking his protection while delivering a valuable diamond necklace. They share a brief romance and a sensual moment in his living room. *Faye* at first seems sincere, but in the end, her obsessive hunger for the finer things in life reveals her true intentions.

Robert B. Sinclair directed this *Staccato* segment, in which Lizzie has some memorable lines as *Faye Lynn* that, if they don't quite reflect her reality off-camera, certainly reference it.

For example, regarding her failed and insincere relationship with *Johnny*, *Faye* tells him: "We tried to make a go of it. It's just one of those things!" He says, "Faye—you've seen too many movies," and she replies: "That's right, Johnny . . . too many movies with too many glamorous people, wearing glamorous clothes and going to glamorous places. But that's what I want, Johnny. I want it so very much."

In reality, of course, Lizzie could not have cared less about those things . . . except attending movies, at least when she was a child. She always wished she could have seen more films in her youth, something her parents prevented her from experiencing.

Meanwhile, Lizzie as *Faye* shares a passionate kiss with Cassavetes as *Johnny* in one scene, probably the most sultry scene from her entire body of work.

Seven

The Europeans

"Only then in Europe could she begin to see Robert as a father, a person separate and different from the famous star."

—Writer Jacqueline Starr, *Screen Stars Magazine*, August 1967

In 1979, Lizzie appeared in two very different TV-movies: *Act of Violence* and *Jennifer: A Woman's Story*. *Violence* was in keeping with her post-*Samantha* traumatic plot choices (a woman is assaulted and turns bitter); *Jennifer's* story was somewhat more uplifting (a wealthy woman loses her husband and takes over his successful company).

That same year, Lizzie's friend Lee Remick was featured in a film called *The Europeans* which was the initial presentation of Merchant Ivory Productions, headed by producer Ismail Merchant of Bombay and American director James Ivory, who later directed such acclaimed and stylish films as *Howards End* (1992) and *The Remains of the Day* (1993).

The Europeans was the first in this series of movies to address the pertinent balance of social graces and reserved emotions—the kind Elizabeth had been addressing her entire life, as instructed by her parents, most certainly her father.

Remick was born in Quincy, Massachusetts, the daughter of Gertrude Margaret Waldo, an actress, and Francis Edwin "Frank" Remick, a department store proprietor. She appeared on six episodes of *Robert Montgomery Presents*, during which she and Lizzie developed their friendship.

Although the two young actresses never performed together on *Presents*, Remick made her Broadway debut with *Be Your Age* in 1953, the same year Lizzie debuted on Broadway in *Late Love*. They later appeared in a fanciful rendition of F. Scott Fitzgerald's novella *The Diamond as Big as the Ritz*, adapted by William Holdack for an episode of NBC's *Kraft Television Theatre*. Airing September 28, 1955, the story was broadly played by all cast members including Lizzie as a seemingly pre-*Serena*-esque character named *Jasmine*, who's unimpressed with her family's wealthy status.

Remick played her sister *Kismine*, alongside Lizzie's future TV-movie co-star William Daniels (from 1974's *A Case of Rape*) as her brother. Rounding out the cast was Signe Hasso and George Macready, as Lizzie's on-screen parents, and Mario Alcalde as Remick's boyfriend.

Lizzie has a free-for-all as *Jasmine*, reciting biting dialogue with such flare to her arrogant pretend mother and father, as if hoping her off-screen prestigious real parents would take a listen.

Here's a sample, regarding *Jasmine's* father:

"There's a look about not feeding the animals all over Father's face"
"It would just take a twist of Father's wrist to put you back in the pit again"
"Oh, now Father, you're just getting yourself upset about nothing"
"You mustn't mind Father. He's a bit theatrical"
"That would be a good one on Father."

To *Jasmine's* mother:

"Mother, why do we always have to have wealthy people visit us? They're such bores"
"Mother, why don't you send *Kismine* to college?" ("It's only for boys, dear.")

In several scenes, *Jasmine* is seen reading *Cinderella*, one of many fairy-tales, Disney-related or otherwise, that Lizzie loved; and at one point *Jasmine* says to her mother:

Mother, don't you think *Cinderella* is divine? It's the only book that is worth anything, well except the one about the little girl who has to sell matches to support her father [*The Little Match Girl* by Hans Christian Andersen]. Oh, I love that one.

And then:

I think *Cinderella* is the best. Only I think everybody ought to be poor in the end instead of rich. I think it would be much better that way.

To her sister *Kismine* near the end of the episode:

You don't expect me to go on living in this house, doing stupid things and meeting stupid wealthy people, while you're out in the world, poor and having fun, do you?

And later, when she wants to accompany her sister and Alcalde:

I won't be a nuisance. I'll help all I can. And we will be poor, won't we . . . like the people in books. And I'll be an orphan, and utterly free. Free and poor. What fun!

Dialogue from the other characters also must have proved compelling for Lizzie upon her first read of the script. Remick's boyfriend says: "Everybody's youth is a dream," to which Lee adds, "How pleasant to be young."

The most telling non-*Jasmine* dialogue that might have hit a nerve in Lizzie's father/daughter dynamic was voiced by Macready's parental TV role: "Cruelty doesn't exist where self-preservation is concerned."

In January 1954, *TeleVision Life* published the article, "Our Name Is Montgomery" by Norma Gould, in which Elizabeth talked about her how her parents viewed her career. She had expressed how much her father tried to discourage her from acting, painting the bleakest possible picture of the entertainment industry. "He said it was the most heartbreaking field you can go into," she recalled. However, her father added that it could also be quite satisfying.

These comments were voiced the year Elizabeth debuted in "Summer

Love," an episode of *Robert Montgomery Players*, the summer replacement series for *Robert Montgomery Presents*. It was in "Love" that she co-starred with John Newland, who spoke glowingly of Lizzie, who called him a "wonderful performer." When asked if they had ever dated, she replied, "Well, we've had drinks together after rehearsals at the Barberry Room. We're just good friends."

Her ideal man, as explained in the article, was one with personality, character, ease, and a nice wardrobe. "She also prefers older men," Gould wrote, as was later more than evident when Lizzie married Gig Young and then Bill Asher.

But at the moment, her father was the only older man in her life; and for the most part, he approved of her life and career. He kept a close eye on each of her performances, including those on *Robert Montgomery Presents* and the *Robert Montgomery Summer Theatre* shows. As for her mother, "Well, I guess she's pleased," Elizabeth said. "You know how it is; she's never actually sat me down and said, 'Elizabeth, I want to tell you how pleased I am with what you're doing.'"

In September of 1967, *TV Radio Mirror* magazine published the article, "An Old Beau Tells All about Liz Montgomery's Past," by Jane Ardmore. It profiled a former boyfriend of Elizabeth's from New York, a physician who—because the American Medical Association apparently then frowned upon the personal publicity of its members—was clandestinely identified as "Bud Baker."

Baker used to dance at various high society balls with Elizabeth; he had attended St. Mark's High School in New York with Lizzie's brother Skip and then later went to Harvard with a young sophisticate named Frederic Gallatin Cammann, who graduated in 1951.

In 1950, after her parents divorced, Lizzie moved with her family to New York. Her father was despondent over the lack of Hollywood roles for forty-something men his age and he had high hopes for a lateral career move on the East Coast. He was also now married to the socially prominent Elizabeth "Buffy" Harkness, an heiress who just happened to be close friends with Cammann's mother, who according to Tom McCartney, was known as Mrs. H. Thomas Richardson; Cammann's father was Frederic Almy Cammann.

While it is uncertain as to who exactly introduced Lizzie to Frederic, who would in time become her first husband, it was most likely Buffy, who was slightly class conscious. But Lizzie and Cammann had many mutual professional and personal connections, and they saw one another at various social functions and dances in New York, the same debutante gatherings that were periodically attended by Bud Baker. As Baker told *TV Radio Mirror* in 1967, "I'd always be on the stag line," where he would see Lizzie whom he described as "very, very pretty, very popular."

"You couldn't dance with her one minute straight without some other guy cutting in," he said. "And she always seemed so above it all; bored stiff, really." Or so she appeared. In reality, the high society game wasn't Lizzie's style. Only later did Baker understand that she was a country girl at heart, someone who loved horses and dogs, any animal, and the wide open spaces of the Montgomery compound in Upstate, New York.

"The social game was new to her," he said. Her entrée was, he confirmed, by way of her stepmother Buffy Harkness, "and of course, everyone knew she was Robert Montgomery's daughter. But Liz was a bright light in her own right. She had this built-in radiance."

Bud had first met Lizzie when his cousin escorted her to a prom at St. Mark's—a cousin who apparently still treasured her picture in his year book. "And let me say," he clarified, "that my cousin wasn't any big romance of Elizabeth's. He was a *fun* friend. That's what I was, too."

That's how dating was defined in those days; you attended dances and proms with platonic friends, most of the time never sharing the slightest kiss or even holding hands. At least such was the case for this younger wealthier set . . . from the outside looking in.

Baker then recalled another dance, this time at the River Club, down by the water on New York's East End Avenue. The summer before, he had met Lizzie's father and brother. His family owned a home on the shore and someone invited the Montgomerys, including Robert and Skip, to join them. Bud said they were both "great . . . easy-going," Skip, in particular, "always was."

Bud hoped such associations would have proved fortuitous, if only so he could cut in line to dance with Lizzie at the River Club, approach her and say, "Hey—you know, I met your dad and your brother this summer."

More times than not, however, and to his great disappointment, she would be unimpressed, which made him think, "*She's really snooty.*"

Bands headed by Meyer Davis (who died in 1976), or Lester Lanin (who died in 2004, but was still going strong into his nineties) would be playing in the background, and Bud would try again. "Great band, isn't it?" Still, Lizzie would give him that "above-it-all look."

"To tell you the truth," he said in 1967 at the height of *Bewitched's* popularity, "she wasn't as much fun as she is now." And apparently, she wasn't as attractive to him then as she had become. "Her figure was always okay, but her face was sort of babyish and kind of pouty, especially when you mentioned her father. It wasn't from any lack of love for him, though. Through the years I've discovered that. She adores her dad. But who wants to talk about a famous father?"

Probably not Lizzie; but Bud wasn't "hung up" on those dances. He didn't get carried away and he never thought Lizzie did either. The only reason he attended those dances was to dance with her and a few other gals.

Although Lizzie was very reserved, and more insecure than she let on, according to Bud, she danced like a dream. She was a coordinated athlete who looked and was totally feminine. She wore lovely discreet clothes, in excellent taste. "You figured she'd marry young . . . someone with a great family name behind him and become one of the social set on the East Coast."

She did. Frederic Gallatin Cammann, Baker's upper-class Harvard acquaintance whom he said came from "a great family," namely Albert Gallatin, Cammann's maternal great grandfather, and a former Secretary of the Treasury. According to the U.S. Department of the Treasury:

> Born to an aristocratic Swiss family, Albert Gallatin (1761–1849) emigrated from Switzerland to America in 1780. Elected to the House of Representatives in 1795 and serving until 1801, Gallatin fought constantly with the independent-minded first Secretary of the Treasury Alexander Hamilton. He was responsible for the law of 1801 requiring an annual report by the Secretary of the Treasury, and he submitted the first one later that year as Secretary. He also helped create the powerful House Ways and Means

Committee to assure Treasury's accountability to Congress by reviewing the Department's annual report concerning revenues, debts, loans, and expenditures. Appointed Secretary of the Treasury in 1801 by President Jefferson and continuing under President James Madison until 1814, Gallatin was in office nearly thirteen years, the longest term of any Secretary in the Department's history.

In the meantime, Fred Cammann became friends with Lizzie and the Montgomery brood before his service to the United States. After graduating from Harvard, he enlisted in the army and was stationed in Korea. Once discharged from the service, Cammann was reintroduced to Lizzie in 1953, when he was hired as a stage manager-turned-casting director for *Robert Montgomery Presents*.

It has been suggested that Cammann was drawn to Lizzie primarily because of her entertainment affiliations, as his career interests leaned toward the industry, specifically in the casting department. But *why* they got together didn't matter to Robert Montgomery. According to Dominick Dunne, Elizabeth's father was just plain "thrilled" that his daughter was interested in as well-bred a man as Cammann. At least that's what Dunne told MSNBC's *Headliners & Legends* in 2001.

Like Cammann, Dunne started out in show business as a stage manager on *Presents* and the two were friends. Robert Montgomery had also befriended Dunne and placed a great deal of trust in him, and held him as a confidant. As Dunne explained it, Robert told him that Cammann was "the kind of guy I want my daughter to marry."

This time, Lizzie was all too eager to bend to her father's will. She and Cammann started dating and then, according to *Newsweek Magazine*, March 29, 1954:

> Engaged: Elizabeth Montgomery, 20, actress, daughter of movie actor and TV producer Robert Montgomery, and casting director Frederic Gallatin Cammann, 24, obtained a marriage license in New York, March 18.

The wedding was held on March 27, 1954, at St. James Protestant Episcopal Church in New York. When asked in 2011 about his life with Lizzie, Cammann was cordial, but brief: "I'm in my eighties now, and that was a long time ago. It's in the past, and that's where I'd like to keep it."

Sally Kemp, however, remembers Lizzie's wedding to Cammann as if it happened yesterday. It was a not-so-great marriage that was at least preceded by a happy and reverent ceremony, and an elegant and festive reception. Lizzie had been a bridesmaid at Sally's first wedding, and when Lizzie decided to marry Cammann, Sally returned the favor. She recalls:

It was a beautiful wedding. We all arrived at her mother's apartment. Our dresses had been purchased for us, along with the petticoats that went under them, pearl necklaces, all exactly alike. White kid gloves all exactly alike . . . the little headdresses that we wore, and white satin shoes . . . because it was a white wedding. I had never seen a totally white wedding before, but we were each adorned with these beautiful ivory dresses. We all dressed together, and usually bridesmaids have to pay for their own way, but not this time. Everything including the underwear was paid for—including the stockings! And we all had the same shade of nylon stocking. I was very nearsighted, but too vain to wear my glasses. So I really didn't see a whole lot. (But) She was an incredibly beautiful bride. She was always both enchanting and adorable, but not like Jarmila (their fellow student from the New York Academy). Elizabeth did not have that kind of beauty. She was like a pixie . . . a little gamine when she was young, even as she got older. She had beautiful eyes, a beautiful mouth, and that cleft chin. But she didn't have that grand kind of beauty. But she was the most beguiling and amazing looking bride. I thought Freddie was going to faint when he saw her. He really loved her. But they all did (men in general). I couldn't imagine how they couldn't.

Academy Award–winning actor Cliff Robertson loved Lizzie, too, but as a platonic friend. The two performers remained close through the years and, like Sally, Cliff was there when Lizzie married Cammann:

It was very festive. St. James Church was on the upper Eastside in New York, and I specifically remember her walking down the aisle, because I had an aisle seat. And right after when she and Freddie were pronounced man and wife, she walked passed me, and with that ring on her finger, gave me a big ol' wink, as if to say, *I got the man I wanted!* It was fun to watch. Everyone was there, including her brother (Skip), who was dancing the Charleston. Freddie was a nice guy. He was brought up in the East. He was very ambitious to learn the TV production work and he utilized his assets rather wisely on Madison Avenue. But they weren't married too long.

Robertson had "no idea" why Lizzie's first marriage failed, but he detected it might have had something to do with her theatrical ambitions.

Cammann's career choices were periodically described as a stage manager, TV producer, casting director and/or executive; he wanted an old-world wife and Lizzie wanted to be a newfangled actress. That was something she worked hard to achieve, and not by exploiting her father's famous name. According to Robertson, she was determined not to be labeled a society actress. "And I think that came from her mother's side," he said. "Her mother was a Southerner, and her aunt (Martha-Bryan), who was a dear friend of mine as well, was from I think Tennessee, and she had all the graces of a Southern lady."

In other words, Lizzie had a strong sense of pride and wanted to succeed as an actress on her own merit. "Freddie was very upper crust and old-fashioned," Sally Kemp says. "The marriage probably would have lasted had Elizabeth decided not to become an actress."

If anything, Elizabeth's marriage to Cammann proved to be benchmark in her friendship with Kemp. They were moving in different directions. By the time Lizzie married Freddie, she and Sally did not see one another that often anymore. In the pre-Cammann days, the two women would have dinner, lunch, or get together somehow several times a week. "When we each married," Sally laments, "things changed."

To anyone who knew Lizzie, the idea of her being identified as a stay-at-home wife, minus any form of career, was slightly absurd, at least at this time in her life. Only later would she more readily embrace the sequestered home life, and sometimes crave it. But that transpired after she became a star on *Bewitched*, when she was able to better balance and appreciate the finer and simpler things in life.

In the beginning, Cammann made an effort to support her theatrical endeavors. According to *Cosmopolitan Magazine* in July of 1954, he was in the Service when she made her TV debut on that "Top Secret" episode of *Robert Montgomery Presents* (December 1951). She explained:

To be specific, he was in the Army and he had been on KP for eighteen hours. He was so anxious to see me on television that he sneaked out of the kitchen to see our show in the recreation room. The mess sergeant caught him. And thanks to me, he had to stay on KP for the next two days.

When he was relieved of the KP duty, and upon eventually leaving the Army, he and Elizabeth were busy with decorating their new apartment on New York's Upper East Side. When asked if he objected to Elizabeth continuing her acting career now that they were married, he replied, "Not at all. How else can we pay for all the furniture she's ordered?"

Certainly, no one on either side of their family had to worry about meeting such payments. The main concern, at least for Lizzie and Cammann, was meeting eye to eye on the marriage in general, which just simply never came to be. As one of their mutual friends concluded in an article for *The Saturday Evening Post* in 1965, "Freddie just couldn't measure up to her father." But it wasn't all Robert Montgomery's fault.

Lizzie's marriage to Cammann was unstable from the onset. Although wired for show business, Cammann cut such ties away from the set. In Lizzie, he envisioned a stay-at-home wife, much like *Darrin* hankered for *Samantha* to remain earthbound on *Bewitched*. But the actress, unlike her most famous TV counterpart, wanted a full-time job, outside of the home, specifically, an acting career. And she wanted to take it to the next level . . . in California, but he didn't want to leave New York, so the marriage went south.

Had the two met later in life, the bond may have stuck. Instead, their wedded bliss unraveled, commencing with his ousting from the elite social circles to which he had become accustomed. Close colleagues and friends were aghast at his alliance with Elizabeth, whom they incorrectly labeled as a common actress. It was not a personal attack on her, but rather a general displeasure with her profession. His peers were simply unimpressed with the theatrical world, even when such a world revolved around so endearing a performer as Lizzie.

On the home front, the two bickered constantly, with their first major disagreement proving to be nothing less than outright jarring. He apparently became so upset he packed his bags and went home to mother. *Samantha* had at times threatened to do the same on *Bewitched*. In such a case *Darrin* would exclaim, "What for? Your mother's always here!" *Samantha* was usually supportive of her mortal husband, but would be appalled at his attacks on her mother.

In contrast, Lizzie was stunned at Cammann's inaugural retreat to his mother's.

Following each minor or major altercation, he would storm out only to return to his newlywed wife, time and again. After what ultimately became the final intense bout with his packing ritual, Lizzie allegedly—and we can only assume, gently—placed her derriere upon his suitcase in order for it to lock properly, which paved the way for his final exit. Immediately following, she purportedly filed for divorce.

At least this is what Gig Young, her second husband, apparently told his sister, according to Young's biography, *Final Gig: The Man Behind the Murder* by George Eells.

That said, a brief item in the press, "Star's Kin Asks for Divorce," appeared in a Las Vegas newspaper on August 10, 1955, stating that Lizzie, now 22, and referred to as "Robert Montgomery's daughter," had obtained a divorce from Cammann, now 26, whose profession was listed as "a television executive." Although terms of a property settlement were not disclosed, she charged cruelty and was granted restoration of her maiden name.

Lizzie's break-up with Fred Cammann was coined a *quickie* Nevada divorce, the criteria for which was met by her fulfilling a residency requirement in that state for thirty days. After that, she left for Hollywood to work with Gary Cooper on *The Court-Martial of Billy Mitchell*, her big screen debut.

In an interesting twist, this film shared several aesthetic similarities with *The Rack*, a motion picture from 1956 starring Paul Newman, Walter Pidgeon, Cloris Leachman (*The Mary Tyler Moore Show*), Robert F. Simon (who played *Darrin's* father on *Bewitched*), and a fair-haired Anne Francis.

Mitchell was based on a true story of the American general (Cooper), and his court martial for public complaints about High Command's dismissal and neglect of the aerial fighting forces during World War I. *The Rack* was a fictional account of *Captain Edward Hall* (Newman) who returns to America after two years in a prison camp during the Korean War. But both films dealt with the military and alleged insubordinate behavior of its lead screen soldiers.

About a decade after working on *Mitchell*, Lizzie would star in *Bewitched*, which debuted on ABC in 1964. Some years following her work in *The Rack*, Francis would find TV fame with another ABC show called *Honey West*, which debuted in 1965 (if only running one season to *Bewitched's* eight). In *The Rack*, Francis played a troubled woman struggling with the death of her solider husband, a successful brother to Newman's ultimate poor soul. In *Billy Mitchell*, Lizzie portrayed an emotionally torn woman struggling with the loss of her husband at the apparent misguided hands of the Navy Brass.

The Rack was a superior film, with Newman delivering an A-list performance at the on-set of his career. In *Billy Mitchell*, Cooper gave a tired performance near the end of his career. (Four years later, he would appear with Lizzie's *Bewitched* co-star Dick York in the 1959 film, "They Came to Cordura," during which York suffered a permanently damaging back injury that ultimately forced him to be replaced by Dick Sargent as *Darrin* in 1969).

In either case, Elizabeth was gripping as the grieving wife in *The Court-Martial of Billy Mitchell*, potentially pulling emotions (via her preferred training in "method acting") from the turmoil she was experiencing off-screen with her failed union to Fred Cammann.

For the time being, too, there was a rumor circulating that Cooper, well known in Hollywood as a Lothario of sorts, went chasing after her on the *Mitchell* set. According to Montgomery archivist Tom McCartney, Cooper was "driving pretty hard to the hoop." The actor frequently flirted with Lizzie and was "on the make." At one point, "Coop," as he was sometimes known, was nowhere to be found, even after a stage manager completed an extensive search on the set. The stage manager finally knocked on Cooper's dressing room door, which was locked. Finally responding to the interruption, the actor popped opened the door—with Lizzie reportedly in view inside his room. Although it appeared that she was ultimately seduced by Cooper's various charms, the hearsay of their alleged affair was just that and never was substantiated.

There was additional supposition of a potent off-screen romance between Lizzie and the historically womanizing crooner Dean Martin when they co-starred in 1963's *Who's Been Sleeping in My Bed?*, a salaciously titled film with a slightly daring plot for its time:

> Actor *Jason Steele* (Martin) is not a doctor, but plays one on TV. He's so convincing in the role, women of all shapes and sizes, including the alluring

Toby Tobler (Jill St. John), find him irresistible. His poker buddies (some played by Louis Nye and Jack *Barney Miller* Soo) may envy him, but his fiancée, art teacher *Melissa Morris* (Lizzie), isn't the least bit impressed. In fact, she's quite upset; although she eventually learns to hold his attention by implementing an inventively affable bedside manner of her own, which she partially introduces with a seductive dance sequence.

In 1989, Lizzie remembered that sequence with a smile, and posed, "Wasn't that funny? And that was strangely enough one of the more difficult things I had to do." The actual dance moves were not an issue. She was always athletic and had studied dance for years. But it was the precise choreography that forced her to face the music. She clarified:

> It wasn't like dancing today, which is freewheeling. And Jill St. John (who also danced in the film) did it better than I did. But my character was supposed to be a wonderful dancer, so that was cool. If they had me out there riding a horse or playing eight sets of tennis I would have been much better. Or if we filmed it today, I'd have been out at some disco dancing. That would have been no problem either. But it was difficult for me because you get so kind of confined when you have to do it and the *clicks* (dance measurements) are going and the music starts and stops, and the dialogue starts and the music stops. But it was fun. I enjoyed it. I enjoyed being pushed into the pool at the Beverly Hills hotel. That was really funny because there were a couple of people who couldn't swim, and I found myself in this bridal gown which must have weighed 900 pounds, saying, "It's okay. I can swim. And I'll be right here." It was a very nice experience. It was a feature, which was fine—and it was one of those things that you did.

Elizabeth had worked with Martin one previous time, in another feature film, but to a much lesser and somewhat odder extent, in 1960's *Bells Are Ringing,* directed by Vincente Minnelli (once married to Judy Garland and father to Liza):

> A Brooklyn phone service operator (Judy Holliday) seeks to improve the lives of her clients by relaying between them various bits of information. In the process, she falls in love with playwright *Jeffrey Moss* (Martin), whom

she is determined to meet. Problem is: he only knows her on the phone as "Mom!"

Lizzie's credited role? *Girl Reading Book*, one of the strangest cameos in big screen and small screen history; one of the oddest appearances of any performer on record, anywhere; she's seen with her head down, collapsed over a table in a tavern. It may have had something to do with her love for reading, a practice her father had instilled in her ever since she was a child. Either way, entertainment historian Ken Gehrig tries to make sense of it all:

> Having already made *The Court-Martial of Billy Mitchell*, and many guest-starring roles on television, it's a mystery that Liz would appear in this wordless role where she virtually seems a mannequin. In a very long take at an actor's hang-out in New York, Judy Holliday's character is trying to convince the Brando wannabe actor played by Frank Gorshin to drop *the method*. Liz is in the foreground screen left; no dialogue, no movement, no expression; very much concentrating on her reading matter. What? Was it the opportunity to work with Oscar-winners: actress Judy Holliday, director Vincente Minnelli and/or producer Arthur Freed? Sadly, this was Judy's last film appearance and the last MGM musical of Minnelli and Freed. So unwittingly this was Liz's only opportunity to do such a film. Also, it's unlikely anyone knew that in hindsight this film is early exposure for future TV people: Jean Stapleton (*All in the Family*), Frank Gorshin (*Batman*), Hal Linden (*Barney Miller*) and Donna Douglas (*The Beverly Hillbillies*). Ironically, Liz has less to do onscreen than all of these others—and yet, her concentration on her actor's *goal* seems relentless. None of the posturing of Holliday or Gorshin distracts Liz from her book!

As to any alleged affair with Martin, during production of this film or *Who's Been Sleeping in My Bed?* Lizzie mentioned not a word. However, Montgomery archivist Tom McCartney points out that various revealing documents from the files of famous Hollywood gossip columnist Hedda Hopper are now accessible online. Among the papers is a transcript of an alleged telephone conversation between Lizzie and Hopper during which Hedda threatened to expose the alleged affair that Lizzie had with Dean.

Into this mix, actor J. Anthony Russo, who had a small role in *Bed*, chronicled his own observation about a Montgomery/Martin connection in his book, *Creativity and Madness: The Passion of a Hollywood Bit Player* (BookSurge Publishing, 2005). According to Russo, one day at lunch between filming scenes for *Bed*, Lizzie apparently jumped onto Martin's lap and began to smother him with kisses. When she left, Martin turned to all of those who would listen and supposedly intoned, "Don't mind her. She's a little stunod," which is Italian for "a little drunk."

That said, if the rumor of Lizzie's purported affair with Martin had been addressed elsewhere, which it has not, she may have been on the rebound from Gig Young just before falling in love with and later marrying Bill Asher, whom she met on the set of *Johnny Cool* (which was filmed the same year as *Bed*). By then, her relationship with Asher was her only real documented affair, a dalliance that transpired after she and Young separated.

Concurrently, according to George Eell's book, *Final Gig*, Young was having a very public—and one could only assume also a very wild—fling with Sophia Loren. He and Lizzie then reunited for approximately six months, after she which she divorced him for good.

On February 15, 1954, Lizzie appeared with Sally Kemp and Cliff Robertson in "Our Hearts Were Young and Gay," an episode of *Robert Montgomery Presents*. The episode was based on the book by actress Cornelia Otis Skinner and journalist Emily Kimbrough. Originally published in 1942, the book is about their European tour in the 1920s when they were fresh out of college at Bryn Mawr. It spent five weeks atop the *New York Times* Best Seller List in the winter of 1943, and was adapted for the big screen in 1944, starring Gail Russell as *Cornelia*, Diana Lynn as *Emily*, and Charlie Ruggles (a future *Bewitched* guest-star) as *Otis Skinner*, Cornelia's father.

In the TV version on *Presents*, Lizzie played *Cornelia*, Kemp was *Emily*, and Robertson was *Paul Smith*, a romantic interest for *Emily*. Each actor brought youthful buoyancy to their roles.

Lizzie, Sally, and Cliff made many appearances on *Robert Montgomery Presents*, and appeared in the show's first summer stock theatre group that included an orchestra conducted by Al Kemp (not *Hal* Kemp, Sally's father). Cliff enthusiastically recalled it all in 2011:

One summer, Robert decided to form the *Robert Montgomery Playhouse* with a particular number of actors, and I was one of the few lucky ones to join in. And we got to do a number of shows. It was very nice, if a little bit isolated and insolated from Hollywood. Bob preferred the East, as it were. But we all worked so well together, and it was a romp! We never took each other too seriously. We just plain had a ball performing in a play called *Our Hearts Were Young and Gay*, written by a very good writer named Rod Crawford [although sources document Nathaniel Curtis as penning the teleplay]. Both Elizabeth and Sally were a delight to work with. They were very close, like sisters. And Sally was a lovely friend . . . to both of us.

Sally adds:

Our Hearts Were Young and Gay was a surprise. We were all so young and *green*! And sweet Cliff Robertson; I saw him again a couple of times when I moved back to New York City; sad to lose him last year (2011). At least there were glimpses of talent on all our parts. I went on to specialize in classical roles, Shakespeare, Shaw, Wilde, etc., mostly in theatres in L.A. and New York, keeping me in non-luxury, but great satisfaction; Elizabeth and Cliff achieved a far wider audience.

From 1962 to 1993, whenever a young comedian impressed Johnny Carson during an appearance on *The Tonight Show*, the heralded late-night king of talk shows would invite them over to his famous sofa. In the same way, Robert Montgomery would periodically invite key players from a given episode on *Presents* to join him at the show's end to bid farewell to the home audience until the following week. After they performed to their *Hearts* desire, a very young and bubbly Lizzie and Sally joined Robert at the end of the show. All three were beaming. Robert was proud of their performance, which pleased Elizabeth, but also surprised her. Robert spoke directly to the camera, but she did not, nor did Sally, who recently had a chance to see the episode nearly sixty years after she appeared in it:

It was good to see Elizabeth (in her interviews) looking lovely and warm and charming. She seemed to be at ease in spite of confessing to nerves. But that's what we do. Not just as actors, but for the backgrounds we were both from. You try to make your guests (or interviewers) feel at home.

If anything, it's pleasing to see Lizzie interact so honestly and joyfully with her father and her best friend. The latter dynamic, unfortunately, would later change.

In the days before she met and married Fred Cammann, Lizzie's friendship with Sally was solid enough for Robert Montgomery to consider Kemp a member of the family. "He treated me as though I were his other daughter," she says. "I absolutely adored him and his (second) wife Buffy. From the day Elizabeth and I met, she didn't live with her father. And he and Buffy had the most beautiful duplex penthouse on East 72nd Street, not far from Fifth Avenue."

Lizzie lived with her mother during the week and would visit her father for regular weekend trips in the country, and Sally tagged along. The Montgomery East Hampton abode "was always very impressive," she says in recalling a playful interchange that usually transpired between the two prior to such excursions:

> The phone would ring. My mother would answer, and this voice on the other line would say, "This is Robert Montgomery's secretary. I'm calling for Mr. Montgomery. Can Miss Kemp come out to play in the country for the weekend?"

It was Lizzie, of course, on the other end of the line, disguising her voice.

Sally's mother was always frustrated that she never had the chance to meet Robert Montgomery, but gave her consent: "Well, of course Sally can go to the country."

"I practically lived with them when I wasn't at home," Sally recalls of the Montgomery visits, which periodically expanded into trips abroad.

After Lizzie married Fred Cammann, her father and Buffy would go sailing, or take summer European excursions. Along for the ride would be Annie, Buffy's daughter from a previous marriage, and a random classmate of Annie's. Both were about 18.

Then in 1954, when Lizzie and Sally were both 21, the Montgomerys planned a trip to Europe that ultimately proved a milestone in their relationship. According to Sally, Lizzie called her and said, "Daddy and Buffy are leaving for Europe and they're having a bon voyage party on this huge ship. Let's go to the party.'"

Sally had never traveled on a great ocean liner, although she was supposed to have done so on an earlier trip with her mother and stepfather that never transpired. "So, I went with the Montgomerys," she explains. "I adore the old luxury liners. But not those great big things like the new Queen Mary or the Queen Elizabeth. They're too big. But the old ones are heavenly."

Sally arrived on this one particular classic luxury liner, the kind of which she was so fond, and there were the Montgomerys "in their beautiful suite, with champagne and lots of elegant people and some press standing around." She and Lizzie remained over in one corner, taking all of it in, hoping, "Someday, we'll get to do this, too." Much to the surprise of both young ladies, that day and moment had arrived—when Robert, minutes later, walked up to Sally, startled her, and asked if she was 21.

"Yes. I just had a birthday a few months ago."

"And do you have some money of your own?"

"Yes."

"All right, then . . . why don't you fly to London and join us and come on the trip?"

Upon viewing this interchange between Kemp and her father, Lizzie naturally assumed that she, too, would be joining her parents and her best friend on the trip. "Oh, Daddy," she said. "What a divine idea!"

At which point Robert looked at her and said, point-blank, "Elizabeth—you just got married a few months ago. You are *not* coming with us to Europe for six weeks. You're going to stay with your husband." Lizzie was stunned into silence. Sally, however, was putting a call into her parents who were out of town.

"Mommy . . . may I go to Europe with the Montgomerys?"

"Of course, Darling, but what are you going to wear?"

When it came time to depart, Sally made certain to find the proper attire, then packed it all into a suitcase, and flew to London. Her plane landed in the U.K., and the Montgomerys, who arrived beforehand, sent a customs official to greet Sally before any passenger was allowed to exit the aircraft. A man dressed in uniform approached her, and said, "Miss Kemp . . . I've come to escort you through customs."

As the two deplaned, Sally was carrying her mother's treasured Elizabeth Arden alligator make-up case. She and the customs representative made their way across the walkway, where Robert and Buffy Montgomery were waiting at the entrance. Upon running to greet them, she triggered loose the handle on her mother's make-up case, and out onto the ground rolled various crystals and other cherished items. "I was so embarrassed," she recalls. "I tried to pick them up and fit them into the hem of my skirt. It was terrible." That is, until she reached the Montgomerys, who eased any minor mortification. "Never mind," Robert told her. "We'll get another make-up case for you."

"They were just lovely," Sally recalls of Lizzie's parents, who were waiting for her in a Rolls Royce, driven by a chauffeur wearing a uniform with boots, a tunic, and a cap. They drove the long way in order for Sally to see Buckingham Palace and places like the Connaught, one of the great, elegant London hotels which, though reasonably small is still her favorite.

And it was at the Connaught she stayed, along with Buffy's daughter Anna and her friend Jill—all expenses paid by the Montgomerys, another gift, this time as a gesture to encourage a sense of freedom for three young girls on an exciting trip abroad. Sally remembers:

> We went all over Europe. And everywhere we'd go, everybody knew who Bob was. We had dinner with people like the American Ambassador of Paris, and attended parties where we were the only people who did not have *titles*. We went to Sutherland and saw the incredible mansion of the Duke of Sutherland, which was later purchased by J. Paul Getty. And I had the great opportunity to be there when the Duke was home. It was an extraordinary time.

Yet not so much for Lizzie, who remained back in the States while her parents vacationed in Europe with her best friend. "I don't think Elizabeth ever forgave me for that," Sally intones. They were still friends, but that vacation slight ever lurched in Lizzie's memory. The two never broached the subject until decades later during what became their final meeting. "The last time I saw Elizabeth was the only time she talked about that trip," Sally explains of an awkward encounter that took place in Los Angeles sometime in the 1980s.

A decade or so before that landmark day, Sally portrayed *Nurse Ratched* in the 1970 first revival of the play, *One Flew Over the Cuckoo's Nest*, directed by Lee Sankowich at the Little Fox Theatre in San Francisco, where it ran for five years. By this time, Sally had divorced her first husband Bob Grant and was now married to actor Paul Jenkins, who was playing *McMurphy* in *Cuckoo's Nest*. A few years passed and a production of the play, with Sankowich back as director, was presented at his proprietorship, the Zephyr Theatre in Los Angeles, where Sally and Jenkins had relocated. Only this time, circa 1980s, the role of *McMurphy* was played by Robert Foxworth, who had been with Lizzie since their meeting in 1973 on the set of the ABC TV-movie *Mrs. Sundance* (which debuted in 1974; Foxworth would perform in 1975 with *Star Trek: Deep Space Nine* actor Salome Jens in yet another production of *Cuckoo's Nest*, this one at the Huntington Hartford Theatre in Los Angeles).

Sally never had the chance to see the 1980s edition of *Cuckoo's Nest*, but her husband did. And on closing night after the curtain came down, there was an on-stage party for all present and previous cast members. "But we arrived late," Sally recalls. "And I found myself walking into this dim theatre, where there wasn't much light. I approached the stage where the party was taking place, and all of sudden, I heard this voice from the shadows saying, 'Well, as I live and breathe, it's *Scary* Kemp.'"

That was Lizzie's nickname for Sally, who immediately recognized her old friend's voice. As such, she replied in kind, with a pronounced Southern accent, posing into the dark hall, "Elizabeth Victoria Montgomery? Is that you in the corner?"

They both ran into the middle of the stage, fell into each other's arms, and stood there for what Sally approximated as about 15 to 20 minutes, catching up on the twenty or so odd years since they had last seen each other.

Lizzie opened the chit-chat: "I've had three children."

"I know. I've heard from your cousin. I only have one. My husband died."

And on they went, until an awkward pause froze the memories of times gone by.

"We were still holding one another, face to face," Sally intones. "But then Elizabeth pulled back a little bit and said, 'My father always loved you more than he loved me.'"

Now, it was Sally who was stunned into silence, as was Lizzie decades before, when Robert Montgomery insisted that she remain in the States with her then-new husband Fred Cammann (while her best friend galli-vanted throughout Europe with her parents).

"I thought I was going to die," Sally says, upon hearing Lizzie's state-ment. She was hurt when Lizzie said that, and protested, "Elizabeth, you are so wrong. Your father adored you. You were so like him in so many ways."

But such sounds fell on deaf ears, which as Sally explains, was par for the course:

> Even though she embraced me that day on the stage, and we ran into one another's arms on that stage, she still resented that I went to Europe all those years before, while she did not. But there were a lot of people who Elizabeth eliminated from her life. She kind of had a way of dropping peo-ple. There were no second chances with her. And this also even happened with her cousin Panda, who had grown up with Elizabeth like a sister. I don't know what that was in her. As young girls, we couldn't have been closer. I never really had as close or as loving and supportive a relationship as I had with Elizabeth. That's why it was so strange when she was no longer in my life. I never even heard from her when Gig died, and certainly not when her father died. Nothing. The last conversation we had was when she dropped that bombshell on me about her father, which I called ridicu-lous, because he did love her so much. And we still loved each other.

While the two women stood face to face on that dark stage in 1980s with their arms wrapped around each other's waists at the after-party for the final curtain call for *One Flew Over the Cuckoo's Nest*, the situation was if not *crazy* then certainly strange. "Who's your agent?" Lizzie asked.

"*Oh, Elizabeth,*" Sally thought to herself. "*You don't want my personal phone number? And you won't give me yours. You just want to know how to contact me, should you ever need to.*"

So, instead, she said, "Elizabeth—don't worry about it. We'll see each other again."

"I suppose so," Lizzie added.

"We then embraced one last time," Sally recalls. "And I never saw her again." In hindsight, it appears Lizzie never stopped loving those whom she had ever cared about, but she was so sensitive a human being that if she felt offended or possibly threatened by someone, even in the slightest, unintended way, a defense mechanism would kick in, ensuring that she would not place herself in that vulnerable position again. "I think, too," Sally surmises, "it was a little bit of the *out of sight, out of mind*" train of thought. Her life was very busy, especially when she first went out to California and started doing *Bewitched*. Then she had three children. That's an awful lot to deal with and it's certainly understandable that we drifted apart at least for those reasons."

Meanwhile, Lizzie eventually traveled abroad, if not with her father. Ironically, on May 19, 1967, *TV Guide* later compared her and Bill Asher to world-renowned foreign royalty in explaining the great power they amassed in Hollywood by way of her *Samantha* success. After *TV Guide* reporter Arnold Hano noted, "The Ashers run *Bewitched*," the studio spokesperson declared, "They are like the crowned heads of Europe!"

Eight

~

Spirits and Demons

"Are you starting a rumor, or merely repeating one?"

—*Ann Evans*, as played by Elizabeth in "Patterns,"an episode of
NBC's *Kraft Television Theatre*, January 12, 1955

Ghosts played an integral role in Lizzie's life, long before she'd encounter them as *Samantha* on *Bewitched* ("*Tabitha's* Cranky Spell," 3-28-68; "The Ghost Who Made a Spectre of Himself," 10-27-71). As she explained to *TV Photo Story* magazine reporter Laura Wayne in June 1971, she had apparently seen a real live ghost in a hotel, shortly after arriving in England where she was visiting her parents. Here's how it went:

She was about to open her hotel room door, when she became conscious of someone hurrying down the hall. A few days later the same thing happened. Again, she was just vaguely conscious of feeling someone hurry by her, but by the third time it happened, she "definitely saw a foot and the bottom of a skirt as it disappeared around the corner." Swiftly, she rushed to the corner and looked down the hall. There was no one there and, as she assessed, it would have been impossible for anyone to have reached and entered one of the doors in that hall in so short a time.

She returned to her room, and contemplated what had transpired. She then became certain that whoever, or whatever, she had seen was not dressed in the fashion of the day. The "ghost's" skirt was long and full, and the foot and ankle which had disappeared around the corner were clad in a high-buttoned shoe.

The housekeeper entered her room a few minutes later and when Lizzie relayed what she had experienced, the housekeeper said, "Oh, you've seen her. She has been here for many years, ever since this house was new," and passed the incident off casually.

Lizzie concluded, "I never learned the name of my ghost or her story."

Author and professional namedropper Dominick Dunne had befriended Elizabeth when he served as a stage manager on *Robert Montgomery Presents*. In his book, *The Way We Lived Then: Recollections of a Well-Known Name Dropper* (Crown, 1999), he recalled, among other things, working on *Presents*, her marriages to Fred Cammann and Gig Young, and his developing friendships with Cliff Robertson and Arlene Francis, both of whom starred with Lizzie in the hit Broadway play *Late Love* (from October 1953 to January 1954). Dunne was delighted with *Love's* success, and intrigued by the bond that formed between Lizzie and his wife Lenny, a relationship that he said would have "twists and turns in years to come."

For the moment there were only ups and downs, as the newlywed Cammanns lived in the New York apartment above the space Dunne shared with his mother, who one night hosted a party to celebrate *Late's* success. Dunne claimed that he and his mother were good friends with Lizzie, as he had served as an usher at her wedding to Cammann, a fellow stage manager on *Presents*. Both Dunne and his wife Lenny were so close to Lizzie that, after the birth of his first child (actor Griffin Dunne), she would often baby-sit, a fact which Dominick said his son to this day takes delight in revealing. Yet those intimate proximities would soon contract and fade.

In time, the Dunnes moved to a larger apartment on East 76th Street, Lizzie disengaged Cammann in Vegas, and on December 28, 1956, in that same fast-paced, high-living Nevada city, she wed Gig Young of whom her father was not the least bit fond. As Dunne told *Headliners & Legends* in 2001, "Bob Montgomery hated Gig Young, and was . . . distressed" about Lizzie's romance with the older actor. "I think that put the first strain on their father-daughter relationship."

In the interim, the Youngs moved to Los Angeles, and Cammann married again (to Nora Franke) in yet a second ceremony for which Dunne served as an usher.

By the time all of this transpired, Lizzie's old friends, like Bud Baker, had lost track of her. She extricated herself from him and others as she had from Sally Kemp. Occasionally, after she married Young, Baker, for one, would run into her at waving distance in some mob scene when she and Gig were on the East Coast. But other than that, she was a no-show. She turned the page. Seemingly, with each new relationship came a new crop of friends, and a new era was born for the actress who liked to draw. A fresh canvas awaited her at each new brush with fame.

When Elizabeth was living with Gig Young in their rented furnished New York apartment, she fell in love with a white dishtowel decorated with blue butterflies. As writer Arnold Hano observed in the *TV Guide* article, "Rough, Tough and Delightful," May 19, 1967, "This was no doubt a climax in the life of Liz Montgomery. When she wiped something, it turned out to be with an item totally domestic, albeit festooned with butterflies."

In that same article, Hano made note of a poem Elizabeth composed when she was only in third grade:

> Creepy, crawly caterpillar
> You are very funny.
> You will be a butterfly
> When the days are sunny.

When Hano asked her about that poem, and which animal she most identified with, the caterpillar or the butterfly, she replied, indignantly, "Goodness, surely not the butterfly!" Meanwhile, her marriage with Young was at times like living in a cocoon.

She first met the actor, twice married and divorced, after he had recently ended an engagement to actress Elaine Stritch and began hosting the anthology TV series *Warner Brothers Presents*. According to George Eells' biography of Young, *Final Gig: The Man Behind the Murder* (Harcourt Brace Jovanovich, 1991), Gig's show was filming on the same Warner's lot that Lizzie was shooting her first motion picture, *The Court-Martial of Billy Mitchell.*

To celebrate signing contracts for Gig's new series, Warner Bros. staged a dinner at the Beverly Hilton Hotel at which studio executive Gary Stevens requested the actor's presence. Gig consented but was uncertain about his potential escort. Since she was on the lot, Stevens suggested Lizzie who was then all of twenty-two. Gig was born November 4, 1913, which made him forty-two, approximately, because like Lizzie he was known to tally his age with a minus-five-year span that was left open to the imagination.

In either case, Gig was apprehensive about the potential date. He simply did not want to give the impression that he was too old to be dating a young starlet. Assured by Stevens that such would not be the case, Gig invited Lizzie to join him for the studio dinner. As it turned out, she was excited about the idea. Apparently, she had seen one of his recent film performances and said to anyone who would listen, "I think he's the most attractive man on the screen and I intend to marry him."

While most shrugged off the remark, fate seemed to play against Lizzie's hopes for a romance, let alone a marriage. At the time of her first date with Gig, she was scheduled to return to New York shortly to begin rehearsing a play. More importantly, she was not totally legally free from her marriage to Fred Cammann.

That said, and as Eells explained in his book, it was obvious to many that Gig's appearance and mannerisms were oddly similar to those of Robert Montgomery. The two had met when Gig guest-starred in an episode of *Robert Montgomery Presents* called "The Sunday Punch," which aired October 19, 1953:

> One-time fighter *Tony Marino* (Young) is on his way down the boxing ladder but can still throw a mean "Sunday punch." After his manager (played by Frank Wilson) attempts to bribe him to "take a dive" in a fight with up-and-comer *Kid Walker*, *Tony* becomes infuriated and almost wins the fight, but then suffers a dangerous head injury that may have lasting repercussions.

Three years after *Punch* aired, and approximately twelve months after Lizzie met Gig, she performed in an episode of his show, *Warner Brothers*

Presents, titled "Siege," which aired on February 14, Valentine's Day, 1956. On camera, she played a country schoolteacher whose class is held captive by an escaped convict. Off-camera, her young heart was held captive by Gig and the two were married the following December 28, and her father Robert Montgomery was nowhere in sight. He would not attend his daughter's second marriage.

Meanwhile, Lizzie and Gig decided they wanted to have children of their own, immediately, if possible. But to alleviate certain health issues he had had a vasectomy when he was only twenty-five. He would later reverse the procedure but his relationship with Lizzie, which lasted six years, still did not prove fertile.

What it did produce was a lot of turmoil, largely due to the fact that Gig was a chronic alcoholic. What's more, it was challenging for him get over the loss of his second wife. In 1949 he and his first wife, Sheila Stapler, were divorced after nine years of marriage. In 1951, he wed drama coach Sophia Rosenstein, who died of cancer one year later.

Number three was up when Gig met Lizzie. He was immediately hypnotized by her sophisticated ways and flattered by the attention she showered on him. When she returned to Broadway to replace the ingénue in *The Loud Red Patrick*, they were constantly on the phone.

After finishing his stint on *Warner Brothers Presents*, Gig received an offer to go into the legendary Jean Dalrymple's revival of *The Teahouse of the August Moon* at the New York City Center. He wasn't as impressed with Dalrymple as he was with Lizzie. So, he leapt at the opportunity to be near the future *Bewitched* star. The *Moon* revival didn't spark any interest, but his romance with Lizzie was set afire.

Charismatic and confident, her charms were evident wherever she went. As author Eells uncovered in his book on Young, the actor found Lizzie alluring but somewhat intimidating. But she helped to fill a void and loosened him up socially. At times they were like two little kids, according to Bob Douglas, a mutual bystander and friend to the couple.

One weekend, for example, Lizzie took Gig and Douglas to her family's attractive country home in Patterson, New York. Upon arrival there, and after several drinks, Gig blurted out, "What about dinner?"

At which point, Lizzie ventured into the kitchen, returned and said, "Well, we really don't have much of anything." They discussed going to a restaurant, but apparently that wasn't an option. After a time, she appeared with three plates, on which were three hamburgers. Everyone tasted them, and Gig said,

"Mmmmmm, don't think much of these."

"What?" Lizzie wondered. "I don't think much of these," Gig repeated.

As Douglas recalled, the meat patties were "absolutely filthy." Lizzie had made them out of dog food!

Out of such shocking hijinks as this their romance increased and became serious. According to Douglas and his wife Sue, it was Lizzie who pushed to be married, but Gig was uncertain. Sharing the secret of his 1938 vasectomy with her was not easy. His wife Sheila had resigned to the information calmly and rarely made reference to it. With his wife Sophie, it wasn't an issue at all, since she had undergone a hysterectomy before they married. Elaine Stritch had assured him they would be together even it was not possible for him to father children. But with Lizzie, Young felt old. He became increasingly concerned about his masculinity which, as he viewed it, was diminished by the vasectomy. But he finally told her the truth, and she didn't care. They would breed dogs, she said. Sue Douglas in *Final Gig*:

> She went into the marriage with her eyes wide open. She was so nuts about him. I don't think anything would have made any difference. I think he was a little scared of the marriage, but not Liz. She adored animals and in some way believed they would take the place of children, which, of course, is ridiculous thinking.

According to an early studio bio, Lizzie and Gig did at least own a collie, which they named *Willie Grogan*, in honor of the principle character he played in 1962 Elvis Presley feature film *Kid Galahad*. They also had a goat named *Mary Chess*, which happened to be a trade name for a then-line of perfumes. At the time, they lived in Sunset Plaza, a fashionable mountain-side residential area above Sunset Strip, where Lizzie maintained her green thumb . . . for mint, which she grew in her backyard.

The two-page bio also went on to explain her principal hobby was painting. She had sold watercolor works of art and was working on an assignment to illustrate a children's book. She was a collector of antiques and had "no particular liking for modern art, although she respects it."

As Eells explained in *Final Gig*, a band of "loosely connected couples" from the entertainment industry surrounded Lizzie and Young in Manhattan, including the Dunnes, Howard and Lou Erskine, Betsy Von Furstenberg and Guy Vincent, and Bill and Fay Harbach.

Husband and wife actors William Daniels and Bonnie Bartlett were also part of that group. Married for over fifty years, Bartlett and Daniels had known Lizzie and Gig from their days in New York when they performed in guest-star roles on *Robert Montgomery Presents*. Although Lizzie made frequent appearances on her father's show, none were with Daniels and Bartlett. The two would not work with her until years later. Daniels, best known to classic TV fans for his regular stints on *St. Elsewhere* (NBC, 1982–1988) and *Boy Meets World* (ABC, 1993–2000), as well as being the voice of *K.I.T.T.* on the cult car show, *Knight Rider* (NBC, 1982–1986), appeared with Lizzie in her 1974 NBC TV-movie, *A Case of Rape*. Bartlett, a heralded actress in her own right with countless TV and film appearances under her belt, worked with Elizabeth in her 1975 TV-movie for ABC, *The Legend of Lizzie Borden*. "So Bill and I just happened to be in two of her biggest hits," Bartlett says.

Decades before, Elizabeth and Gig visited Daniels and Bartlett in their New York apartment:

"Gig was a rather elegant and charming gentleman," Bartlett recalls. "But he drank too much. *Everybody* drank too much. They were both drinking a lot, but I never saw her drunk, while he was pretty hopeless. She was good to get away from him."

Actor/author J. Anthony Russo had chronicled in his book, *Creativity or Madness*, that Dean Martin believed Lizzie to be intoxicated on the set of *Who's Been Sleeping in My Bed?*, and now Bartlett remembers Lizzie once revealing that her mother "drank a lot." "She had a nice way of saying it, so it wasn't coarse," Bartlett explains, "but she said, 'I told Mother I was going to cut her off at the bar.' And I believe at this point, her mother lived with her. She adored her mother."

Upon hearing this, Sally Kemp, has an epiphany: "My mother, I realize now, like Elizabeth's, was an alcoholic."

But while studies have shown that alcoholism is both a disease and hereditary, Sally questions if Lizzie had a substance abuse problem:

Elizabeth and I usually sat next to each other in classes at the Academy and always had lunch together. I *never* smelled alcohol on her and would have known instantly. I was very wary and conscious of it. I wasn't aware of her drinking much until she was trying to extricate Gig from Elaine Stritch. She had a tremendous crush on him and there was a big age difference between them . . . I don't know how many years . . . and [her father] was against the match. I saw less of her by then since I was pursuing my own life. I saw them occasionally once they were married and they seemed happy. Gig was very charming until he'd had too much, then he'd kind of blur. I think Elizabeth *did* try to keep up with him, partly to lessen the age difference. I think she was far more intelligent than he was. He had a suave, sleek surface, but I've no idea what was beneath it, or even if there was a beneath. If she was unhappy or becoming unhappy, she never shared it and once they moved to L.A. all contact ceased and I know nothing of hers or their life together. When I heard the horror story of Gig's death, I was deeply grateful she was well out of it. I don't know about her life from then on except that she and Bill Asher had three children, which must have made her very happy . . . she always had a lovely childlike ability to create fun. I heard rumors of [her] drinking with [Bob] Foxworth, but they were only rumors and there are always rumors about celebrities. I knew as an actress myself that she couldn't keep up her work schedule, raise three children, and look beautiful if she was incapacitated by booze. I wish our lives hadn't gone apart, that's all I can say.

Biographer George Eells in *Final Gig*:

If the Young-Stritch affair played itself out as a bittersweet Neil Simon, then Gig and Liz's mad marriage radiated Noel Coward savoir faire: communal dashes to the martini fountain after screenings, croquet matches and other games. To those who knew them both, it seemed that Liz was intent on matching Gig's capacity for drink, as though it were some kind of contest.

Agent Martin Baum represented both Lizzie and Gig while they were together. Baum to Euell in *Final Gig*:

As a couple, Gig and Liz were a delight. There was a childlike innocence about him that was totally refreshing. There was little guile, no jealousy or resentment of others who were doing well. A dear person. Of course, that was the surface Gig. I noticed when we were out on an evening socially, he drank excessively by my standards, and Liz was drinking right along with him. But they seemed happy.

In late summer of 2011, Lizzie's good friend Cliff Robertson described her relationship with Gig as "very warm and passionate," adding:

> They seemed to get along very well. He was a charming fellow and a good actor. I would see them out on the West Coast for a while, when she was spending most of her time out there. But then she and Gig split up and she called me in New York, where I was still living at the time. She'd call every once and a while [to] say, "Are you coming to town?" And I'd tell her when and we'd often meet at a restaurant to catch up. She would tell me about her latest exploits and what not. But I never had any indication of whether or not there was trouble in the marriage. And when they did split I was sorry to hear that. I knew that they had been very happy, though clearly not for a long period of time.

Loyal until the end, Robertson believed Lizzie handled every circumstance throughout her life with "grace and charm. She showed a lot of spunk for a girl who was brought up with creature comforts." Once more, it was Lizzie's unaffected demeanor that marked her appeal, specifically with Gig. "That was probably one of the main things that he saw in her," Robertson surmised. "That she was so well-grounded."

Montgomery archivist Thomas McCartney:

> Her background helped to ground her, especially in that industry, which allowed her to survive where as so many others within it perished, literally. Her inner strength allowed her to continue to focus on her work when all around her crashed and burned in her personal life, this again came from being fundamentally strong, stable, and secure within herself and who she was as a human being. She was able to float with ease from one to any other social interaction, no matter if it was a lunch-bucket crew member or someone with high social standing to the point of royalty itself. She mainly drank with Gig to be able to be close to him on an emotional level so he would not shut her out, this being to keep loneliness at bay and to make Gig emotionally available, otherwise he shut down emotionally and shut her out. All addicts like company and pressure those around them to take

part in their addiction. In this case, the pressure to do so came from Liz herself to retain access to Gig, so he would take her along on his magic carpet rides rather than leave her behind. Drinking like they did, as with Liz's mother, was the norm then; in those days, no one would bat an eye at someone who drank a half a dozen hard drinks a day. Point being that the way Liz and her mother drank then was not noticeable. That's what people did and society almost expected [it] of one. It was the norm. Now, we know better, but then they did not, nor would they be aware that their actions would be taken with anything more than a shrug of the shoulders.

McCartney makes a valid observation: In the 1950s, 1960s, and 1970s, on-screen and off, daily alcohol consumption was considered socially acceptable and *cool*, as was smoking. But the devastating health ravages of such vices were not yet fully calculated.

As with many dramas and sitcoms in the 1960s, specifically, *Bewitched*, characters were frequently seen drinking or inebriated. Certainly, whenever *Darrin* felt overwhelmed by his wife's witchcraft, he made himself a *double* or a *triple*, once even asking *Sam* to fix him a *quadruple* (in the fifth season episode, "I Don't Want to Be a Toad; I Want to Be a Butterfly," where he says, "Make it a quadruple and finish the story after I pass out"). In fact, actor Dick Wilson, better known as *Mr. Whipple* from the famous Charmin bath tissue commercials, was considered nearly a semi-regular on *Bewitched* due to his more than fifteen appearances as a drunkard, either at *Darrin's* favorite bar, trying to pick up *Samantha* outside a restaurant (while *Darrin* fetched the car in "If They Never Met"), or as a neighborhood bum who thought *Endora's* down-sized version of *Darrin* was a leprechaun (in "*Samantha*'s Wedding Present").

Consistent drinking also took place on 1960s shows like *That Girl*, *I Dream of Jeannie*, even on the daytime gothic soap, *Dark Shadows* (which Johnny Depp and director Tim Burton recently resurrected for the big screen), where a glass of sherry was the gothic drink of choice. Acting and song legend Dean Martin, Elizabeth's co-star in the 1963 film, *Who's Been Sleeping in My Bed?*, had a reputation as a chronic drinker and he brought that role to the party every week on his very successful TV variety hour, *The Dean Martin Show*. Additionally, one of the *Martin* program regulars was comedian Foster Brooks who, like Dick Wilson on *Bewitched*, became famous for making light of the drinking-man persona.

Later into the 1970s, drinking appeared regularly on sitcoms like *The Paul Lynde Show*, which just so happened to star a former *Bewitched* regular, which was produced by *Bewitched's* Bill Asher, who also just so happened to be Elizabeth's third husband. Lynde's anxiety-ridden attorney *Paul Simms* would frequently ask his wife *Martha* (played by Elizabeth Allen, but not Lizzie's mother) to fix his regular dose of martini.

However, the devastating health ravages of weekly if not daily inebriation were not fully explained because the statistics just weren't there at the time. It was an ignorant era and ignorance was bliss, or maybe just blind, even after 1964, when *Smoking and Health: Report of the Advisory Committee to the Surgeon General of the United States* was published. Unfortunately, before the 1970s, tobacco advertising was legal in the United States and most of Europe. In America in the 1950s and 1960s, cigarette brands frequently sponsored TV shows, from all-family fare such as *The Dick Van Dyke Show, I Love Lucy,* and *The Beverly Hillbillies,* to the celebrity-laden game shows *To Tell the Truth* and *I've Got a Secret.*

Flash forward to two interviews in the early 1990s, and Lizzie seemed to have made a startling realization of her own. Two times she was asked if she ever got tired of people asking her to do the twitch, and with both replies, she mentioned the topic of wine. In 1991, when she sat down with Ronald Haver for their *Here Comes Mr. Jordan* laserdisc conversation, she mused, "Well, it depends on how many people I ran into," then adding she'd be unable to nose-wriggle if she had a drink. "If I wanted to get sloshed on the (*Bewitched*) set," she continued with a laugh, "I would have never been able to [do the] twitch. So, I can't do it if I'm tired or if I've had a glass of wine. Isn't that funny?"

In 1992, during her chat with John Tesh for *One on One*, she laughed, and said:

> If I'm tired, if I've had one glass of wine, or if I'm inclined to get the giggles, there is no way to do it. Now, you can figure out which one is my excuse now. Obviously, I haven't had a glass of wine, I'm not tired—yet—and I mean, sitting here (trying to do it, when asked, on camera, and not in character as *Samantha*) . . . it's very hard.

☆

According to a variety of sources including the March 1962 issue of *Photoplay Magazine*, Thomas McCartney, and www.elvispresleynews.com, music superstar Elvis Presley, who certainly had his own issues with substance abuse, may have undermined the foundation of Lizzie's relationship with Gig Young. It appears that a tense situation developed on the set of *Kid Galahad*, the 1962 motion picture starring Presley, and a purportedly very agitated Young. Although *Kid* is considered some of Presley's best work on screen (1956's *Love Me Tender* and 1958's *King Creole* notwithstanding), it's startling to conceive how it ever completed filming considering Gig's antics.

Apparently, Lizzie was a daily visitor to the *Kid* set and while Gig was busy filming, she'd chat up a "storm" with Elvis, so much so that one time Gig became enraged and caused a scene. Green with "Elvis envy," he nearly physically attacked Elvis, while Lizzie was crushed at Gig's accusation and burst into tears. At which point Elvis reached out to comfort her, which only further infuriated Gig. The two men exchanged threats and then Elvis called Gig "an asshole" and ordered him to "grow up!"

At some point, Elvis had his fill of the daily Liz/Gig quarrels and he was not at all pleased with Young's unprofessional behavior. He was getting so fed up with Young, that he felt like it wasn't worth completing the movie. But he did. He would often hear Young verbally abuse Lizzie. But he didn't intercede. He just hoped that one day she would "come to her senses." Ultimately, he was relieved that the movie was over because as he saw it, "I never want to work with Gig Young again."

But such was not the case with Lizzie, whom Elvis attempted to cast in at least one of his films approximately one year after meeting her on the *Kid* set. But studio big-wigs kept passing on pairing the two, specifically in 1961's *Blue Hawaii*, in which Joan Blackman was cast instead, and which Lizzie later described as one of her favorite Elvis films.

There was also some talk that hip-twisting Elvis was indeed romantically interested in the future nose-twitching Lizzie. He was allegedly envious of Young's marriage to Lizzie. "If she was single," he was to have stated, "I would certainly pursue her."

When asked how she felt about Presley, Lizzie replied at the time:

I think Elvis is very attractive and yes, if I was single I would date him. Even though he isn't my type, I would have given him a chance and who knows what it could have led to? Let's face it, what girl wouldn't want to date Elvis? I do want to work with Elvis one day, if the studios would let me. But it doesn't seem likely at this present moment.

Three weeks after *Kid Galahad* completed filming Gig was still adamant that Lizzie had slept with Elvis and continued to argue with her about the alleged antics. At one point, the disagreements became so intense, Gig apparently left town for a few days to see a friend named Helena, a development he sardonically implied would allow Lizzie to spend time with her new "lover!" Now lonely and neglected, with tears turned to anger, Lizzie allegedly hurried to Elvis' side, stopping short of having the affair that would have manifested Gig's worst nightmare.

Around the same time, rumor had it that Lizzie found Gig in their bed with some random nimble naked young blonde. Upon viewing said scene, Lizzie apparently instructed the woman to dress and leave, and in the process tossed Gig out on his ear—without any nose-twitching assistance on her part. That would come later, when she wed herself to *Bewitched* and married Bill Asher, which was another relationship for which Elvis reportedly had a measure of envy. While Asher claimed in 2003, for an interview with Terry and Tiffany DuFoe (today of www.cultradioagogo.com), that such was not the case, because he "didn't know Elvis," he did have one issue with him. Apparently, Elvis was supposed to have starred in one of Bill's films. "It was a pretty good story," Asher recalled, "and he had agreed to do it." The motion picture would have apparently given the singing sensation the opportunity to play a "heavy," which was very different from the more carefree persona he created in most of his films. But right before he was scheduled to work on the movie, Elvis made his famous television debut on *The Ed Sullivan Show.* Consequently, his representatives advised against their client portraying the darker role, and the young superstar pulled out of the film.

Gig Young was four years older than Vernon Presley, Elvis' father, not to mention two decades older than Lizzie. As Sally Kemp has said, she believes her friend was attracted to Gig mostly as a father figure and recalls further how Robert Montgomery was none too pleased with his daughter's decision to marry the senior actor:

> I think he was very angry that she married Gig. He wasn't that much younger than Bob, who probably saw what Elizabeth couldn't see. And

what no one else really saw. It was a challenge to look past Gig's great charm. But he must have hurt her, because she left him.

Indeed, according to various sources when Robert learned of Lizzie's intention to wed Gig, he became incensed. Their relationship somewhat mercurial, he was ardently against her marrying someone he once called "almost as old and not one quarter as successful as I am."

As time passed Robert's disdain for Gig did not subside, and Lizzie and her new love seemed to relish this fact, devising little schemes that incensed her father. As Dominick Dunne's wife Lenny explained in *Final Gig*, during one particular visit to Los Angeles, Robert invited the Youngs and the Dunnes to dinner. It was not the most tranquil of evenings, because neither Robert nor Gig was able to be cordial—sincerely or otherwise. "But after we finished dining," Lenny relayed, "Nick and I invited everyone back to our house for a drink. They came, some more eagerly than others."

But Lizzie had an early call the next morning for a TV show and, after a respectably lengthy visit with the Dunnes, she and Gig begged their good-byes, though not before approaching and kissing her father with a simple, "Goodnight, Daddy Bob." Mimicking the move, Gig swiftly leaned toward his father-in-law, smacked him right on the lips, and echoed Lizzie's words, "*Goodnight, Daddy Bob!*"

"Well," recalled Lenny Dunne, "I thought Robert Montgomery was going to have a stroke."

The cards may have held a similar fate for Gig. According to Eell's biography, he suffered from skin cancer and was Valium-dependent. His career failing, he was paranoid about the future and, as Lizzie's friends Bonnie Bartlett and Sally Kemp had assumed, he was an alcoholic.

Although Sally did not know Young "that well at all," it was clear to her that he did have a "huge drinking problem. And that was always a mystery to me how that horrible, horrible thing happened with him later. I was never around him that much and I never knew him that well. So I never saw that side of him. But anyone who drinks like that has to have major demons."

The "horrible, horrible thing" to which she refers here and to which she previously referred as the "horror story of Gig's death" was the murder/suicide that involved him and his fifth wife, a thirty-one-year-old German woman named Kim Schmidt. Schmidt was hired as the script girl on Gig's final movie, *The Game of Death*, which was released in 1978. On September 27 of that year, the two were married. Three weeks later on October 19, 1978, in the Manhattan apartment they shared, Gig shot Schmidt in the head, killing her instantly. He then shot himself. The police theorized that it was a suicide pact, but were baffled by the additional three revolvers and 350 rounds of ammunition found in the apartment. After the investigation the police stated Gig had definitely acted on the spur of the moment and his actions were not planned.

Clearly, Elizabeth's marriage to Gig was troubling and trouble-making, but it could have ended much worse than it did. Because of Gig's vasectomy, the union did not produce any children. Finally and fortunately, and after repeatedly denying she was even estranged from Gig, Lizzie confessed in April of 1963 to what would become her second "quickie" divorce in Nevada. She met Gig in 1956 while she was filming *The Court-Martial of Billy Mitchell* and she left him while working with Dean Martin in *Who's Been Sleeping in My Bed?*

Nine months after his divorce from Lizzie, Gig married real estate agent Elaine Whitman who was pregnant with his first child, a daughter, Jennifer, who was born in 1964—the year *Bewitched* debuted. While Lizzie was making new magic as *Samantha* (and a baby of her own with William Asher, namely William Asher, Jr.), Gig proclaimed his first child's birth a "miracle," validating his reverse surgery as a success.

Although the Gig was up, the joy didn't stick. On November 23, 1966, Whitman filed for divorce. Frequent court battles over child support led him to publicly deny Jennifer was his daughter, claiming he was duped into his marriage to Whitman, but because he had claimed Jennifer as his own in the original divorce papers, he had no legal recourse in the matter.

According to George Eell's book, when Lizzie and Gig were still married, she envisioned having children who would have inherited his large gray eyes and dark wavy hair. When the issue of his paternity suit later became Hollywood news, she was purported to have then said to a friend: "(Jennifer's) not Gig's child. Believe me, if Gig didn't get me pregnant, he didn't get anyone pregnant."

In *The Way We Lived Then*, Dominick Dunne said Lizzie and Gig were "wildly happy" for a long while. Dating back to his days as script supervisor for *Robert Montgomery Presents* and shortly beyond, he and his wife Lenny were friends with the Youngs and then "something happened." But the Dunnes hadn't a clue as to what that was, as neither Lizzie nor Gig were the type to disclose private information. Apparently, she left their house in one direction and he went the opposite way, "furious with each other," Dominick said, and that was that.

Conversely, Lizzie dearly loved her fourth and final husband Robert Foxworth who once had his own take on her marriage to Young. As he explained on A&E's *Biography* in 1999, her relationship with Young was unpleasant and "some domestic violence" was involved. Fortunately, as Foxworth pointed out, Lizzie was intelligent and strong-willed enough to break away from Young's grip.

According to George Eells in *Final Gig*, Lizzie's marriage to Young was not the perfect union that was sometimes portrayed in the press. "The first hint that trouble was brewing came early on, back in the golden days in New York." Helena Sterling, Gig's old friend from the Louis Shurr West Coast office, had moved to Manhattan at the Youngs' request and found herself spending a great deal of time with Elizabeth, whom she at first considered as Eells put it, "scatterbrained." "Then," Sterling told Eells, "I realized she was lonely." Writer Lily Brandy offered this conclusion in the article, "I Hope This Spell Lasts," published October 1966, in *Inside Movie* magazine:

> Gig Young . . . gave Liz something of an inferiority complex. His career was riding high during their marriage . . . and he was much better known than she was. She tried to subordinate her own ego and ambitions to his. It didn't work. She was truly her father's daughter. The acting bug hit her hard and despite the setbacks, the false alarms, the disappointments, she determined to persist. Significantly, her star really began to rise after her divorce from Gig.

Nine

∽

Two Plus Hundreds

"Precrassny."

—The Russian word for *pretty*, as spoken by Elizabeth as *The Woman*, who has the only line of dialogue in *The Twilight Zone* episode, "Two," airing September 15, 1961

Between Lizzie's "Top Secret" premiere segment of *Robert Montgomery Presents* (December 3, 1951) and her initial twitch in *Bewitched* (debuting September 17, 1964), she made over 200 diverse guest-star TV appearances. Some of those shows include: *Boris Karloff's Thriller* (NBC, 1960–1962), *Alfred Hitchcock Presents* (NBC, 1958, "Man with a Problem"), *Johnny Staccato* (ABC/NBC, 1959/1960, "Tempted"), *One Step Beyond* (1960, "The Death Waltz"), *Wagon Train* (1959, "The Vittorio Botticelli Story"), *Rawhide* (1963, "Incident at El Crucero"), and *77 Sunset Strip* (1963, "White Lie").

She also delivered stand-out performances in ABC's *The Untouchables* (for "The Rusty Heller Story" episode that aired October 13, 1960, for which she received her first Emmy nomination in 1961); the series premiere of NBC's *Theatre '62* edition of "The Spiral Staircase," which aired October 4, 1961 (in which she starred as a mute, alongside a very vocal character played by her then-husband Gig Young); *The Twilight Zone* episode two, which CBS broadcast September 15, 1961 (and in which she delivered yet another muted performance, this time with Charles Bronson, who also did not speak a word of dialogue); and for the "Mr. Lucifer" segment of *Alcoa Premiere* that aired on ABC, November 1, 1962 (when she literally "danced with the devil," played by none other than famed hoofer Fred Astaire, who also hosted the series).

Produced by Everett Freeman, "Mr. Lucifer" was written by Alfred Bester and directed by Alan Crosland, Jr. who would years later helm episodes of *The Six Million Dollar Man*, *The Bionic Woman*, and *Wonder Woman*; among others. Not only is the entire episode classified as a fantasy comedy, which was a rare segment for any anthology series of the day, but it is laden with *Bewitched*-like special effects with items and props "popping in and out"; "Mr. Lucifer" even snaps his fingers and stops time as did *Samantha* many times on *Bewitched*.

As to the actual premise of the episode, and Lizzie's character, she played *Iris Haggerty*, the devil's assistant (a.k.a. "a legitimate moon goddess"). Apparently, *Iris* did her thesis (wherever that was) on moon goddesses: "I always thought it was rather unfair when the Christians turned her into a demon. But in mythology that's the way the banana splits."

Upon review of "Mr. Lucifer," it immediately becomes clear just how much Lizzie reveled in the performance, as she delivered what could be described as an early, energetic pre-witched take on *Serena*, *Samantha's* look-a-like cousin on *Bewitched*. *Iris* is hot, snippy, loose, fun-loving, free-spirited, and devious. We see her as platinum blond, a raven-haired beauty in elegant evening wear, and in a bikini. At one point, she even says it straight out, ". . . I'm on the loose, and I just may take off."

Other dialogue is as revealing, and somewhat more representative of Lizzie's real life. At one point, she begins a telling conversation with Astaire's *Lucifer*: "All I can say is they don't make men like they used to. When I was a moon goddess . . ."

But he interrupts her: "When they made *you* they broke the mold."

Another of *Iris's* lines which slightly bespoke Lizzie's life: "I always thought that every woman should marry, and no man"; "When you're independent it costs you."

But probably the most interesting sequence of "Mr. Lucifer" is when Lizzie as *Iris* and Astaire as the *Devil* are literally monitoring on screen the life of the mild-mannered *Tom Logan* (Frank Aletter), who they so very much want to bring over to the dark side. Here, the audience is introduced to *Jenny Logan*, Tom's wife, on whom *Iris* and *Lucifer* set their sights to use as a pawn in his seduction.

When *Mr. Lucifer* wonders how to first seduce *Jenny*, *Iris* suggests summoning *Don Juan, Casanova,* and *Ben Casey*, the latter of which was a popular TV doctor of the time played by Vince Edwards. But *Lucifer* rejects the idea:

"You don't corrupt the young American girl with matinee idols."

"Oh," *Iris* replies, "you don't?" (a possible wink to Robert Montgomery).

What proves more provocative about this sequence is that the role of *Jenny* is played by none other than actress Joyce Bulifant who, years later would not only go on to star as Gavin MacLeod's spouse on *The Mary Tyler Moore Show* (CBS, 1970–1977), but would become William Asher's wife in real life after his divorce from Lizzie. As *Lucifer* and *Iris* discuss Bulifant's character, Iris looks none too pleased, if not downright jealous, and says of *Jenny*: "She's the kind of wife women hate. She designs and makes her own clothes, speaks three languages, she's a fine cook, a charming hostess; and she's writing a novel in her spare time."

An additional noteworthy, if not lengthy, appearances from this early era of Lizzie's career was when she performed in the "Patterns" segment of another live anthology series, NBC's *Kraft Theatre* (1947–1958). "Patterns" aired January 12, 1955, and was written by the prolific Rod Serling and directed with great skill by Fielder Cook. The episode, which was remade as a theatrical feature film the following year, proved so popular, it was first re-performed live on TV February 9, 1955, a rare development for the small screen at the time. Usually, live segments were broadcast only once; even recorded editions of the same episode never aired twice. But such was not the case with "Patterns," which also just so happened to be the five hundredth episode of *Kraft Theatre*.

Here, Lizzie played the small role of a secretary named *Ann Evans*, alongside a cast that included a young Richard Kiley (*St. Elsewhere*), Ed Begley (father to Ed Begley, Jr., also from *St. Elsewhere*), Everett Sloane, Joanna Roos, Jack Starter, Victoria Ward, June Dayton, Jack Livesy, and others.

Fred Staples (Kiley) is the newest executive in a large firm who befriends *Andy Sloan* (Begley). Staples is good at what he does, and the company's head *Walter Ramsay* (Sloane) is content with his performance on the job. But the situation soon becomes stressful, delicate, and then ultimately tragic, when *Ramsey* tells *Fred* he's been hired to replace *Andy*, who has dedicated his life to the company, at the expense of his family.

One of Lizzie's opening lines (to a fellow secretary) sets the stage for the entire premise. Even though we never hear too much from her again, she says: "No sign of the new genius, I suppose?"

Her most memorable line in the episode: "Wow . . . you never know when you're going to hit a nerve"; which, off camera, proved telling of her sometimes too frank conversations with her father—or anyone else who was in the room.

Other than that, she said little else to say or do in "Patterns," and although it was a small part, she made it her own. She was helped along, of course, by Cook's clearly defined direction and the densely written script by Serling, with whom Lizzie would work a short time later on her now famous "Two" episode of *The Twilight Zone*.

Arguably her most prominent and best known pre-*Samantha* TV spot, "Two" debuted on CBS September 15, 1961, and co-starred a young and pre-superstar Charles Bronzon as the only other cast member. Author Marc Scott Zicree summarized the episode in his excellent book *The Twilight Zone Companion* (Silman-James Press, 1992):

While searching for food, a young woman wearing the tattered uniform of the invading army encounters an enemy soldier—one intent on declaring peace. Initially, she is violently distrustful of him—a situation which only intensifies when they remove two working rifles from a pair of skeletons. Later, though, when she admires a dress in a store window, he removes it and gives it to her. She goes into a recruiting office to slip it on. Unfortunately, the propaganda posters within rekindle the old hatreds; she rushes out and fires off several rounds at him. The next day, the man returns, dressed in ill-fitting civilian clothes. To his surprise, the woman is wearing the dress. Finally having put aside the war, she joins him and the two of them set off, side by side.

As Zicree appraised, "Two" was penned and directed by the multitalented Montgomery Pittman (1920–1964). Pittman's first assignment in the *Zone* was helming "Will the Real Martian Please Stand Up?" But it was "Two" that demonstrated the full extent of his abilities. Here, he presented an optimistic story set in a substantially dark, post–World War III desolated town inhabited only by the dead, with the exception of two enemy soldiers. Zicree explains how fairly obvious it becomes that Bronson signifies an American soldier and Lizzie a Russian. "In fact," he writes, "her single line is 'precrassny'—Russian for 'pretty.' This is a gritty and realistic story of survival, told with a minimum of dialogue yet with the emphasis always on characterization."

The "Two" characters "go against the stereotype," Zicree goes on to say. It is Bronson's character, "broad and muscular, with a face like an eroded cliff, who is the pacifist." On the other hand, he labels Lizzie's character as "one who is suspicious and quick to violent action. Those who remember her from *Bewitched* might be shocked by her appearance here: long brown hair, smudged face, pretty in a peasant-like way, but not at all the glamour girl."

Pittman's widow Murita also comments in the book, saying Lizzie "was so dedicated to her art. Most girls want to look really pretty for the camera. Monty had to fight her, really, because she wanted to make her eyes really black. She got too much makeup on; she was making herself too haggard."

Maybe so, but her dedication to the role was more than evident. "It was not an easy part by any means," Zicree concludes.

And Lizzie embraced the challenge. "You find yourself reacting to things you never reacted to before," she said at the time. "You find it difficult not to exaggerate every look, every action. You think nobody will notice you unless you ham it up. You have to underplay every scene in a play of this type. But I must say I never enjoyed doing a show as much as I did 'Two.' "

According to *The Twilight Zone: Unlocking the Door to a Television Classic* by Martin Grams, Jr. (OTR Publishing, 2008), Lizzie thought making "Two" was "creepy. I couldn't help thinking what it would be like if I went around the corner and there actually wasn't anyone there—nothing but rubble, grass growing in the streets, the debris of a dead human race."

On September 18, 1961 *The Hollywood Reporter* offered its review of "Two":

> Some confusion at CBS as to whether Friday's *Twilight Zone* was the season's debut, the confusion caused by a sponsor change next week, methinks. . . . But this was the first new one of the season, starring only Charles Bronson and Elizabeth Montgomery in "Two," a tale of the only two survivors in an atomic war—Bronson, essaying one of us, and Liz, mute but effective as an enemy soldier . . . Seg was interesting but not as powerful as other short-cast *Zones*, particularly the one where Robert Cummings carried the show solo ("King Nine Will Not Return," 9-30-60).

As Grams pointed out in his *Zone* guide, *Variety*, the other industry trade, had a policy of reviewing all season premieres of television programs and was also confused. The magazine ended up reviewing next week's episode instead of this one.

Elizabeth made two appearances on yet another anthology series, this one titled, *Appointment with Adventure*, which aired for only one season on CBS, from 1955–1956. Filmed live each week, *Danger* gave viewers a glimpse of drama and adventure from around the world and from the distant and not-so-distant past. Subjects of the weekly plays included the American wars, as well as conflicts of far-away countries, and were performed by a number of well-known stars of the time.

The episodes in which Lizzie starred were called "All Through the Night" (2-5-56) and "Relative Stranger" (11-20-55). In "Night," she performed with her friend John Cassavetes (an alumnus of the New York Academy of Dramatic Arts) and actress Tina Louise (who would later play movie star *Ginger* on *Gilligan's Island*).

"Relative Stranger," however, stands out. Written by Irving Werstein and directed by Paul Stanley, the episode also starred William Windom, who would later take home an Emmy for his lead in the ground-breaking if short-lived sitcom, *My World and Welcome to It* (NBC, 1969–1970). He also appeared as *Commodore Matt Decker*, commander of the doomed USS *Constellation* in the famous 1968 *Star Trek* episode "The Doomsday

Machine," and in the 1980s–1990s portrayed the curmudgeonly *Dr. Seth Hazlitt* opposite Angela Lansbury's mystery-writing/solving *Jessica Fletcher* on CBS' *Murder, She Wrote.*

But for the moment, he was married to Lizzie, and found himself involved in the mysterious escapades of "Relative Stranger":

> After her father dies and leaves an inheritance, *Helen* (Lizzie), a young married American married woman, visits relatives in Copenhagen who prove to be more than unfriendly, if not downright corrupt and violent. Fortunately, her husband *Dan* (Windom) arrives at a dire moment, and just in the nick of time.

The anthology's main title (*Appointment with Danger*) was melodramatic, but it must have appealed to Lizzie's adventurous side, while the specific episode title ("Relative Stranger") was an ominous description of how Lizzie at times perceived Robert Montgomery in her youth (as she once admitted not knowing he was an actor until learning so from a fellow Westlake classmate).

The paternal dialogue in "Relative" was clear as a bell. *Helen* tells *Dan* things like: "I'm kind of nervous about meeting Dad's cousins for the first time. I hope they like me"; "I've never had a large family. There's just mother and dad and me"; and "I don't mind talking about Father. Of course it has been rather lonely without him" (which may have specifically echoed Lizzie's feelings as a child when her father spent months making movies abroad or serving in the Air Force).

Upon arrival in her relative's homeland, *Helen* loses a favorite necklace, explaining: "My grandmother gave it to me," mirroring the relationship Lizzie had with her grandmother Becca who gifted her with many things (like a cherished broach that Lizzie wore throughout her life), but most importantly the gift of understanding priorities.

In later, more violent scenes, Lizzie's *Helen* is seen tied-up with her hands behind her back, spread across a bed on her stomach. It's a scene that would be repeated, down to camera angles, in her 1992 TV-movie, *With Murder in Mind*, in which she played real-life real estate agent Gayle Wolfer who was assaulted and traumatized by a client.

But *Helen* in "Stranger" was the first of many victimized characters Lizzie played before Wolfer in *Mind*. Eventually, she played *Kate Wainwright* in

The Victim (1972), *Ellen Harrod* in *A Case of Rape*, and *Catherine McSweeney* in *Act of Violence* . . . . as well as *Helen Warren* in the *Theatre '62* segment, "The Spiral Staircase," in which Lizzie delivered one of her more outstanding performances from this early, pre-*Bewitched* television era.

"Staircase" debuted as part of NBC's *Theatre '62* in on October 4, 1961. In this small screen remake of the 1945 film (starring Lizzie's friend Dorothy McGuire), she plays *Helen Capel*, who, because of a childhood trauma, has not spoken a word in decades. It's an old-fashioned mystery with dark hallways, flickering candlelight, rain storms and lightning, and with it, Lizzie delivers one of her most riveting, pre-*Samantha* dramatic performances. Although the characters are different, the cinematic mood is the same when she plays the murderess *Lizzie Borden* in the 1975 TV-movie *The Legend of Lizzie Borden*. But little wonder, as both productions were directed by the talented Paul Wendkos who on "Staircase" also guides the likes of Lizzie's co-stars Lillian Gish, Edie Adams, Eddie Albert and Gig Young.

Playing a mute character is always a challenge and tour de force for any actor and Lizzie had the chance to do it twice. First, for "Two" on *The Twilight Zone* and in "Spiral." As with many of her other roles, the dialogue she heard in "Spiral" proved telling and insightful into Lizzie's life.

At one point, *Helen* is told: "Don't settle. Don't hide out." Lizzie never did the former, and infrequently performed the latter.

Elizabeth enjoyed gardening in real life. As *Helen*, she heard Eddie Albert's character tell her: "You like to make things grow, don't you?"

Lizzie had boundless energy, and yet she was one to pick and choose not only her friends but her topics of conversation. And if she didn't like what she was hearing, for whatever reason (mostly because it may have been negative), she'd switch topics (how Freudian!). That's why it proves so intriguing when Lillian Gish's character tells *Helen* on screen: "You change the subject faster than anyone I know."

Albert's character later tells *Helen*: "You're imperfect, and there's just no room in this world for imperfection."

Yet, Lizzie embraced the imperfect populace of the world. She campaigned for the downtrodden and disadvantaged.

But it's Gish that has the best "Lizzie-life" dialogue, even though she doesn't speak it to Lizzie. Rather, she says it to Gig Young's character,

Steven, whom Gish believes is a scoundrel. In the end, we find out otherwise. But before that she tells him:

"You're an insect, Steven . . . a carrier . . . a breeder of disease and disorder. You should have stayed away."

Young, in real life, proved to have those similar traits. If only Elizabeth had never met and married him. Fortunately, she found the courage to divorce Young and ultimately stayed away from him.

Even in these pre-witched television days, Lizzie had her choice of material, many times receiving personal requests to work with top directors, including a young Sydney Pollack, who years later, went on to become a feature film legend with, among other movies, romantic classics like *The Way We Were* (1973), *Tootsie* (1982), and *Out of Africa* (1985).

As she expressed to *TV Guide* in August of 1961, she was uncertain about one particular role Pollack had in mind for her.

> I don't know whether I want to do this script or not. It's a strange kind of a thing, really; Sydney Pollack's directing it. It's for *Frontier Circus* (a CBS series that debut the following September). But it's really incredible. I was telling (Pollack) today the last three things I've done have all come from directors. *The Untouchables* I got through Wally Grauman, and then last week I did a *Twilight Zone* ("Two," scheduled to open *Zone's* new season also on CBS in September). I'm absolutely mad (about writer and director) Monte Pittman. I don't know what it is all of sudden.

What it was was that she was "hot," and not only in her physical appearance. In spite of her good looks, which were a given, she had talent, and everyone who was anyone in television wanted to work with her, including Pollack for his episode of *Frontier Circus*, which was created by future *Star Trek* writer Samuel A. Peeples. The series was about a one-ring circus that traveled through the American West in the 1880s. The segment Pollack had in mind for Lizzie, "Karina," was written by Jean Holloway, and broadcast on November 9, 1961, and she may have decided to do this episode for several reasons, possibly on a subconscious level:

Karina Andrews (Lizzie) becomes a fugitive after shooting *Jeff*, her abusive husband (played by Tod Andrews). A first, she hides out in a circus wagon. But owner *Col. Casey Thompson* (Chill Wills) later allows her to join his camp as the target in a knife-throwing act, just as a local lawman and his vengeful spouse are soon hot on her trail.

It's a stock and interesting entry in a series that held much potential, but it's more intriguing that Elizabeth would opt to perform in this episode about an abusive husband, while in the midst of an abusive marriage to Gig Young. In fact, Young was pictured and interviewed with her for the very same article in *TV Guide* in which she talks about this new *Frontier*. At one point during the interview, the doorbell rang; as Lizzie explained, albeit playfully, it was the "liquor store man. Mr. Young's been shopping."

Lizzie would later play out the "abused" aspect of the *Karina Andrews* character in future TV-movies like *The Victim* (1972), *A Case of Rape* (1974) and *Act of Violence* (1979), while the fugitive aspect of the *Karina* role becomes a precursor to similar plights of Lizzie's future parts in the post-witched TV-movies, *Mrs. Sundance* (1974) and *Belle Starr* (1980).

The parallels may have easily been made: Lizzie was in the midst of what ultimately turned out to be a failed marriage to Bill Asher, which was in the process of ending right around the time she agreed to star in *The Victim*. *Etta Place*, a.k.a. *Mrs. Sundance*, as well as *Belle Starr*, were "on the run," while Lizzie went into hiding with *Bewitched* director Richard Michaels upon learning of Asher's affair with actress Nancy Fox (during the eighth season of *Bewitched*).

A few years before she took the lead in *Karina*, Elizabeth had played *Millie* who was experiencing a "Marriage Crisis," in that 1959 episode of *The Loretta Young Show*, a dramatic anthology series hosted by the actress (who also appeared in various episodes). By the time of "Crisis," Lizzie had replaced one real-life marriage drama (with Fred Cammann) with another (Gig Young). What's more, also appearing with Lizzie in the "Crisis" episode of the *Loretta* show was future *Hawaii Five-O* actor Jack Lord playing her husband *Joe*, who was also her on-screen spouse in her first feature film, *The Court-Martial of Billy Mitchell* (1955). In that movie, Lord's character dies. In real life, Cammann is alive, but Lizzie leaves him, and later walks out on Gig, who later dies in a tragic murder-suicide.

However, beyond all of that dire news, Lizzie's involvement with the "Karina" episode of *Frontier Circus* further solidified her spirited interest in circus stories. One of her favorite feature films was the 1953 classic *Lili*, starring Leslie Caron (whose lead character joins the circus), and she starred in the 1981 TV-movie, *When the Circus Came to Town* (in which her character, *Mary Flynn*, a bored housewife, joins the circus).

Lizzie's most prominent pre-*Bewitched* TV performance is that of her Emmy-nominated lead as a prostitute in *The Untouchables* episode, "The Rusty Heller Story," which was directed by the aforementioned Wally Grauman, and which aired on ABC October 13, 1960. A little background on the series in general:

The Untouchables ran from 1959 to 1963 and featured Robert Stack as *Elliot Ness.* Stack went on to become the popular host of the documentary series, *Unsolved Mysteries*, (NBC/CBS, 1988–1999), while *The Untouchables* was adapted into a feature film in 1987 and then returned to television as a new syndicated weekly edition in 1991. But in 1959, its original version was considered shocking programming.

Authors Tim Brooks and Earle Marsh explain as much in their *Complete Directory to Prime Time Network and Cable TV Shows: 1946 to Present* (Ninth Edition, Ballantine Books, 2007):

> With the chatter of machine-gun fire and the squeal of tires on Chicago streets, *The Untouchables* brought furious controversy—and big ratings—to ABC in the early 1960s. It was perhaps the most mindlessly violent program ever seen on TV up to that time. Critics railed and public officials were incensed, but apparently many viewers enjoyed the weekly bloodbath, which sometimes included two or three violent shoot-outs per episode.

TV Guide observed that, if anything, *The Untouchables* was consistent:

> In practically every episode a gang leader winds up stitched to a brick wall and full of bullets, or face down in a parking lot (and full of bullets), or face up in a gutter (and still full of bullets), or hung up in an ice box, or run

down in the street by a mug at the wheel of a big black Hudson touring car.

Either way, Lizzie relished in the opportunity to appear in the "Rusty Heller" segment, which also happened to feature a guest stint with future *Bewitched* regular David White. On *Bewitched*, White portrayed the conniving ad-man boss *Larry Tate*. In "Heller," he was *Archie Grayson*, right hand man/attorney to gangster *Charles 'Pops' Felcher* (played by Harold J. Stone). Ultimately, *Rusty* used *Archie* to get to *Pops*—who was the man with the real power. When Lizzie was reminded in 1989 that *Rusty* was responsible for *Archie* losing his tongue, she said, "Well, he got his tongue cut out, and I squealed on him so he could." She also remembered one of her favorite lines as Rusty:

"I'd rather walk barefoot through a snakepit."

With his tongue intact in 1989, White only praised Lizzie's performance in the episode, stating very simply and to the point: "She was very good in it." A synopsis of the episode reads:

> *Rusty Heller* is a nightclub performer who envisions a better life which, in her case, means attaining a lot more money. So she sets her eyes on mobster *Charles 'Pops' Felcher*, who has ambitions of his own. With the recent arrest of Al Capone on tax evasion charges, *Pops* seeks to become the top mobster in Chicago. But when he shows little interest in *Rusty*, she settles for his attorney, *Archie Grayson*. Although *Pops* eventually comes around, *Rusty* starts to live and play more dangerously; she ups the ante, as it were, and decides she can make more money by selling the same information to both *Pops* and the Capone mob.

In his biography, *Straight Shooting* (McMillan, 1980), *Untouchables* star Robert Stack said the "Rusty Heller" story was one of his favorite segments in the series, mostly because of working with Lizzie:

> One of the best episodes was "The Rusty Heller Story." When it came time to cast the lead, the producers drew up a list of actresses as possible stars. The last name on the list was Elizabeth Montgomery. I had known Liz's father Bob Montgomery; I went shooting with him, and took him to Dad's duck lodge when I was a kid. I'd only known Elizabeth as a young

socialite. When the girls at her finishing school talked about making a debut, I'm sure they weren't thinking about the kind Liz made in her first appearance on *The Untouchables*, in the role of a tough young southern hooker. I'd learned from parts I'd lost that you must be objective in your judgment; the fact that I knew this girl and her background was no reason to disqualify her from consideration for the part. The producers didn't always ask my opinion about casting, but in this instance, I'm glad they did. Anyway, she took the part and ran away with it; she got an Emmy nomination and, I think, should have won it. Dame Judith Anderson won the award for *Medea*, which was shot in Scotland on location over a thirty-day period. Liz turned in a smashing performance in six days. It was the only time that *Ness* got emotionally involved. The episode had a touching and gentle poignancy to it.

As *TV Guide* noted at the time, this *Untouchables* segment and Lizzie's Emmy-nominated performance doubled her "acting price." She also attained a feature film contract, was inundated with TV scripts, and, after a decade of hard work, all but established Robert Montgomery as "Liz Montgomery's father." But she, then married to Gig Young, was all but surprised by the attention. As she recalled at the time, Stack had approached her while working on the show and said, "Liz, if you don't get an Emmy nomination for this, I'll be surprised." She replied:

> Oh, Bob, for heaven's sake. It was the last thing I did in 1960 before Gig and I left for New York (Young appeared on Broadway for six months in *Under the Yum Yum Tree*). Then last spring Gig and I were driving back from New York and we stopped in Arizona. Gig said, 'There's a Los Angeles paper,' and I said, 'Oh, I just can't wait to see who's been nominated for all those statues.' And I looked down and saw Ingrid Bergman—Judith Anderson—and me. I knew Judith Anderson would get it. It wasn't a wish. I just knew it.

Anderson won that year for "Outstanding Single Performance by an Actress in a Leading Role" for her interpretation of *Lady Macbeth* in the Hallmark Hall of Fame production of *Macbeth*, which aired on NBC. It was Hallmark's second version of Shakespeare's classic play with a different supporting cast, but the same two leads (Anderson and Lizzie's future *Bewitched* father, Maurice Evans), and the same director (George Schaefer).

Lizzie's other fellow contender that year was Ingrid Bergman, who was nominated for her role in CBS's *Twenty-Four Hours in a Woman's Life*. Bergman's *Clare* was grandmother to *Helen Lester* (played by Helena de Crespo) who was in love with a man she had known only 24 hours, a playboy who spent time in jail for passing bad checks. Although the man has promised to change, most of her straitlaced relatives are up in arms. Bergman's *Clare* says the girl is free to join the man she loves on one condition: that she listen to the story of a day in *Clare's* own life and of a man she tried to change.

Bergman's *Clare* was a character of great texture, as certainly was Anderson's *Lady Macbeth*, and both actresses were stellar veteran performers, even then. Lizzie, however, was still somewhat of a newcomer and pigeon-holed as her father's daughter. Those were two strikes that may have worked against her in the eyes of Emmy academy.

What's more, the twitch ties to *The Untouchables* were manifold if not yet realized.

The Untouchables was produced by Desilu, the powerhouse studio run by Lucille Ball and Desi Arnaz, the latter of whom gave Bill Asher his big break in TV directing for *I Love Lucy* (CBS, 1951–1957). A few years after her *Rusty Heller* stint on *Untouchables*, Lizzie, coming off of two failed marriages, fell in love with Bill on the set of *Johnny Cool* in 1963, shortly before they worked together on *Bewitched*. It was a match made in magic, as two very different but somehow similar people were brought together to form what eventually became one of the most successful Hollywood business partnerships this side of Ball and Arnaz.

Not only did Bill direct episodes of *I Love Lucy* and *Bewitched*, but there were other similarities between the two shows. The famous *Lucy* episode, "Job Switching," was remade as a *Bewitched* segment called "Samantha's Power Failure." Just as *Lucy* squealed, "Well!" to her husband *Ricky* on *Love* at some impending doom, so did *Samantha* to *Darrin* on *Bewitched*; *Lucy* and *Ricky* were of different cultures as were *Samantha* and *Darrin*. Lucy employed her wit and special prowess to resolve any particular situation, as did *Samantha*.

In any case, Asher was the "third man in." Freddie Cammann had long been out of Lizzie's life; Gig Young, like Cammann, was not able to live up to the qualities of the idealized man Lizzie envisioned to be her husband. Now it was up to Asher, and everyone wondered if he'd be able to pull it off.

LITTLE TWITCH: A one-year-old Elizabeth Montgomery is held by her mother Elizabeth Allen in 1934. SMP—Globe Photos

EARLY ELEGANCE:
Elizabeth at age 2 in 1935.
Supplied by SMP—Globe Photos

SHIPPING AND NEAR-MISHANDLING: Lizzie and her brother Skip were in
Europe when World War II broke out in 1939, the same year their father Robert
Montgomery was filming *The Earl of Chicago* in England. He joined the American
Field Service, and was attached to the French Army as an ambulance driver.
Her mother Elizabeth Allen went to work as a volunteer for the Red Cross. The
Montgomerys had booked Lizzie and Skip on the Athenia steam ship to go back
to the States. But the reservations were jumbled, and the children were given
passage on the Arandora Star steam ship leaving the same day. According to *TV
Star Parade* magazine in October 1956, world headlines reported the sinking of
the Athenia, and there was no word from the Arandora. Under censorship the
liner couldn't break silence at sea. For twelve frantic days, the Montgomery parents
waited for news. Finally, the cable reported Lizzie and Skip's safe arrival home to
their grandmother Becca. Courtesy of Everett Collection

DASHING, DEBONAIR, AND DAUNTING: Robert Montgomery strikes an intimidating pose in this publicity photo from 1932. It was a look and a "feeling" that would impress, haunt, and taunt Lizzie long after he died in 1981. Photographed by George Hurrell, courtesy of Getty Images

CLEAR AS A SOUTHERN BELLE: Elizabeth's natural beauty was as fresh as the country air in this, her first publicity TV photo from the early 1950s. Supplied by SMP—Globe Photos

TOP SECRET: Elizabeth and Margaret Phillips in a (behind-the) scene from the famed "Top Secret" episode of *Robert Montgomery Presents*, which aired on December 3, 1951, and which marked Elizabeth's television debut. Supplied by SMP—*Globe Photos*

THE EYES HAVE IT: Elizabeth, her father, and their famed matching "arched eyebrows" are ready for the cameras in this publicity still from 1953 for *Robert Montgomery Presents*. Supplied by SMP—Globe Photos

SUMMERY SMILES: Some of the Summer Stock Players of *Robert Montgomery Presents*: Elizabeth with (from left) Vaughn Taylor, Margaret Hayes, and John Newland in 1953. Supplied by SMP—Globe Photos

A SOPHISTICATED LADY AND GENTLEMAN: Elizabeth and her first husband, high-society roller Fredric A. Cammann, on their wedding day in New York City, March 27, 1954. AP Photo—Tom Fitzsimmons

POISE AND POSTURE: Elizabeth was no "slouch." Robert Montgomery would never allow it. He always insisted she carried herself with class and distinction, all of which is evident here in this publicity shot taken for her first feature film, 1955's *The Court-Martial of Billy Mitchell*. Supplied by SMP—Globe Photos

NOT INTERESTED: Elizabeth rejected Gary Cooper's alleged romantic advances on the set of *The Court-Martial of Billy Mitchell*, 1955. Supplied by SMP—Globe Photos

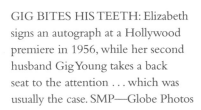

GIG BITES HIS TEETH: Elizabeth signs an autograph at a Hollywood premiere in 1956, while her second husband Gig Young takes a back seat to the attention . . . which was usually the case. SMP—Globe Photos

HER MAN PRE-TATE: Elizabeth was a romantic interest for future *Bewitched* actor David White (*Larry Tate*) whose character, attorney *Archie Grayson*, had it bad for her hooker-with-a-heart role in "The Rusty Heller Story," the 1960 episode *of The Untouchables.* For this she received her first Emmy nomination. ABC Photo Archives, courtesy of Getty Images

DANCING IN THE DARK: Elizabeth's dazzling *Iris Hecate* literally dances with the *Devil*, played by the ever-dashing Fred Astaire, in the 1962 *Alcoa Premiere* episode titled "Mr. Lucifer." As *Iris*, Lizzie delivered one of her finest and most versatile pre-*Bewitched* TV performances. The character also imbued shades (in hair color and personality) of *Serena, Samantha's* somewhat more mischievous cousin who Elizabeth would later play on *Bewitched*. Courtesy of Everett Collection

COOL LOOK:
Lizzie displayed her "sexier side" in the 1963 big screen cult film classic *Johnny Cool*, where she met and fell in love with director Bill Asher, whom she would marry and later team up with for *Bewitched*. UA/Photofest

A VARIETY OF ROLES: Elizabeth embraces famous "Rat Pack" member Dean Martin, while real-life future best friend Carol Burnett awaits her turn in this publicity shot for their 1963 feature film *Who's Been Sleeping in My Bed?* Lizzie's blond look in this film offers shades of things to come for *Bewitched*, which debuts the following year. Meanwhile, both Martin and Burnett would go on to star in very successful TV variety shows, both in which Lizzie politely declined invitations to perform. She got her start in live theater and would return to the stage post-*Bewitched*, but she would make her only variety show appearance with a guest-host stint on *The Hollywood Palace* (with guest star Paul Lynde) in 1966. mptvimages.com

PART II

Bewitched

"This is Elizabeth Montgomery. Stay tuned
for *Bewitched*. Next! In color."

—Elizabeth Montgomery, in on-air promos for *Bewitched*

Ten

~

Lizmet

"There's one thing that makes *Samantha* easy to play . . . she's as
much in love with *Darrin* as I am with Bill (Asher)."

—Elizabeth Montgomery, *Look Magazine*, January 1965

In 1985, Bill Asher directed his final feature film, *Movers and Shakers*, written
by Charles Grodin, who also appeared on-screen in the movie, along with
Walter Matthau and many classic TV legends: Gilda Radner (*Saturday Night
Live*), Bill Macy (*Maude*), Tyne Daly (*Cagney & Lacy*), Vincent Gardenia
(*All in the Family*); with cameos provided by Steve Martin and Penny Mar-
shall (star of *Laverne & Shirley*, co-producer of 2005's *Bewitched* feature film):

> Hollywood studio president *Joe Mulholland* (Matthau) makes a slightly silly
> promise to his dying friend *Saul Gritz* (Gardenia), most of which involves
> making a movie using the title—if not the content—of a best-selling sex
> manual. *Joe* ultimately hires down-and-out writer *Herb Derman* (Grodin)
> and off-beat director *Sid Spokane* (Macy) to formulate a concept, but soon
> realizes he may have over-promised his friend *Saul*.

Twenty years before, in 1963, Asher was keeping promises to Lizzie on
the set of *Johnny Cool*, although it wasn't exactly love at first sight. In fact,
upon first meeting, they loathed one another. As Asher told *TV Circle* magazine in August 1970, "It was a case of instant hate. I was late for our appointment. She didn't like that and I didn't think it mattered whether she liked

it or not. So it was rocky going at first, until we began working. Then after a while, bam! There we were." As Asher concluded on MSNBC's *Headliners & Legends* in 2001, after he cast her, he was pretty well "gone," in other words, head over heels in love.

However, just prior to their mutual Cupid encounter, Bill and Lizzie were preoccupied with other relationships. As he expressed to *The Saturday Evening Post*, March 13, 1965, "We were both emotional basket cases when we met. Maybe Liz had never been loved, never been happy before. I don't know. I wouldn't want to speculate."

No speculation required. In 1951, Asher married actress Dani Sue Nolan, who made over thirty film and TV appearances between 1949 and 1988. (She played William Holden's secretary in his famous Asher-directed *I Love Lucy* episode, "L.A. at Last," in which *Lucy* burned her nose with a cigarette). They had two children: Liane (born 1952) and Brian (born 1954).

By 1963, they'd been separated for approximately two years, but feelings lingered. Elizabeth, meanwhile, had recently separated from Gig Young, feelings depleted.

In retrospect, Lizzie meeting Bill on the set of *Johnny Cool* turned out to be a blessing, if at first in disguise.

Compared to the previous men in her life, he was the opposite of the dashing Fred Cammann and Gig Young, not to mention her debonair father Robert Montgomery. Writer Joe Hyams explained it all that spring in *The Saturday Evening Post*. Asher was muscular, stocky, and tan, but he had bushy eyebrows and closed-cropped hair. He resembled more of a "retired prize fighter than a director." Although Hyams called Asher the "antithesis" of Lizzie's first two husbands, like Cammann, Young, and her father, he was also "a strong and dominating presence."

Also like Young, Asher was in his forties and Lizzie liked older guys, this older guy, in particular, whom she called "the greatest director I know, because he's a sensitive, compassionate person." Consequently, after smoothing the initial bump on the hot road to their *Cool* romance, they became inseparable. Lizzie liked the great outdoors. So did Bill. She loved to play tennis. So did he. In fact, it was one of the many things they had in common. They even shared the same sense of humor. They loved each other. They loved to work. They loved working together, and when they did so, it was magic. Asher, in particular, was a master of making it all work, on-screen and off. As a man, he knew how to please the ladies. As a director, he was one of the greatest conductors to orchestrate media magic in TV history. Before and after *Bewitched*, he was a heralded presence in the industry.

Born William Milton Asher on August 8, 1921, Bill was the son of Ephraim Asher, an associate producer of the classic 1931 horror films *Frankenstein* and *Dracula*, as well the original 1935 edition of *Magnificent Obsession* starring Irene Dunne and Robert Taylor (which was remade in 1954 with Jane Wyman, Rock Hudson, and *Bewitched's* Agnes Moorehead). His mother Lillian worked as a clerical assistant for MGM.

As chronicled in *Palm Springs Life* magazine December 1999, Bill lost his father when he was just eleven years old and "the excitement of a life in the new and daring film industry" was supplanted by the bottle for a Catholic mother whose Jewish associate producer–husband had died young and left her the burden of rearing children during the Depression. At fifteen, Bill enlisted in the Army, lied about his age, and forged his mother's consent.

After four years with the Signal Corps as a photographer during World War II, he left the service, which he said probably saved his life because he was one to fight authority.

Consequently, he headed for Hollywood where he approached "some guys" his father knew for help. They slammed the door in his face. At which point, he left Tinscltown for the low-rent, basic living of the Salton Sea area east of Palm Springs. There, he began writing short stories for magazines, which he had done in the Army.

In 1948, he co-directed with Richard Quine the feature film *Leather Gloves*, starring Cameron Mitchell, Virginia Grey, and a young aspiring actor named Blake Edwards. Like Asher, Edwards would later marry an actress best known for playing a supernatural woman: Julie Andrews (*Mary Poppins*). (Also like Asher, Edwards would become one of the industry's most prominent directors; *10*, *S.O.B.*, *The Pink Panther*, *Victor/Victoria*, *The Man Who Loved Women*).

In addition to feature length movies, Asher also wrote short films, five-minute reels that were utilized as interstitials in theatres for a new growing sensation called *television*. This resulted in a call from CBS officials who were familiar with his work and seeking directors for this new small screen medium, then a foreign concept in the industry. But within six weeks, Asher had returned to Hollywood, where he was directing shows like *Racket Squad* (1950–1953, syndicated CBS), and *Big Town* (1950–1954, CBS/NBC). He also completed a pilot for a new TV series called *Our Miss Brooks* (1952–1956), featuring big screen star Eve Arden, recreating her hit show from radio.

On the sound stage next to *Miss Brooks* was another infant CBS show called *I Love Lucy* which was about a relatively diverse married couple. He was *Ricky Ricardo*, a Cuban bandleader played by the multifaceted Desi Arnaz; she was his wife *Lucy*, daffy-but-crafty Hollywood-obsessed American redhead embodied in the one and only Lucille Ball. Despite such combined talent the show's immediate future was in doubt. But Lucy and Desi remained calm in the midst of the storm, preserved the honesty of their *Love* and, in the process, the series became the cornerstone for an entertainment empire called *Desilu* (a company title that combined its proprietors' first names).

One of the first bricks placed to solidify that creative foundation was by a vigorous Asher who, in 1952, was hired by Arnaz to direct a few *Love* episodes. By the end of its first season, *Lucy* was a monster hit and was renewed for an additional year. Bill was asked to direct the show for $500 per episode. "In those days if you were making $200 a month, you were doing well," he told *Palm Springs Life*. "I was in my mid-twenties, unmarried, working on *Our Miss Brooks* and *I Love Lucy*, making $1000.00 a week from both shows combined. I lived like a drunken sailor! You can believe I spent the money."

But he also spent time honing his craft, in the process blazing the trail for a new medium that would change the way the world communicated. Once turned away by his dad's false friends, Bill eventually connected with the TV greats of the era: Danny Thomas on *Make Room for Daddy* (ABC/CBS, 1953–1965); *The Dinah Shore Chevy Show* (1956–1963; for which he won an Emmy); Sally Field on *Gidget* (ABC, 1965–1966; for which he directed the pilot and several episodes); producer Sidney Sheldon on *The Patty Duke Show* (ABC, 1963–1966), and countless others.

By 1963, he ventured into directing movies first for TV (*Mickey and the*

Contessa), and then features, beginning with *Johnny Cool*, in which he met and cast Lizzie, who shared the lead with actor Henry Silva. The film was co-produced by Asher's friend Peter Lawford, who was married to Pat Kennedy, sister to President John F. Kennedy, and party to the famous celebrity *Rat Pack*: Frank Sinatra, Dean Martin (Lizzie's co-star from *Who's Been Sleeping in My Bed*, which filmed that same year), Joey Bishop, and Sammy Davis, Jr., who both had supporting roles in the movie (while Davis performed the title song). Adapted from the novel, *The Kingdom of Johnny Cool*, by John McPartland, the movie follows this story:

> Gangster *Salvatore Giordano* (Silva), his future fortunes and misfortunes, were planted in his youth, growing up in the hard climate of World War II Sicily defying both the government and the mafia. When he was but a boy, his mother was shot in the crossfire—and from then, his gun was his only family. (At least, that's how the English subtitles translated the Sicilian dialogue in the film's prologue.) Years after his mother is killed, an adult *Salvatore* is crowned *Johnny Cool* by an ostracized American gangster named *Johnny Colini* (Marc Lawrence)—the *first* Johnny Cool—who in turns sends his replacement to America to whack those responsible for his exile. Upon arriving in New York, the new *Mr. Cool* proceeds with *Colini's* vendetta, and begins to make the required assassinations. But complications arise after he hooks up with divorced socialite *Darian "Dare" Guiness* (Lizzie).

While hardcore *Bewitched* fans may liken her character's name to *Samantha's* "what's-his-name" mortal husband, *Dare* was also the name Elizabeth once considered giving her first daughter. But that never panned out (she ultimately decided on *Rebecca*, after her grandmother).

As to the film itself, it's the kind of violent project to which Lizzie would later cling, post-*Bewitched*, with TV-movies like *A Case of Rape* and *Act of Violence*, both in which her characters were severely beaten—as was *Dare* shortly after meeting Johnny.

In fact, when *Cool* was released, an item in the press singled Elizabeth out as possibly the "most bruised actress in pictures as a result of her co-starring role opposite Henry Silva in the electric dramatic thriller."

The item went on to explain how in one day's filming Lizzie's *Dare* was beaten in a "frighteningly realistic violent scene," which was followed by another scene in which a car door slammed on her hand upon entering the vehicle (after fleeing a pool bombing). In the next day's filming, she was then called upon to leap from a pier to a small dinghy in Los Angeles Newport Harbor, and that's when things really turned ugly. Poor Lizzie failed to clear the pier and fell forward with a shuddering thud. Consequently, she received contusions on her arms and legs, and that last scene was cut from the final print of the film.

But as the press release stated further, "true to the acting heritage of her family name, Miss Montgomery, famed Bob's daughter, showed up bright and early for the next day's filming, and the shooting of *Johnny Cool* proceeded on schedule."

Into this mix, however, Lizzie's *daring* portrayal of *Guiness* continued to fit her choice of roles that somewhat resonated with her reality. For example, upon first meeting Silva's *Cool*, *Dare* offers this telling introduction:

> I'm twenty-seven. I grew up in Scarsdale with all the advantages . . . braces, dancing school, riding lessons . . . the whole bit. I've been divorced for about a year from a boy who grew up the same way.

Beyond the inconsistent age reference in 1963 (when the film was released that year, Elizabeth was thirty years old) and the braces (she always prided herself on her uniquely chipped front tooth), it was Lizzie all over, at least until she met, married, and then divorced Fred Cammann.

The same year *Cool* was released, Asher directed his first *Beach Party* movie, which spawned *Muscle Beach Party* and *Bikini Beach*, both in 1964, and *Beach Blanket Bingo* and *How to Stuff a Wild Bikini*, both in 1965, the latter in which Lizzie made a cameo doing her then newly famed twitch.

Through it all, there was additional *Cool/Rat Pack* intermingling involving Sammy Davis, Jr., Peter Lawford, and Frank Sinatra, who was then entertainment counsel to President Kennedy's Inaugural. Not only did Lizzie meet Bill on the set of *Cool*, she was introduced to the *Pack* via Bill's friend Lawford, who was Kennedy's brother-in-law. From there, she went with Bill to Washington for JFK's Inaugural on January 20, 1961. Approximately eighteen months later, on May 19, 1962, Asher produced, directed, and supervised the President's birthday bash at which Marilyn Monroe performed her sultry ditty "Happy Birthday Mr. President." Asher recalled in *Palm Springs Life*, December 1999:

Lawford was a good guy. Marilyn was a wonderful woman. She really cared about people. She also cared about the work. All she really wanted to do was be the best actress she could be . . . Jackie Kennedy didn't like many in the Hollywood crowd but she liked me. Actually she barely tolerated anybody else.

Suffice it to say, Elizabeth and Bill's friendship with the Kennedys was solidified at the President's Inaugural—and nearly three years before the tragic political incident that would send shockwaves around the world—just as a particular magical mayhem would step in to help ease the fray.

The pilot for *Bewitched* began rehearsals on November 22, 1963—the fateful day on which President John F. Kennedy was assassinated.

The night before, Elizabeth and Bill Asher were at home, wrestling with what in perspective was a minor frustration, but one that later became a major magic snag: they had yet to conceive of a unique and identifiable gesture with which *Samantha* could manifest her magic.

Fortunately, a creative spark provided a proverbial light when, Bill, from the living room, shouted to Lizzie, "That's it!" Upon hearing her husband scream, she rushed to his side to offer comfort during what sounded like a pressing tragedy. But that was yet to come. For now, upon her arrival at his side, Bill simply asked, "What's that thing you do with your nose?"

Clueless as to what he meant, she queried in return, "What *thing*?!"

"When you become nervous, you move your nose in a certain way," Bill prodded.

"He thought I just didn't want to do it or something," she remembered in 1989, and she was still confused, and downright aggravated. "The next time I do this (thing)," she told him, "let me know."

At that moment, Lizzie became so flustered she instinctively performed what has today transmuted into one of the world's most recognizable facial tics. Bill then went on to explain what he had seen, and what she had done and, in those joyful moments, *Samantha's* nose twitch was born, igniting the eventual birth of *Bewitched*—if on the night before a catastrophic incident that would change the world.

Elizabeth remembered that fateful November day in 1963, which began like any other, if at first unique only because she was preparing to leave for her first *Bewitched* rehearsal. As the early hours passed, the events of this new atypical day expanded. As she recalled in 1989, she was brushing her hair in the bedroom and heard Bill scream from the living room. But this time, it wasn't a good thing.

"No! It can't be true!" he said.

"For some reason," she said in 1989, "I felt it had nothing to do with family. But it's as if I inherently knew what had happened. The whole thing was very strange, but to keep on working did seem to be the right thing to do."

So, that's exactly what they did. Lizzie and Bill pushed forward, and went on to the set of *Bewitched*, which filmed at the Sunset Gower Studios in Hollywood. She remembered:

> We went ahead and had the first reading of the script. It was very interesting. There wasn't one person that didn't show up. There weren't any phone calls made. It was like everyone on the set just needed to talk with each other. We needed to be there, working. It was like a little memorial service that hadn't turned that yet. Everyone was there supporting each other (during) this horrendous thing.

Essentially, Lizzie, Bill, and the rest of the *Bewitched* cast and crew did what should always be done in the midst of tragedy: realize that, for the living, life must go on.

On July 24, 1964, the summer before *Bewitched* debuted, Elizabeth and Bill welcomed a 7 lb. 6 oz. baby boy they named William Allen Asher, Jr. On October 5, 1965, Elizabeth gave birth to their second child, a 7 lb. 2 oz. boy named Robert Deverell Asher. On June 17, 1969, the Asher's youngest was born: a beautiful 7 lb. 13 oz. girl they named Rebecca Elizabeth Asher.

Through it all, on the other side of the screen, *Samantha* and *Darrin's* little *Tabatha* (later changed to *Tabitha* with an "i") was born on January 13, 1966 in the episode "And Then There Were Three." *Tabitha's* brother *Adam* later materialized on October 16, 1969 in the episode, "And Something Makes Four."

In reality, Billy Asher, Jr. arrived during *Bewitched's* first season which began production in the summer of 1964—some eight months after Lizzie filmed the show's pilot in November 1963. For that initial episode, she was showing slightly, and strategic camera angles and wardrobe choices were utilized to conceal her condition.

In June, July, and August of 1964, she was in a fully expectant/recovery/rest period that forced her to miss most of the shooting schedule for the show's first full season. She then returned to the set the first week of September 1964, just in time to complete filming of the episode, "Be It Ever So Mortgaged."

Elizabeth became pregnant with her second child Robert (named for her father), around New Year's Day, 1965 (the second part of the first season of *Bewitched*), and worked through the following summer, taking maternity leave from September 10 to December 10, 1965.

She became pregnant with her third child Rebecca (named for her maternal grandmother) in mid-October 1968 during production of *Bewitched's* fifth season—and beginning with the non-*Darrin* episode, "Marriage Witches, Style," which began filming on January 20, 1969. To allow Lizzie some headway on this her third pregnancy, *Bewitched* filmed four episodes early in March and April 1969: "*Samantha's* Better Halves," "*Samantha's* Yoo-Hoo Maid," "*Samantha* and the Beanstalk," and "*Samantha's* Curious Cravings." Following Rebecca's birth, Lizzie returned to the *Bewitched* set on August 22, 1969 to film "*Samantha's* Caesar Salad."

Ultimately, Lizzie's first pregnancy (Billy, Jr.) was hidden from the TV viewers, while her second (Robert) and third (Rebecca) pregnancies were written into the show when *Samantha* became pregnant with *Tabitha* (Robert) and *Adam* (Rebecca). Although most people associate twins Erin and Diane Murphy with the role of *Samantha* and *Darrin's* daughter, there have actually been ten little witches on the show since 1966. Cynthia Black, who was two-and-a-half weeks old when she appeared on the series, played Tabatha in episode 54, "And Then There Were Three." Then, twins Heidi and Laura Gentry took over the part the following week. The Gentry girls were born on August 16, 1965.

A few weeks later the role of Tabatha was given to slightly older twins Tamar and Julie Young, and they stayed for the remainder of the second season. The Young girls were born on June 24, 1965. The last set of twins,

Erin and Diane Murphy, became cast members at the start of the third season. The Murphy girls (fraternal twins) were born on June 17, 1964, so the now-spelled Tabitha had physically aged more than a year between seasons two and three. This was necessary as the part would expand once it was announced that she was indeed a witch.

However, before all that transpired, the birth of *Bewitched* itself became just as intricate.

Resulting from an extended *affair* between several pertinent parties, the seeds of *Bewitched* were planted by Columbia/Screen Gems studio executives William Dozier and Harry Ackerman, the latter who had long-envisioned a supernatural sitcom that he titled *The Witch of Westport*.

In early 1963, Dozier and Ackerman, both of whom died in 1991, hired writer Sol Saks to write the pilot script, "I, *Darrin*, Take This Witch, *Samantha*," and *Bewitched* was born.

Dozier, then Vice President of Screen Gems West Coast operations, detailed *Samantha's* genesis for *TV Guide*, January 27, 1968, in the article, "The Man Who Helped Deliver a $9,000,000 Baby Tells How it All Happened."

With periodic meetings in 1963 Dozier and Ackerman discussed potential new TV projects, one of which was about a mortal wedded to a supernatural who did not reveal her persuasion until their honeymoon.

Shortly after these meetings with Ackerman, Dozier lunched with George Axelrod, the author of the 1952 play *The Seven Year Itch*, starring Vanessa Brown and Tom Ewell (who later reprised his role in the 1955 feature film adaptation starring Marilyn Monroe). It was then Dozier suggested the concept for a sorceress sitcom, the notion of which delighted Axelrod who very much wanted to write the pilot, which was not yet titled *Bewitched*.

An agreement was bartered with Axelrod's agent Irving Lazar and work was to commence immediately. But there was an issue. Lazar had also managed to cut a significant deal for his client to write, produce, and potentially direct several feature films for United Artists, which also wanted Axelrod to start work at once.

To alleviate the conflict a generous Dozier released Axelrod from his Screen Gems commitment and then met with writer Charles Lederer who, like Axelrod, immediately recognized the potential of a weekly witch series. But Lederer was also too involved with another job in this case, writing the screenplay for MGM's 1962 feature, *Mutiny on the Bounty* (starring Marlon Brando).

In stepped Sol Saks, with whom Dozier and Ackerman had both worked at CBS where he had penned *My Favorite Husband* for Ackerman and *Peck's Bad Girl* for Dozier. Now Saks was commissioned to write the pilot script he tentatively titled *Bewitched*.

Around the time Saks was hired, New York actress Tammy Grimes was under contract to Screen Gems. Then the star of Broadway's hit, *The Unsinkable Molly Brown*, Grimes had signed not only to do a series for Screen Gems, but one or more films for its feature film unit Columbia Pictures. Upon reading his witch script, Grimes requested changes from Saks, who sent along revisions after she returned to New York.

While that transpired, Dozier had separate business in that same city, where he was approached by an enthusiastic agent named Tom Tannenbaum who wanted very much to team his clients with a show for Screen Gems. Those clients were Lizzie and Bill Asher.

As fate would have it, Dozier was a friend to Elizabeth with whom he had long wanted to do a series and Ackerman, Dozier's Columbia colleague, was a CBS executive during the reign of *I Love Lucy*, countless episodes of which Bill had guided. Now with Screen Gems, Ackerman was executive producer for a host of the studio's very popular TV programs, not the least of which was *Father Knows Best*, co-starring Elinor Donahue, who would become his wife in real life.

Who would *Darrin* wed on *Bewitched*? That die was yet to be cast. For the moment, Dozier and Ackerman were working on finding *Samantha*.

By this time, the Columbia-contracted Grimes was considering the lead in playwright Noel Coward's new Broadway musical, *High Spirits*, which he had also signed to direct. Based on his previous hit play, *Blithe Spirit*, *High Spirits* centered around a female ghost, and like *Bewitched*, embraced a fantasy-comedy premise.

Grimes' choices were similar but different: Would she portray a sorceress or a spectre? She ultimately chose the latter and, like writer George Axelrod, was released from her contract with Columbia.

In 2007, she told writer Peter Filichia and *Theatre Mania's* online magazine, "I vetoed the script they gave me." In 1963, she told the studio, "This *Samantha* has all these powers? Well, then why isn't she stopping wars? Why isn't she fixing traffic in Los Angeles, saying to all of those drivers, '*Just a second—I'll soon get you all home.*'"

However, she said, Columbia didn't agree with her, so they "went to Elizabeth Montgomery."

When asked if she regretted the decision, Grimes replied: "No, but I used to wonder what would have happened if I'd done it. I probably would have done far more television and less theatre. So it's all right."

Yet as Harry Ackerman recalled in *The Bewitched Book* (Dell, 1992), Grimes did indeed regret not starring on *Bewitched* as *Samantha*, who when she read the script was named *Cassandra*. "I run into her every two or three years, and she's still kicking herself for not having done (the show)."

In 1989, Lizzie said she "met Tammy in New York when I was about fourteen." Although she years later decided to end *Bewitched*, and made every creative attempt to distance herself from the series after it ended, Elizabeth threw herself into the role of *Samantha* and felt "eternally gratefully" to Grimes for rejecting it. "I didn't get the part because I beat out hundreds of women in some huge casting call which was painstakingly narrowed down to me," she explained. "Tammy said *no*, I said *yes*, and I was simply at the right place at the right time."

That "right time" occurred shortly after she and Bill Asher completed production on *Johnny Cool*, in which she starred and he directed, and during which they fell in love. Enamored with him, she at that point became disinterested in acting, mostly because of the grueling schedules and distant film locations that meant extended periods of time away from the new love of her life. Bill, however, did not want her to disengage from her craft. "I felt that would have been a great loss," he said in 1988. "She had a lot to offer the industry, and she should be working, for herself, as well as for her contributions to the business."

Consequently, he suggested the possibility of working on a series with her during which there would be no periods of separation. "And Liz was all for that," he added.

Although Lizzie and Bill met for the first time on the set of *Johnny Cool*, she was well-aware of his work. As she recalled in *Modern Screen* magazine in 1965, she had rejected a number of series and always said if she did decide to do a show, "it would be wonderful to get William Asher."

Got him, she did. But initially Bill wasn't all that excited about "getting" Lizzie, as a thespian, that is. He always said the last thing he'd ever do was fall in love with an actress. Yet, as he too told *Modern Screen*, he soon realized that Lizzie was "special, very definitely special. She has none of the *personality* which usually goes with a personality. She doesn't possess the slightest affectation. She isn't affected by adulation. She's first of all what she is. Second, she's an actress."

"What he means," Lizzie chimed in at the time, "is that the only drive I have is to get home." Still, she often wondered if it was possible to be both a good actress and a happy woman. When she met actress Julie Andrews, whom she deemed "enormously talented," she knew it was possible. In her view, Andrews appeared "extremely happy."

Like Lizzie, Andrews would for years be associated with an iconic magical female role, this time, on the big screen as *Mary Poppins*, co-starring Dick Van Dyke, released in 1964, the same year *Bewitched* debuted on the small screen. It was produced by Walt Disney, for whom Lizzie as a youth had long desired to be hired as an artist.

"The Fun Couple" . . . that's what Lizzie and Bill were considered in and around Hollywood, and that's the title of the TV show on which they intended to work together when they first approached Screen Gems. *Couple* was based on the novel by John Haase, who later teamed with writer Neil Jansen to adapt the book for a Broadway play (that opened and closed within three days at the Lyceum Theatre in October 1962).

Bill's TV edition of *Couple* featured a character named *Ellen*, the world's wealthiest woman who falls for "an average Joe" actually named *Bob*, who was an auto mechanic. Fiercely independent, *Bob* was intimidated by *Ellen's* elite status. As Bill explained it in 1988, *Couple* was "a real Getty's daughter–type thing," which was set at the beach where "nobody really knows each other's last names." In this way, *Couple* was a kin to his *Beach Party* movies of the era and the *Gidget* series he directed for ABC, Columbia, and Acker-man. It also sounded an awful lot like Lizzie and Bill's reality, minus the auto-mechanic aspect.

Notwithstanding, somewhere between the first *Beach* movie and *Gidget*, Bill brought *Couple* to Dozier, who later gave the green light to high con-cept Twentieth Century Fox shows for ABC like *Batman* (1966–1968) and *The Green Hornet* (1966–1967). He liked the *Couple* premise, but suggested that Bill meet with Ackerman. "He's got something in mind that's very similar," Bill recalled Dozier saying, "and you might like it better."

Dozier, of course, was referring to *Bewitched*, which was an opposites-attract comedy that featured an attractive young woman who just so hap-pened to be a witch. *Couple* was an opposites–attract comedy that featured an attractive young woman who just so happened to be rich. Consequently, Dozier's instincts proved to be "on the nose." Bill not only favored *Bewitched*, he said he and Lizzie "flipped over it."

In retrospect, it appears Columbia merely stored the *Bewitched* pilot until Lizzie and Bill arrived on the scene. Due to Ackerman's *Lucy* affiliation with Bill, the studio was aware of his strength in directing TV female leads. The studio also respected Lizzie's artistic body of work, and as she perceived it, those in power merely saw the writing on the wall. "Columbia purely felt that Bill and I would work well together," she intoned in 1989 with a wink and a smile. "An extraordinarily good producer/director teamed with someone who at least looks like she could do the job."

While a few key players viewed the near "breech birth" of *Bewitched* with ease, creative conflicts continued to arise which almost thwarted the game. Beyond the basic script and casting decisions, the series was having issues with budget and the Writers Guild, the latter of which claimed the show's premise was lifted from the 1942 feature film *I Married a Witch*.

A revered fantasy comedy classic, *Married* is considered to be one of the best English-language motion pictures of its time. As directed by French film maestro Rene Clair, the ingenious story (based on a novel by *Topper* author Thorne Smith) cast the enchanting Veronica Lake as *Jennifer,* a sexy seventeenth century sorceress, who appears in modern day New England to haunt a gubernatorial candidate played by Fredric March, a descendent of the Puritan who condemned her. But she falls for him instead. Adding to the fun, March portrays various incarnations of his character through the years, which only adds to the film's style, wit, and inventiveness.

After the pilot for *Bewitched* was filmed, Bill Asher was asked if he had seen Clair's masterpiece. He had not. "And besides," Bill clarified in 1988, "there wasn't any valid comparison between the two concepts, certainly none which would have invited any legal ramifications. *Bewitched* began where the movie ended. Our story was about a married couple and the movie was about a courtship."

One bullet was dodged, at least until former child star turned studio executive Jackie Cooper came into the fold. According to what *Bewitched* director Richard Michaels said in 1988, "Bill was the unnamed producer of the show from the beginning." But when Jackie Cooper replaced William Dozier as a top executive for Columbia, the studio sought to avoid bestowing series control to husband and wife business teams due to a not-so-positive experience with *The Donna Reed Show*, which was produced by its star and her spouse Tony Owen.

"Jackie came in and saw me controlling things from a distance," Bill explained in 1988. "He tried to institute a policy which would prohibit Liz and me from working on *Bewitched*, and we damn near didn't do the show."

Cooper alluded to the derision in his autobiography, *Please Don't Shoot My Dog* (Morrow/Avon, 1981), and learned rather quickly the "art of dealing with people, and specifically, how to be an executive." He also never doubted *Bewitched's* potential and was eager to work with Lizzie, whom he had met when she was just a teenager years before *Robert Montgomery Presents*. She was "already beautiful and already very strong and positive," he said; and she would remain so when they met on two future occasions: first, when she was married to Gig Young, and later when she was with Bill Asher whom Cooper, like Harry Ackerman and many other industry insiders, had known as the director of *I Love Lucy*.

In January of 1964, two months after filming was completed on the *Bewitched* pilot, Jackie and Lizzie reconnected, at her invitation. She wanted to discuss a business matter. He suggested they have lunch at the Beverly Hills Hotel. After the meal, her tone apparently became formal and she requested that Cooper honor the promises allegedly made by William Dozier, his Columbia predecessor:

She wanted Bill to be secured as *Bewitched's* core producer and show runner, with Harry Ackerman serving as executive producer. She had her own ideas of which direction *Bewitched* should go and she wanted those concepts incorporated into future scripts. She was to retain casting and director approval, and wanted Bill to direct the first eight or nine episodes.

Cooper thought such "promises" sounded quite unlike Dozier. In response, Lizzie apparently just glared at him with what he described as her "big blue eyes," which were actually green and could become "very steely when she wanted them to."

Lizzie's animated pupils merely added to her arsenal of unique facial expressions which, according to Cooper in this instance, emphasized a very straightforward decision not to do *Bewitched*. "It's too bad," she told him upon leaving their lunch/meeting. "It would have been a nice little show."

Back at his office, Cooper contacted her agent, Tom Tannenbaum, and said he'd have to inform Columbia's New York office head Jerry Hymans of the recent developments. Hymans would then be obligated to notify ABC which undoubtedly would cancel *Bewitched* before it hit the air—unless a mutually satisfactory lead replacement actress could be found, which Cooper assumed would be highly unlikely. Needless to say, Tannenbaum was concerned. "Please, hold the fort," he told Cooper. "Don't do anything until I talk to her."

A short time later, Tannebaum called back with what Cooper expected to be a mere confirmation: Lizzie was indeed quitting. But Cooper stood his ground. As he wrote in *Please Don't Shoot My Dog*:

> There were good reasons not to go along with her demands. Ackerman was a tried-and-true TV producer. He should be in charge. No way was Billy (Asher) going to direct the first eight or nine shows—nobody in his right mind did that. Casting and director approval? Not in my studio. And if she had ideas as to the direction in which the show was going, fine, but let her funnel them through the producer.

Cooper made further calls, next to Tom Moore, then head of ABC. "Tom was a good, level-headed person, not given to hysterics," he said. Cooper explained what had transpired, and despite the odds, Moore thought there was a possibility of finding another actress to play *Samantha*. Consequently, Cooper instructed his casting office to start looking for another actress who would fit Lizzie's age and type. He didn't tell the press of the recent developments, and neither did Lizzie, which he was pleased to learn. But still somehow there was a leak.

In those days, Hollywood gossip columnists had "moles" in every studio on the payroll. Consequently, the story seeped into the trades, stating that "Elizabeth Montgomery was unhappy at Screen Gems," and no one denied it.

During the casting search, the studio found three actresses who proved they could play *Samantha*. Screen tests were arranged, a director was hired, and Dick York, already signed to co-star, was brought in to work with the potential new replacements, all of which was funded by Screen Gems, at a not inconsiderable sum.

But the day before the screen tests were to commence, Cooper claimed a messenger appeared at his office door, bearing Lizzie's handwritten note of apology. Apparently, she realized that her demands were incongruent with her contract, and that she should have respected and trusted Cooper's discretion. She promised not to insist that Bill produce or direct, and she would work well with Harry Ackerman. She hoped Cooper would keep Bill in mind for the future.

In Cooper's eyes—and hands—Lizzie's note was a victory, but he wanted to officially secure her words. So he brought the note to the studio's legal department and integrated it as a new contract addendum, which she agreed to and signed.

From that day forward, and for the first five seasons that *Bewitched* was on the air, Lizzie never spoke to him again. "On the other hand," he explained in his book, "she was never late, she always knew her lines, she never caused anybody any trouble, she was a perfect lady, and she made the show a huge success." Also, too, Cooper ultimately agreed to Lizzie's previous creative "suggestions": Bill ended up directing the first fourteen episodes of the first season and, by the fourth year, was promoted to producer, ultimately supplanting producer Danny Arnold, who switched over to ABC's other popular female-driven sitcom, *That Girl*, starring Marlo Thomas. Arnold later created and produced *Barney Miller* for ABC in 1975.

On the other hand, Harry Ackerman was executive producer from day one.

During those early tense contract negotiations with Jackie Cooper and Screen Gems/Columbia, Lizzie and Bill Asher required at the very least a strong Hollywood player in their corner. Consequently, in stepped none other than Lizzie's father, Robert Montgomery. "I asked him if he'd back me up," Bill acknowledged in 1988. "I told him that Columbia didn't want me to do the show and that Liz wouldn't do it without me."

Without hesitation Robert consented to support his daughter and son-in-law in any way possible, which meant helping to schedule a meeting between Bill and Jerry Harmon. In that meeting, Bill promised Harmon that he would be financially responsible for all of *Bewitched's* production costs and that Columbia would own distribution rights and overhead. "I was accountable from a creative and financial standpoint," Bill said. "But from a logistical standpoint, the studio owned the copyright, which is something I really shouldn't have let happen" (though Bill later controlled even that).

That provision proved an attractive choice for Screen Gems, and it was not dismissed. With a final agreement signed and sealed, all parties were in accord, and as Bill acknowledged in 1988, "The studio backed off, I proved them wrong and, on a very precarious note, Elizabeth and I began to shoot the show."

Eleven

~

Remember the Mane

"It's a gossamer thing; and there are so many factors involved. They just mesh . . . and I certainly appreciate his talent. He's incredible."

—Elizabeth, describing then-husband Bill Asher,
Modern Screen Magazine, 1970

In the second half of its first season on May 20, 1965, *Bewitched* aired an episode called "Remember the Main," directed by William D. Russell and written by Mort R. Lewis. It featured an actor named Edward Mallory who in 1967 married actress Joyce Bulifant (who later married Bill Asher after his divorce from Lizzie in 1974).

In the "Main" segment, the *Stephens* family gets involved with the political campaign of a local candidate running for office:

At *Darrin's* suggestion, hopeful *Ed Wright* (Mallory), challenges his opponent *John C. Cavenaugh* (Byron Morrow) to a public debate for a seat on the city council. The issue at hand: illegal fund allocations for a new drainage system. When a water main bursts, subsequently securing an easy win for *Wright, Darrin* suspects *Samantha's* handy witchcraft. Not so, she says. It's *Endora* who's to blame.

While the episode represents Elizabeth's political ideals off-camera, and certainly *Bewitched's* general message of democracy and equality on-camera,

"Remember the Main" invites a play on words with insight into Lizzie's emotional metamorphosis with each new marriage, signified by something as simple as the change in style and color of her hair.

For example, by the time she and Bill Asher became involved with *Bewitched*, their relationship was sealed. She appeared more at peace than ever, a contentment that seemed to coincide with her decision to go blonde. When she and Asher first met on the set of *Johnny Cool* in 1963, her hair was brunette. After *Cool* and before *Bewitched*, she had a very *Samantha*-like blonde hairstyle in a few episodes of *Burke's Law* (one in which, in fact, she subconsciously does her famous twitch—even before she brings it to *Bewitched!*).

In general, Lizzie's real hair color was best described as "ash blonde, dirty blonde, or on the blonde side of brunette."

As a young girl, she had very blonde hair—what they used to call *tow-head blonde*—but as she grew older, her hair grew darker, as is usually the case with tow-heads (although knowing Lizzie, her sense of humor, and her love for animals, she probably called herself a "toad-head").

At various intervals in her adult life, she experimented with different shades that seemed to somehow match not only her mood, but her professional objectives, and indeed sometimes her husbands.

During her first marriage to Fred Cammann, she was wet behind the ears and inspired, but restless and inattentive. Her hair was merely streaked with blonde, possibly signifying her ambivalence to this union to the wealthy sophisticate, which she ended after only a year.

For a good portion of the time she spent with second husband Gig Young—in what could certainly be described as a dark marriage—Lizzie dyed her hair a dark brunette in hopes of being cast for darker, more textured characters. The strategy worked as she went on to play the war-torn *Woman* from "Two" on *The Twilight Zone*, the prostitute *Rusty Heller* from *The Untouchables*, and the devil's assistant in *Mr. Lucifer*. Ironically, of course, for her role in *The Spiral Staircase*, in which she co-starred with Young, she was a lighter brunette. But her off-screen troubles with Young outweighed whatever professional strides she made, and this marriage ended after six years.

A decade or so later, when she appeared in 1975's post-*Bewitched* TV-movie, *The Legend of Lizzie Borden*, her hair was a shade of red, which distinguished her from playing an all-blonde *Samantha* while still adding a unique tone to help ease the transition from comedy to drama. She wanted to distance herself from *Bewitched*, but not from her audience.

By this time, too, she was living with a brown-haired Robert Foxworth. They weren't yet married and would not be for years to come, but he was then the love of her life, and her darker blonde hair was a better match for his brown locks.

But in that first season of *Bewitched*, back in 1964, shortly after losing her heart—and dark hair—to director Bill Asher on the set of *Johnny Cool*, it was if the all-blonde Lizzie had the best of all worlds. For her, at the time, blondes did have more fun.

Before that, non-actor Cammann wanted Lizzie to give up her beloved acting craft (like *Darrin* would ask *Samantha* to give up witchcraft). And although she viewed the thespian Young as a father figure—and he certainly respected their combined theatrical craft—it was director Asher who would guide her most succinctly, on and off camera. In short, she was bored with Freddie, exhausted by Gig, and the happiest with Bill.

As writer Joe Hyams pointed out in *The Saturday Evening Post*, March 13, 1965, with Bill, Elizabeth was leading a rich, full life without the stigma of being "a poor little rich girl." She still did all her favorite things—like ride horses, paint, and play tennis—which as previously mentioned Asher also enjoyed. But she found in *Samantha* a role that fit her like a glove—and a husband in Asher who, although slighter in physical stature, stood just as tall as her father in commanding a room.

As her old friend Bud Baker told *TV Radio Mirror* in September of 1967, at the onset of *Bewitched's* fourth season—and the fourth year of her marriage to Bill—Lizzie was "so alive now; so completely honest." There was no "above-it-all" attitude like when she was as "a kid at those parties. No faking the phony social stuff the way she had to with Freddie. No trying to adapt to Gig's very nice quiet reserve. She's Billy's girl, and absolutely honest; nothing to fear. Every actress has to have a pretty strong ego, but you can't overpower a guy like Bill."

Baker further explained:

> She's changed. She's really radiant, fulfilled. And it isn't just a matter of having found herself professionally. That's great, but she takes it in stride;

she has what most show business people I've met never have—perspective. She knows glamour for what it's worth, knows how many women scramble for careers because they aren't happy enough in other areas of their life. Acting is normal and natural to Liz—both her father and mother had the talent—and it is something fun to *do*, not something to sacrifice your life *for*. No, what changed Liz is this guy Bill Asher. He's the right kind of man for her; a gutty guy, a real man-type guy who is strong. They are ideally suited to each other, totally in love. He doesn't try to lock her up, he doesn't have to. They are both whole people with everything in the world in common, and it's great they got together.

"Together" is putting it mildly. They were joined at the hip, at home and at the office.

According to what *Bewitched's* publicist Harry Flynn told *TV Guide* writer Arnold Hano in 1967, Bill Asher was tough and tender for all the right reasons: "If you make a mistake, he can give you a rough time. He's especially hard on phonies"—as was Lizzie. "If an interviewer is not her cup of tea, she can't sit down and be pleasant. She loathes pretensions."

In effect, the Ashers were refreshing, direct, and honest. If they reminded you less of the crowned heads of Europe, Hano said, they reminded you more of the Kennedys. Like the Kennedys, they were brisk, businesslike, tireless, hard-nosed, competent, personable, pragmatic, and intelligent; and they liked to play touch football.

They were also in tune. When Lizzie performed as *Samantha*, she kept her eyes glued on Asher, who would feed her the cues. If he beamed, she beamed; he nodded, she nodded; he smiled, she smiled. Asher judged actors within a strict margin, and Lizzie was on his scale. "As an actress," he said, "there is nothing she can't do." Lizzie added, "Bill is the best director I've ever worked with."

More than anything, as Hano detected, they were two people in love. They also *liked* each other, and were subsequently perceived as a combined breath of fresh air in Hollywood—living proof that opposites attract.

Again, they were "the fun couple"—not the series idea, but the actual people. She was the rich Beverly Hills girl and he was the not-quite-poor boy from Manhattan. She was tall, slender, blonde, and beautiful, the cool-eyed girl who danced until dawn at all those New York balls in 1951. He was short, squat, thick-necked, and balding, like your friendly neighborhood wrestler. She went to swank finishing schools, danced with Andover boys and Harvard men, summered in England with her father, and began her career at the American Academy of Dramatic Arts. Asher never finished high school. But decades later on *Bewitched*, as far as Lizzie was concerned, Asher graduated at the top of his class, and they became an unstoppable team.

Once they got rolling on *Bewitched*, Lizzie and Bill had their life and art down to a science. Although she once said that her "art belonged to Daddy," that is, Robert Montgomery, Bill Asher was the new "daddy" in town.

According to *TV Guide* in 1967, their work day began at 5:30 AM and lasted until 7:15 PM, when they'd arrive home to see the kids: first-born William Jr., followed by Robert and then Rebecca. After play time Elizabeth would study lines while Bill planned the shooting schedule. From there it was dinner and bed.

On weekends they played golf, tennis, or both, they'd drive down to Palm Springs to party, and were usually the last to leave any festivity. Lizzie decided at one gathering to play the piano, just before dawn. "She does not really play the piano," a friend said. "She attacks it."

Early the next morning they romped through a game of that Kennedy-esque touch football on the lawn to loosen their muscles for countless sets of tennis.

"We work hard during shooting days, to have more free time in the evenings and on weekends," Asher said. "Our private life comes first."

Lizzie agreed. And although *TV Guide's* Arnold Hano described her as a "reasonably headstrong girl," she deferred to Bill in nearly all matters. Just as her old friend Bud Baker had concluded, her alliance with Asher created a new Lizzie. The one-time social butterfly now seemed to be locked in a cocoon.

Although they still enjoyed a night on the town, Lizzie and Bill were old-fashioned, maybe like Fred Cammann had once envisioned he and Lizzie might be during her first marriage. But now, with Asher, she was ready to settle down.

"If I am asked to make a publicity trip and Bill can't go along, I don't go," Lizzie told *TV Guide*. "It's all right for the man to go off by himself. The man is head of the family."

In short, Mr. Asher would never be known as "Mr. Montgomery." When explaining *Bewitched's* appeal to *TV Guide*, it sounded like he was tooting his own horn. But the fact was, he knew his stuff. "The show," he said, "portrays a mixed marriage that overcomes by love the enormous obstacles in its path. *Samantha,* in her new role as housewife, represents the true values in life. Material gains mean nothing to her. She can have anything she wants through witchcraft, yet she'd rather scrub the kitchen floor on her hands and knees for the man she loves. It is emotional satisfaction she craves."

When asked whether he was defining his own philosophy of life and marriage, Asher replied, "Completely."

While their material gains may have meant nothing to Lizzie or Bill, as was explained in *TV Guide*, neither was discarding the luxuries. By the spring of 1967, the close of *Bewitched's* third hit year, they had four vehicles: a Mercedes 220 SE coupe (his), a Jaguar XK-E (hers), a Chevrolet Corvette (his), and a Chevy station wagon (theirs). The latter two were company courtesy cars (Chevrolet was a *Bewitched* sponsor).

The Ashers' Benedict Canyon home (which Lizzie would later share with Robert Foxworth and retain for the rest of her life) was massive, and located directly across from Harold Lloyd's fabled estate.

They also owned land in northern California. But most importantly, they retained 20 percent of the profits of *Bewitched*. At the time, 20 percent of any television show going beyond the third season (as *Bewitched* certainly did) was worth approximately $2 million.

Lizzie was raised in wealth, but her newfound money was something else again. It would be a lot to expect for her to refrain from using it to ease even the slightest burden.

In today's world, statistics show that many marriages dissolve due to lack of money. Conversely, many stay together because of lots of money. It wasn't all that different during the reign of *Samantha* and *Darrin,* and Lizzie and Bill.

Bewitched was a success. They were in love. They had a happy marriage and a happy show. In the midst of it all, the *new* Lizzie had arrived. She had kowtowed to Asher's rule and found emotional satisfaction, at least in 1967.

In the later years of the series, she played a more active role in the business aspect of their relationship. The show became a co-production of Screen Gems/Columbia Studios and Ashmont Productions, which was initiated in 1965. Then in full swing, Ashmont rivaled the much larger Desilu Productions in name only. The title Desilu was formed by the first names of Desi Arnaz and Lucille Ball; the shingle "Ashmont" was shaped from the last names of Bill and Lizzie. Still, Ashmont—the company and the happily married couple—were a force to be reckoned with . . . at least until the "twitch hit the fan."

Twelve

~

Double Double . . .

"Every little breeze seems to whisper Louise."

—Dr. *Bombay* to *Samantha*, in the *Bewitched* episode, "Mixed Doubles" (3-4-71)

Beyond the fact that there were two *Darrins* on *Bewitched*, there were several *twin aspects* of the series that were concocted or just plain happened . . . on camera and behind the scenes.

After Alice Pearce died in 1966, Sandra Gould stepped into the role of nosy mortal neighbor *Gladys Kravitz*. Alice Ghostley's bumbling witch maid *Esmeralda* replaced Marion Lorne's blundering sorceress *Aunt Clara* following Lorne's death in 1968. Kasey Rogers was hired to play *Louise Tate*, after Irene Vernon exited the role in 1966. Multiple sets of twins played little *Tabitha* over the years, notably sisters Erin and Diane Murphy, while twin brothers David and Greg Lawrence played the part of *Tabitha's* younger sibling *Adam*. And, of course, Elizabeth herself played both *Samantha* and her look-alike cousin *Serena*.

Into this mix, a few episodes of *Bewitched* imbued a "doubles" premise, such as "Mixed Doubles," which aired on March 4, 1971, and was directed by William Asher and written by Richard Baer:

> *Samantha* can't sleep. She's concerned about *Larry* and *Louise* (Rogers), who are having marital troubles. But the next day, she has troubles of her own. She finds herself in bed with *Larry,* while *Louise* is at the *Stephens* home

with *Darrin*. Somehow, *Samantha* and *Louise's* souls have switched bodies. Consequently, *Sam* calls *Dr. Bombay* (Bernard Fox), who remedies the situation which, he says, was caused by something called "dream inversion."

"I always thought those [type of episodes] were kind of fun," Lizzie said in 1989. "I just hope that we didn't do too many of them. And I don't think we actually did, but they were fun because I think audiences enjoyed all that kind of nonsense. I always enjoyed watching stuff like that, too. It's fun to watch other people behaving like they shouldn't behave."

In 1980, music legend John Lennon released what would become his final recording: *Double Fantasy*, an album that in many music circles was labeled a love letter to his wife Yoko Ono, who by then was also a member of his band.

Years before, Lennon and his original "mates," The Beatles—Paul McCartney, George Harrison, and Ringo Starr—made their American television debut on CBS' *The Ed Sullivan Show*, February 9, 1964, approximately seven months before *Bewitched* debuted on ABC.

Bewitched and The Beatles offered entertaining escape from the turbulence that infested the 1960s. The Beatles wanted everyone to hold their hands to forget their troubles; *Samantha* made everyone wish they could twitch away their heartache. Off-screen, Lennon married an Asian princess in the form of Ono; on-screen, *Darrin* married the queen of the witches in the guise of *Samantha*.

Both were mixed marriages that fell victim to third parties who sought to create a great divide. McCartney, Harrison, and Starr blamed Ono for the breakup of The Beatles. *Endora* desperately desired *Samantha* to leave *Darrin*. The Lennons represented racial equality and sang to give peace a chance. *Samantha* advocated for conciliation among TV's top two races— witches and mortals.

Lizzie and *Bewitched*, and Lennon and The Beatles each strived for some sense of familial and universal tranquility. It was a double fantasy, and a dark reality. But somehow, we all came out of it a little better and none the worse for wear. We were delivered by a music superstar (who commented that The Beatles were more popular than Jesus Christ) and a supernatural TV series that delivered a fantastical solution for a subpar world.

Magic was welcomed wherever it could be found, and with Elizabeth and *Samantha, Bewitched* provided the perfect forum—a forum that still stands today, if born amidst the controversy of yesteryear.

When *Bewitched* debuted, September 17, 1964, certain network, studio, and advertising executives expressed concern as to whether or not the show would be perceived in the Bible Belt as a platform for Satanism. The notion may today seem absurd, particularly because at its core the series was a romantic comedy, certainly more human and humane than much of contemporary television.

But if *Bewitched* had any serious evil overtones, Lizzie's co-star, Agnes Moorehead, would have been the first to voice any objections. Passionately opinionated, the fiery redhead was the daughter of Dr. John H. Moorehead, a Presbyterian minister who, by present standards, would be considered a Pentecostal Christian Fundamentalist. Charles Tranberg, author of *I Love the Illusion: The Life and Career of Agnes Moorehead* (BearManor Media, 2005) explains:

> It seems a contradiction because Agnes was such a fundamentalist Christian in her upbringing and throughout her life. But she loved playing *Endora*. [She] even came up with the name of the character and liked to come up with all kinds of ideas. She also had played witches before, in an episode of *The Shirley Temple Playhouse* for example, and later on an episode of *Night Gallery*. She really never thought of *Endora* as "evil" but as mischievous, and somebody who was simply pointing out the foibles of mortal life.

Moreover, if anyone had the "right" to object to Lizzie's portrayal of *Sammy's* supernatural ways, it most probably would have been Britain's Sybil Leek, then the world's top-ranking self-professed, real-life witch.

Fortunately, as Lizzie explained in 1989, Leek had visited *Bewitched* set and granted her sorcery seal of approval. "Sybil gave us her blessing and was very sweet."

"Oh, Darling," Leek told her, "I've seen so many of these *things* (other media witches) and I really can't stand them. But I just love your show. You're so nice and have such a sweet way about you. You're doing everything just perfectly."

Had Leek not sanctioned her performance, Lizzie mused, "I would not have shown up for work the next day."

On September 13, 1970, reporter Lorraine St. Pierre profiled *Bewitched* for *The Boston Sunday Advertiser* to commemorate the show's first on-location filming in Salem, Massachusetts, a city that *TV Guide* once named "the witch capital of the world." The article was published in tandem with the airing of eight *Bewitched* episodes from the seventh season involving *Samantha's* trip to a witches' convention, and St. Pierre described Lizzie's *Samantha* as "a cute prankster."

In her *Book of Shadows* (Broadway Books, 1998), author and real-life Wiccan priestess Phyllis Curott wrote, "A witch is anyone who cultivates divine and sacred gifts." She also deduced that television programs like *Bewitched* are important because "they're showing witches are good."

Fortunately, while working on *Bewitched*, Lizzie agreed.

Exhibit A: She vetoed the name *Cassandra* which, inspired by the sorceress from Greek mythology, was *Samantha's* original name in the *Bewitched* pilot. Lizzie "hated that name. It's terrible; a real *doom and gloomer. Boo . . . boo. Hiss . . . Hiss*," she said in 1989.

The other suggestion was calling her *Elizabeth*, but she was just as adamant about that not happening. "*No, thank you*," she intoned. "I mean, isn't that the stupidest thing you ever heard? Having the character's name be the same as the actor's name? I find it distracting. It doesn't separate the character from the actor. And I think it smacks of a rather appalling ego."

Despite Lizzie's strong opinion on the matter, there was a kinship of sorts between *Samantha* and *Cassandra*. *Cassandra* and other gods of Greek mythology abided by a strict and specific mystical doctrine; *Samantha* and her supernatural peers followed a particular code of ethics found in the *Witches' Book of Rights* (as relayed in the *Bewitched* episode, "Long Live the Queen"). Both *Samantha* and *Cassandra* possessed the power to foretell the future (although the *Bewitched* creative team decided there would be no conflict if *Sam* chose not to engage this particular foresight).

That leaves one last *Samantha-Cassandra* affinity. In the Greek myth, the god *Apollo* places a curse on *Cassandra*. Eons later, it would seem *Samantha* got caught in the fall-out. Like *Cassandra*, she always knew of some forth-coming disaster but was helpless to avert it, namely, Agnes Moorehead's *Endora*.

Moorehead was part of the equally legendary Orson Welles and his esteemed Mercury Theatre group, a band that eventually transferred their unbridled talents into several classic films, not the least of which was 1941's *Citizen Kane* (considered in many a cinematic circle as one of the best mov-ies ever made).

In August of 1965, *Bewitched* entered its second hit season. Moorehead talked with reporter Earle Hesse of *Screen Stars* magazine about working with Lizzie, saying: "She keeps us all on our toes. I play a witch also on that show, and it takes some doing to out-witch and out-charm her. She's a born scene-stealer." And she was, literally, in two "double aspect" episodes of *Bewitched*, initially, in a first-season Dick York episode called "Which Witch Is Which," and then in "The Mother-in-Law-of-the-Year," during the middle of Dick Sargent's second year (but the show's seventh season). Sum-maries for each episode are as follows:

"Which Witch is Which?" (3-3-65) Written by Earl Barrett. Directed by William D. Russell: *Samantha* is unable to make a dress-fitting appointment, so *Endora* transforms herself into her daughter's double and shows up in her place. While being fitted, *Endora-as-Sam* catches the eye of *Bob Fraser* (Ron Randell), a friend of *Darrin's*. *Mrs. Kravitz* (Alice Pearce) sees the two together, and thinks *Samantha* is cheating on *Darrin*. In the end, *Endora* pops in at the *Stephenses* in her *Sam-guise* and leads *Fraser* to believe that she and *Samantha* are "identical twins."

"Mother-in-Law-of-the-Year" (1-14-71) Written by Philip and Henry Sharp. Directed by William Asher: *Samantha* is forced to impersonate *Endora* who in a unique display of emotion feels neglected by her son-in-law. To get on his good side, she creates and stars in an ad campaign called the "Mother-in-Law-of-the-Year" for *Bobbins Bon Bons*, his new client at *McMann & Tate Advertising*. At first, *Mr. Bobbins* (John McGiver) is smitten by *Endora's* creative charms, but the tables turn when she grows bored with the mortal festivities. At which time, *Samantha* replicates her mother's image, and literally inserts herself into the "Mother-in-Law-of-the-Year"

TV commercial. *Endora* then rematerializes in the commercial, and everyone sees double.

Off-screen, however, Lizzie sometimes saw red, as she and Moorehead,
aka *Aggie*, were not always on the same page. Both were independent think-
ers and rarely backed away from confrontation, although in 1989 Lizzie was
quick to make clarifications:

> People were always trying to create fights between us and said that Aggie
> and I hated each other or that Aggie and Maurice (Evans) hated each other,
> or that Maurice and I hated each other. And none of that was ever true.
> Even Mabel (Albertson, who played *Darrin's* mother) and Aggie got along
> fine, mostly because Mabel wouldn't put up with any bullshit. And it was
> great because Aggie would always try to push it (the limits) with the women
> that would come on the show. And I would just sit back and say, "Well,
> let's see how this turns out."

Elizabeth believed Moorehead enjoyed the challenge of their relationship "because she knew I loved her dearly," and that "Aggie's bark was
worse than her bite."

But Moorehead chomped at the bit when Dick Sargent was hired to
replace Dick York as the new *Darrin* in the fall of 1969. Sargent's new term
on the show began on a foot of edgy hostility. Set in her ways, Moorehead
was not at all pleased with his presence. She was fond of York and his
talent, and respected his New Age-like spirituality. Even though such beliefs
countered her conservative Christian viewpoint, Moorehead felt his presence was key to the show's success.

As was explained in *TV Guide*, May 29, 1965, with the article, "He's
Almost Invisible in the Glare of Success," York many times invoked religious items into sculpting, an art he practiced in his spare time. He described
one of his pieces as "four-dimensional":

> I try to incorporate all religious teaching, the Old Testament, the New
> Testament, Confucius, Buddha, The Agnostic, one figure representing all.
> In the front you see Adam, a cloud-like Adam. Eve is beside him on the
> ground looking into an empty cradle. As you revolved around it, the back
> of Eve's head becomes Woman. And Adam, from the back, is the crucified

Christ. Then Eve becomes the Virgin Mary from another angle. There are six different perspectives.

It seemed a convoluted concept, but Moorehead respected York's vision, which in her view, contributed to her understanding of the man behind the vision:

I probably understand him better than others. He's rather profound, you know. He has a spiritual quality. I am a religious girl. I have a great faith. This creates a rapport between us. Actors who have this spiritual quality often understand each other without much communication.

Adds Moorehead biographer Charles Tranberg today:

Aggie Moorehead absolutely loved Dick York! And this never wavered. They both had a deep spirituality. Aggie's was more of a conventional God-based spirituality which was developed from a childhood as a minister's daughter. She was a fundamentalist. Dick was not. He was spiritual, but he was more of a deep thinker. He was the type of guy who could find God anywhere. God is being outside looking at a beautiful mountain range. He was interested in all kinds of philosophies, not only the Christian faith. But still Aggie saw him as a fellow seeker of wisdom and somebody who felt that there was a supreme being. They had lots of conversations on the set, between scenes, on things like this. When Dick left the show, she was not happy. She felt he was a big part of the success of the show and even said that he had the hardest part of all because he had to make all these supernatural things happening to him seem real, and that took real acting, another thing she appreciated. She thought he was a superb actor.

With specific regard to the *Darrin* switch, Tranberg adds:

Aggie didn't like the *Darrin* switch. She hoped it wouldn't happen, but she accepted it, because this type of thing does happen in the theatre all the time as she noted. She took out her disappointment on Dick Sargent, who was hired to play the new *Darrin*. For a while on the set she made his life difficult. He wasn't happy about the way she treated him either. She certainly didn't have the rapport on-screen that she had with York. Eventually as time went by, she did mellow somewhat, even inviting Sargent to her annual Christmas–Birthday bashes, but there certainly wasn't the same bond with Sargent that she had with York.

Although Agnes Moorehead claimed no lack of communication between herself and Dick Sargent, or any personal objection to him replacing Dick York, David White, the irascible *Larry Tate* on *Bewitched,* recalled things differently.

In the fall of 1970, the *Bewitched* cast and crew traveled to Salem, Massachusetts (the show's first on-location filming) for an arc of episodes having to do with *Samantha* attendance at a Witches' Convention. On the plane-ride back to Los Angeles, White was seated next to Sargent, who he said, had a tear in his eye. Apparently, something Moorehead said had made him cry. "He was very upset," White said.

It was like that from the beginning. At the first table script-reading with Sargent the year before, in 1969, White said Moorehead rose from her seat, turned to all of those who would listen, and stated pointedly, "I am not fond of *change.*"

In 1992, Sargent granted an interview to author Owen Keehnen, which appears in Keehnen's book, *We're Here, We're Queer* (Prairie Avenue Productions, 2011). According to Sargent, Moorehead said, "They should never meddle with success."

> "Meaning," Sargent explained, "Dick York should never have been replaced, which I thought was a very cruel and unthinking thing to say in front of me. But that was her. She came to rehearsals with a Bible in one hand and her script in the other. She was certainly the most professional woman in the world, and she was so good [an actress]. Thank God we became friends eventually."

In 1989, Sargent only praised York's performance as *Darrin,* calling him "excellent!" In 1992, Sargent told Keehnen that he was set to play the famous *Mr. Stephens* before York, and even actor Richard Crenna (*The Farmer's Daughter*), who was in the running for the role. "I had the interview and by the time they got back to me, I had already signed on a series called *Broadside,* so Dick York got it. But I was the original choice."

One year before, in 1988, York assessed Sargent's take on *Darrin*. Although York wanted the summer of 1969 to "rest up" in order to continue playing the part through that fall and for the remainder of the series, he had nothing but kind words for Sargent: "The man had a job to do, and he did it well. He was an actor, and he did a fine job. I never held anything against him."

As to York's relationship with Elizabeth, *Bewitched* writer Doug Tibbles recalls:

> He was quiet, and now looking back, that was because of the pain he was in. He did not seem loaded the way people on pain medication [do]. It didn't seem that way at all. He just seemed like a nice quiet professional. He was semi-detached. Through my eyes, his relationship with Elizabeth was simply professional. I mean, they were kind of almost sweet. But you couldn't tell if it was just two polite people or two people just being polite. I didn't see tons of closeness and I didn't see tons of distance. It was somewhere in the middle.

That's kind of where Elizabeth found herself when she ultimately confronted Moorehead about her mistreatment of Sargent, of whom Lizzie was fond and enthusiastic about his joining the *Bewitched* cast. She made every attempt to keep peace on the set. At one point early on, she walked with Sargent to see Moorehead, who proved to be nothing less than unwelcoming. As Lizzie explained in 1989, upon greeting Sargent, Moorehead outstretched her arm and instructed him to kiss her hand, as if he was greeting royalty. Lizzie was stunned. "Oh, Aggie," she said with a ting of sarcasm. "How wonderful . . . I can always count on you to make people feel at home."

Moorehead responded with an icy glare, but Lizzie would have none of it. "Don't you look at me that way," she told her.

Lizzie thought "Aggie's response was great, because that meant we were really communicating."

Later that day, she walked into Moorehead's dressing room, something she rarely did, and communicated some more:

> Now, you know how you can be, and I know how you can be. So, I don't want you to be like you and I know you can be. Obviously you're being

difficult because you know what I'm telling you is true, and that I should have never come in here . . . and that we should have never had this conversation, because it may sound like I think you're stupid. And if that's true, well, then, I'm sorry. I do apologize. I didn't mean to hurt your feelings by telling you something that you already know.

As Lizzie went on to explain in 1989, Moorehead feigned ignorance. "She pretended as if she didn't understand what I meant and was a little aggravated."

A short time later, she and Moorehead were back on the set, and ready to shoot a scene. Suddenly, in the middle of rehearsal, Moorehead turned to her TV daughter and said, "You're right."

"That was all that was ever said about the incident," Lizzie recalled. She believed Moorehead enjoyed the challenge of their relationship because "she knew I loved her dearly. We really did have a mother-daughter relationship. I truly did adore Aggie. She was heaven."

A few graffiti artists in Hollywood would have agreed. Sometime in the mid-1980s, the phrase, "Agnes Moorehead is God," was canvassed across the side of a Tinseltown structure, once standing opposite the Capitol Records building on Vine Street. Upon learning this in 1989, Lizzie's eyes widened and smiled in bemusement. "Huh!" she said, "She finally made it, eh?"

In playing opposite two *Darrins* on *Bewitched*, Elizabeth shared unique interplays with Dick York and Dick Sargent. But off-screen, she may have considered Sargent more of a friend. According to what *Bewitched* third-season producer William Froug revealed to www.emmytvlegends.org, documented on September 14, 2001, Lizzie had issues with York. Froug said executive producer Harry Ackerman hired him on the show to "take the fall," to buffer any personal tension that transpired on the set—between Lizzie and York, as well as between Lizzie and Bill Asher. Froug explained:

> Asher and Liz were in a troubled marriage . . . They lived together, they drove [into work] together, but there was tension there that nobody but them could know about. So they needed someone in the [producer's] chair.

And I was the guy they chose. It was [a] perfect [fit]. Nothing to lose for them, and nothing to lose for me.

Consequently, Ackerman hosted an initial meeting with Froug, Asher, and Lizzie; and as Froug went on to explain:

> The first thing out of Liz's mouth was, "We've got to get rid of *him!*" Now, I'm brand new, and I'm wondering, "Who the hell is *him?*" So, after the meeting . . . I finally had to say to Bill, "Who is *him?*" And he said, "Dick York. Liz can't stand him."

As Froug perceived it, "Dick was madly in love with Liz," and whenever York was forced to rest between filming, due to his severe back ailment, he would glance over to Lizzie, "longingly."

"It was pretty clear he was very smitten," Froug said, "and it was equally clear that she couldn't stand him because of that. Liz was the kind of woman that if you loved her, you were in trouble," Froug concluded. "She was a tough cookie!"

Beyond Froug's somewhat indiscreet personal opinion from behind-the-scenes, on-screen, Elizabeth and Dick York were pure magic.

Charles Tranberg profiled York for *Classic Images* magazine in October, 2011. As he sees it, Lizzie had veto power over casting the show's pilot. Had she not approved of York, he would never have made the initial cut, much less come to play the role. Tranberg explains:

> I think she thought that he was a strong counterpoint to her, and certainly their scenes together were magical. They had on-screen chemistry from day one. Whatever problems they might have had off-camera never showed up on-camera—not even towards the end when York was increasingly ill due to his back problems and the psychological effects that the medication he was taking was causing. She probably became frustrated with him due to missing some shows, but when they worked together on-camera . . . the chemistry was spot-on.

Tranberg also says York recognized in Elizabeth a trace of his wife Joey, the former actress known as Joan Alt, and whom he had known since they were children:

I think that always had a great effect on him and how he worked with and perhaps acted around Elizabeth. He realized how good they were together on camera. I think her interpretation of *Samantha* appealed to him both as an actor and maybe a bit as a man.

No maybes about it. As York acknowledged in his memoir, *The Seesaw Girl and Me*, (New Path Press, 2004), he "first fell in love with Elizabeth Montgomery by leg distance," after seeing her perform with Tom Poston in the "Masquerade" episode of Boris Karloff's anthology series, *Thriller*. "My God," he thought, "what a pretty dark-haired girl. And those legs! Oh my God!"

A few years later he auditioned for *Bewitched*, and had a chance to get a closer look, when Lizzie was sitting outside the casting office that housed Bill Asher and Harry Ackerman. "She unfolded those gorgeous legs and looked at me," York wrote, "and I saw her in person for the first time. She had full lips and dark, soft hair. She was sex all over."

A few minutes later, he and Lizzie walked in to read for Asher and Ackerman. By this time, of course, Lizzie already had the part. This audition was for York, who told her right before they read together, "Oh, God, you'd be wonderful" for the part of *Samantha*.

York also noted in his book, "I've known Elizabeth Montgomery all my life, and she's kind of been my wife because she reminds me of Joey." He explained how he walked into the audition "more confident than I've ever been in my life."

At this point, he had his arm around Lizzie, and quipped to Asher and Ackerman, "I don't know about you guys, but this girl is perfect. Let's sit down and read this turkey and see if I'm the right guy for her."

York's confidence paid off. He was more than right for the part. He was perfect.

Off-screen, as Charles Tranberg assesses, Lizzie's relationship with York was also ideal.

At least, in the beginning, she reportedly invited the Yorks to play tennis and socialize every now and then. But they were a private couple, and when away from the set, he liked to spend time with Joey and their children. Tranberg explains:

I don't think Elizabeth resented this, because she was a strong believer in family first, too. But as the time went by something, and I'm not certain what it is, soured their off-screen relationship. Not to the point that Elizabeth was demanding that they get rid of Dick, she knew how important he was to the show, as did Bill Asher. I don't know what it was; that she was getting fed up with his illnesses and I'm not sure how much empathy she had for his pain. They accommodated him on the set, certainly.

I do know that she felt the show was stronger when it was focused on *Samantha-Darrin*, and that when he was sick and missed shows it affected the balance of the show. I recall Mrs. York telling me, and I don't think she would mind my revealing this, that when Dick was nominated for an Emmy . . . finally! . . . in 1967, the cast, as usual, had a table at the awards ceremony. Elizabeth was also nominated as was Agnes Moorehead and others associated with the show.

But Dick was not there, so, at some point, Elizabeth excused herself and called Dick's house to see if he was coming. Apparently she was told that the whole family was gathered around the master bed watching the telecast on TV, and they were having more fun doing that. My guess is that Elizabeth probably didn't think that was being a professional and showing support for the show.

Into this mix, David Pierce, author of *The Bewitched History Book* (Bear-Manor Media, 2012), assesses Lizzie's alternate interpretations of *Samantha* in playing opposite first York then Sargent:

Many fans of *Bewitched* have varied opinions of the chemistry between Elizabeth Montgomery and her TV husbands, Dick York and Dick Sargent. I think she she had more chemistry with the former but I think the reason for it wasn't so much because of him, but because of what was going on in her life at the time she worked with him. Liz had just recently married Bill Asher and they were just starting their family. By many accounts, Bill and Liz were very much in love and Liz had mentioned how much she loved being a mother. Being able to work with her beloved husband who worked her schedule to make it easier to be with the children made her very happy, and that I think that translated into her acting with Dick York. The show was successful which would also have contributed to her happiness. With Dick Sargent, I think she had great chemistry with him as well, at least at first. However, her personal life starting going into shambles with the breakdown of her marriage, and though I think she could've maintained the energy, she didn't have it in her. Therefore, though Dick Sargent gave it his all, I personally believe Liz didn't, and it shows in her performances toward the end.

In 1989, Elizabeth herself concluded of the dual *Darrin* days:

I don't know who anyone's first choice was [to play *Darrin*], all I know is that, Dick York, Dick Sargent, and Richard Crenna were there. And any one of the three I would have been totally delighted with. . . . It's really difficult to compare a couple of actors like that when you've been that close to them. But I felt that Dick Sargent was a more easy-going presence, actually. But don't forget, too, by the time he came in, that marriage was five-years old. So the characters themselves changed automatically. The newness of the relationship was done, and the relationship matured. So, I felt that *Darrin*, in any case, was becoming more of an easy presence, which made the problems even funnier at times. And he would sort of lapse into this kind of complacency, whenever he could. It was almost as if *Darrin* grew in the relationship . . . he felt maybe he wouldn't have to be on his guard as much. So, when he was suddenly confronted with something . . . like five years into the relationship . . . he wasn't quite the nervous wreck [as when York played him]. It was a marriage that had worked for six years [by the end of spring of 1970, Sargent's first season]. I mean, how many of those do you find around, especially with a mother-in-law like *Endora*.

Beyond the *Darrin* debacle, Lizzie found it challenging to address other issues with Agnes Moorehead, *Endora's* alter ego. For one, she said it was "impossible to talk politics to her . . . so you'd stay [away] from all sorts of really complicated areas like ice cream and religion."

But *Bewitched* writer Doug Tibbles rememberd Moorehead as "kindly and polite . . . removed and semi-serious. I don't think it was directed at Elizabeth. It was simply her carriage."

Lizzie remembered how such carriage led to a terse, if comical, interaction between her and Aggie when film legend Ida Lupino was hired to direct the *Bewitched* episode, "A is for Aardvark," the plot which Bill Asher once said represented the message of the entire series.

Darrin is home sick in bed. Tired of running up and down the stairs to cater to his every whim, she grants him the gift of witchcraft. At first he goes wild with the power, but ultimately discovers that having material things without working for them is meaningless. And once he's feeling better, he buys her a watch (with money he earned from *McMann & Tate*), that's inscribed, "I love you every *second*." *Samantha* cries real tears, and their love is stronger than ever.

However, as Lizzie acknowledged in 1989, there was no love lost between Lupino and Moorehead, nor herself and Moorehead while filming this episode. Lizzie thought Lupino was "terrific, and really liked her, but she had her hands full with Aggie."

Elizabeth recalled Moorehead standing up against the television set in the *Stephens'* living room, and having "one of her snits. She had that attitude," which Lizzie felt was exacerbated by Moorehead's heavy eye make-up, or "whatever it was that (make-up artist Ben Lane) used to paste on her eyelashes. I just never understood how she could (have) . . . all that gook in her eyes." So Lizzie finally asked:

"Aggie, can you take a nap?"
"What do you mean?"
"How can you close your eyes with all that shit up there?"
"Don't talk to me that way!"

"It was amazing, because she was giving Ida this really kind of weird look," Lizzie went on to remember.

But Lupino was legitimately concerned about Moorehead's well-being. "What's the matter, Darling? Are you okay?"

Elizabeth intercepted those questions and said, "I think she's got something in her eye."

"And Aggie was fuming," Lizzie mused. "She almost popped her eyes, because she couldn't say, 'How dare you?'"

The situation became progressively worse from there, especially with Moorehead backed up against that television. Finally realizing that Agnes was sincerely upset, Lupino was more desperate than ever to address her concerns.

"Is there anything we can do?!"

And Lizzie was "just sitting there on the sofa, trying to stifle a laugh."

At which point, Aggie turned around to leave the set and, as Lizzie said, "She looked like an owl . . . her head almost went in a 180 degree turn. And she looked at me and I just looked at her, and she stomped off, away to her dressing room and slammed the door. And boy those violets (Moorehead's favorite flower, based on her favorite color) in that dressing room just went *boooogooogoooosh*."

Another jolting conversation took place between Elizabeth and Moorehead on the *Bewitched* set during the potent Sylmar earthquake of 1971. "There were still aftershocks," Lizzie recalled. "So we were all still kind of nervous, and I asked her if she was scared."

"No, of course not!"

"You weren't the tiniest bit scared?!"

"No! Why should I be scared? God takes care of me! God protects me through anything!"

"Well, that's good. So, what was the first thing you did when you felt the quake?"

"I grabbed my Picasso plate and put it underneath the piano."

"I see . . . God would take care of you, but you wouldn't trust God with your Picasso plate, eh?"

"Oh, Elizabeth! Really!!"

At which point, according to what Lizzie recalled in 1989, Moorehead "flounced off into her dressing room!"

Elizabeth also remembered how Agnes would sometimes employ a slight affectation in her voice when reciting certain words. "It's like when she hit us that day with 'Meami' instead of saying 'Miami.' I said, 'You just came back from *Meami*?' And I thought, *If anybody says anything, I'm gonna kill 'em*. Because I didn't think I could handle that. I just went, 'Oh, give me a break!'" While filming the episode, "Double, Double, Toil and Trouble," on September 28, 1967, something or someone was going to *break* for sure. In this segment:

Samantha, now Queen of the Witches, has to hold court at her house. When *Darrin* arrives home and sees the unusual proceedings, he orders every witch and warlock, including *Endora*, to vacate the premises. Infuriated, Endora enlists *Serena's* help to rid *Samantha* of *Darrin* forever. So, while

Sam attends a church fundraiser, *Endora* and *Serena* impersonate *Sam* [mak-ing] every attempt to drive *Darrin* away. Later, when their plan fails, Endora and *Serena*, along with *Samantha* and *Darrin*, [each] receive a pie in the face, during a free-for-all that takes place after *Sam* brings home a few baked goods from the church fundraiser.

The pie-throwing scenes were ignited when *Darrin* mistakenly threw a pie at *Samantha* who he thought was *Serena*, and the mayhem just expanded from there. And when this episode is viewed closely, Lizzie, who received a pie in the face twice, first as *Samantha* and then as *Serena*, is seen laughing so hard, her lines had to be dubbed twice. She and York clearly enjoyed filming this episode, but as Lizzie recalled in 1989, Moorhead was none too pleased about receiving a pie in the face:

It was instant fury and amusement at the same time. It was totally beneath her dignity when it happened to her. She wasn't the least bit happy. She was seething, and not a happy camper . . . And yet it happened to everybody else and because she was an actress that's the only thing that saved it. But there was no reason she should have been happy *all* the time. We would accommodate her in the schedule when she really had something to do like her one-woman show. Even though she confessed to me once that when she first read for [*Bewitched*], she thought well, *It's a job. I'll take it. It's going to be a failure anyway.* And then of course she was kind of hoping that it wouldn't have been a success, and then [when it was] she said she only wanted to do seven episodes . . . Then after doing [those seven and more], she said, *What do you mean, only seven episodes?* I always knew that once she was hooked on it, she wasn't going to go away too much.

But that's exactly what Moorehead eventually would do with her cross-country one-woman stage show tour, and it ultimately annoyed Elizabeth.

We'd do the schedule around her and everything. And she was cranky. I used to think, *I can't believe this. Why are we accommodating this woman?! If I'd try to do this, everybody would say, 'What?! Get your ass on the set, and stop behaving like an ass!'* Right? And of course I wouldn't have done it anyway, but that used to bother me (that Moorehead did it). And then she would get really nasty about stuff sometimes. And Bill would say, *Oh, come on, now, Liz . . . she's lonely.* And I'd be like, *Dammit—it's her own fault!* She's lonely and feeling put upon. Because I always tried to really make her feel terrific. I mean, I'd argue with her and stuff like that. I mean, why not? . . . Because that was fun.

Clearly, there were highs and lows, bonds and gaps between Lizzie and Aggie. But more than anything, as Charles Tranberg confirms, the two women had a solid professional relationship. Lizzie, in particular, "did little things" for Moorhead, sent cards, flowers, etc. "But off the set, except for an occasional party, such as one of Aggie's lavish Birthday-Christmas parties, they really didn't hang out together. If anybody was the daughter Agnes never had it was probably Debbie Reynolds."

As Tranberg sees it, Lizzie's association with Moorehead could have been more competitive on Aggie's part:

> But Elizabeth took great effort to make sure that Aggie felt comfortable as a member of the *Bewitched* family. She would send her cards for holidays and birthdays and flowers and funny little notes, just to let Aggie know that she was thinking of her. Aggie, I think, came to like Elizabeth very much so. At first she might have been a little dismissive of Elizabeth's talents. She once, reportedly, told Elizabeth that she basically plays herself, while when Aggie was Elizabeth's age she was *always characterizing*.
>
> I think Elizabeth took that kind of comment with a grain of salt and as time went on Agnes came to revise her opinion of Elizabeth's talent. She would have been greatly impressed, had she lived long enough, to see the many diverse and different types of roles that Elizabeth took on after *Bewitched*—and how well she did in them.

Tranberg says Moorehead always perceived Lizzie as a refined woman with good manners and a funny bone:

> Aggie loved a good sense of humor and Elizabeth could have a wicked one—as could Aggie. Neither, I believe, suffered fools gladly. They were both professionals who came to the set on time and knew their lines; Aggie certainly appreciated this about Elizabeth. Certainly as people that they had a respect and certain affection towards one another. As artists, I'm sure that Elizabeth was proud to be on a series that included an actress of Aggie's

stature. Aggie could be a bit jealous, however, that she was not the *star* of the show. It's somewhat revealing that in her correspondence to her secretary, Aggie repeatedly refers to *Bewitched* as *my show*. It's kind of funny.

Lizzie and Aggie were at the very least strong-willed, if not competitive. The competition, Tranberg says,

> . . . would be mostly on Aggie's side. Elizabeth was proud to be associated on the series with her. In fact, she was the one who suggested Agnes for the role of *Endora* and actually approached her about doing it. Agnes, at least from her private letters, seemed to feel that at times her contribution to the show was less appreciated than say, [that of] Elizabeth and Dick York.

In 1968, both women were Emmy-nominated in the lead actress category, possibly leaving room for Moorehead's vindication because, as Tranberg goes on to explain,

> . . . she felt it was her rightful place to be; even though Elizabeth, quite frankly, was certainly the lead actress and appeared in every episode. Whereas Agnes, who was brilliant as *Endora,* didn't appear in every episode [only two-thirds] and in some of those in which she did, she might just 'pop' in and then 'pop' out again. My guess is that when Agnes was, afterward, nominated in the supporting category again, it was a disappointment to her."

Another interesting cross-tone between Lizzie and Aggie was Robert Montgomery, an actor for whom both women had a great deal of respect. In the 1940s, when Moorehead was new to Hollywood, a columnist, "perhaps it was Hedda Hopper or Louella Parsons," Tranberg suggests, asked her to name a few actors she admired and the elder Montgomery, a Republican, was on her list.

> Politically, Agnes grew more conservative as the years went by. Early on she had greatly admired Eleanor Roosevelt and even had provided the voice of ER on radio with *The March of Time*, but by the 70s Agnes was openly supporting Richard Nixon and Ronald Reagan. She had previously thought that actors shouldn't be publicly involved in politics, but she truly

MAGICAL: No other word better describes Elizabeth in this publicity still from 1962.
Frank Bez—Globe Photos

A NEW ADAM AND A NEW EVE: Lizzie's "The Woman" struggles with Charles Bronson's "The Man" in "Two," her famous episode of *The Twilight Zone*, which originally aired September 15, 1961. No dialogue was spoken in this apocalyptic story except for one word by Elizabeth's character: "precrassny," which is Russian for "pretty." CBS/Photofest

BELOVED: Like every aspect of her life and career, a modest Elizabeth never gave herself credit for being a loving, kind parent. But she was. Just ask her children, two of whom she is seen with here in 1966 (on the grounds of her Beverly Hills home), all of whom she had with William Asher: Robert Asher, named for Lizzie's father (sitting on her knee), Billy Asher, Jr. (playing with the grass), and her daughter Rebecca, the youngest (not pictured), who would come along in 1969. She would be named after Elizabeth's beloved grandmother Becca. Globe Photos

THE EYES AND EARS OF COMEDY: Elizabeth and Dick York struck gold with their on-screen chemistry in *Bewitched*. They are seen here in a publicity shot from one of the show's most *end-ear-ing* episodes, "My, What Big Ears You Have," which originally aired on December 7, 1967. ABC/Photofest

BEDEVILED: Many of Lizzie's post-*Bewitched* performances were much darker roles than *Samantha Stephens*. But none were as diabolically evil as her TV-movie characters from 1975's *The Legend of Lizzie Borden*, 1991's *Sins of the Mother*, and *Black Widow Murders: The Blanche Taylor Moore Story* (as pictured here), which aired May 3, 1993. Interestingly, in both *Mother* and *Widow*, Lizzie sported a very *Serena*-like hairdo, short and teased. In this photo from *Widow*, her hair is short and auburn. In *Sins of the Mother*, her hair was short and exactly *Serena*-black. Picture-Alliance/Newscom

WITCH UPON A MOON: A statue of Elizabeth as *Samantha* was commemorated by TV Land in Salem, Massachusetts (*the witch capitol of the world*), on June 15, 2005. The design combined the visual of the *Bewitched* animated opening credits sequence of *Samantha* flying on a broom past the moon through a starlit sky with the live-action sequences in which she was dressed in regular mortal clothes. TV Land

felt that America was on a moral decline and felt that people like Nixon and Reagan would implement policies that would turn this around.

In that way, she was probably closer to Robert Montgomery than to Elizabeth—who was a lifelong liberal. I doubt very much that Elizabeth and Agnes ever discussed politics. I can't really document it but I have a feeling somewhere along the line Agnes might have told Elizabeth, "You did a good job in that scene. Your father would be so proud!" But then again, if she felt that there was a hint of Elizabeth and Robert Montgomery having problems in their personal relationship—she might not say anything to Elizabeth about him.

Tranberg concludes that both actresses were bright, funny, strong-willed, and talented women who came to like each other a great deal and enjoyed working together. "Agnes probably thought that Elizabeth got a few more perks and consideration due to the fact that her husband, Bill Asher, was the director and later producer of the show. She alluded to it a couple of times in letters to her secretary regarding this." But in general, he concludes, Lizzie and Aggie complemented each other well. "You could see really in their performances that they could be mother and daughter. They brought a lot of affection and love to their scenes together."

Meanwhile, the following twitch-bit of information proves intriguing:

According to entertainment historian Rob Ray, the name *Endora*, bestowed upon Moorehead's *Bewitched* character, refers to the Biblical *Witch of Endor*. Ray says this sorceress, sometimes called *The Medium of Endor*, was "a woman who apparently conjured up the spirit of recently deceased prophet Samuel, at the command of King Saul of the Kingdom of Israel, in the *First Book of Samuel* (28:3–25)," although the witch is absent from the version of that event recounted in the deuterocanonical *Book of Sirach* (47:19–20). If anything, that seemingly fits Moorehead's religious personal profile (which also includes her coaching actor Jeffrey Hunter for his role as Jesus in the 1961 movie, *King of Kings*).

Ray further explains how William Shakespeare is nicely added into the witch's brew here, specifically Act IV, Scene 1 of *Macbeth*: "There's that infamously popular moment in *Macbeth* when those three witches cast a spell to bring a double amount of 'toil and trouble' to the king"—a moment that concurs with Lizzie and *Bewitched* in more ways than one, mostly because she caused her father a periodic measure of heartache, and vice versa.

Thirteen

. . . Toil and Trouble

"Do I look like *Mary Poppins* to you?"

—*Serena*, in the *Bewitched* episode,
"*Serena's* Youth Pill," February 5, 1972

Lizzie loved to watch science fiction/fantasy programs like the original *Star Trek* (NBC, 1966–1969) and the gothic daytime soap *Dark Shadows* (ABC, 1966–1971), the latter of which featured another blonde sorceress (*Angelique*, played by Lara Parker). After *Bewitched*, she delighted in shows like *The Incredible Hulk* (CBS, 1978–1982), which co-starred Bill Bixby and Lou Ferrigno in a double lead role.

To tone her own theatrical twin muscles on *Bewitched*, she'd don a black wig and some funky 1960s wardrobe to play *Serena*, *Samantha's* look-alike and somewhat wilder cousin.

The idea for Serena was generated early on in the series. In 1989, Lizzie explained the *Samantha-Serena* transformation process:

> Melody McCord was my understudy. We would go into my dressing room and go over dialogue, so she could get the timing right, so there wouldn't be any gaps. She was exactly my height and looked very much like me. That's why we could do the wonderful crossover (scenes on camera). We were lucky that she worked out that way. There are times when you have an understudy that doesn't look anything like you at all, except for light

coloring. She and I are built alike, same coloring. Then they would have to tie-off all the cameras and wait until we changed clothes and makeup. For her, makeup was no problem unless we were using ³/₄ of her face, and not just changing her wig. With me, it would be a complete makeup change. It was always easier to go from *Sam* to *Serena* than *Serena* to *Sam*. *Serena* wore a lot more makeup . . . that crazy person.

Whenever *Serena* showed up, Lizzie was billed in the credits as *Pandora Spocks*, a subtle nod to the famous Greek myth of *Pandora's Box*.

Pandora's Box was an artifact, taken from the myth of *Pandora's* creation as it is explained around line 60 of *Hesiod: Works and Days*. The "box" in question was actually a large jar given to *Pandora* (translated as "all-gifted") which contained all the evils of the world. When Pandora opened the jar, the contents were released, except for the virtue of hope.

Today, opening Pandora's Box means *to create evil that cannot be undone*. In *Serena's* world on *Bewitched*, it meant Lizzie's interpretation of *Samantha's* free-spirited cousin would be significantly hipper than her performance as the more conservative *Sam*. Lizzie played *Serena* to the hilt, further amusing herself with the *Serena/Spocks* billing.

"I just thought I was so clever when I came up with the name," Lizzie said in 1989, even though a *Bewitched* co-worker had another suggestion when doing the show.

"Why don't you just call her *Pandora Box*?"

"Um, I don't think so," she replied. "My choice is a little subtler and funnier."

She was also clear on another matter: Her real-life cousin Amanda did *not* serve as the prototype for *Samantha's* cousin *Serena*. She explained in 1989:

> We had always been very close as kids. But she was not the inspiration for *Serena*. And instead of making *Serena* out to be *Samantha's* long lost sister, I thought to make her *Samantha's* cousin.

However, another *Bewitched* character, *Uncle Arthur*, played by Paul Lynde, had at least been named after Lizzie's real-life relative. "I always adored my Uncle Arthur," she acknowledged in 1989, while she also thought highly of Lynde. "I got along very well with Paul," she said . . . almost to a fault.

One morning on the set of *Bewitched*, the two shared a laugh so hard, director Bill Asher screamed, "I give up!" called for lunch at 10:30 AM, and walked off the set. That's when Lynde pointed to her and said, "It's all *her* fault."

"We were a mess, just an absolute wreck," Lizzie mused in 1989, recalling the incident during which they behaved like childhood playmates reprimanded by a grade-school teacher.

One of her favorite *Bewitched* episodes was the first season episode "Driving Is the Only Way to Fly," which featured Lynde in his first guest-star appearance on the show, not as *Uncle Arthur,* but as *Harold Harold,* a very nervous mortal driving instructor for *Samantha.* Lizzie recalled:

> "Driving Is the Only Way to Fly" was one of my favorites! I mean, I totally truly enjoyed that. When you're working with somebody who's totally off the wall like [Lynde was], it gives you a lot of [creative] freedom. And Bill having known Paul for a long time, trusted him a lot and vice versa. So stuff that we would do also bled over into [Paul's performance] . . . His instincts were fascinating. I wish he would have known. I wish he [had] understood how important he was despite all of his problems [alcoholism, manic depression]. I tried to help him. . . . It was wonderful because when you work with somebody really like that you find yourself kind of using another part of your imagination that you don't use with people that you [usually work] with. It was on a different level [with Lynde].

No doubt Lizzie laughed a lot with Lynde whenever he played opposite her as *Samantha,* be it as *Uncle Arthur* or *Harold Harold.* But he hardly cracked a smile whenever she portrayed niece *Serena* to his *Uncle Arthur.* "Paul couldn't stand *Serena,*" Elizabeth admitted. "His attitude was very different when I played her as opposed to when I played *Samantha.* But so was everybody else's. I'd walk on the set as *Serena* and the crew acted entirely different toward me than when I was *Sam.*"

Vi Alford, the wardrobe designer, not only functioned differently around Lizzie when she donned the *Serena* black wig and garb, she would periodically fail to recognize the actress. "There were times, when Vi would forget that I was playing *Serena*," Lizzie recalled. "I'd be standing right next to her, and she wouldn't even know I was there."

Former actor Peter Ackerman is a married Episcopalian priest with children who serves as Rector of St. Christopher's Episcopal Church in Springfield, Virginia. In the 1960s, he was the child of a TV star and a network executive who oversaw nearly every hit Columbia/Screen Gems series of the era, including *Hazel*, *Dennis The Menace*, *I Dream of Jeannie*, *Father Knows Best*, and *Bewitched*.

Peter is the son of *Bewitched* executive producer Harry Ackerman, who also served as the head of Screen Gems (and before that CBS) and actress Elinor Donahue, best known for her roles on *The Andy Griffith Show* and *Father Knows Best* (the latter during which she met and married Harry). So, like Lizzie, he's the offspring of noteworthy parents in the entertainment industry, parents who raised him with strong family values at the height of their Hollywood careers. Again, like Lizzie, Peter's interest couldn't help but be piqued by the industry that surrounded him. He recalls a rare show business party at the Ackerman home with all the trimmings—caterers, bartenders, servers, TV stars, athletes, and more:

> I remember waking up as a little kid, practically invisible to a discussion with a fellow who had just returned from Africa studying pigmies. I still remember where I was standing in the house when I said to myself, "This is what I want to be a part of when I grow up."

He was afforded the luxury of visiting the sets of Columbia's most classic shows, namely, the adventures of *Samantha* and *Darrin*, where he would meet and chat with Lizzie, Dick Sargent (the second *Darrin*), Agnes Moorehead ("She clearly liked kids"), and Paul Lynde (". . . did not like kids").

One day, Peter visited the *Bewitched* set when Lizzie was in her *Serena* guise. "I was probably the most gullible kid in those days," he recalls. "And it didn't help that outside my Dad's office were two autographed photos, one of and signed by Liz, and one of and signed by Liz as *Serena*."

When he finally did meet Lizzie as *Serena*, "she couldn't have been nicer," he says. But then someone, probably Bill Asher, yelled from the set, "Hey—where is Liz?!" At that point, Lizzie/*Serena* turned to Peter and said, "I think she went to tinkle," politely excused herself and then left to see if they needed her on the set. "For years," Peter concludes, "I told my school friends that Liz and *Serena* were two different people, and I was convinced!"

Upon its debut, *Bewitched* had immediately established itself as a hit for ABC. So much so, rival network NBC and *Samantha* proprietor Columbia Studios sought to regurgitate the magic formula, at first requesting the assistance of *Sam*-scribe Sol Saks, who declined. "I had already created one show about a witch," he said in 1988. "I didn't want to do another."

Consequently, NBC approached producer Sidney Sheldon, who had befriended Bill Asher on *The Patty Duke Show*, which they had co-created. Sheldon agreed to do a new supernatural sitcom, and suggested to Columbia and NBC a concept that ultimately became *I Dream of Jeannie*, starring Barbara Eden as a female genie in love with her male master played by Larry Hagman. But Sheldon was concerned that Asher might object to *Jeannie's* similarities to *Bewitched*. "Sidney was very polite about the whole situation," Bill explained. "He came to me and said, 'How do you feel if I do a show about a genie?' And I told him I didn't care."

Lizzie, however, was irate. When she first got wind that Sheldon was developing *Jeannie*, she gave it little thought—until, that is, she and Bill met for a social chat with Sheldon in Beverly Hills.

As she recalled in 1989:

Sidney was a friend of Bill's, and he invited us to lunch. The more Sidney talked about what he was going to do with his show, the more I sat back in my chair in awe. I thought to myself, "Elizabeth—are you hearing this right? Are you really listening to this conversation?" I was in such a funk. And when I heard Sidney say, "I must think of some way for her (Jeannie *blinked* her eyes) to motivate the magic just like *Samantha* does (with her nose twitch)," I just couldn't believe it. I had to prop my hand under my chin to keep my mouth from falling open. I was annoyed. That doesn't mean I was annoyed with Barbara Eden and Larry Hagman. I was annoyed with Sidney. I was struck dumb. And I usually have something to say. But as I recall, it was a silent drive home.

Despite such a detour, Sheldon's show enjoyed a smooth ride with home viewers. Like *Bewitched* on ABC, *Jeannie* proved to be a ratings dream for NBC—from the moment it debuted in the fall of 1965. What's more, *Samantha's* training reels were not derailed, as *Bewitched* continued to inspire *Jeannie*. Lizzie offered her double-play of *Samantha* and her mischievous raven-haired look-alike cousin *Serena*. Eden later delivered a twin take as *Jeannie* and her brunette doppelganger sister, all of which further infuriated Lizzie. "People were even laughing about *that one*," she said in 1989, particularly because *Bewitched* and *Jeannie* were filmed at the same studio. "Had I been Barbara, I would have said, 'No, sorry. How can I do this? How can I play the dark-haired double to this character?'"

By this point, Lizzie was "flabbergasted," and thought, "Sidney Sheldon should have said, *Wait a minute. I've known Bill Asher for years, and I'm his friend.* ("At least I think they were," she added.) *I can't go in there and steal from this other show,* which is in essence what it was."

Although Lizzie was always cordial to Barbara during the *Bewitched-Jeannie* cross-over years, she was periodically annoyed with her, particularly in the Screen Gems makeup room that both women shared while working on their respective shows. For a time, actress Sally Field was there right beside them, during her time on *Gidget* and *The Flying Nun*, both of which, like *Bewitched* and *I Dream of Jeannie*, were produced by Screen Gems, and aired on ABC in the 1960s.

When Field appeared on *The Rosie O'Donnell Show* (May 10, 2001), she talked about having her makeup applied in that room, while she sat between Lizzie and Barbara. Apparently, Barbara liked to sing, which she happened to be doing a lot of this one particular morning, and it got on Lizzie's nerves. According to what Field told O'Donnell, when Barbara left the makeup room one day, Lizzie turned to her in frustration and said, "Does she have to sing *all the time*?!"

In her memoir, *Jeannie Out of the Bottle* (Crown/Archetype, 2011), which she wrote with Wendy Leigh, Eden apologized to just Sally and not Elizabeth for the musical annoyance. Apparently, Eden used her *Jeannie* time in the makeup room to rehearse for a nightclub act she was performing in

Las Vegas. "Sorry, Sally! If only I'd known, I'd have practiced in the shower instead."

On September 21, 2005, a few years later, Eden appeared in the second episode of TV Land's *TV Land Confidential* series. She mentioned the morning makeup sessions, some baby talk, and ignored the singing sensationalism. In the *Confidential* segment "When Real Life and Screen Life Collide," Eden explained how she'd frequently see Lizzie in the makeup department. "In fact," she said, "we were pregnant together. She had many babies on that show [*Bewitched*]."

Still, those in the *Bewitched* circle tried to calm Lizzie's nerves regarding the general intermingling of their show and *I Dream of Jeannie*. David White thought Lizzie riled herself up for nothing. In 1989, he said:

> There was little noteworthy comparison between *Bewitched* and *I Dream of Jeannie*. *Samantha* and *Darrin* were trying to lead a normal life with their children. There was a great deal of love within the *Stephens'* household, and there wasn't that kind of love on *Jeannie*. And the humor on *Bewitched* was less impacted. It didn't hit you over the head with one-liners as much as it allowed the humor to develop from the situation.

Years after *Bewitched* and *I Dream of Jeannie* completed their original network runs, Lizzie still felt a measure of contempt for the witch-inspired genie series, particularly when in 1985, Bill Asher, from who she had long been divorced, signed on to direct the NBC TV reunion movie, *I Dream of Jeannie: 15 Years Later*. Produced by Sidney Sheldon, the film became one of the highest rated small screen flicks in history, surpassing Lizzie's 1974 NBC film, *A Case of Rape*. "You should have heard Liz," he recalled in 1988 when discussing his work on the film. "She said, 'You idiot!'"

She wasn't upset that the movie was a hit, or that it surpassed *A Case of Rape* in ratings, or any of that. Bill says she was just upset that he was involved with the movie at all.

However, in 1989, when she was reminded of his association with the film, Elizabeth remained loyal to her ex-husband (the father of her three children), saying, "I didn't care about that. That was his business. And they could not have picked a better person to do it."

After the *Jeannie* reunion aired, she was frequently approached about doing a TV reunion movie of *Bewitched*. Various networks offered her a substantial salary to reprise the role of *Samantha*. But as she explained in 1989, she never considered it even a slight possibility, despite the potential cash flow:

> Absolutely not; it's not about the money. That has nothing to do with it; for the networks and studios that might not be the case, but screw that. I'm approached about this all the time. And I know there are people out there who really want to do this . . . but there's not a shot in hell . . . forget it. I think once you've done something, you've done it . . . and that's fine. And I'm proud of it. But now, let's just, as my grandmother used to say, "Leave it lay where Jesus flung it!"

Or as she later and less passionately relayed to writer Ed Bark of *The Dallas Morning News* on March 26, 1994:

> I wouldn't want to do it again. It's still playing all over the place in reruns. It was a wonderful experience, and I had a blast doing it. But when you've done something like that, let it have its life and let it go where it's going.

Media steward Rob Ray offers his take on the *Sam-Jeannie* doubles debacle:

> The conceit of one actor portraying multiple roles is probably as old as the acting profession itself. Classic playwrights in their work as varied as William Shakespeare's *King Lear* to James M. Barrie's *Peter Pan* have created multiple parts designed to be played by the same actor. The idea that one actor could play two roles simultaneously was born near the dawn of film-making and achieved early renown in the films of Mary Pickford. Pickford, known as *America's Sweetheart* with her long curls and petite five-foot frame, could play children as easily as adults and often performed in movies requiring her to age from childhood into adulthood. In several films, such as *Stella Maris* and *Little Lord Fauntleroy*, surprisingly sophisticated split-screen effects were used to enable her to appear onscreen in two roles at the same time. In *Little Lord Fauntleroy*, the petite Miss Pickford portrays the title male role and his own mother and in one scene we actually see Miss Pickford as a

boy kiss the cheek of Miss Pickford as the mother using a split-screen technique as sophisticated as any used today. Later, in 1921, Buster Keaton played nearly every role in his two-reel short entitled *The Playhouse*. In the fifties, Alec Guinness played eight roles in *Kind Hearts and Coronets* and Peter Sellers played almost as many in 1964's *Dr. Strangelove*. Examples of one actor portraying twins are too numerous to mention, but *The Parent Trap* is one of the more famous examples. However, the idea of one actor playing identical *cousins* may go back to the first silent version of Anthony Hope's *The Prisoner of Zenda* in 1913, which has been remade countless times. In that story, the heir to the throne of a mythical European kingdom is abducted just before his coronation and his identical British cousin, a commoner, is drafted by the palace to pose as his royal relative until the kidnappers can be thwarted. To the baby boomer generation, the most famous identical cousins may be *Patty* and *Cathy Lane*, both portrayed by Patty Duke in *The Patty Duke Show* from 1963 to 1966, a series that Bill Asher and Sidney Sheldon co-produced. Imitation is the sincerest form of praise, one might say!

Maybe so; but it simply bothered Lizzie that *I Dream of Jeannie*, an already blatant replica of *Bewitched*, would go the next step and showcase the brunette and slightly-more lascivious relative look-alike scenario. It got to the point where *Bewitched* writers were ordered to stay away from *I Dream of Jeannie*. Unfortunately, one of *Samantha's* main scribes didn't adhere that ruling—and was subsequently fired as a result of writing a *Jeannie* segment behind Lizzie's back.

The *Bewitched/I Dream of Jeannie* scenario was never more evident as when, on July 16, 1994, *TV Guide* ignited *The Great Jeannie vs. Samantha Debate*. The magazine essentially invited its readers and Nick at Nite watchers to respond to this poll:

Which magical blonde is more powerful: *Samantha* the witch on *Bewitched* or *Jeannie* the genie from *I Dream of Jeannie*? Exactly 810,938 out of approximately one million Nick at Nite viewers voted *Samantha* the stronger supernaturalist. But editors of the *Guide's* popular "Cheers & Jeers" column were astounded by the results:

Are you crazy? *Sam* didn't even have enough wattage to keep the same *Darrin* for the run of her show. She also received frequent paranormal assists from *Endora* and her TV coven. Meanwhile, bottled *Jeannie* not only kept *Major Nelson* (Larry Hagman) in a trance for five seasons, she wed him, kept her evil sister in check, and did it all with nothing but her crossed arms. We think *Tabitha* was stuffing the ballot box.

Two weeks later, Lizzie fans were livid and fearless and continued with their *strong* opinions, which *TV Guide* had no choice but to publish. In the issue dated, July 27, 1994, the editors wrote:

What a fuss! When Nick at Nite sponsored a '60s sitcom showdown pitting *Samantha* against *Jeannie*, we weighed in with our opinion. We chided the 810,938 viewers who picked *Sam*, and boy, did we hear it. Since we couldn't make the letters go away by blinking, we decided to devote this page to your most(ly) bitter rebuttals.

Some of which were as follows:

Don't you realize that *Bewitched* all but put the ABC network on the map? Get a grip, *TV Guide.*—Mason Cargone, North Chili, New York

Put them in a sealed vault, which one do *you* think would get out?—Yancy Mitchell, Ardmore, Tennessee

Bewitched appeared a year before *Jeannie*, so there wouldn't have been a *Jeannie* if not for *Bewitched*, nor a blink if there hadn't first been a twitch.—Randolph Sloan, Greece, New York

Whoever wrote that Jeer, was male and prefers a pleasing-you-pleases-me-syndrome slave to a loving, equal partner in relationships.—Wendy Martin, Owosso, Michigan

Any woman who calls her husband "Master" is already a loser.—Jimmie Welt, Gunter, Texas

Of course *Samantha* had more power than *Jeannie*. She didn't have to rely on a skimpy costume to keep ratings high!—Mary Campbell-Droze, San Mateo, California

How many women are powerful enough to replace their husbands—unnoticed—with someone who not only goes by the same name but is a foot and a half taller?—John Moreland, Pasadena, California

Fourteen

~

Public Broadcasting

"I grew up in Hollywood, so I've seen what
kinds of damage loose talk can do."

—Elizabeth Montgomery, *The Advocate Magazine*, July 30, 1992

Lizzie could just as easily chat with the "go-fer" on any studio set as mingle at the most elegant Hollywood affair. But book her on a talk show? No way. Such appearances were "too personal" for her shy nature. As she explained to *Picture Life Magazine* in December 1971, "They terrify me."

It was an emotion she would mention time and again when addressing live TV performances, interviews, or personal appearances of any kind. On December 21, 1985, she went on *Entertainment Tonight* to promote her CBS TV-movie, *Between the Darkness and the Dawn*. Reporter Scott Osborne asked if she enjoyed doing interviews ". . . like this one."

"Not really," she replied. "In fact, you have no idea just how panic-stricken I am right now."

On February 6, 2012, *Time Magazine* published a fascinating cover story, "The Power of Shyness: The Upside of Being an Introvert (and Why Extroverts are Overrated)" by self-admitted introvert Bryan Walsh who wrote:

Shyness is a form of anxiety characterized by inhibited behavior. It also implies a fear of social judgment that can be crippling. Shy people actively seek to avoid social situations, even ones that may be inhibited by fear. Introverts shun social situations because, Greta Garbo–style, they simply want to be alone . . . Caution, inhibition, and even fearfulness may be healthy—and smart—adaptations for the overstimulated person, but they're still not characteristics many parents would want in their children, especially in a society that lionizes the bold. So it's common for moms and dads of introverted offspring to press their kids to be more outgoing, lest they end up overlooked in class and later in life. That, however, can be a mistake—and not just because our temperaments are difficult to change fundamentally.

Still, Lizzie did somehow manage to show up that day in 1985 with Scott Osborne on *Entertainment Tonight*, and she made four other rare appearances on TV talk shows with live audiences. She was by no means a frequent talk show guest, like Totie Fields, Burt Reynolds, or Zsa Zsa Gabor, but there she was on: *The Dennis Miller Show* (in 1992 with Robert Foxworth), *The Merv Griffin Show* (in December 1970 to promote her favorite *Bewitched* episode, "Sisters at Heart"), *The Joey Bishop Show* (in 1967 with Michele Lee, who would later appear with Elizabeth in the 1976 TV-movie *Dark Victory*), and *The Mike Douglas Show*, on November 4, 1966, an especially riveting segment in which she proved telling, honest, and protective, all at once.

Here are some highlights from the *Douglas* interview in particular, by far her most fascinating talk show appearance:

> Douglas opened the show with his routine musical number, she emerged from behind the program's sliding stage doors with a strange companion: a small statue of a fox's head that Bill Asher had purchased for her at an antique shop. She brought it with her for good luck, and kept it on her lap when not in her hand.
>
> The figurehead worked like a charm. She, Douglas, and his co-host Cesar Romero (then playing *The Joker* on ABC's camp classic *Batman*) played darts, and she won.
>
> Later, Douglas turned to the studio audience (and the home viewer) and said, "I'm not sure if any of you know this, but Elizabeth is the daughter

of Robert Montgomery." The studio audience applauded in recognition, while she smiled and said, "I like him, too."

When Douglas wondered if she felt her father played a role in her career, she went on to address several key aspects of the core relationship with her father:

"Probably—because it was in the family my interests peaked. I don't think you can be around something like that and either not love it or just give it up entirely. My brother (Skip) tried it for a while and just decided it really wasn't for him. And I think probably he's the only sane member of the family. But Dad helped. And people say it is a help or a hindrance to have a parent who is known. And it's definitely a help. I think it's silly to say it isn't, because I know it certainly helps open doors that [would] not necessarily open that easily or maybe never. Afterwards, I guess, it depends on ability. But certainly it helps and I've always been very proud of him."

Douglas asked her to talk about her father's former duties as the appointed television advisor to President Eisenhower (a topic which author Steven J. Ross had touched upon during his CPAN interview at the 2012 Los Angeles Festival of Books). She said that her dad helped the President with makeup, eye-glass selection, and the teleprompter. But she couldn't remember if Eisenhower wanted to use one of those "tricky things," because she certainly never saw their benefit. "I don't trust them," she said. "They make me very nervous." If she was forced to count on the electronic cue-card machine for important presidential-like speeches, she'd be a "nervous wreck" because even the thought of using one forced her to have visions of "kind of snarling into a hole or something."

Romero chimed in and wondered if her father helped the President with speeches and diction. "Yes," Lizzie replied. "I believe he did. And it was funny because he was getting teased, unmercifully, when he was doing makeup for the President."

At one point, she explained when her father called her up and said, "Meet me at the White House," which sounded strange to her.

"That's just crazy."

But she agreed, on one condition: If he'd meet her in the makeup department.

She was kidding, but he wasn't amused. "I think that's a terrible thing to say," he complained.

No matter. She enjoyed her meeting with President Eisenhower: "It was very exciting." She walked into the Oval Office, and he was sitting at that "marvelous desk in that beautiful room."

At some point, the President rose from his chair, and the first thing she noticed was his casual attire, specifically, that he wasn't wearing a tie, which she thought "seemed kind of strange . . . He had on like a golf shirt—with the three little buttons and things."

Sure enough, before she met the President, he had asked her father, "Do you think I should put on a tie?"

After Lizzie detailed her travels to Washington, Douglas asked her about the challenges of raising children with Bill Asher amidst their busy *Bewitched* schedule. She replied: "Oh, yes, well . . . it's a little rough and thank goodness they're young. You know, the oldest one (Billy, Jr.) is a little over two; and the youngest one (Robert, named for her father) is one year old October 5. So they're quite a handful. But the children's hours are so peculiar. But I don't think it matters as long as we have enough time to really be with them if they're kept up a little later at night as long as they get their sleep. We see them every night when we come home. We're up at 5:30 in the morning which is before they ever get up."

Later, Cesar Romero, whom *Bewitched* producers once considered to play *Samantha's* father (a role rejected by Lizzie's father and later won by Shakespearean actor Maurice Evans), interjected how he and Asher had roomed together when they were starting out in the business, and how he had once worked for Asher's father, a producer, at Universal Studios.

The interlocking topics, though not known to all, continued when legendary theatre producer David Merrick, famous for *Hello Dolly*, later appeared with writer Abe Burrows to promote their new musical, *Holly Golightly*, based on *Breakfast at Tiffany's*, and starring Mary Tyler Moore and Richard Chamberlain.

At the onset of his interview with Merrick, Douglas ignited an odd conversation with the somewhat controversial and very opinionated Merrick which caught him and most probably everyone else off-guard. With Lizzie sitting opposite him, and with Merrick smack dab in the middle, Douglas said, "David, your image with actors is a father image."

Lizzie's reaction remained hidden from the camera, but she might not have displayed one at all. In those days, talk show guests handled themselves with decorum and were not as outlandish, abrasive, and brutally honest or as "shock-expressive" as they are in today's "anything goes" style of reality TV. It was monumental enough that Lizzie was appearing on a talk show, let alone partaking in a segment that might open a potential can of worms.

In either case, Douglas' father-figure reference and Merrick's subsequent reply most assuredly gave her pause, considering her relationship with her dad, not to mention her then-present marriage to Bill Asher, and her prior nuptials with Gig Young—both of whom were older than she.

In response to Douglas, Merrick said:

"Well, I think that's what a producer is, sort of a father image of the whole project (in this case, *Holly Golightly*). To get it launched and to get the entire creative team together. . . . and when it gets into trouble . . . the show I mean . . . and it surely does very quickly, they come looking to the producer to keep it together and also to be sort of a referee in the fights. And perhaps that's the reason for the father image."

As if to add insult to injury, Douglas then wondered if Merrick watched television. The producer responded forthrightly that he did not—again, while seated directly beside Lizzie, who was then at the peak of her popularity with *Bewitched*—the television show that all but put ABC on the map. Despite the fact that it was established in 1948, the "alphabet web" was still the youngest of the networks and it needed a hit like *Bewitched* to solidify its status.

Merrick was granted a chance to recover his dignity in Lizzie's company when Douglas asked him about beautiful women. At which point he turned to the beloved actress, glanced back at his host, and said, "Here's a beautiful woman—and a beautiful witch is best of all."

Shortly after that, Merrick's colleague, the flamboyant Burrows, joined the panel, and brought along with him a glimpse of that future shock-expressive mentality. Within seconds of taking the stage, he mimicked "zapping" Lizzie with his hands—right before asking if she'd like to take the lead in his next play.

Possibly intrigued by the suggestion, she responded with only a giggle (and what looked like almost a twitch), certainly aware that her *Bewitched* schedule might not allow for such outside demands. Also, appearing in Burrows' next production might not have been a wise career move.

Holly Golightly, which he and Merrick were on the *Douglas* show to promote, did not become the hit it was intended to be (which may have been one reason why Merrick appeared so testy). It starred Lizzie's TV contemporaries, Richard Chamberlain and Mary Tyler Moore, both of whom had just finished successful series runs (*Dr. Kildare* and *The Dick Van Dyke Show*, respectively). Unlike Lizzie, however, they could more easily forget *Golightly* and pursue other such assignments. But as it turned out *Holly* failed to pay off, which may have already been evident to the wise and perceptive Lizzie.

Another guest proved to be an even more intriguing addition to the panel: Reverend Rudolph W. Nemser, then the Pastor of a Unitarian church in the suburbs of Washington, D.C., and otherwise known as the "Divorce Pastor," was seated right next to Lizzie, who was most certainly reminded of her previously failed marriages to Gig Young and to her first husband, Fred Cammann.

Former *Douglas* associate producer Kenneth Johnson would later produce and direct sci-fi TV classics like *Alien Nation* (Fox, 1989–1990), the original *V* series (NBC, 1984–1985), the original *Bionic Woman* (ABC/NBC, 1976–1979), and *The Incredible Hulk* (CBS, 1978–1982), the latter of which was one of Lizzie's favorite shows ("I absolutely love it!").

Johnson remembers the week Lizzie appeared on the Douglas show with guest co-host Cesar Romero, "mostly because (fellow producer) Roger Ailes and I took Romero out to see Sammy Davis, Jr. in performance. And then we all spent three hours in Sammy's dressing room afterward."

As Johnson recalls producing the daily *Douglas* show, he was one of three producers who divided the guests amongst themselves. But as he explains:

Elizabeth did not fall to me that day, so I didn't have that much communication with her. But the confluence of discussion on the show that day was truly happenstance and it's interesting in retrospect to see how it dovetailed with Elizabeth's own life. I do remember that we were delighted to have her on and that she was charming and the audience loved seeing her.

As it turns out, many fans of Lizzie and *Bewitched* are also fans of Johnson's original *Bionic Woman* series starring Lindsay Wagner (and not the NBC remake from 2007), and have for years compared the two shows and the characters of *Samantha Stephens* and Wagner's cybernetic *Jaime Sommers*. For one, performing and visual artist Ray Caspio:

Bewitched is the first TV show I remember watching. It was on a small color television in the front room of my grandma's house when I was probably three years old, if that. The animated opening sequence combined with the music transfixed me, and when Elizabeth appeared on the screen, she did the same. There was something very accessible, yet private about her. Her heart was open and something deep was going on within. Elizabeth, as *Samantha*, represented possibility to me. Anything I wanted, I could have if I worked for it. She had the magical abilities to obtain whatever she wanted whenever she wanted, but she wasn't satisfied with that. Her power was in herself: a theme that ran through many of her characters, and a theme that runs through characters I've been inspired by since childhood, such as Lynda Carter's portrayal of *Wonder Woman* and Lindsay Wagner's *Jaime Sommers*.

Johnson explains why Wagner was cast as *Sommers*:

She had a truly real, girl-next-door quality and brought a refreshing spontaneity to the scripted material. She had a facility for really making it sound like she was making it up as she went along. Part of that came from me listening carefully to her idiomatic speech patterns and writing the character of *Jaime Sommers* in a fashion that Lindsay could most easily embrace.

A similar strategy was utilized by Bill Asher and the other *Bewitched* powers that be with Lizzie's interpretation of *Samantha*, whether it was strategizing on how to transfer her real-life nose wriggle into *Samantha's* twitch, or with phrases like these from *Samantha* that stemmed from her real-life colloquialisms: "Well," "Oh my stars!" and "Good grief" (although Lizzie relayed in 1989 that she lifted that last one from *Charlie Brown* and the animated *Peanuts* cartoon by Charles Schulz).

That said, Johnson never watched *Bewitched*, so he "can't accurately compare Elizabeth's acting style, but certainly both Lindsay and Elizabeth became America's darlings and deservedly so," he says.

As fate would have it, Johnson later served as the producer/director of *The Incredible Hulk* TV series starring Bill Bixby and Lou Ferrigno. As Lizzie expressed to *TV Guide* in 1979, *Hulk* was one of her favorite shows and she had at one time played opposite Bixby in a pre-*Incredible* segment of *Password* (April 5–9, 1971). Johnson's response:

It's very nice to hear that Elizabeth was a fan of *The Incredible Hulk*. High praise, indeed. We certainly labored to make each episode as meaningful and substantive as possible. Our largest audience was actually adults—with women as the largest single group. Working with Bill and Lou was always a treat. We all cared a lot. I'm glad it impacted on her so favorably.

As to the general adventures in working on *The Mike Douglas Show*, and the irony of those guests who appeared with Lizzie on her particular segment, Johnson concludes: "There is a wealth of stories from those years that range from the sublime to the ridiculous."

Lizzie's appearance on *The Merv Griffin Show* in December of 1970 was much less involved than *The Mike Douglas Show*, because her reason for doing the show outweighed her actual appearance. It was here she discussed her favorite *Bewitched* episode, "Sisters at Heart," a Christmas story that originally aired on December 24, 1970. Written by a multiracial tenth grade English class at Thomas Jefferson High School in Los Angeles, the episode condemned prejudice and rallied against injustice.

The idea for "Sisters at Heart" was generated after Lizzie and Bill Asher responded to a phone call from a twenty-three-year-old California teacher named Marcella Saunders. As documented for *TV Picture Life Magazine* in December 1971 (when ABC aired its second and final screening of the episode), Saunders had alarming news: only six students in each classroom were reading at the proper level. At Jefferson High School, less than 1 percent were reading at the ninth grade level; 44 percent read on the third grade level and the other approximately 65 percent were either down or slightly up from that figure. The problems didn't end there. Many of the students were not writing nor comprehending at the high school level. If able to read their textbooks, they often were unable to understand what they read.

Saunders had a solution, and her twenty-four African-American children went on to reap the benefits from what ultimately was Lizzie and Bill's compassion and concern. Upon first speaking with Saunders, the Ashers learned that *Bewitched* was her students' favorite show. Consequently, the class, all of whom did not have cars, and many of whom did not even have the money for bus fare to Hollywood, were invited to the show's set, with Bill and Lizzie making certain the students arrived safely by chartered bus. "They were so shy at first, withdrawn," she said at the time, "but so well behaved; so courteous and polite."

After a relaxing lunch with the Ashers at the studio commissary, the youngsters returned to the set, relaxed, and full of meaningful, intelligent questions. They had discovered something that held their interest. The apathy had vanished, as if by magic. They had been invigorated, and wanted to know as much about television production as possible. Suddenly, children who could never write before, were writing three pages. During rehearsals, kids who could not read were now doubling up on scripts and fighting over who would portray *Samantha* and *Darrin*.

Saunders asked the students to write compositions detailing the studio experience. The papers, the way she described them, "were fantastic," and the class returned to the *Bewitched* set on three different occasions; each time they were welcomed by Bill and Lizzie who said, "They seemed more interested, more eager to know about the technicalities of the production. What kids! Just marvelous. Outstanding!"

As to the actual script for "Sisters at Heart," the students knew it had to be unique. Beyond solid writing and good grammar, it had to say and mean something. So they worked together and eventually created this story:

> *Tabitha* (Erin Murphy), *Darrin* and *Samantha's* little sorceress, befriends *Lisa* (Venetta Rogers), the African-American daughter of one of *Darrin's* clients (Don Marshall) who stays with the *Stephens* while they're away on a business trip with *Larry*. After she and *Lisa* are bullied in the park for being of different colors but still wanting to be sisters, *Tabitha* employs *wishcraft*, and *wishes* they could become siblings. Consequently, white polka dots appear on *Lisa*; and brown polka dots appear on *Tabitha*, literally painting them as equals. In the most poignant scenes in the episode, *Samantha* tells *Tabitha* and her friend, "All men are brothers; even if they're girls."

When the script was completed, the students made a trek back to the studio to present their gift-wrapped present to the Ashers. "We were overwhelmed," Lizzie said at the time. Not only because of the magnitude of the gesture, but because the script was so impressive. "Really," she added. "We've had bad scripts submitted by professional writers that weren't as well written or creative."

"Sisters at Heart" became an official *Bewitched* episode, a secret the Ashers shared only upon being certain the script could be utilized. To move things along, Bill hired professional scribe Barbara Avedon, who had written for *Bewitched* (and other family shows like *The Donna Reed Show*). She helped to expand the story into the required length of a 30-minute teleplay.

In 1989, some eighteen years after "Sisters at Heart" debuted, Lizzie reflected on filming the episode and its core theme of prejudice, which she also view as the central theme of the entire series:

> Yeah . . . this is what *Bewitched* is all about . . . how people can sometimes get off track, and [get on] the outside trying to belong. It was also one of the few things that *Samantha* and *Endora* agreed on. . . . There were times when I certainly would have liked to have gotten a little bit more political (on *Bewitched*). But there were just certain parameters that we could not pass. Also, the underlined theme was the exaggerated promises-that-you-make-and-can't-quite-keep-sometimes. And the feeling that *Maybe if I do help, maybe getting caught doing something you promised you wouldn't do won't be so bad if the end result is oka*y. I mean, people have that in everyday life. *Bewitched* was not about cleaning up the house, zapping up the toast . . . and flying around the room. It was about a very difficult relationship. (*Samantha* and *Darrin's* marriage) was a very tough match. I mean, who the hell would want to go through that kind of stuff? It wasn't the easiest of relationships. It had to be very difficult for *Darrin Stephens* to be married to this woman who could have anything that she wanted . . . and chose not [to] . . . except sometimes. It was a love story. But that's not all of what it was. That was a part of what it was.

In other words, the romantic notions of *Bewitched* were only part of its charm—and Elizabeth's. Despite her shy demeanor, she went on the *Griffin* and *Douglas* shows and her appearances were and remain riveting, if only for the fact that she was not one to grant such personal, non-scripted TV spots.

Conversely, *Bewitched* co-star Agnes Moorehead once served as co-host for an entire week on the *Douglas* show. Charles Tranberg, Moorehead's biographer, explains:

> For a private woman, Agnes was quite public. She did like appearing on talk shows, but she gave instructions about what she would and what she wouldn't discuss. She wouldn't discuss her marriages or her private life—except for social things she did. She loved, however, to discuss her career, she loved to discuss what she thought was the declining morals of the theatre and of younger people in general. She was very opinionated on the social issues of the day—usually from a more conservative point of view. Elizabeth was equally private. She had been married several times and didn't

want to discuss those marriages. She really didn't even want to discuss, openly, her upbringing and her father, Robert Montgomery—all that much. When she wasn't working she wanted to be there for her kids—and she was, by and large. By most accounts, Elizabeth was a wonderful mother. So being on talk shows or game shows (although she did enjoy guest-spots on *Password* and *Hollywood Squares*), wasn't a priority.

PART III

Disenchanted

"I'm likely to have my share of flops as well as successes . . .
as long as I don't have to wriggle my nose for eight years again."

—Elizabeth Montgomery, to journalist Steve Jacques,
during an interview to promote *A Case of Rape* (1974)

Fifteen

To Twitch Or Not To Twitch

"She hated it when people asked her to twitch her nose."

—Liz Sheridan, chatting about Elizabeth's post-*Samantha* disdain on
Bewitched: The E! True Hollywood Story, 1999

By the mid-1960s, TV shows had switched from black and white to color, and *Bewitched* was not any different. In later seasons, Elizabeth would preface each episode with voice-over and visual promos, each of which she instilled with a vivacious energy that encouraged the viewer to watch with eager anticipation. "This is Elizabeth Montgomery," she'd say. "Stay tuned for *Bewitched*. . . . In color."

The show's first color episode was "Nobody's Perfect," which opened the third season, airing September 15, 1966. This episode also introduced *Samantha* and *Darrin's* daughter *Tabitha* as a full-fledged young supernatural. Consequently, *Samantha* was forced not only to curtail her own powers, but her daughter's as well, mostly instructing her with the phrase, "Mustn't twitch!"

Upon first hearing that, *Endora* pops in and says, "Oh, how charming. When every other mother in the world is telling her child, mustn't touch, you'll be saying, 'Mustn't twitch!'" Simultaneously, off-camera at home in Beverly Hills, Lizzie was parenting her real-life children.

In an interview with *Photoplay Magazine* in 1968, she acknowledged the challenges facing a working mother. At the time, she and Bill Asher only had the two young boys, Billy, Jr. and Robert, but because of *Bewitched's* heavy workload, it was not always possible to give her sons a so-called *normal childhood*.

Still, she was determined to maintain as regular an environment as possible under the circumstances. She wanted her sons to feel the same way about her work. One day, she invited Billy, Jr. to visit her at the studio, but he wasn't all that impressed by the Hollywood glitter. It was just a place where his parents went to work. He liked to come to the studio, but only to play with Erin and Diane Murphy, the twins who played *Tabitha*. They were the same age, and Lizzie said they had "a perfectly fine time."

She tried to avoid the pitfalls that accompany being a working mother. At the time, the major concern was finding a nurse who could be firm-but-friendly to her sons. As she told *Photoplay*, "We have one now who is a gem. She knows just when to crack down on the boys and when to let them alone. That's important."

Lizzie had experienced nurse troubles before. They expected her to supply the discipline when she arrived home from *Bewitched*. "*That* would have been great!" she mused. "Here the mean old Mommy came home and whacked them for something they did at 10:00 o'clock that morning and had already forgotten about."

Then there was the day she came home and found Billy, Jr. pouring a glass of water on the living room carpet.

"Don't do that!" she told him.

"Nanny let me," Billy replied.

Lizzie turned to the nurse and asked, "Is that true?"

"Poor little thing, what harm can he do?" the nurse wondered.

Lizzie exploded: "What harm can he do? In the first place, he's playing with a glass and could cut himself if it broke. In the second place, he's ruining the rug." Needless to say, the nurse's services were no longer required.

She tried to "remain firm with the boys," she said, but it wasn't always easy. When she came home at night she had a tendency to indulge them, to compensate for her absence. "That's a mistake," she admitted.

When she wasn't working, she gave them as much time as she could. On the weekends she and Bill, Sr. were home most of the time, and on their off days during the week, they were with little Billy and Robert. One time, she and Bill, Sr. went to Palm Springs for a few weeks without the kids, if only because she felt it was easier than "uprooting the boys."

"They didn't mind," she told *Photoplay*. "They prefer being at home."

Years later, Lizzie still felt she could have done more as a mother to all of her children. As she expressed to John Tesh on *One on One* in 1992, "Parenting is probably the toughest job anyone could ever have. I haven't been very good at it. But I think I've gotten better."

However, after she passed away, Billy Asher, Jr. appeared on MSNBC's *Headliners & Legends* in 2001, and said she was a "great parent." And although she believed she wasn't maternally accessible because of her career, from Billy's perspective, she provided nothing but unconditional love.

Each of her children acknowledged how fortunate they were to have had Lizzie as their mom; just as the *Bewitched* cast and crew appreciated working with her on the set.

As the show's executive producer Harry Ackerman said in 1988: "We were the luckiest people in the world to have someone as warmhearted and appealing as Elizabeth Montgomery."

Echoing what her friend Sally Kemp said upon first seeing Elizabeth do the "bunny nose" when they were kids, Ackerman concluded, "No one could twitch her nose like she did. Believe me, we all tried."

Once Lizzie walked away from *Bewitched*, she walked away for good. She would not twitch again on screen, except for a series of Japanese TV commercials in the 1980s, and American public service announcements for the visually impaired in the early 1990s. Beyond that, her famous facial tic became a harness around her adenoids. Over the years too many negative nose encounters took their toll, ad nauseam, and she could not always wriggle her way free.

According to what her friend Liz Sheridan said on *Bewitched: The E! True Hollywood Story* in 1999, Lizzie was not at all pleased when people asked her to twitch her nose.

But what was she to do? She retained one of the most dedicated followings in TV history—and in turn felt obligated to her fans. "They have given me what I have, and I'm grateful," she told *Screen Stars* magazine in 1965.

She liked a "normal amount of privacy," but she wasn't the "dark-glasses type" who scurried behind hedges or ducked out back doors every time a fan approached her for an autograph. If they were "reasonably courteous," she intoned, "I felt I should be also."

Years later, in 1989, she said, "People are nice. They really are . . . most of the time." Other times, not so much, as when a random parent would force their child to say hello. "This inevitably happens at least once a year," she said, "and it's heartbreaking."

On one occasion, she was shopping and a somewhat abrasive woman, with her reluctant preteen daughter in tow, approached Lizzie and made a scene. "You come over here and say 'hi' to Miss Montgomery," the mother insisted to her offspring.

"No," the child responded. "I don't want to."

Yet the woman insisted how much her daughter wanted to meet *Samantha*.

"If that's true," Lizzie wondered, "why is she yelling to the contrary?"

"She's just shy," the mother replied, and then to threaten her child, she said she'd told her that if she refused to greet the *Bewitched* star, the actress would twitch her nose and "turn her into a toad."

Lizzie was livid: "You told her *what*?! How *dare* you say such a thing? No wonder she's scared to death!"

Upon hearing that, the mother grabbed her daughter by the hand, and scuffed away in a fit of anger.

Another time, early in *Bewitched's* run, Elizabeth was filming a promotional spot on the set of *Bonanza*, as both series had the same sponsor (Chevrolet). "Every time I did the twitch," Lizzie remembered in 1989, the director of the spot would yell, "Cut!"

She thought, "What the hell is the matter? I'm getting bored with this. I thought I could do this in one take and then get out of here!"

No such luck. Suddenly, the director turned to someone on the set and said, "I don't know how she's ever going to do a series. She's got this terrible *twitch*!"

"Everybody was like, 'Oh, my God . . . he doesn't know,'" Lizzie laughed in recalling the awkward moment. "He saw the storyboards but just never made the connection. He must have been the most humiliated person. But I was hysterical."

A third uncomfortable public twitch encounter, this time, somewhat more intrusive, less comical, and downright insulting, occurred shortly after *Bewitched* debuted. As Elizabeth revealed in 1989, it happened one night in the ladies' room of Chasen's Restaurant in West Hollywood. "Of all the weird kinds of old fashioned places to be in," she said, "Right?"

"I was powdering my nose or whatever it was I was doing," she went on to explain, and this woman kept pacing back and forth in front of her. Lizzie was like, "What is going on here?"

She found out, when the woman approached her and said, "Pardon me, but I just have to ask you . . . *where did you get your nose job?*"

"Being the quick thinker that I am," she mused to herself, "Oh, God— what do I say? Don't say (anything like), 'My Mummy and Daddy gave it to me.' "

Instead she replied, "The Farmer's Market," which only further confounded the woman. But Lizzie continued taking delight in sending her inquisitor on a detour: "You know, there's a place called *The Coral Reef*, and right in back of that little kind of hut . . . there's a doctor's office . . . and it's absolutely amazing what they can do. I was only bruised for like a couple of days. They're fantastic."

"In California you can just find anything," the woman replied sincerely, if a little befuddled.

Lizzie recalled in 1989:

> To this day, I still think of that woman, because I knew she had to be a tourist. And then I thought, Why did I say "The Farmer's Market?" It just popped into my head . . . and I just had to make something up. But she was like, "Oh, wow! That's really great." And I just pictured this poor woman wandering around The Farmer's Market (looking for just the right plastic surgeon).

David White listened to Lizzie tell this story, and said the *nosy* woman should never have questioned his famous twitch-witching friend about such a delicate subject, not to mention, operation:

> She should have known that you didn't, if she looked at your nose, she would have realized that nose jobs sink after a while. A girl I knew in New York had one, and she was beautiful when she just had it done (but only) for a few years afterwards. And then I saw her later, and it had sunk . . .

because they take the bone out . . . and they put gristle in there or something. So it isn't as sturdy a bone like the bridge of your nose . . . Your nose is just like your Dad's.

While filming *Bewitched*, he and Lizzie would meet in the makeup room every morning, "And there she'd be," he said, "without any makeup on, and her hair pushed back. I used to think, 'She could never say *Robert Montgomery isn't my dad.*'"

"People do say that I look like him," Lizzie interrupted.

"Yes, around the eyes," David said.

"My Mom and Dad both had these (arched) eyebrows."

Overall, Lizzie may have shielded many aspects of her personal life from the press, specifically with regard to her marriages and other personal issues that she may have had, but a fine balance of her trademark humor and decorum ever lurked behind the scenes. On occasion, if selectively so, she was refreshingly honest and self-deprecating, whether discussing, for example, her father or her appearance. She cheerfully addressed both topics during an interview with *TV Radio Mirror* magazine in January 1965, concluding:

> I myself believe there was some kind of hocus-pocus afoot in my getting to be a TV star. In spite of my being Robert Montgomery's daughter, the odds were against me. I'm no Hollywood glamour girl, and my so-called "beauty" calls out for a plastic surgeon. I feel sorry for the poor makeup man in the morning. I'm his greatest challenge.

At the start of *Bewitched's* third season, executive producer Harry Ackerman offered the position of story editor to then-twenty-six-year-old *Bewitched* writer Doug Tibbles, who penned a few segments of the show including the "Nobody's Perfect" episode that introduced the catch phrase, "Mustn't twitch." But Tibbles, now seventy-two, turned down the job. He explains:

> I just didn't want to do it. I felt like I was good at the dialogue, but I just didn't like the show. It just didn't hold my interest. I just didn't care about it. It didn't mean anything to me. And I had a string of money coming in, which dried up later. But at the time, it seemed like I could pick and choose.

Because Tibbles rejected the promotion, Ackerman offered the position to Bernard Slade, who later became famous on Broadway for writing *Same Time Next Year* and for creating *The Partridge Family* for ABC in 1970. "To be honest," Tibbles says, "Slade was 'more qualified' for the job. I was too young. I was good with the dialogue and that's what I was known for. My trick was to 'make 'em laugh out loud' twice on a page, even if they couldn't use it, or even if Standards and Practices threw it out for some reason."

But according to how Lizzie felt about Tibbles' talents, his words weren't going to land anywhere except in the mouths of the *Bewitched* actors. For example, there's a "perfect" moment between *Samantha* and *Tabitha* that is quite touching and eloquent, and representative of the core "acceptance" message of the entire series. When *Sam* catches her daughter using witchcraft for the first time she experiences a circle of emotion, but ultimately pride and joy. She says:

> Oh, I know . . . I know what it is like to be part of the magical life, to have so much at your fingertips. But we're living in a world that isn't quite used to people like us. And I'm afraid they never will be. So, I'm going to have to be very firm with you. You're going to have to learn when you can use your witchcraft and when you can't. Now, your wonderful daddy wants us to be just plain people. So you're going to have to stop wiggling your fingers whenever you want something.

Besides "Nobody's Perfect," Tibbles penned "I Don't Want to Be a Toad, I Want to Be a Butterfly" and "*Samantha* the Sculptress," all of which he wrote while only in his mid-twenties.

"*Samantha* the Sculptress," from the fifth year, 1968–1969, involved very odd special effects that featured talking-head clay busts of *Darrin* and *Larry*. It was a quirky entry, just this side of *The Twilight Zone*.

"Toad/Butterfly," also from the fifth season, turned out to deliver what Lizzie considered to be one of the funniest lines in the entire series. The episode aired on December 12, 1968, and featured Maudie Prickett as *Mrs. Burch*, *Tabitha's* mortal teacher who talks with *Ruth Taylor* (Lola Fisher) about her daughter (and *Tabitha's* fellow classmate) *Amy Taylor* (played by Maralee Foster, and named for Doug Tibbles' real-life daughter).

Ruth Taylor: I understand about playing in the forest, I understand why
   you wanted to make my Amy a toad instead of a butterfly. But the fact
   is that my child is still missing.
Mrs. Burch: But I have never lost a child in all my years as a teacher.
Ruth Taylor: And you start by losing mine.
Mrs. Burch: Look—somehow I'll make it up to you.
Ruth Taylor: I'm calling the Police.

It was that second last line, "Look—somehow I'll make it up to you,"
to a parent about the misplacement of their child to which Lizzie took a
liking. "For whatever reason," Tibbles explains, "she loved that line."
Whether or not her appreciation of that line had anything to do with the
troubled kinship she experienced with her father Robert Montgomery is
left to the imagination.

In the meantime, Elizabeth's other core relationship of the day, her marriage to Bill Asher, may have already been in trouble. According to what
Tibbles can remember, the Montgomery-Asher-Richard Michaels triangle
began long before the final season of *Bewitched*. He, like William Froug,
saw signs of tension as early as season three, while working on "Nobody's
Perfect."

But before discussing the details of what Tibbles recalls about that complicated relationship, it's pertinent to provide some background on his own
fascinating life and career:

Doug is the son of the very successful writer George Tibbles, who
penned the pilot for *My Three Sons* (which starred Fred MacMurray) and
that sitcom's subsequent first season. He also wrote episodes of fantasy shows
such as *The Munsters*; both to which Doug would also contribute scripts.
Doug also wrote episodes for *Happy Days* and, just as with *Bewitched*, he
was offered the story editor position on that show. This time, however, he
accepted the job. For five hours. Then, as he recalls, "I said to myself,
"That's it! I'm never doing it [writing a TV sitcom] again!"

"It was my father's business," he explains, "and I just jumped into it
because I needed the dough. My dad was a piano player who always wanted
to be a writer, and I was a drummer who never wanted to be a writer. But
I didn't like writing, even though I was successful at it."

Because of his father's musical and subsequent writing success, from the time he was a child and on into his twenties, Doug found himself hobnobbing the Hollywood party circuit. His father played the piano in the 1940s and toured with the likes of the legendary Eddie Cantor. Doug accompanied him to the crossroads of the Los Angeles Union Station, where he would meet Cantor, as well as Charlie Chaplin, Ed Gwynn, and Lou Costello, all with whom George Tibbles had been associated. "And I was only seven years old!" Doug exclaims. "It was an amazing time. I mean, we used to go to places like [director] Walter Lang's house, just to play cards. I even remember playing cards with a twenty-year-old R. J. (Robert) Wagner, and Fred and June MacMurray before my Dad even really knew them or did *My Three Sons.*"

Others on the Tibbles party circuit included the iconic Elizabeth Taylor and Alan Ladd. It was Ladd who starred in the classic 1953 feature film, *Shane,* which as Bill Asher explained in *The Bewitched Book,* was the basis of the "*Shane* Theory":

Shane was a gunslinger who only used his weapons as a last resort; first he would address the issues at hand with his wit, his intelligence, even his humor. When all else failed, then he would bring out the big guns and save the day. That's how Bill explained the power of the twitch to Lizzie who was initially impatient with *Samantha* holding back her witchcraft. She should not overuse the twitch, Asher cautioned. "You're *Shane!*" he told her. "You don't twitch until the audience wants you to."

Doug Tibbles, meanwhile, was not holding anything back, and his perspective as a child and teenager growing up in Hollywood was always clear. Except occasionally . . . as when he'd confuse Lizzie's father Robert Montgomery with George Montgomery, both of whom frequently visited the home of early film idol Van Johnson, where Doug and his family attended parties.

Doug recalls one party in particular at the home and pool of Dean Martin, Lizzie's co-star from *Who's Been Sleeping in My Bed?* Standing by the pool at Martin's home, Tibbles was approached by none other than actress Janet Leigh. "Doug," she began to ask, "would you like a drink?"

"Want a drink?" he reiterates today. "I don't even know how she knew my *name?!*"

However, everyone at the party certainly knew Leigh's identity. She was a respected actress, who became best known for two creations, both of which are connected to Lizzie: Leigh's *shower-stealing* performance as *Marion Crane* in Alfred Hitchcock's classic 1960 film, *Psycho*, which starred Anthony Perkins, who was good friends with *Bewitched's* Dick York; and Jamie Lee Curtis, Leigh's daughter with actor Tony Curtis, who also fathered David and Greg Lawrence (though not with Leigh), the twins who played *Darrin* and *Samantha's* son *Adam* in the last three seasons of *Bewitched*.

Also, too, of course, Martin was a member of the Rat Pack, which included Sammy Davis, Jr., Peter Lawford, and Frank Sinatra, all of whom knew Lizzie. . . . and Doug Tibbles. He remembers visiting Sinatra's home:

> We knew his daughter Nancy, and Dean Martin's kids, too. We knew all of them. You see, to grow up in L.A. at that time, if you were our age, and went to our high school (Hollywood High), you would have gone to Sinatra's house, too.

At one point, Doug had also befriended Jim Mitchum, younger brother to classic screen idol Robert Mitchum. As he recalls:

> Bob Mitchum called my house and spoke to my Mother, as I was standing right next to her. He wanted to take me to Greece with the Mitchum family. But I didn't want to go, and I told my Mother that. I knew they just wanted me to keep Jim busy, and I didn't feel like playing babysitter to Jim Mitchum.

On yet another occasion, Doug had made contact with another legendary actor. He explains:

> Marlon Brando was having a meeting with director Walter Lang. But we didn't even look at him. It was no big deal to me and my friends. We grew up with movie stars' kids. By that time, we were teenagers, and all we cared about was looking at pretty girls. Other than that, we really didn't give a shit. I was numb and desensitized to the whole celebrity game.

Flash-forward a decade or so to *Bewitched*: From Tibbles' perspective, he had known and grown up with A-list movie stars. So when he arrived on the *Samantha* series, he explains, he still felt the glitter and glamour of the big screen, and television was a step down for him. But he was still impressed with the small screen charisma of the stars of *Bewitched*, namely, Lizzie and Dick York.

"Dick was a nice guy," he says, ". . . a gentleman," while he remembers Lizzie as "not the least bit arrogant." In fact, Doug continues, "she was one of the kindest people in the entire business, along with Andy Griffith and Dean Martin" (both with whom he had collaborated on various projects). "She was always lady-like, always polite and down to earth. And she was always very nice to me."

So nice, in fact, it used to rile Bill Asher, especially one day, when Lizzie approached Doug and said, "We think you're marvelous!" She was referring to herself and Asher, who was standing beside her. But according to Doug, "Bill didn't seem to take that too well. He just seemed like a jealous husband. It was seemingly a rough time in their marriage . . . he was very on edge."

Shortly after Lizzie complimented Doug, he met with Asher and Michaels to discuss one of his scripts. Bill asked Doug to rewrite a few pages of dialogue. Doug agreed, but apparently, not to Bill's immediate or complete satisfaction. "Okay, Bill," he said, "but I'm not going to fake it and pretend that I can come up with a few lines now; let me go home and think it over."

Asher went ballistic, and screamed, "You're a professional, Doug! And you should be able to come up with something on the spot!"

Taken aback by Asher's response, Doug thought, "What is *wrong* with him?" Upon hearing Asher's tantrum, Doug didn't know what to think and he had a knee-jerk reaction. But in time, he saw the big picture. He explains:

> I got so mad, that I took the script—which was not bound, and threw it in the air; and it came fluttering down all over the floor, and I left. Young and impetuous, I was saying things like, "[Forget] this! I'm not doing this shit!" And I ran out the door and out onto the Screen Gems lot. It was Richard Michaels who then chased after me, running outside into that lot. I just remember him saying, "Doug, please come back." And I may be wrong about this, but I thought something was going on *then* between Richard and Elizabeth, and I don't know how well known it was. There was definite tension in the offices, not so much on the set. But you could feel it in the offices, especially with Asher. I mean, here I am a young guy, and Elizabeth was saying I was marvelous, and I'm not making myself out to be Rock

Hudson. All I'm saying is that when she paid the slightest bit of attention to someone else in any way, it seemed to bother him.

When asked why Asher didn't fire Michaels if he knew about the affair with Lizzie at this stage of the game, Doug replied:

> But that's just it. I don't think he knew. That's my guess. He might not have believed it. It's like after we all found out none of us could believe that she would do that. I'm not saying that she wouldn't have done it out of fear of Bill Asher, but that she didn't seem like the kind of "fooling-around" girl. I mean, the way she looked, she didn't seem like the kind that would go sneaking-around. That's just my perception today.

In further retrospect, Doug finds it ironic that it was Michaels who chased him down on the Columbia studio lot to reconcile with Asher after their confrontation. He explains further:

> Dick Michaels was a really nice guy and very level-headed no matter what happened. And to clarify, I had no idea what exactly was going on. I just noticed a jealous man in Bill Asher. And only later did I piece things together. But you wouldn't have pictured Dick Michaels in an affair with Elizabeth, and you wouldn't have pictured her in an affair with *anyone*. And I hate to say this, but either way, I really didn't give a shit. I was like, "Just get me out of here!"

Today, Tibbles is living his musical dream. With songwriter wife Barbara Keith and stepson John Tibbles, they headline the respected trio, *The Stone Coyotes*, based in Greenfield, Massachusetts. Barbara is on the electric guitar and vocals, John plays bass, and Doug plays drums.

In Tibbles' *Bewitched* episode "To Twitch Or Not To Twitch," which aired in the show's fourth season, *Samantha* and her ad-man husband *Darrin* bicker over the use of witchcraft. It's an especially dicey disagreement this time, because her not doing so ultimately causes him embarrassment at a client's dinner party.

Whether or not certain impediments had developed behind the scenes in previous seasons, by the show's eight and final year, 1971–1972, all hell broke loose. Lizzie was growing if not tired of *Bewitched*, at least slightly weary of the notoriety that came along with the "nose job." She was also hurt. Her marriage to Bill Asher was in trouble. As Asher told A&E's *Biography* in 1999, "The show itself was not as strong as it had been. And that bothered her, and so she said, 'I don't want to do it anymore.'"

Sixteen

Temperatures Rising

"We enjoy each other. Our interests are the same; I think our
temperaments go together."

—Elizabeth, describing her relationship with Bill Asher, two years
before they separated, *Modern Screen Magazine*, July 1970

According to *The Schenectady Gazette*, in the fall of 1971, Bill Asher had
noticed an attractive professional ice skater–turned–New York actress in a
toothpaste commercial. She was the perfect fit for the role of a female expert
skater he was seeking to cast for the *Bewitched* episode "*Samantha* on Thin
Ice." Upon his invitation, Nancy Fox flew to the West Coast, on her dime,
for an interview. Charming and talented, Fox could act and skate at the
same time, and she won the role, Asher's heart, and a regular spot on a new
series he was developing.

But he was on thin ice with Lizzie. Their days were numbered and by
the summer of 1972, they separated. Hollywood columnist Marilyn Beck
confirmed the news, August 4, 1972:

> [While the] Elizabeth Montgomery–Bill Asher estrangement continues,
> Asher is managing to snap out of the blues a bit with the help of actress
> Nancy Fox. She is the young cutie who portrays the nervous student nurse
> in Asher's new *Temperatures Rising* ABC series. His attentions on and off the
> set are making her feel much less nervous about her first shot at stardom.

And this from *The Los Angeles Times*, August 30, 1972:

Now Nancy Fox, who plays the nurse in *Temperatures Rising*, is said to be helping raise Asher's temperature lately.

He was working overtime on *Rising*, developing another sitcom, *The Paul Lynde Show*, and allowing his marriage to Lizzie to fizzle. Consequently, it was now clear that she had found at least a measure of comfort in the arms of Asher's *Bewitched* protégé Richard Michaels, who explained it all to *Entertainment Tonight* (E.T.) in 2006. By the eighth and final year of *Bewitched*, his and Lizzie's friendship had developed in a "deeper way," he said. It was something they both tried to "repress. But as the year went on, it became more and more compelling."

So they moved into a one-bedroom apartment in West Los Angeles and kept their affair hidden. Reports in the press suggested she had retired and moved to Europe. But Michaels said such was not the case. Lizzie simply did not want to be hounded by the tabloid media. So they kept their relationship a secret.

By 1986, Asher hired Michaels to direct an episode of his CBS drama series *Kay O'Brien*. According to what Michaels conveyed in 2006 on E.T., any animosity that may have existed between the two men had dissolved. "That was then," Asher told him. "This is now."

Michaels said he and Lizzie were friendly until the end. It proved challenging, but "anytime something like this happens, it's always tough on the principals," he said, as if they were actors performing in a play. "It was tough saying good-bye. But absolutely we were on good terms when it broke."

It's been nearly five decades since he and Lizzie were together, but as Michaels told E.T., he still thinks of her as *Samantha*, even though he knew her as Elizabeth all those years before. "I don't think any of us can forget the sweet lady who could twitch her nose and make everything okay in the world," he said.

Michaels, who retired from directing in 1994, lives in Maui, Hawaii. Ironically, his daughter, Meredith Michaels-Beerbaum, shared a love of horses with Elizabeth, as she was the first woman to be ranked Number One in the world in equestrian show jumping.

In time—if not *just* in time—Bill Asher realized his liaison with Fox was a mistake and blamed himself for his divorce from Lizzie. In 1999, he appeared on A&E's *Biography* and admitted that ". . . the whole thing was my fault. I was going to work every morning and she was doing nothing. And it got to her. And she finally took off. I was very angry that she left. So I left."

Apparently with Fox, and then Lizzie divorced him in 1974. But in 1976, Fox was out of the picture and Asher married actress Joyce Bulifant, who subsequently divorced him in 1993. Since 1998, he's been married to Meredith Asher.

Through it all, Lizzie had found a "fox" of her own—Robert Fox-worth—whom she met on the set of *Mrs. Sundance* in 1973. He became the only other man in her life, the one she frequently referred to as the love of her life.

Nancy Fox, a childhood friend of *Charlie's Angels* star Jaclyn Smith, would continue acting, at least through the 1980s, when she'd appear in films like, ironically enough, *Warlock*, released in 1989. It was in 1982 that she appeared in what is arguably her largest role: the lead for *The Sonja Henie Story*, a feature film based on the life of the Norwegian blonde Olympic star and ice-skating movie queen of the 1940s.

Beyond that, she was never heard from again, at least publicly. She now leads a quiet life in New York, which is how she always wanted it. In November 1977, she repeated to *The Youngstown Vindicator* almost exactly what Lizzie said to *Look* magazine in 1965: "I don't care about being a big star. I don't even think I'd like that. I just want to stay well-adjusted and happy."

While Lizzie and Nancy may have had more in common than either may have realized, *Bewitched* co-star Irene Vernon felt left out in the cold, pushed to the curb. She had played *Louise Tate* on the show before she was replaced by Kasey Rogers or, as Vernon said in 1988, "I was fired!"

Apparently, it was because of her friendship with Danny Arnold, the show's original producer. According to Vernon, Bill and Lizzie were not at all fond of Arnold. So, they let her go in the spring of 1966, the end of the second season. "Devastated," Vernon then left Hollywood, geographically and figuratively, and gravitated towards a more successful career, in real estate, in Beverly Hills.

In the big scheme of things, some actors are willing to do whatever it takes to make it in Hollywood. Others, like Fox and Vernon, vote against a *no-holds-barred* approach and leave show business behind, savoring their lives and their sanity in the process.

Performers like Elvis and Michael Jackson, for example, were not so lucky. They didn't know when to stop. They succumbed to the intoxicating environment the entertainment industry provides, almost like a drug; and in some cases, exactly like a drug. There's so much opportunity, so much potential to succeed, and when that success arrives, it simply becomes too much to handle.

Fortunately, in Lizzie's case, she was never forced to choose between a career and personal happiness. She was born into wealth and status that stabilized her life, at least financially. Although her father was demanding and she for many years lived in his shadow, Elizabeth would later carve out her own brand of stardom that allowed her the luxury to pick and choose to work as she pleased. In short, even with her various issues, she had her head on straight.

Entertainment curator Rob Ray explains it all:

One type of performer is the tenacious, career-is-all person with the determination to succeed at all costs. They will succeed at anything they strive hard enough to do because nothing else in their life matters. Most classic stars like Bette Davis, John Wayne, and Lucille Ball fall into this category . . . today, maybe even George Clooney, Tom Cruise, and Oprah Winfrey, certainly. Another type is the person who has the drive but can't cope with the pressures of the business. As a result, they crash and burn with their life ending in tragedy. Marilyn Monroe and Judy Garland and now, unfortunately, Whitney Houston, are classic examples of vulnerable souls who couldn't handle the pressures. But most people fall into a third category. They have the desire to make it, but whether they succeed or not, once they realize what sacrifices and struggles a career entails, they decide for their own personal happiness and survival to leave the table. Their survival instinct impels them to move on. Greta Garbo is the ultimate example from the classic film era, and I suspect Irene Vernon and Nancy Fox, and even Elizabeth herself, to a certain extent, fell into this third category, too. For most people, career isn't everything. Personal happiness and fulfillment is. For that group, life is too short to deal with the stress of show business day in and day out, and Elizabeth knew that.

Cliff Robertson was Lizzie's good friend in the early, pre-*Bewitched* portion of her career. Other than that, he didn't know much about, for one, her relationship with Bill Asher, because as he said, "I didn't know him. But I do know he was very possessive, and a rather domineering figure, although he was a little fellow. And maybe because he was so short a fellow, he had a complex?"

During the *Bewitched* years, Robertson didn't see much of Lizzie, whom he affectionately referred to as "Lizbel" (as if she needed yet another nickname!). "She went into an envelope," he says and the closest he came to her in those days was through mutual friends whom he'd periodically stop and ask, "Have you seen Lizbel?"

One day, however, at a restaurant in Santa Monica, he finally ran into her, walking out the door with Asher. By that time, Robertson was set to marry his second wife, Cynthia Stone, who was by his side. "I wanted to introduce Elizabeth to my new bride-to-be," he said. When his Lizbel caught sight of him, much to Asher's displeasure, she shrieked, "Oh, Cliff! It is so great to see you!"

"We hugged," Robertson recalled, "I guess, in what would be perceived as a typical Hollywood encounter. I don't think Bill was too pleased. He seemed a little bit impatient with her as if to say, 'Quit talking to this silly actor.' But I didn't give a damn, because I was just seeing an old friend." From this brief encounter, and from what he heard through the Hollywood grapevine, Robertson perceived that Asher was exerting a "certain control" over Lizzie. "He was very protective of her in that way. From a professional standpoint, at least from what I can gather, it proved beneficial for her. From a personal standpoint, I don't think he ever had it so good."

Bewitched actor David White agreed. In 1989, while in Lizzie's presence, White assessed the Montgomery-Asher marriage/business relationship in one sentence: "She was tremendously supportive of him almost to the point of sainthood."

Upon hearing that, Lizzie added: "Bill was such a good director and if it hadn't been for him, [*Bewitched*] wouldn't have happened anyway. But I tell you, there were times when I was frustrated, and I'm sure there were times when he was just as frustrated with me."

As if on cue, David then recalled when Bill directed a scene with him and Lizzie. He was proud of his performance that day, and assumed Bill was going to say "Print!" after the scene was completed. "But he didn't," David recalled.

Lizzie chimed in with each account of his memory of that day:

> David: One time Liz and I did a scene and it was just marvelous. She was so spontaneous and she was so great. And we didn't quite finish, and suddenly Bill says, "Cut! Now, quit horsing around, Liz!" Remember that?
>
> Lizzie: I sure do.
>
> David: And she looked at me like, *Who's crazy here?*
>
> Lizzie: I was like, "What is going on?"
>
> David: Well, I thought I'm gonna get him a book on directing. You're supposed to watch the actors.
>
> Lizzie: Boy, that was funny.
>
> David: It was so beautiful, you know.
>
> Lizzie: I remember that.
>
> David: You were in shock.
>
> Lizzie: I know. Asher always figured that I should know what he meant even when he didn't say anything, which wasn't true, necessarily.
>
> David: Not necessarily.
>
> Lizzie: He was wonderful with the guest actors and stuff. He could always think of nineteen different ways on how to tell them to open a door if that was absolutely necessary.
>
> David: And he did often.
>
> Lizzie: Yes, he did.

To David's surprise, Lizzie recalled a tense moment of her own with Bill on the *Bewitched* set, when they weren't exactly on the same page . . . of the script. The incident transpired while filming the fifth season segment, "*Samantha's* Power Failure," during which Lizzie happened to be pregnant with their last child, daughter Rebecca, while Bill was about to have a baby all on his own:

> We had a short day for some reason, and there was some party being given on the next stage. And I had been running back and forth between stages to check the lighting for a lengthy scene that Bill planned to direct on the following day.

However, he surprised her and said, "Well, as long as we're set up for it, let's do that speech where you appeal to the Witches Council." It was an intricate special effects–ridden scene that would also include Agnes Moorehead, who would be stationed at a lower level of the set, glancing up at Lizzie as *Samantha* chatted with the Council. But Lizzie was unprepared to shoot the scene and shocked at Bill's demands.

"*Holy shit!*" she thought. "*What does he mean? I haven't even looked at that scene!*"

So she told him, straight out:

"I don't know it."

"Well, why not?"

"Because I wasn't supposed to know it until tomorrow."

"You mean you don't look ahead?"

"Bill!! What do you mean, 'I don't look ahead?' Of course, I do. But this is a long scene."

"You can handle it. Just throw yourself into the witches' robes [the black frock or 'flying suit' that *Samantha* was prone to wear when she meant serious witch business], and let's get going. Let's not waste any more time. We've got another forty-five minutes."

Lizzie was furious, but as usual, she deferred to Bill's discretion, and did what he requested. She retreated to her dressing room to change and to give the script a quick study or, as she said, "To look at this damn thing, and try to memorize it, feverishly."

But there was more trouble ahead. Suddenly, there were visitors on the set and not just regular visitors, but crew members' wives. "And wives of the crew are never trustful of their husbands, anyway," Lizzie recalled. "They really aren't."

By this time, she's uncomfortable for several reasons. 1) She's frustrated with Bill's impatient demands for her to know lines she did not need to remember until the next day. 2) She's feeling the various physical discomforts of being pregnant. 3) Potentially jealous crew members' wives are now roaming the set. 4) The watchful eye of Agnes Moorehead is ever present.

When Bill finally said, "Okay—let's get through this once," Lizzie was out of sorts to say the least, but trudged on to face the music—or at least the conductor.

"Can we just go ahead and shoot it?" she asked.

"No!" Bill insisted. "I just wanna go ahead and *run it!*"

Lizzie caved, "Okay."

She then found her mark on the set, readied her lines, and with "Aggie standing right there in front" of her, she heard this woman say, "Jesus Christ! She's fat. I had no idea she was that fat!" A jealous crew member's wife had spoken—and Lizzie was her victim.

Oh, how nice, Lizzie thought upon hearing that hurtful phrase, just as Bill was about to scream one very important word: "Action!" But instead, he yelled "Cut!"

Lizzie was trying to concentrate on her lines and they went through the scene twice. But after hearing that disturbing comment, as she recalled, "I just couldn't remember what the hell I was doing, and Bill blew up":

> You're not concentrating! This is ridiculous. There is no reason under the sun why you shouldn't be able to do this.

"Under any other circumstances I would have agreed with him," she mused in 1989.

But at least there was a break in the clouds and no one was more surprised than Lizzie at what transpired next:

> Do you know that Aggie turned to me and said, "Don't let him get you down. You can do it!" And that was the first time she ever said anything like that to me, because she knew it was beginning to get to me. So I took this big deep breath and said, "Okay—let's go then!"

The result? One of the most beloved scenes in the entire series:

> *Samantha*, in her elegant ebony and emerald robe, defending herself, *Cousin Serena* and *Uncle Arthur* before the high court of the Witches Council, which has stripped them of their powers. By this time, *Sam* had ignored the Council's demand that she end her mortal marriage, and her cousin and uncle stood firm in support of their favorite relative. Mouthing words that represented the core message of *Bewitched* as well as Lizzie's own philosophy, *Sam* said to her magical elders: "Remember the Witch burnings at Salem? Remember the innocent who were condemned simply for being different? Remember your rage at that injustice? Well, aren't you guilty of

the same injustice? Aren't you condemning me simply because I choose to be different? You can take away my powers but I'll always be a witch. It's you—the highest of all courts—who are taking the risk—[risking] your integrity—your right to sit in judgment."

Three years later, in what became *Bewitched's* swan season, 1971–1972, ABC had scheduled its once-supernatural powerhouse against CBS's new reality-based sitcom ratings' giant *All in the Family*, which though it began with a slow start in 1971, became the "eye" network's staple of newly crowned contemporary comedies. By this time, the network had rid itself of country-geared hits like *Mayberry R.F.D.* (1968–1971; a spin-off and continuation of *The Andy Griffith Show*, which had debuted in 1960), *The Beverly Hillbillies* (1962–1971), *Green Acres* (1965–1971), and *Petticoat Junction* (1963–1970); each perhaps more realistic than the fantasy fare presented by *Bewitched*, but nowhere near the edgy modern truths that would mark the scripts of producer Norman Lear's *All in the Family*, and his subsequent CBS spin-offs like *Maude* (1972–1978), *The Jeffersons* (1975–1985), and others of this ilk.

The issue-laden adventures of *Archie* and *Edith Bunker* (played by the Emmy-winning Carroll O'Connor and Jean Stapleton) on CBS' *All in the Family* were very different than the magic escapades of *Samantha* and *Darrin* on ABC's *Bewitched*. The television landscape had changed, right along with the times, and viewers were apparently ready for the alterations, although *Bewitched* executive producer Harry Ackerman once relayed how the networks were too quick to make such sweeping changes. "There was room for all kinds of programming," he said. Most assuredly, he was referring to *Bewitched*, which in fact, was renewed for three more seasons in the spring of 1970, the end of its seventh year.

But Lizzie had first resigned from the show in the spring of 1969, the close of its fifth season which just so happened to be Dick York's final semester as *Darrin*. At that point, certain terms were renegotiated in a new four-year deal that was put in place for seasons six and seven with a mutual option for seasons eight and nine. An additional *Bewitched* TV-movie would then follow in the tenth year, but only if both sides—Columbia, and Lizzie and Bill Asher—agreed upon all terms. If not, one party could not then force the other to undertake the optional year.

Before season seven commenced in the fall of 1970, that year would be designated as its final semester. Screen Gems and ABC then renegotiated another deal with Lizzie and Bill, granting them close to 80 percent of the show's ownership, along with complete creative control, which in effect they had always had, except that now it was official. It was also a way of sticking it to Jackie Cooper for the way he had treated them in 1963, when the show was first developed.

Consequently, in March of 1971, it was announced that *Bewitched* would be back for its eighth season, and *that* would become its last year in production. Somewhere in the midst of that final season (circa March 1972), Lizzie consented to a ninth year and then, after everyone else had agreed to move forward, she changed her mind. ABC once more met with their favorite star and offered her the farm, as it were. She politely listened, thanked all attending parties, but declined their generous offer, and that was that.

In the interim, Bill Asher admittedly made some personal and professional missteps. He spent too much time on the sets of ABC's *Temperatures Rising* and *The Paul Lynde Show*, both of which he and Lizzie bartered to produce in place of *Bewitched* through their Ashmont production company which was still in operation. At which point, Richard Michaels could have easily stepped in as *Samantha's* core producer/director, if not Lizzie's potential next husband.

Peter Ackerman remembers hearing a conversation between his parents, *Bewitched* executive producer Harry Ackerman and *Father Knows Best* actress Elinor Donahue, who were unaware of his close proximity. It had to do with Lizzie and another crew member, possibly Michaels, approaching his father about continuing *Bewitched*, "obviously pushing Bill Asher out."

He explains:

My dad, as loyal a man as you could ever meet, determined not to stab Bill in the back like that, and kindly but firmly told Liz and the other fellow "no." I recall another part of that same conversation between my parents which, if true, is a bit salacious and would only be seen as gossip today. So I will keep that to myself. I do recall that on this very same day Bill Asher and his kids came over to the house, probably to commiserate with my dad. I was out playing with his and Liz's kids and I told Willie, their oldest son about what I overheard; both what I shared here and what I did not. And I realize now that it probably got back innocently to one or both parents. Again, we were young and would not have had the filters to keep things to ourselves. I still believe to this day that I may be the reason that the Asher kids never came to play with us again. Years later Bill mentioned that right after that visit, Liz made it clear that their kids were no longer to go to our house. It could be that Willie shared what I said to him with his mom and dad and because of that, or perhaps only because Liz was disappointed that my dad did not continue the show with her and the other fellow, [that] made her decide to separate herself from the Ackerman family as much as possible, including not having her kids play [with us].

As time went on, Peter never sensed any hard feelings between the two families. "My parents would see Lizzie at events," he says, and in 1975, his father took to him visit her on the set of *The Legend of Lizzie Borden*, "and she could not have been nicer to me or my dad."

Harry Ackerman passed away in 1991 and Lizzie entertained the idea of attending the service, for which Bill Asher hosted the post-funeral gathering with his then-wife, actress Joyce Bulifant, *Marie Slaughter* on *The Mary Tyler Moore Show*, and mother of John Asher (former husband to Jenny McCarthy). "But ultimately," Peter says, "Liz decided not to attend."

In 1997, the Asher family organized a surprise seventy-fifth birthday party for Bill, who was by then divorced from Bulifant, and now married to Meredith Asher. Peter was invited to the bash, along with many of the *Bewitched* crew. Also in attendance were two of the Ashers' adult children, Billy, Jr. and Rebecca, both with whom, Peter says, he "happily, and most importantly, was able to reestablish contact." Unfortunately, he says, the Ashers' middle child, Robert, did not attend the gathering.

There was likely a large list of directors/producers who could have easily taken the *Bewitched* reigns in Bill Asher's absence, even with another actor besides Dick York or Dick Sargent potentially playing a *third Darrin*. But there was only one *Samantha*, and she was portrayed by the irreplaceable Elizabeth Montgomery—who was simply not interested in moving forward with the series.

Consequently, ABC developed and aired *The Paul Lynde Show* and what ultimately became *The New Temperatures Rising Show* with Lynde replacing James Whitmore from the old *Temperatures Rising* sitcom, all of which aired in place of *Bewitched's* nonexistent ninth season and subsequent TV-movie sequel (intended for the 1972–1974 seasons).

But when *Bewitched* switched to Saturday nights in the fall of 1971 to do battle against *All in the Family*, Lizzie had chosen not to continue with the series, even though ABC had opted to renew it. She was tired and viewing episodes from that eighth year, that became abundantly evident to the audience. Beyond the "liberated woman" braless look that she was sporting by that time (as was Marlo Thomas as *Ann Marie* in the final season of ABC's *That Girl*, 1966–1971), Lizzie looked as though she was dragging her feet in every scene. By this time, too, Dick Sargent was into his third season playing *Darrin,* and the show started reworking previous Dick York episodes. It remains puzzling as to why Bill Asher and company simply did not hire an entirely new batch of writers to create all new scripts. Instead, many of the show's episodes in that final year were mere retreads of previous segments.

Essentially, the rewriting of such scripts paved the way for the writing on the wall, and the end was near for *Bewitched*. Peter Ackerman remembers those final hours:

> Although I was young I had a sense then that it had run its course. I remember watching a "new" episode with my grandmother, in which *Darrin* was squawking through his living room dressed as a chicken or something and I recall thinking, "This show is starting to get too silly," although I never told my dad that.

In the eyes of Ackerman, the *Bewitched* cancellation "cancelled something else. With it or, more to the point, because of it, Bill and Liz ended their marriage."

By then, Screen Gems/Columbia was co-producing the series with Ashmont Productions, Lizzie and Bill's company that took its cue from Desilu Productions, presided over by Desi Arnaz and Lucille Ball. A pattern was beginning to take shape, for better and for worse, with female TV stars and their business partner/husbands, one that Jackie Cooper had first recognized with Donna Reed and her business partner/husband Tony Owen and their power struggle over *The Donna Reed Show.*

Yet, whereas Reed and Owen stayed together until after the *Donna* show's demise, the end of Ball's half-hour weekly series *I Love Lucy* in 1957 was followed by her real-life marriage dissolution from husband and show producer Arnaz. Twenty years later when *The Mary Tyler Moore Show* ended its CBS run in 1977, Moore called it quits with her show producer/husband Grant Tinker. After CBS gave the pink slip to *The Carol Burnett Show* in 1978, Carol gave walking papers to her husband and *Burnett* show producer Joe Hamilton. When Sonny & Cher ended their famous *CBS Comedy Hour* in 1974, so did they end their real-life once wedded bliss. Now *Bewitched* was closing its doors, and so soon would be the Montgomery/Asher love affair.

As writer K.V. Burroughs expressed in *Movieland and TV Time* magazine, September 1972:

> If I were to repeat rumors of reasons the Ashers may have decided to call it a day, it would be talking about something I simply know nothing about and refuse to pass along. It really isn't important and is between Liz and Bill. It is sad and obviously must be painful to both of them. Divorces are very painful and create a sense of failure in both parties. There are always the questions, *Where did we go wrong? We were so much in love. How could it be gone? Was it my fault?* Sometimes there just are not good answers to any of these questions, but they still torture the two who are going through the death of their love. It is even worse if love is still strong in one of the parties and not in the other. At any rate, no divorce comes about overnight. It takes years of marriage erosion to cause two wonderful people like the Ashers to decide to call it a day. It takes a lot of intolerable living to be convinced that the children would be better off with two separate parents than one unhappy pair trying to hide their marital trouble from the eyes of their little children. If it is true that they have decided to divorce, it is a great tragedy for them and we are sorry to hear it. Liz would not be the first wife to deny trouble in her marriage right up to the last minute. There have been cases in Hollywood where stars denied splitting even on the day they filed for divorce. So far as we know, Elizabeth is resting after a long run in a very popular TV series. The Ashers should have no money problems because the series has made them wealthy. It is a time for resting and thinking and reviewing their lives. Perhaps in the more relaxed atmosphere they will decide to go on together. We'll all know soon enough. Meantime keep your fingers crossed. I am.

As an item from *The Daily Star* reported in 1974, Burroughs' noble words and heartfelt wish did not prove prescient.

> *Bewitched* actress Elizabeth Montgomery has divorced her husband of 10 years, director William Asher. The reason for the divorce is unknown at present. In the divorce settlement, Liz was given the house and full sole custody of their three children, William, 10, Robert, 9, and Rebecca Elizabeth, 4. William Asher was given full unlimited access to their children. Elizabeth does not wish to discuss her divorce. All she will say is, "I had to divorce Bill. It was too painful to continue, and I think our children would be better off with two separate parents than one unhappy pair trying to hide their marital troubles from them. I do have my children to consider. They are so young, especially Rebecca. I have to think of what's best for them."

Lizzie was always thinking what was best for *everyone*. And whatever personal or professional relationships she established by way of *Bewitched*, whether with Bill Asher, Agnes Moorehead, Dick York, Dick Sargent, David White, Paul Lynde, Richard Michaels, or any number of the cast and crew, she made a lasting impression on each of them. As R. Robert Rosenbaum, one of the show's directors, explained in *The Bewitched Book*:

> Elizabeth was a very caring person. She was one of the most loved actors in our business. It was fun working on *Bewitched*, and she helped make that happen. The whole crew adored her. She was sincerely interested in the welfare of everyone and their families.

In that same publication, Michaels added:

> Liz was the darling of the *Bewitched* set. She was just as friendly with the go-fer as she was with the director. She immediately disarmed people, and not everyone is like that, especially in the entertainment industry. She was a dream come true.

Actor Art Metrano (*Joanie Loves Chachi*, *Baretta*) was featured in several *Bewitched* episodes, initially, "*Samantha's* Wedding Present," which aired in the fifth season. In 1990, he summarized his years on the series, as well as the show's series of events:

Bewitched was the second show of my Hollywood career. Bill Asher became a big supporter of my career. He hired me in early 1970 to play a garbage man on my very first *Bewitched* show. I kiddingly said to him, "Please let me know when this will air so I can call my mom in Brooklyn." Bill did let me know when it would air and hired me for many other episodes of *Bewitched*. I would say it was Burt Metcalfe who cast the show, and Bill Asher who directed, got my career started in Hollywood. From that show at the Columbia lot, I was hired to do many other TV shows. Elizabeth was always nice to guests on the show and years later her daughter Rebecca and my daughter Roxanne became friends during their high school years. I remember Dick York as always being in pain and David White and Dick Sargent as being two terrific guys.

In the end, the rise and fall of *Bewitched*, as well as the Montgomery/Asher marriage, was a learning experience for all, especially Lizzie. As she explained at length in 1989:

I learned a lot from being on *Bewitched* . . . People were so willing to let you in on their secrets or their not-so-secret likes and dislikes about what they were doing . . . from props to the gaffer . . . to lighting . . . to cinematography. It's not like it was this closed kind of shop where they didn't want to share their expertise. They enjoyed telling other people how good they were and what they did, and they had a damn good right to be proud of what they did because everybody did it so well. I have fond memories of these people and the reason is because we shared so much. It's not like we were isolated. You'd be hard-put to be isolated from anybody you'd worked with for eight years unless you're a total *do-do.*

I always thought it was like going to college. It really was like taking a course, and I learned an enormous amount on every level. And I don't think I ever missed a day. And the thing I found most amazing, was that any member of any crew at any given time is infinitely more important than the actors on the set, because they are so expert in what they're doing. If you ask them, 90 percent of them are more than willing to help, to tell you that this is that . . . and that is what that plug is . . . and that's what that light does.

It's a fascinating business, and what I found so rewarding is that I was never bored . . . never . . . for one minute. And a lot of people can sit around and be bored (on any set). I've noticed that. But there's never any reason to sit around and be bored because there's a whole lot of other stuff you can be doing. I think being bored is extremely boring and unproductive. There's just no excuse for it . . .

I learned about special effects. I learned a whole lot about a whole lot of stuff. I learned about things that I never even thought existed before. It's just a revelation to me. It's just so much more fun. And it makes you appreciate what everyone else is doing. And that the crew is the most important (group of) people on the set. They are what make it come together. It's everybody's production. The harder you work together and the closer you get—the better it's gonna be . . .

Nobody was afraid of making an ass of themselves, particularly me. I figured that's what I'm here for. And it's always nice to have people around who are that secure . . . who will trust. We had a company that really trusted each other . . . that worked that well together. You knew that nobody was out to get you . . . or how to hurt you. And that whatever happened happened because that was what the other person was really feeling should happen. And no one was out to upstage anybody, or snarl at anyone. It was amazing.

Seventeen

Post Serial

"The scenes were pretty much traumatic, and I would find myself
feeling depressed afterwards."

—Elizabeth Montgomery, expressing the emotional and
psychological strain that resulted from filming *A Case of Rape*
(*People Magazine*, March 1974)

When *Bewitched* debuted in the fall of 1964 its main commercial sponsors
were Chevrolet and Quaker Oats cereal. After Lizzie ended the series in the
spring of 1972, she would appear in various other television productions
with all new sponsors. Namely, her TV-movies, which she addressed in
summary in 1989:

> All of them have been different from each other, except perhaps *Act of
> Violence* and *A Case of Rape*. They've all had different kinds of "feels" to
> them, and that's one of the reasons that I've done them. I get letters from
> people saying, "The wonderful thing that we like about what [you do]
> since you left *Bewitched* is that we never know what you're going to do
> next." . . . [The movies] are all strange. (I'm) not being pigeonholed, which
> is good. And being afforded the luxury to do that is nice, to be able to pick
> and choose and only do what you want to do. Audiences really like that.

In 1993, she told journalist Bart Mills in short, "I can wait to do another
series. I'm happy doing movies for television."

248

As research has shown, Lizzie became the *Queen of TV-Movies . . .* by retaining a high *Television Quotient Rating,* or *TV-Q.* In fact, according to Ronny Cox, her friend and co-star in the small screen movies, *A Case of Rape* and *With Murder in Mind,* she had the "highest TV-Q of anybody."

TV-Q scores are a research product of New York–based business, *Marketing Evaluations. Qs,* as they are now known, were originally developed in the early 1960s for television programmers to calculate awareness of and favorability toward those public personalities on or associated with *The Ed Sullivan Show* and *The Tonight Show Starring Johnny Carson.* Over time, the panel survey was extended to include all broadcast and cable network shows and stars, sports celebrities, products and brands. In each case, the key factor was the likeability quotient, with collected data analyzed and summarized by the various perceptions accumulated on and by consumers into a single measurement.

For example, Tom Hanks topped the charts as the most likeable overall actor since 1995 and his TV-Q score has consistently been at least double the score for the average thespian in any medium. As another example, the CBS drama series, *NCIS* finished the 2010–2011 season as the top-rated scripted show on network television. When the latest TV-Q ratings of the most popular actors in prime time were released on August 4, 2011, it came as little surprise that a *NCIS* cast member or two ranked high on the list.

Pauley Perrette, who plays the "gothic" forensic scientist *Abby Sciuto,* earned the top spot on the survey; followed by Cote de Pablo, who came in second; Mark Harmon in fourth place; and David McCallum (originally known on TV from *The Man from U.N.C.L.E.*) in fifth place. The only non-*NCIS*-actor in TV-Q's top five for that season was Jim Parsons, who plays *Sheldon* on *The Big Bang Theory,* another CBS show (this one, a comedy).

While Marketing Evaluations believes the Q popularity measurement is a better indication of viewers' fondness for a show versus more traditional methods like TV ratings, networks are able to barter their compounded Qs to charge higher ad rates during their programs.

In short, TV-Qs, which are conducted twice annually, calculate how much the general public likes or dislikes a particular TV star. With specific regard to Lizzie's reign on television, author Michael McWilliams stated it another way in his book *TV Sirens* (Perigee, 1987): "Montgomery is to the tube what [Greta] Garbo is to the cinema. She's as emblematic of *TV actress* as Garbo is of *movie actress*."

Despite those small screen calculations which could have projected wide screen margins, post-*Samantha*, Lizzie shied away from feature film work beyond her narration of the controversial documentaries *Cover Up* (1988) and *The Panama Deception* (1992), and for many, this was a disappointment.

Bewitched writer John L. Green, who created *My Favorite Martian* (CBS, 1963–1966, a show that once included a "twitch" reference), once compared her special brand of TV quality to journalist Jane Pauley. "You can just see the intelligence in her eyes," he said.

And Lizzie stayed with television because she enjoyed it, she wasn't overly ambitious with regard to her career, and there were few big screen parts available for women.

In 1988, *Bewitched* writer Richard Baer said of Lizzie, "I think she wanted to be Jane Fonda. She sure looked like her, but it wasn't meant to be. *Bewitched* came along and, though she never admitted it, I think she was tired of doing the show after the first few years."

In 1978, Elizabeth went on a promotional tour for her NBC mini-series, *The Awakening Land*. While she believed the film-TV comparison was an odd thing, she never really thought in those terms. She left that up to network and studio executives. She continued working because she loved her job. And she was in a position to pick and choose projects at will. She was frequently granted first choice on various projects and many times rejected significant offers for both television and film. She went by her instincts and never regretted any decisions for TV or the big screen.

With regard to feature films in particular, she welcomed opportunities when they presented themselves, but she was never compelled to do one. In 1988, Columbia Pictures approached Sol Saks about doing a *Bewitched* feature film. The studio approached Elizabeth about the idea, and Saks said she was "intrigued." But as it turned out, Saks owned the TV rights, but not the motion picture rights. Consequently, thirteen years later, a very different *Bewitched* feature film hit theatres, a movie that got a lukewarm reception by critics, but which nonetheless paid loving tribute to Lizzie's memory.

Back on the small screen, between 1972 and 1993, Elizabeth was satisfied with the work at hand. For her, the quality of television movies was closing in on theatrical motion pictures. Her success from *Bewitched* had allowed her to work as she pleased, even on a limited basis, doing two TV-movies a year. For her, money was never a concern and she never felt underpaid.

Instead, all that mattered was the quality of the script and production. An astute judge of material, and a severe critic of what she managed to have and not have produced, Lizzie thought television executives never gave enough credit to the home audiences, whom she believed craved sophisticated programming like PBS' once-popular and somewhat suggestive British series, *I, Claudius*. But airing such risqué programming on any mainstream American network in 1977—and for a few years to come—wasn't going to happen, and she knew it.

Truth be told, Lizzie constructed a solid career in television because she was talented, charismatic, and female, and because audiences had separate perceptions of the small and big screens. At the time, TV projects were not usually given the green light unless there was significant indication of a solid female interest. In fact, many TV-movies of today, specifically for networks like The Hallmark Channel or Lifetime, are still geared specifically toward a female audience.

In Elizabeth's core TV-movie era, the mainstream target audience for feature films was, with few exceptions, young adults with limited female appeal. At the same time, television proved to be an extraordinary challenge because of its boundaries, and although she never felt too confined by the small screen's size, she particularly embraced daring subject matters, which she viewed as strategic career moves.

In 1961, she may have once dubbed TV a "mediocre medium," but by 1994, when she chatted with reporter Ed Bark and *The Dallas Morning News*, she had clearly changed her mind:

> I love television. I like the pressure. I like the lack of wasting time. I would love to do a feature, but that's a whole other animal. I'm lucky to be able to kind of hang in there and wait a bit for really good scripts. I like to try to pick something a little unlike anything I've done before.

Certainly, her first post-*Samantha* screen performance in the 1972 ABC TV-movie, *The Victim*, a nerve-wracking thriller, reflected that decision:

A wealthy *Kate Wainwright* is trapped on a rainy night at the home of her sister, *Susan Chappel* (Jess Walton), whom she soon discovers has been murdered and stuffed in the basement. And *Kate* may the next victim.

The Victim debuted in what would have been Lizzie's ninth year on *Bewitched* had she agreed to her extended contract with the series. Instead, twitch-fans were treated to her take on *Kate*, who looked like *Samantha Stephens* and dressed like *Samantha Stephens*, but who wasn't *Samantha Stephens*. Not by a long shot. Lizzie's hair as *Kate* was as it was styled in the final season of *Bewitched,* but the happy, chipper *Samantha* persona, although subdued in that last year, was nowhere to be seen when Lizzie played *The Victim*. Her break from *Bewitched* was loud and clear, and she wanted *Samantha* fans to hear her cry of freedom.

In 1977, Leonard Nimoy, star of the original *Star Trek*—one of Lizzie's favorite TV shows—authored *I Am Not Spock* which he hoped would send a message of independence to "Trekkers" the world over. With *The Victim* Lizzie followed suit, as if to say, "I Am Not *Samantha*"; it's considered one of her best movie portrayals since her big screen debut in 1955's *The Court-Martial of Billy Mitchell.*

But in playing *The Victim*, she may have frightened more than a few viewers in the Bible Belt, which certain studio and network executives thought she had already done with *Bewitched*.

Although the violent themes and scenes of *The Victim* are considered mild by today's standards, there are still some solid scares in the film, which offers a strong supporting cast. Besides Jess Walton as Lizzie's on-screen sister, George Maharis (*Route 66*) played her brother-in-law, *Ben Chappel*, and veteran actress Eileen Heckert was a slightly sinister housekeeper, *Mrs. Hawkes.*

Through it all, the entire cast and crew enjoyed near-perfect weather conditions, as the movie was shot on location on the Monterey Peninsula in California. But that didn't help the film's premise, which was centered around a treacherous rain storm. Lizzie explained to *The Florence Morning News* on March 2, 1974:

"The lack of rain meant that we had to create our own deluge. Over 100,000 gallons of water (was) used on the location and each time they set up the rain towers it was an expensive job. My major concern was the problems that would result if re-takes were necessary. My hair would have to be re-done, the wardrobe dried and the area re-dressed. I've always tried to be a one-take actress," she said, "but with this film that objective proved especially challenging. I felt easy coming back to drama after so many years, but there were special problems that made this the toughest story I have ever done. The technical work was the best I have ever seen, but it was so complex that the crew and I had to have absolute perfect timing to make everything work properly."

When it was all said and done, irony refused to take a holiday. Only seven days after *The Victim* completed production, near-monsoon-like rains flooded the area.

But rain or shine, working on the movie boosted Lizzie's performance stamina, while her career received a breath of fresh air. In 1964, she was playing *Samantha*; in 1974, she decided that television drama in particular was "as good or better than it was ten years ago. The advances in the technical areas are almost staggering. I saw some of them on *Bewitched*, but on this film I saw how new cameras and lenses can be a tool of both the director and the actor."

Between *Bewitched, The Victim,* and her other 1970s TV-movies, she was still approached about resurrecting *Samantha* in some way, even as a supporting character on a short-lived ABC spin-off called *Tabitha*, the pilot for which debuted on May 7, 1977. The show was about *Samantha* and *Darrin's* now grown-up magical daughter, and it featured future *Knots Landing* star and aspiring singer Lisa Hartman (today married to country crooner Clint Black). William Asher had directed a previous *Tabatha* (with an "a") pilot segment starring Liberty Williams, which aired on April 24, 1976. This edition was actually more mystical than *Bewitched*, but it didn't sell. However, a second pilot with Hartman caught ABC's fancy and it went to series. Asher set the stage, premise, and the theme of the spin-off, but was not hands-on involved following his work on the first pilot. He later directed a few episodes of the series (in which *Bewitched* originals Sandra Gould, George Tobias, and Bernard Fox reprised their *Gladys, Abner Kravitz*, and *Dr. Bombay* roles), but other than that, Asher only became an advisor on the show.

Lizzie's presence as *Samantha* was requested in both editions of the *Tabitha* series, but she declined, even in a guest-star capacity. The sequel faced many casting challenges.

On the later years of *Bewitched*, the child *Tabitha* was played by twins Erin and Diane Murphy until the show ended in 1972, when the character was only eight years old. By the time the *Tabitha* series debuted, she would have only been thirteen years old. A hallmark of the original series was that, despite its fantasy premise, whatever transpired within its fabricated world made sense. There was always "logic within the illogic."

As Elizabeth explained in 1989:

> Ease is facilitated only by construction. If it's not constructed well, you find yourself walking into blank walls, and tripping and falling down. And there's just no way to rescue anything unless something's been constructed [well]. And that's why with ease we could flip from one thing back to another [mortal to the witch world]. That was one of the great advantages of our kind of format. It opened itself up into many ideas, and we could really pretty much go in any direction, as long as we kept to the ground rules.

Needless to say, such ground rules were feet of clay on the *Tabitha* series, which didn't have a logical-within-the-illogical leg to stand on. Meanwhile, too, making the *Tabitha* character twenty-something in 1977 also went against the basic premise idea that witches are immortal and tend not to age swiftly.

As Elizabeth continued to explain in 1989, such confusing plot developments and other aspects of *Tabitha* were troubling for her as well as fans of the original series:

> First of all, I didn't see the show, but I heard that she didn't twitch as well as I did. I kept getting mail from people were who outraged, saying, "Where is Erin Murphy? What in the world (is going on)?! This woman is 25 . . . this doesn't make any sense." I was getting mail from people like it was my fault, although also saying, "Thank God you didn't have anything to do with this." I wrote every single person who sent me letters like that. They felt betrayed. I thought, "How can you be betrayed by a TV show?" But they were irate. I got almost as much mail about that as I get about

anything else. It was very funny . . . ranged from kids who hated it to grownups who said, "This is the stupidest thing I've ever seen."

Like it was all my fault. I'm saying (to myself), "Why are they blaming me for this? I had absolutely zero to do with this." People were getting pissed off at me. I remember walking into stores and having people say to me, "Did you know they were going to do this? How could you have allowed this?" All I said [was] "I didn't want anything to do with this." People were getting downright nasty to me . . . People were just annoyed.

Ten years after the *Tabitha* series failed, Bill Asher began to develop yet another *Bewitched* off-shoot, this one called *Bewitched Again*, about an entirely new witch and mortal love affair. Whereas *Darrin* on *Bewitched* prohibited *Samantha's* use of her special powers, the mortal on the new show would do nothing of the sort. Instead, he encouraged his supernatural love to practice her craft.

It was a fresh take on the original series and, to help jumpstart the program, Bill had convinced Elizabeth to make a cameo in the pilot. She was to reprise her role as *Samantha*, introduce the new witch/mortal couple, and then pop off forever. Her consent to become involved with *Bewitched Again* was monumental and enticing, and Asher placed a great deal of energy into the project. Unfortunately, the intended new series, which was to be produced in the U.K., lost its financing and the idea was shelved.

To help ease the stress that resulted from *Tabitha*, her divorce from Bill Asher, and the general anxiety that accompanies the life of a major television star, Lizzie made frequent appearances on game shows like *The Hollywood Squares* hosted by Peter Marshall and *Password* hosted by Allen Ludden. According to what *Bewitched* producer/director Richard Michaels said in 1988, "She loved that stuff!"

For many of the *Password* spots, which were videotaped live, she played opposite her good friend Carol Burnett whom she met on the set of 1963's *Who's Been Sleeping in My Bed*. In Burnett's wonderful book, *This Time Together* (Crown, 2010), the super-talented redhead recalled one particular *Password* game with Lizzie in the section "Viewer Discretion Advised." It had to do with Burnett's team-partner on the show, whom she referred to in the book as Louis, and his somewhat improper, although innocent, use of the word "twat."

Burnett delicately defined the word as an unflattering term that referenced a particular body part of the female anatomy. In either case, she, Lizzie, and *Password* host Allen Ludden (who was married to Betty White, then of *The Mary Tyler Moore Show,* later of *The Golden Girls,* and today of *Hot in Cleveland*) were in hysterics by the end of the segment.

In 1989, Lizzie remarked just how much she enjoyed her frequent *Password* game play-on-words with Burnett: "Oh, we were terrific, weren't we? In print I know that sounds terrible, but we were! Carol is just a super wonderful lady, and I really appreciated the fact that we did become friends."

However, post-*Password*, their bond somewhat loosened. Lizzie explained:

> It's a funny thing, because so many friendships are like that in this town and anywhere. You work together so closely and then you hardly ever see that person again. Well, it's true. Carol and I don't see each other very often—but when we do, it's always nice. And I think instinctively she knows that if she picked up the phone and called me at 3:00 in the morning and said, "Can you be here?" I think she knows that I would be there for her, which is odd, as I say, when you don't see somebody that often. But I wouldn't respond with [as if she were annoyed], "Oh, Carol, what is it?!" I'd say, "Ok, I'll be there as soon as I can." There's certain people you feel that way about.

Despite her close friendship with Carol, and extensive comedy experience, Lizzie continuously rejected invitations to guest-star on *The Carol Burnett Show* (CBS, 1967–1978). As she went on to say:

> It's one of the many regrets I have, though it's not really a regret because even today I wouldn't do it. I'm just too terrified of that kind of stuff. She asked me to do it, and I said, "I just can't." I would have been so panic-stricken. It's not as though I haven't done stuff like that. It's not like, "No—I don't like spinach." "But have you tried it?" "No, but I don't like it anyway." It's that I know how terrified I get on the live stage. And it's just not worth it to me.

While promoting her singing performance as *Serena* in the *Bewitched* episode, "*Serena* Stops the Show," Lizzie addressed her TV variety show conundrum with *The Los Angeles Herald Examiner* for the article, "Liz Montgomery Makes Night Club Debut, but on TV," published February 9, 1970. "I've always thought of some big Miami Beach or Vegas hotel for my singing engagement," she mused. "I'd have settled for Joe's Bistro in Toluca Lake."

At the time, she had been asked to create a nightclub act and was offered a TV special of her own in which she was to sing and dance, but ultimately nothing came of the idea. "To me," she said, "a nightclub appearance or a special would involve more rehearsal time than I can afford. And I wouldn't want to go out and fall flat on my face because I hadn't prepared sufficiently."

Instead, she decided to utilize her harmonic vocal chords in a more controlled atmosphere . . . on the set of *Bewitched*, in character as *Serena*, singing "Blow You a Kiss in the Wind," by 1960s pop stars Boyce and Hart (who were under contract to Columbia and made a guest appearance in the episode). Her performance was a one-shot segment in a half-hour sitcom as opposed to the hour-long continuous song-and-dance routine that would be required in a variety show format.

"Who could resist that? It was like having your cake, et cetera, et cetera," she joked about the *Serena* segment that ultimately became a choreographed production number with psychedelic lighting which transformed *Samantha* and *Darrin's* living room into a nightclub.

It all proved so puzzling, if consistent with her unpredictable spirit. She'd sing as *Serena* on short *Bewitched* segments, but was reticent about appearing on the *Burnett* show; and come March 19, 1966, things became more confusing.

That's when she hosted *The Hollywood Palace*, which featured frequent *Bewitched* guest-star Paul Lynde with whom she got along famously. She enjoyed Carol's company, too, but Lynde's presence on *Palace* may have proved more comfortable because: 1) He was hand-picked from Lizzie's *Bewitched* stable, and 2) *Palace* aired on ABC, *Samantha's* home network, whereas *Burnett* aired on rival CBS. Also, her *Palace* spotlight as host allowed for more creative control as opposed to only being a guest on *Burnett*.

After her early appearances with Carol on *Password*, Lizzie became less enthusiastic about the game after it changed formats. The original show debuted on CBS with host Allen Ludden in 1961 and ran until 1967. ABC brought it back with Ludden from 1971 to 1975, during which it briefly became the celebrity-drenched *Password All-Stars*. NBC did an update in 1979 with a new edition called *Password Plus*, which also ran with Ludden though only until 1981 when failing health (stomach cancer) forced him to relinquish his hosting duties. NBC tried once more in 1984 with *Super Password*, now hosted by Bert Convy, and this new format ran until 1989.

Lizzie's final *Password* appearance was with actor Wesley Eure (*Land of the Lost*, NBC/CBS, 1974–1977) within the *Plus* format, hosted by Ludden, airing August 3, 1979. But throughout each of the editions, as bonus rounds were added along with elaborate sets, the once simple and popular word game became overly puzzling or, as she said in 1989, "It all just got kind of convoluted. It was so pure the other way, when it was what it was."

During one of those pure *Password* games, specifically, the week of November 19–23, 1973, she appeared with Robert Foxworth, whom she met and fell in love with on the set of the ABC TV-movie *Mrs. Sundance* (which aired in 1974 but filmed in September 1973). Although they later played *Password* within the 1979 *Plus* format, it was their 1973 session that proved most advantageous. "When Bob and I did the show that year," she recalled in 1989, "we raised $11,000 for the L.A. Free Clinic, and no one would play with us anymore because we just got so good at it. I guess when you're together a lot you kind of think on the same level."

She and Foxworth were together a great deal. He contributed to her comfort zone when they appeared at charity events or on talk shows like John Tesh's *One on One*. It was to Tesh she explained her attraction to Foxworth (who most recently provided the voice of *Ratchet* in the *Transformer* feature films): "He's got one of the most wonderfully inquisitive minds . . . of anybody I've ever met. And he's compassionate. He cares about things. He also cares a great deal about his career. He's got a wonderful sense of humor."

Before and after his best known role as *Chase Gioberti* on *Falcon Crest* (CBS, 1981–1990), Robert Foxworth had numerous screen and stage performances, including his television debut in the 1969 *CBS Playhouse* drama, *Sadbird*. After starring in *The Storefront Lawyers* (aka *Men at Law*), a 1970–1971 series for CBS, he appeared opposite Faye Dunaway in "Hogan's Goat" (NET Playhouse, 1971).

Besides his appearances with Lizzie, his TV films included but were not limited to: *The Devil's Daughter* (ABC, 1973); *The FBI versus Alvin Karpis* (CBS, 1974); *Act of Love* (CBS, 1980); *Peter and Paul* (CBS, 1981); *The Memory of Eva Ryker* (CBS, 1980); and *The Questor Tapes* (NBC, 1974). The latter project, also known as just *Questor*, was written by *Star Trek* legend and Lizzie-favorite Gene Roddenberry.

Intended as NBC's answer to ABC's super popular superhero series *The Six Million Dollar Man* (1974–1979), *Questor* was a slightly more imaginative tale than Lee Major's earthbound bionic cyborg *Col. Steve Austin*. Foxworth's *Questor* was an all-robotic philosophical character in search of his alien creator. He was *The Fugitive* meets *Kung Fu* on the way to Brent Spiner's *Data* from Roddenberry's *Star Trek: The Next Generation* (syndicated, 1987–1994). As it turned out, Bob later appeared in more shows from the Roddenberry/*Trek* sector, including *Star Trek: Deep Space Nine* in 1996 and *Star Trek: Enterprise* in 2004. In fact, Foxworth, like Lizzie, has become a legend in the sci-fi/fantasy world with additional guest-star spots on shows like: *The Sixth Sense* (ABC, 1972); "Frankenstein" (ABC's *Wide World Mystery*, 1973); *Tales of the Unexpected* (1977); *The Outer Limits* (syndicated, 1996); *Stargate: SG-1* (syndicated, 2003); and feature films such as *Beyond the Stars* (1989).

Besides lending his voice to *Ratchet* in all three *Transformer* movies (2007, 2009, 2011), he provided various vocal talents to animated TV shows like *Justice League*, as *Professor Neil Hamilton* (Cartoon Network, 2004–2005) and *The Real Adventures of Jonny Quest*, playing *Race Bannon* (Cartoon Network, 1996–1997). His countless live guest-star appearances date back to small screen classics like *Kung Fu* (ABC, 1974), *The Mod Squad* (ABC, 1971), *Mannix* (CBS, 1971), *Law & Order: SVU* (NBC, 2000–2005), and *The West Wing* (NBC, 2005), the latter in which he portrayed *Senator George Montgomery* (which was a nod to Lizzie's family name, as well as to the actor the public periodically misidentified as her father, George Montgomery, who was once married to Dinah Shore). Other of his theatrical film credits include *Airport '77* (1977), *Damien: Omen II* (1978), *Prophecy* (1979), and *The Black Marble* (1980), and more.

His stage performances include the role of *John Proctor* in *The Crucible* at Lincoln Center, for which he won a Theatre World Award; Off-Broadway productions of *Terra Nova, One Flew Over the Cuckoo's Nest*, and *Mary Stuart* in Los Angeles, and *Long Day's Journey into Night* at Atlanta's Alliance Theatre. In three seasons at the Arena Stage in Washington, D.C., he appeared in twenty productions ranging from *The Skin of Our Teeth* to *Room Service*. He made his name in *Henry V* following work at the American Shakespeare Festival in Stratford, Connecticut.

Unlike the older Gig Young and Bill Asher, and her first husband Fred Cammann (who was only four years her senior), Foxworth was the only younger man she married. Her penchant for all things *Trek* and sci-fi/fantasy may have contributed to her initial attraction to Foxworth, but the actor's diverse talents and varied charms assuredly contributed to his appeal.

In 1992, he expressed his attraction to Lizzie on *One on One with John Tesh*, and noted her ability to see the funny side of life as one of her most appealing traits (as did she of him on the same show): "I would describe her as perhaps the most intelligent woman I've ever met. And one of the things that makes that bearable is that she has a fabulous sense of humor, besides the fact that she's beautiful and sexy."

Lizzie and Bob Foxworth performed together live on stage in a short-lived production of *Cat on a Hot Tin Roof* at the Bell Theatre, Los Angeles, 1978. In the fall of 1989, they were together again on stage, in the play *Love Letters* at the Edison Theatre in Broadway. Only a few months before, *Bewitched* actor David White visited with Lizzie at her home in Beverly Hills, and suggested that she and Foxworth return to the stage.

"Why don't you and Bob do a play? You've done stage work before. Don't you like it?"

"Yeah."

"Here I am messing in her business."

"Oh, you could mess in my business. I don't mind."

"Well, then do one! I think that would be great!"

At which point, Lizzie explained how London's historic Globe Theatre had invited her and Foxworth to perform in Edward Albee's classic play, *Who's Afraid of Virginia Woolf?* In 1966, writer Ernest Lehman had adapted this monumentally depressing play, about a bitter, middle-aged couple who use alcohol as a pawn in and to fuel their already angry relationship, into a feature film directed by Mike Nichols, and starring Elizabeth Taylor and Richard Burton. But Lizzie thought that tackling such a play with Foxworth would have been "totally crazy":

> I'm not sure that two people who really care about each other should do that play. I think it would be better to rehearse it, do it, go home, and then get really kind of attracted to the person that you're working with, so that you're on an entirely different level than to having to live and rehearse with the person doing that play. And when the Burtons did the movie . . . that's different because they didn't have to all be on the same set at the same time.

Needless to say, they turned down Globe's invitation to do *Woolf*, but years before they were on the same set at the same time in *Mrs. Sundance*, the 1974 TV-movie in which she played *Etta Place* opposite his *Jack Maddox*. They met and fell in love while working on this film which ultimately served as a sequel to the 1969 big screen flick, *Butch Cassidy and the Sundance Kid* (in which Katharine Ross portrayed *Etta*).

A review of the film appears in the book, *The Great Western Pictures* (Scarecrow Press, 1976) by James Robert Parrish and Michael R. Pitts:

> It was a catchy gimmick to produce a semi-sequel to *Butch Cassidy and the Sundance Kid* (1969), with Elizabeth Montgomery, the queen of the telefeatures, as the title figure. The intriguing premise had *Etta Place* (aka *Mrs. Sundance*) in a ticklish situation when she learns that the *Sundance Kid* did not die with *Butch Cassidy* but is waiting for her at their old hideout. What makes the set-up so dangerous is that bounty hunters are aware of the planned reunion of the famed outlaw and the schoolteacher of a small Colorado town. Elizabeth Montgomery, very much Robert's daughter, offered a strong performance in this flashy role, giving an enriched characterization in a genre far removed from her days as the star of the teleseries *Bewitched*.

Once more, Lizzie's on-screen performance mirrored her off-stage life, and this time, Foxworth successfully played into the scenario. Although his *Maddox* character was a cagey, weak-spined character who first viewed *Etta* as a way to get out of jail free, he was big-hearted and fell prey to her charms, just as had Foxworth with Lizzie. *Etta's* love may have made *Jack* heroic and strong, but they were always a team, partners for humanity, again, much like Lizzie and Foxworth would be for various charitable causes.

After *Mrs. Sundance*, Lizzie and Foxworth would co-star in two other TV films: *Face to Face* for CBS in 1990 and *With Murder in Mind* for in 1992.

Face to Face was their shining moment, debuting January 24, 1990 under the prestigious *Hallmark Hall of Fame* banner:

Diana Firestone (Lizzie), a brilliant paleontologist, traveled to Africa with a team of assistants in search of the remains of a three-million-year-old man, a potential discovery that would rewrite the anthropological textbooks. *Tobias Williams* (Foxworth) was a rough and ready miner who explored the same territory for meerschaum (a special clay used for making smoking pipes). Sparks flew as they both claimed digging rights in Kenya's high country. She considered him the epitome of a Philistine, narrow-minded, devoid of culture, and indifferent to art. He patronized her "naïve" outlook on life and regarded her as better suited to an ivory-towered academic institution than the African bush. Compromise was out. Occasional attempts to be cordial took mutual turns for the worse. But despite their stubbornness and fiercely independent manner, their hostility gradually changed to reluctant respect and finally to unexpected romantic love.

Lizzie and Foxworth may have played themselves on *Password*, but *Face to Face* marked the first time since 1974's *Mrs. Sundance* that they performed together on screen in character. "It's not the usual kind of romance you see on television," he said of *Face* in a press release for the film in 1990. "It's a mature love story, with two very interesting and very independent characters whose relationship changes from mutual animosity to mutual respect."

The movie was filmed on location in remote Kenya, on the banks of the Engare Odare River. When additional laborers were needed on the set, ten Maasai warriors were hired. Interviewed around a campfire near her tent (her home for the three weeks of filming), Lizzie talked with CBS publicity about the African location shoot. "The innocence, the beauty, the harshness," she said. "It's all here. This is life of another dimension."

Certainly, it was a life that was foreign in terms of her teen years growing up in Patterson, New York, her young adult life in New York, and her later days in Beverly Hills. But she felt compelled by *Face* when, upon first reading the script, she said: "It was so good you couldn't bear to turn the page because you were afraid the next page would disappoint you . . . I kept thinking, 'I hope it stays this good.'" *Face* may have also jogged memories of her youth on the family farm—and even *Bewitched*.

Robert Halmi, Sr. served as the film's executive producer. Jim Chory was the co-producer and actor Lou Antonio directed and also cast himself in a small role. Antonio had first worked with Lizzie on *Bewitched* for an episode called "Going Ape," which debuted on February 27, 1969, in which he played, of all things, a monkey who was turned into a man (the show's slight acknowledgement of the first and most popular *Planet of the Apes* film that had premiered approximately one year before).

Around this same time, Antonio directed episodes of ABC's *The Flying Nun* and *The Partridge Family* (later, NBC's *McMillan & Wife* and *McCloud*, while more recently, *Dawson's Creek, Numbers,* and *Boston Legal*). In 1983, he even directed Lizzie's friends, Carol Burnett and Elizabeth Taylor, in their hit TV-movie, *Between Friends*.

In *With Murder in Mind*, which premiered on May 12, 1992, Lizzie and Bob Foxworth worked together for their third and final time on screen within a scripted format. *Mind* was a fact-based story in which Lizzie played a real-life realtor:

Gayle Wolfer (Lizzie) was shot and nearly killed by a client (Howard Rollins, best known from the TV version of *In the Heat of the Night*, 1988-1994; NBC/CBS). Physically and emotionally scarred from the incident, Gayle remains determined to find her attacker, which she finally does at a county fair. But he's a part-time auxiliary policeman who's established his own security company. The case eventually goes to trial, but at first no one believes her because of his position in the community.

Through it all, Foxworth played *Bob Sprague*, Gayle's longtime live-in boyfriend, which is exactly what he was in Lizzie's real life. He was strong, calm, resilient, logical and practical; loving and family focused; supportive, independent with a strong sense of self even though he was living with his boss. He didn't put up with too much. But he was honest, a straight shooter, and not afraid to speak his own mind. Once again, all qualities which Foxworth also possessed.

In 1989, Lizzie expressed her theories on acting, addressing the more specific challenges of performing comedy as opposed to drama.

> Laughing on screen is more difficult than crying for a lot of actors. It's quite a challenge to laugh on cue in front of the camera. Both laughing and crying are hard for me. There must be something that's easy in the middle of that. Comedy is more difficult on many levels. If you have ten people come into a room and say "I just saw a dog hit by a car in the street." Those ten people are going to go, "Oh, my God." You're going to get the same reaction, presumably, from those ten people. But if someone comes into the room and tells those same ten people a joke, you may get ten different reactions. Some may think it's funny; some may not think it's funny. Some may think it's moderately funny. So you're not hitting the same emotional chord with everyone (compared) with something that might be a very sad kind of event.

Lizzie's friend and fellow-actor Ronny Cox co-starred with her in *With Murder in Mind*, and nearly twenty years before in *A Case of Rape*. He has an upbeat theory on acting that he believes they shared:

> The fun is in the work. The fun of acting is reacting . . . playing off of someone else. I'm not a proponent of rehearsing lines with certain voice inflections or physical gestures. That's distracting. The line can be, "I love you" and I can make it mean "I hate you," depending on how I say it. Therefore, it's presumptuous to decide ahead of time how you're going to say a line . . . until you know how (the other actor) is going to say their line. That becomes the be-all and end-all of acting. I have little patience for actors who over-strategize how they're going to say a line and how they're going to move while saying it. That's not acting. That's robotics. I hate to *see* "acting" and that's what always happens when you see that kind of

work. It's technically very proficient, but lacking in the conveyance of truth. I'm one of the few actors who will vociferously defend American actors over British actors in that respect. Brilliant actors are brilliant actors no matter whether they're British or American. But run-of-the-mill British actors are more technically proficient. They work out how they're going to say the lines. Technically they're way ahead of [American actors] but they don't "invest" in a scene as much as less technically proficient American actors. For my money, if you take the very best of the American actors and the very best of the British actors, the British actors will have far superior technique and American actors will have a far superior grasp of the character! I also don't have much patience with actors who improvise their lines. Acting is like a great piece of jazz. The key to it is listening. You listen to what's being said and allow that to manifest how you're going to reply to what's being said. And I think that's the thing that Lizzie and I were able to do quite well.

It's Cox's brand of passion and love for his craft that contributed to his solid bond with Lizzie while they filmed *A Case of Rape*. In fact, they became so close Cox says "some people on the crew thought we might be lovers." But such was not the case. His wife Mary died in 2006, and they met as children:

Just so everyone knows. I'm a widower now; but I was the most married man you've ever seen in your life. I never had another date. She was, is, and will always be the love of my life! But having said that, Lizzie and I were very close; I was hanging out in her dressing room all the time . . . and I mean all the time. It paid off for us, I think, in the acting (department), because there was this familiarity where we could be at ease. And that ease translated into playing scenes with each other.

In 1979, five years after Lizzie starred with Ronny Cox in *A Case of Rape*, her friend Carol Burnett appeared in the ABC-TV movie, *Friendly Fire*. This acclaimed film was based on the real-life story of Peg Mullen—from rural Iowa who worked against government obstacles to uncover the truth about the death of her son Michael, a soldier killed by American "friendly fire" in 1970 during the Vietnam War.

All of sudden, it seemed, critics heralded Burnett's acting, as if she had never excelled in any worthy capacity for eleven years on *The Carol Burnett Show* (CBS, 1967–1978), on *The Garry Moore Show* (CBS, 1958–1966) before that, or in any of her countless prior stage, TV, or film appearances (including *Who's Been Sleeping in My Bed?* with Lizzie in 1963). This time, because she was performing drama as opposed to her trademark comedy, her talents were praised as if she were royalty. Her crowning as a *Queen of Comedy* was apparently not enough for the critics.

Lizzie received a similar response when she left *Bewitched* behind and ventured into *Rape* and other extremely shocking roles in ground-breaking TV-movies like *The Legend of Lizzie Borden* (ABC, 1975), and *The Black Widow Murders: The Blanche Taylor Moore Story* (1993), among others. Only rarely would she return to the comedic tones and timing that she honed on *Bewitched*, as she did with *When the Circus Came to Town* (CBS, 1981) and in *Face to Face* (CBS, 1990), the latter in which she starred with Robert Foxworth.

In fact, according to her friend Sally Kemp, it was Foxworth who urged Lizzie to delve deeper into these "meatier" roles. She discussed such performances for an interview in 1980 with writer Lewis George of *The Globe*, while promoting her part as yet another female bandit of the Old West in the CBS TV-movie *Belle Star*, which she was initially apprehensive about doing:

> I would rather be known as a serious . . . and good . . . actress now. I've always enjoyed playing real lady creatures like *The Legend of Lizzie Borden*, who was supposed to have axed her family. I also portrayed a lady who was raped in *A Case of Rape*, and a lady beaten up by toughs in my most recent film *Act of Violence*. What concerned me was that the script was stark with dramatic violence. It was such an unusual script. I was afraid executive producer Joe Barbara might have to alter it because of ears of network censorship. My fears were needless. Joe Barbara is just as much opposed to network and creative censorship as I am and agreed completely on the script. An actress can't be anything less than honest when she's working. And I am aware the *Belle Starr* story may be not for the entire family. But this woman had to survive by her own code of ethics in a very difficult environment. She's a fascinating person and very real. She made many drastic mistakes in her life, including murder. There's a certain ugliness about her, but there's also an inner beauty and strength.

In an interview with *The Minneapolis Star Tribune*, on March 30, 1980, she added:

> The real Belle Starr is so clouded by legend and fiction that you can come up with several versions of her life, depending on which history of the old west you study. One thing we do know for sure is that she was an exceptional and amazing woman, if not a good one, and an important figure in the history of the West.

Of all the legends of the west, Starr's was one of the most romanticized by the dime novelists of the day. To them, she was a daring and noble woman who fulfilled the role of a female *Robin Hood*. Her real name was Myra Belle Shirley; she was born in 1848 in a log cabin near Carthage, Missouri. Her family moved to Texas and Belle had not yet grown out of her teens when she began hobnobbing with Jesse James and his gang, and bore one of its members, Cole Younger, a daughter. She then married a horse thief named Jim Reed and bore him a son. After Reed was killed, Starr took up with another gang and moved into Indian Territory (now Oklahoma), where she met and married a handsome Cherokee bandit named Sam Starr. From their hideout on the Canadian River, Belle acted as organizer, planner, and fence for cattle rustlers, horse thieves, and traffickers in illegal whiskey to the Indians. When the law captured her friends, she spent her money generously to buy their freedom. When bribery failed, she would employ her powers of seduction.

After Sam Starr was killed in a shootout, Belle continued her amorous pursuits. To the sorrow of romantic readers from coast to coast, she was shot in ambush in 1889. Her daughter had a monument erected on her grave with a bell, a star, and a horse inscribed on it.

In an early scene in the *Belle Star* film, the lead character is seen encouraging her young daughter to practice the piano. Lizzie explained in *The Minneapolis Star Tribune*:

> She apparently loved music of all types, and had learned to play the piano at the age of eight. She actually was quite a genteel young lady until the Civil War caused her to strap on a gun and change her life, with a little help from her outlaw lover, Cole Younger. But she never gave up her love of music. She displayed her talent at every opportunity, even at church for

weddings and funerals. After the war Belle played the piano in Dallas gambling halls and mastered the guitar. Even after she had become a much-hunted woman, she managed to have a piano in her hideout.

As it was during the *Bewitched* years, Lizzie worked hard on *Belle Starr*, and she maintained a strong sense of priorities and family life for her children. By now, her sons Bill and Robert were in their mid-teens, while daughter Rebecca was only ten years old. She was five years divorced from Bill Asher, and Lizzie and the kids now shared their country-style Beverly Hills home in Laurel Canyon with a beagle named "Who," a cat named "Feather," and Bob Foxworth, who was then starring in *The Black Marble* feature film.

At the time, she and Foxworth were not married. But a decade or so later, and after a twenty-year courtship, that status changed. On January 28, 1993, the two wed at the home of Lizzie's manager Barry Krost, and they remained devoted to each other until the end.

Eighteen

~

Awakenings

"I've just reached another plateau in the type of work I want to do.
It's like a man working all of his life as a gardener and suddenly
waking up to the fact that he wants to be a landscape architect."

—Elizabeth Montgomery, as quoted by Ronald L. Smith in his
book, *Sweethearts of '60s TV* (SPI Books, 1993)

In 2005, Sony Pictures released the *Bewitched* feature film, starring Nicole
Kidman and Will Ferrell, produced by Doug Wick and Lucy Fisher, and
directed by Nora Ephron, who also served as co-writer with her sister Delia.
Penny Marshall (better known in classic TV sectors as the co-star of
Laverne & Shirley) co-produced the movie for which she had originally hired
good friend Ted Bessell (*Don Hollinger* from TV's *That Girl*) to direct. When
Bessell unexpectedly died of an aneurysm in 1996, Marshall was overcome
with grief and the production shut down. By 2003, she had moved on to
other projects, but remained in force with the talented Wick/Fisher/
Ephron team, which ultimately brought *Bewitched* to the big-screen.

Back in 1990, some fifteen years before she dabbled with the possibility
of bringing *Samantha* and *Darrin* to theatres, Marshall directed a motion
picture called *Awakenings*.

Based on the best-selling book by Oliver Sacks, and starring Robert De
Niro, Robin Williams, and Julie Kavner, this film was about a new physician (Williams) who seeks to help a group of patients (including De Niro

and Kavner) who have been comatose for decades, without any sign of a recovery. When he discovers a potential cure, he gains permission to experiment with a new chemical drug that may help his cause. The inspirational film then goes on to showcase the new perspectives that are awakened by each member of this extraordinary group of doctors and patients.

In 1985, Lizzie played a character named *Abigail Foster* in the similarly-themed TV-movie *Between the Darkness and the Dawn*.

Abigail Foster—a young woman who awakens from a 20-year coma only to discover a world that has moved on without her, especially the world she had so lovingly created with her high school boyfriend (David Goodwin) who's now married to her younger sister (Karen Grassle of *Little House on the Prairie* fame). In this new reality, *Abigail* must foster the pieces of her broken life, while coping with a devoted mother (Dorothy McGuire), who knows no other identity than to be her daughter's caregiver before and after she awakens.

In 1978, Lizzie appeared in the acclaimed three-part, seven-hour NBC mini-series, *The Awakening Land*, adapted from Conrad Richter's trilogy of a pioneer family in the Ohio Valley. It aired February 19, 20, and 21, and co-starred the esteemed Hal Holbrook as *Portius* (Holbrook, meanwhile had already chiseled new ground a few years before with the controversial 1972 TV-movie, *That Certain Summer*, in which his and Martin Sheen's characters introduced gay love to the American television mainstream).

Like *Mrs. Sundance* (1974) and *Belle Starr* (1980), *The Awakening Land* was also classified as a western, but far removed from the brightly-brushed Technicolor movie westerns of old. Whereas Lizzie's *Etta Place* from *Sundance* and *Belle* from *Starr* featured slightly more shady traits, her *Awakening* role of *Sayward Luckett Wheeler* was more clearly defined as a pioneer woman.

In 1978, Lizzie wasn't sure if *Sayward* sincerely loved Holbrook's *Portius*. According to Montgomery archivist Tom McCartney, Lizzie believed that *Sayward* needed *Portius*, because he was educated, and a provider for her children. In *Sayward's* day, such a bond was "typical," Lizzie said. It was considered more respectable to first be married, then have children.

Meanwhile, atypical filming for this movie began in September of 1977, and it was grueling. Lizzie, the cast and crew spent the two and a half months on location in the reconstructed post-colonial Village of New Salem, Illinois. Producers were convinced the movie should be made there once the State of Illinois film office persuaded them to peruse the village, and once the Springfield city fathers agreed to fill up a nearby lake so it would resemble the Ohio River.

A vacant Springfield gymnasium was then utilized to house an indoor log cabin for inside shots, as well as extensive prop and wardrobe departments. Other parts of the state got into the act when American Indians from Chicago's uptown were transported to the location to play their forefathers, while hounds, cougars, wolves, and one skunk from the Plainsman Zoo in Elgin were shipped to the location to help legitimize the setting.

As reporter Blecha explained, even the weather in New Salem complied with the production as warm, summer breezes and lush flora and fauna surfaced for the filming of Part 1: *The Trees*, while brisk autumn air and changing colors were there for Part 2: *The Fields*, and dark, dismal winter cold, even with a day of snow, showed up for Part 3: *The Town* (all of which were consecutively broadcast on Sunday, Monday, and Tuesday nights).

According to what Lizzie remembered in 1978, the country was "absolutely beautiful there, but whatever the territory offered, we got . . . viruses, poison oak, bees, mosquitoes, varmints, nettles. It gave us a vague idea of what it must have been like."

She herself contracted a bad case of poison ivy and the shoot overall was physically exhausting (especially on the days in the fields behind oxen and plow). But for Lizzie the most challenging part of portraying *Sayward* was the aging process, learning how to slow down, physically and psychologically.

Despite those challenges, Lizzie gave her usual 100 percent and had great respect for the character:

> *Sayward* wasn't stupid, just uneducated. Her instincts were extraordinary. She didn't say much, but when she did she made a lot of sense. She had a tremendous amount of fortitude. If it wasn't for people like her, you and I wouldn't be here today.

However, Lizzie admitted that the 1880s in the Ohio River held no personal appeal for her. And even though she was a pioneer woman in television, off screen, she had no desire claim the western frontier edition of that title. "No, I definitely would not have liked to have lived then. No one in their right mind would make that choice."

For a live online chat on December 12, 2002, Montgomery archivist Tom McCartney asked *Awakening* costar Jane Seymour, what it was like to work with Lizzie. She replied:

> Elizabeth Montgomery was a wonderful woman and very supportive to me. She was the first, indeed only, star to invite me into her trailer. I remember this as being a very special treat and vowed that if I ever had a trailer, I would share it with younger actresses. It set a precedent for me, one I follow to this day.

Etta Place from *Mrs. Sundance, Belle Starr,* and *The Awakening Land's Sayward* could be described as pioneering female roles for Lizzie (or any other actress) to portray. These were parts for her in particular that fueled ambition, expanded career opportunities, and strengthened artistic muscles. Each of these characters fit into what became her very strategic objective to work with daring projects. And if a network executive or producer objected to a particularly questionable script that may have held her interest, she was further ignited to bring the idea to fruition. "That's the kind of stuff I want to do," she told *Entertainment Tonight* in 1994.

"I think television has grown up," she said to *Tonight* reporter Scott Osborne in 1985, but she believed those "running it" were afraid of doing just that. "I don't know why." At this point, Lizzie was still open to performing in a comedy film, which she believed were "a lot harder [to do] than drama." And such properties were also "very hard to find," she said, partially because "on television there is so much censorship that it's tough to do really sophisticated comedy" that the Standards and Practices divisions at the networks will approve.

While network executives may not have met Lizzie's standards and practices, she dealt with her own challenges head-on, namely her shyness, which she overcame, at least on camera, whenever she assumed a dramatic role in one of her post-*Samantha* TV-movies.

By the time *The Awakening Land* premiered in 1978, *Bewitched* had been off the air six years and she was still mostly known as *Samantha*, the *Queen of the TV Witches.* Now, she had added a new twist to the title: "Lizzie—Queen of the TV-Movies," a crown that would later be bestowed on Valerie Bertinelli (then just exiting the sitcom *One Day at a Time*, today starring in TV Land's *Hot in Cleveland*) and on Jane Seymour (Lizzie's co-star in *Awakening*, who later starred in the family medical western, *Dr. Quinn, Medicine Woman*, a female TV pioneer in her own right).

Due to *Awakening's* success, Lizzie was in a position to command the highest price of any TV star and had her choice of roles. Her acquired wealth from *Bewitched* secured the already stable financial arsenal she amassed by way of her father's inheritance.

Through it all, she not only retained an unaffected demeanor, but remained devoted to her three children. She had it all, and she knew it. But she didn't flaunt it. She didn't have to because everyone else in the industry knew it, too. Long gone were the days when she butted heads with the likes of Screen Gems executive Jackie Cooper at the dawn of *Bewitched*. She was no longer demanding, but in demand. Her success commanded attention. No one could turn away from her, and no one could turn her away.

The Victim, her first TV-movie since leaving *Bewitched*, had attracted a large enough audience for ABC in 1972 that her services were requested for a second film with the network: *Mrs. Sundance*, which premiered in 1974. She was on a hot streak, and the groundwork for her royal TV-movie status was in place.

The free spirit was now a free agent, no longer tied down to one series, one character, or one network. When ratings for NBC's *A Case of Rape* went through the roof and delivered with it her first Emmy nomination since *Samantha*, there was no stopping Lizzie. She was a bona fide legend by the time she'd play yet another one: in ABC's 1975 film, *The Legend of Lizzie Borden*.

After that, came the remake of *Dark Victory* in 1976 on NBC, which also presented the indiscriminate *A Killing Affair* in 1977—all of which garnered upwards of 35 percent of the audience. Today, network suits and producers would kill for such ratings. In the era of *The Awakening Land*, those were the kind of stats they worshipped.

The grungy, gnarled locks, and weathered look of *Sayward Luckett* in *The Awakening Land* are light-years away from *Samantha* on *Bewitched*. Although her age was not yet an issue off-screen, in *Awakening* Lizzie was transformed from a young girl to an elderly woman. *Bewitched* makeup artist Rolf Miller was Emmy-nominated for gracefully aging her (and Dick Sargent) in the December 3, 1970 episode, "*Samantha's* Old Man," which was directed by her friend Richard Michaels.

But now it came time for a dramatic turn, under the insisting guidance of Boris Sagal, who helmed *Awakening* and who, according to Tom Mc-Cartney, she once called "an extraordinary man" and said she would not have done the film without him.

Lin Bolen Wendkos is the widow of director Paul Wendkos, a versatile talent who among other productions guided the Sandra Dee / *Gidget* films. According to *The Los Angeles Times*, he died November 12, 2009 of a lung infection. His career spanned fifty years and covered more than 100 films and television shows, including several episodes of *I Spy*, *The Untouchables*, and the acclaimed 1978 TV-movie, *A Woman Called Moses*, starring Cicely Tyson. He was one of Lizzie's choice directors dating back to the *Playhouse 90* segment "Bitter Heritage" from 1958 through to 1975's *The Legend of Lizzie Borden*, and *Act of Violence* in 1979. Bolen Wendkos has a theory as to why Lizzie took such a dramatic departure with her later work:

> I think she earned the opportunity to do so by playing a very commercial part as *Samantha* on *Bewitched*. In her mind, she may have wanted to give something more of the talent that she was holding back. For example, to play a strong female lead as she did in *Act of Violence*, in which her character (*Catherine McSweeney*) was forced to defend herself.

From 1971 to 1978, Lin served as the first female vice president of a television network when she worked for NBC's daytime operations, bringing the "peacock" network from number three to number one within a two–and–a–half year period when such positions were held mostly by men. Suffice it to say, she knows all too well of what she speaks. As with *Act of Violence*, Bolen Wendkos says Lizzie's 1974 NBC TV-movie, *A Case of Rape*, aired at a time when "women weren't being allowed to tell the truth, or to talk about their inner fears, or to challenge people who treated them in a way that was inappropriate. So Elizabeth was challenging the system and saying 'I am much more than you think and I have something to say, and these characters are going to say it for me.'"

Lin explains how her husband's perspective on *Borden* jibed with Lizzie's theatrical abilities:

My husband worked with a lot of interesting actresses and Elizabeth was definitely one of his favorites. She was a magnetic personality to look at. She captured that character in a way that I don't think anyone else could have. She *became* that person she was playing. If you look at her face in the movie, she had become that character. How many actresses on TV ever did that? Not many. She gave herself to that murderess spirit, and she did not stop until the end. He controlled the set of every movie he worked on. But what he didn't do was control the actress. If the cinematographer, the lighting director or the wardrobe assistant or anyone had something to offer, they would have to wait for Paul's word. But when it came to the actors, he always gave them the opportunity to go on set and do their thing first. Because he knew that's where the picture was. If the actor didn't feel secure in allowing their innermost ideas to surface in that first run-through . . . that first rehearsal . . . then it was a lost cause. He would say to each actor, "What is your character doing in this scene? Let's see it!" He wouldn't just stand there and stare at them. Instead, he'd ride the camera crane, or peer through the camera lens to allow the actor to retain *the privacy of their moment*. He absolutely believed that the photography was very important, and that [it] would need to be real. That's what it made a new creation . . . a real human outline, right there in front of you. He knew the camera had to capture that. So he gave the actors a chance to move around. He didn't just stage a scene and then instruct an actor to walk through it. He let the actor find their moment before he staged the scene and Elizabeth played into that very well.

Actress Bonnie Bartlett performed with Lizzie in the *Borden* film. Although they did not share any scenes together, Bartlett was a fan of her work:

She was an extraordinary actress. She was a major TV-movie star and she could have done almost anything. She was very serious about her work and an extraordinary professional. Every little detail was important to her. She was also a very cheerful person. She came to work with a good attitude, a really good attitude. She really enjoyed being an actress. And I do know that Paul [Wendkos] adored her, and loved working with her. He had that same kind of enthusiastic spirit that she had. The movie was one of his favorite things that he had ever done.

Lizzie's other film with Wendkos was 1979 CBS TV-movie, *Act of Violence*. Originally airing as part of the network's *Special Movie Presentation*, this Emmet G. Lavery production featured Lizzie's *Catherine McSweeney* as a television news writer whose liberal beliefs are challenged when she's brutally attacked by three young gang members, who happen to be Latino. Here's a closer look at the story:

> Divorced, Catherine lives with her young son in a lower-middle class neighborhood. She is assigned to a *crime in the streets* news series with *Tony Bonelli* (James Sloyan), a reporter with zero tolerance for her liberal perspective, so much so, he calls her "ignorant, soft-minded; sheltered." Then, upon returning from work by taxi, she's assaulted in the hallway of her apartment building. A short time later at the hospital, a detective looking into the incident is puzzled by her explanations. "I didn't ask to be mugged," she protests. "Didn't you?" he asks, suggesting that she, the victim, is responsible for the crime. In time, Catherine turns increasingly paranoid, flinching involuntarily at the sight of a minority's face. In effect, she becomes a different person, but not for the better. In the midst of this transformation, *Tony* convinces her to tell her story on TV. So, in a consequent interview, she bitterly condemns her attackers: "I am a bigot, a racist, a fascist, that's what they made me, that's why I hate them." By the movie's conclusion, Catherine regains a measure of her former self.

And Lizzie gains increasing respect as an actress.

Act of Violence aired on November 10, 1979, the same date *TV Guide* published the article, "From *Bewitched* to Besieged," writer Tabitha Chance deduced that Lizzie:

> had undergone more transformations than Henry the Eighth had wives. But unlike some of Henry's consorts, she has kept her charming head intact upon her charming neck—and used it to the dedicated, sensible furtherance

of her profession. Indeed, she is no longer *Somebody's Daughter*—Robert Montgomery's daughter. She is *Somebody*. Elizabeth Montgomery.

She had already proved that, of course, with her stardom from *Bewitched* (on which *Samantha*, ironically enough, had missed by a hair the tragic fate of marrying King Henry—in the two-part episode, "How Not to Lose Your Head to King Henry VIII"). It's safe to say that Lizzie always kept her head in the midst of a storm that frequently encircled the airing of post-*Samantha* films like *Act of Violence*.

Approximately five years before, she appeared in *A Case of Rape*, which Tabitha Chance described as "a fairly explicit examination of the subject, without a happy ending." But Lizzie resented any suggestion that there were (and are) obvious similarities between the two films.

"Comparisons are odious," she said, a trifle royally. "I can't worry about things being similar. As far as I'm concerned, they are two very separate kinds of violations and violence."

On December 21, 1985, Elizabeth talked about her creative choices with reporter Scott Osbourne for *Entertainment Tonight*. She found "fun" in "stretching" herself as an actress and "not feeling safe all the time." She didn't like to feel safe when she worked and believed that actors did their best work when they don't feel safe "because [otherwise] they don't set themselves up for any real challenge."

On May 12, 1992, she appeared on *CBS This Morning* to promote her TV-movie, *With Murder in Mind*, which in some ways was reminiscent of *Act of Violence*. She told *Morning* host Kathleen Sullivan that she liked the "kind of diversity" in each of her TV-movies. "I don't like doing the same thing over and over again. And I like being a little bit scared . . . a little teeny bit."

By "scared," Lizzie once again meant "challenged" with performing in what she felt were unique projects. She wasn't necessarily referring to the fear that some of her characters may have experienced within context of the movies she made or the fear that such films may have instilled in the viewers.

Either way, many of her TV-movies were and remain similar. When she first began making them, each film was diverse: *The Victim. Mrs. Sundance. A Case of Rape. The Legend of Lizzie Borden. The Awakening Land. Jennifer: A*

Woman's Story. Second Sight: A Love Story. The Rules of Marriage. When The Circus Came to Town. And even though it was a remake of her friend Bette Davis' 1939 classic, *Dark Victory* was also a unique addition on Lizzie's distinctive resume.

But the others, not so much: 1985's *Between the Darkness and the Dawn* was derivative of 1976's *Dark Victory* (albeit with a much happier ending). 1979's *Act of Violence* was reminiscent of 1974's *A Case of Rape*, 1980's *Belle Starr* echoed 1974's *Mrs. Sundance*. 1993's *The Black Widow Murders* hearkened back to 1975's *Lizzie Borden*. And again, 1992's *With Murder in Mind* was reminiscent of 1979's *Act of Violence* (not to mention the 1955 "Relative Stranger" episode of the CBS anthology series, *Appointment with Adventure*, in which Lizzie co-starred with William Windom).

Yet while Lizzie did repeat herself with certain performances, each of her post-*Bewitched* TV-movies proved to be ratings blockbusters. So Tabitha Chance wondered:

> Could it be that viewers, on some unconscious level, enjoy seeing an elegant, beautiful woman like Elizabeth Montgomery get mucked up and knocked about by deranged sociopaths? Perhaps her audience wants to see Elizabeth suffer in the roles she assumes on TV. That is one theory.

Psychotherapist Annette Baran shared another with *TV Guide*:

> [Elizabeth] presents a picture of a haughty, independent, prepossessing woman. One sees her as a woman able to take care of herself. Yet even she is helpless and vulnerable—just like anyone else. Women who might feel some awe of her see her as powerless as they would be in the same circumstances. Men, on the other hand, would have a chance to feel chivalrous and protective.

In September 1966, Lizzie explained to *TV Radio Mirror* magazine that she and her cousin Panda were "terribly close":

> I sometimes don't see her for a year but that has nothing to do with it. If I ever had a problem, I can't conceive of having one—I'd call her and there'd be no "why" and "where have you been," we're just close and I guess we always will be.

But according to Sally Kemp, "There was a darkness in Elizabeth's life," a shadow that she believes Panda sensed as well:

> She was as caught up in the mystery of Elizabeth as I am. She was never allowed to see Elizabeth's children. Panda would visit L.A. and they'd have dinner together, but Elizabeth wouldn't wake her children and let Panda visit with them. And Panda never understood why. It was like Elizabeth was two or three other people all mixed into one.

In order to play the darker, more textured roles, Lin Bolen Wendkos believes that most actors have "a hidden story":

> You have to have some kind of experience in your childhood or in your life that was so devastating that you could recall those kinds of feelings. Because, otherwise, how could you play it and how do you become that person? How do you give yourself to a character like that? You're giving yourself over to an audience in such a way that is so . . . inner destructive. That is why so many actors shun the public, and maybe why Elizabeth did, too; because they give so much of their inner selves to the world when they're working that there's not much left when they're not working.

Upon meeting Lizzie in 1979, *TV Guide's* Tabitha Chance said:

> [She had an] air of quiet command and cool amiability. She seemed infinitely unknowable; it is unimaginable to think she might ever be sloppy or have bad breath. At 46 [and marking her birth year as 1933] and easily looking a full sixteen years younger, Elizabeth is smooth of face and perfect of figure. Were one to come upon her suddenly in Saks Fifth Avenue [which she frequented], the conclusion would be that this woman had never done anything more than slice a catered chateaubriand . . . [She was] as carefully nurtured as any rich man's privileged daughter. And yet, breeding, private schooling, riches, looks, and derivative fame were not enough.

Robert Montgomery's shadowy presence still lingered, blurring Lizzie's own identity. But as Chance explained, Lizzie contributed to that stigma. She was no doubt grateful to her father for jump-starting her career. Although she enjoyed drawing and painting pictures, whenever Lizzie said things like, "My art belongs to Daddy," she was talking about her inherited theatrical craft . . . a lucrative craft, one that certainly materialized in a big way via *Samantha's* witchcraft, as well as other performances.

By 1979, Lizzie had negotiated an exclusive contract with CBS to craft two TV-movies a year for the following three years, for which she received more than 1.5 million dollars. That would buy a truckload of art supplies today, let alone over three decades ago.

Of the scripts offered to her in that period, she selected *Act of Violence*. From the minute she agreed to do the movie, Lizzie wanted it shot as written or, as Chance wrote in *TV Guide*, as "sexy, violent; rough in word and deed." While she may have looked like "a tea rose," Chance pointed out, Lizzie was ready to fight network executives, if need be, to keep that approach. "If somebody says no and it's important, you argue," Lizzie said. "But I prefer the word *negotiate*."

Such was the case with *Rape* in 1974, when NBC executives were nervous about a scene involving Lizzie's character, *Ellen Harrod*, and her examination in a doctor's office. "I didn't like doing that scene," she told Chance, "but we fought for it and it stayed in and we were right."

Chance then explained, "Well brought-up women usually don't discuss their private lives with anyone but their mothers, best friends, and hairdressers," and while Elizabeth was willing to bare her soul on camera, she was no exception to that rule, further confirming her intense need for privacy.

She was by this time living happily with Bob Foxworth and felt no need to share with anyone, the press or friends alike, the soap-operatic details of her failed marriages to Fred Cammann, Gig Young, and Bill Asher. But she did enjoy sharing with pals her hilarious, complicated plot recapitulations of daytime TV soap operas.

As she told *TV Guide*, she would indeed "forget" to return phone calls, but she also still wondered if her "Daddy" was proud of her. She remained down-to-earth, but drove a Mercedes, albeit a ten-year-old Mercedes (which was adorned with a "Lizzy" license plate, a misspelling of her favorite nickname). As during her days on *Bewitched*, Lizzie was never late to the set of any of her TV-movies and she was always professional. She readily convinced the crew to adore her by acting like what Chance called "a normal nice person, telling jokes and joining in with the four-letter word patois rampant in Hollywood sets."

"If that bawdiness may seem a strange paradox for the queenly Eliza-beth," Chance concluded, "it isn't. A lady always puts everyone at ease . . ." as opposed to the heartless woman Lizzie portrayed in the 1991 CBS TV-movie, *Sins of the Mother*. Based on the book, *Son*, by Jack Olsen, *Sins* was written for television by Richard Fiedler, and directed by John D. Patterson:

> As a public figure, *Ruth Coe* (Lizzie) is a prestigious socialite. In private, she abuses her adult son, the charismatic Real Estate agent, *Kevin Coe* (Dale Midkiff). The consequences are devastating, when his most recent ladylove realizes he's the serial rapist that has decimated their community.

An especially harsh review of this film appeared in *The Hollywood Reporter*, February 19, 1991:

> Montgomery turns in a peculiarly mannered performance and appears not to have been directed to her best advantage. Though her lines seethe with vitriol and need, she seems disconnected from any emotional underpinning at all, as though she's reading the lines off the page . . . CBS' best shot may be to market it to fans of Elizabeth Montgomery who want to see her play a witch again.

In a strange twist of TV fate in 2001, Mary Tyler Moore, Lizzie's con-temporary classic TV female star of the 1960s (via *The Dick Van Dyke Show*), took the lead in the similarly-themed and titled TV-movie, *Like Mother, Like Son: The Strange Story of Sante and Kenny Kimes*.

Just as some *Bewitched* fans may have been taken aback by Lizzie's por-trayal in *Sins of the Mother*, Moore's admirers (by way of her happy character portrayals of *Laura Petrie* on *Van Dyke* and *Mary Richards* on *The Mary Tyler Moore Show*) may have been just as stunned when she played *Sante Kimes* in *Like Mother, Like Son*.

Sante's childhood abuse and exploitation leaves a legacy of amorality that she passes on to her son *Kenny* (with a "K" played by Gabriel Olds), just as Lizzie's *Ruth Coe's* sins were instilled in her son *Kevin* (also with a "K"; played by Dale Midkiff).

What may prove to be further compelling, and a little confusing, is that Lizzie later played a similar role in 1993 CBS TV-movie, *The Black Widow*

Murders: The Blanche Taylor Moore Story (the subtitle of which is similar to Mary Tyler Moore's real name).

To top it all off, Lizzie and Mary's hair styles are very similar (and the same color) in *Sins of the Mother* and *Like Mother, Like Son*, while all three films are, sadly, based on true stories.

While it may be fascinating how it all worked out, in 1993, journalist Bart Mills delineated the premise of *Black Widow Murders* in particular, and Lizzie's subsequent participation, taking the lead role of *Blanche Taylor Moore*:

> Life was placid in shabby-genteel central North Carolina, where *Blanche Taylor Moore* worked in a grocery store, lived in a trailer park, went faithfully to church, raised her daughters well, gossiped with her friends, and poisoned every man who went to bed with her. When the police finally confronted her with her crimes, she was flabbergasted. How dare they accuse an innocent woman, even though everyone close to her seemed to wind up in the cemetery, stuffed with arsenic? Elizabeth Montgomery is apt casting for this sly, chilling look at psychopathy. Elusive, elliptical, more likely to smile enigmatically than explain exhaustively, Montgomery gets behind the formality of *Moore's* way of speaking and offers convincing hints of the innocence of evil.

Today, Blanche Moore, who told authorities she was sexually abused as a child, has terminal cancer and is on North Carolina's Death Row, convicted of the murder of her long-time lover. Her first husband, her mother, and her father are others whose exhumed bodies revealed large concentrations of arsenic. Her second husband, a minister, who nearly died of arsenic poisoning, testified against her at her trial in 1990.

As Lizzie explained to Mills in 1993:

> Blanche was very lucky. Thirty or forty years ago, she would have sizzled by now. I don't believe they will wind up executing her. She's appealing at the moment. I think she doesn't feel she did anything terribly wrong. It was something she had to do, particularly to the second husband, who was an ordained minister . . . Blanche truly believes she is innocent. No, I mean, she truly believes she is an innocent. She didn't think what she did was wrong, because of the sexual abuse she said she suffered as a child. People

have different ways of dealing with their problems. Once she started on her way, there was no going back.

In 2012, classic TV curator and author, Ed Robertson, host of the popular radio show, *TV Confidential*, put it this way:

> Once *Bewitched* ended she was looking for projects that would allow her to grow as an actress, and further develop her dramatic skills, which she was not always able to do as *Samantha*, particularly in the last couple years of the show. I don't think she was necessarily trying to "shed" her image as *Samantha,* but I do believe she wanted to show audiences (and for that matter, casting directors and the like) that she could do much more than *Samantha*. That's why I think she did *A Case of Rape*, which had aired the year before in 1974, and I think that's what may have attracted her to doing *The Legend of Lizzie Borden*. That, plus the project itself had a strong pedigree. Paul Wendkos had already established himself as an excellent director, plus Fritz Weaver, through his work on such shows as *Twilight Zone*, was an accomplished, respected stage actor. I don't know whether Fritz worked with her father, but I imagine Elizabeth would have relished the opportunity to work with someone like him.

She also embraced the chance to work with screen legend Kirk Douglas in the 1985 CBS TV-movie, *Amos*, which also starred Pat Morita, best known as *Arnold* from TV's *Happy Days* and later as *Mr. Miyagi* in the original *Karate Kid* movies. This time, Lizzie not only played a heartless character, but a seemingly soulless one as well:

> *Daisy Daws* (Lizzie) is a psychopathic abusive nurse at a senior facility that houses *Amos Lasher* (Douglas), her main patient, and *Tommy Tanaka* (Morita), and other seniors who ultimately band against her in a battle for their very lives.

Shortly after this film was rerun in the summer of 1986, a Los Angeles viewer wrote in to the *Television Times* supplement of *The Los Angeles Times*, pining for Lizzie to return to her own "happier days" on screen and her most beloved role. Interestingly, the viewer also addressed what Lizzie later described in 1989 and during other interviews as her personal philosophy about acting. But more than anything, the writer expressed what had been on the minds of countless fans of Elizabeth's and *Bewitched*. In his letter dated August 9, 1986, home audience member Bob Thompson of Burbank, California composed his thoughts and said:

> *Amos* with Kirk Douglas and Elizabeth Montgomery had to be the most brilliant television movie I've seen this year. Montgomery displayed her true talent for portraying a *witch*. Her performance was incredible. However, with all the reunion movies on television lately, I would love to see a revival of *Bewitched*. All I've seen Montgomery do in the last decade is heavy drama. Enough already. Let's see some comedy. I believe it to be her forte. Isn't it harder to make people laugh than cry anyway? What I'm trying to say, I guess, is . . . "*Samantha*, where are you?"

SUGAR . . . Elizabeth as she is best remembered, in this prime photo of her as the pleasant, sweet-natured witch-next-door *Samantha* . . . from the fifth season of *Bewitched*, 1968–1969. ABC Photo Archives, courtesy of Getty Images

. . . AND SPICE: To shake things up a bit on *Bewitched*, Elizabeth periodically played *Samantha's* diametrically opposed (in every way), daring, look-a-like cousin *Serena*, seen here in a publicity shot from the episode, "*Cousin Serena* Strikes Again (Part Two)," which originally aired January 9, 1969. ABC Photo Archives, courtesy of Getty Images

LOVERS AND OTHER ANIMALS: Elizabeth's love for animals was never more evident than on *Bewitched*, during which she worked with, among other critters, dogs, mice, frogs, monkeys, and her favorite . . . horses. In this scene from the episode, "Daddy Does His Thing," which originally aired April 3, 1969, it's a mule into which Sam's father *Maurice* (Maurice Evans) transforms *Darrin*, played by Dick York. It was these kinds of plots that allowed for the absence of York, who had missed fourteen episodes of the series due to the ongoing struggles that accompanied a back injury he acquired while working on the 1959 movie, *They Came to Cordura* (which featured Gary Cooper, with whom Lizzie appeared in her first feature, 1955's *The Court-Martial of Billy Mitchell*). In fact, it was on the set of this *Bewitched* episode that York collapsed, which led to his resigning from the series and being replaced by Dick Sargent the following fall. ABC Photo Archives, courtesy of Getty Images

PEACE, LOVE, AND UNDERSTANDING: Elizabeth flashes the "peace sign" to adoring, if barricaded, young fans in 1969. It's a telling scene. First, in a nod to the times, the peace sign of sorts would show up (in reverse and around the nose) on *Bewitched* as the "witches' honor sign." Second, she appreciated her admirers, but only at a safe distance. And third, she protested the Vietnam War and frequently battled with her father over personal politics. Meanwhile, her political advocacy for various charitable and global causes was renowned. She narrated the controversial feature film documentaries, 1988's *Cover Up* and 1992's *The Panama Deception* (which won the Oscar for Best Documentary), and she was one of the first celebrities to advocate for those suffering with and because of AIDS. ABC Photo Archives, courtesy of Getty Images

PLAYING FAVORITES: Elizabeth with (from left) Janee Michelle, Venetta Rogers, Erin Murphy, David Lawrence, co-stars from her favorite *Bewitched* episode, "Sisters at Heart," which aired on December 24, 1970. The segment was co-written by the multicultural Jefferson High School Class of 1971, and won the Governor's Award that year at the Emmys. The story's premise centered around prejudice which, in May 1989, Elizabeth said was the central message of *Bewitched*. ABC Photo Archives, courtesy of Getty Images

MONUMENTAL MONTGOMERY MOMENT: Elizabeth with (from left) makeup man Rolf Miller, hairstylist Peanuts (with hand on glasses), and Robert Montgomery, during his one and only visit to the *Bewitched* set (with his second wife, Elizabeth "Buffy" Harkness, not pictured). Here, all take delight in the "pig mask" which was adorned by Dick Sargent (not pictured) for the episode, "This Little Piggy," which aired February 25, 1971. In the background: David White (*Larry Tate*) takes it all in from afar. He very much respected Elizabeth and her father, and was pleased to see them together. White was a father himself. But sadly, his son Jonathan (for whom Larry's on-screen son, *Jonathan Tate*, was named) was on board the Pan Am Flight 103 that went down over Lockerbie, Scotland, in 1988. No bodies were ever recovered, and David certainly never recovered from the loss of his son. Courtesy of Everett Collection

FOX IN THE FOLD: Robert Foxworth and charity played interconnecting roles in Elizabeth's life. Here, the two are seen at a charity event in 1974, about a year after they met on the set of *Mrs. Sundance* in 1973. They would ultimately marry . . . twenty years later. Unlike Lizzie's three other husbands, the much older Bill Asher or Gig Young, and even the slightly older Fred Cammann, Foxworth was Lizzie's junior in age. He also shared the same first name with her father and, upon their initial meeting, he had not seen one single episode of *Bewitched*. At the time, that was definitely in his favor as Lizzie was in the midst of divorcing Bill Asher and wanted nothing to do with any aspect of *Samantha* whatsoever. According to Lizzie's friend Sally Kemp, it was Foxworth who encouraged Lizzie to stretch her theatrical talents for "meatier" roles beyond *Bewitched*. Ralph Dominguez—Globe Photos

A SHATTERING PEFFORMANCE: Elizabeth received her first post-*Bewitched* Emmy nomination for her portrayal of the battered housewife *Ellen Harrod* in the groundbreaking television film, *A Case of Rape*, which became one of the highest rated TV-movies in history, and which paved the way for future issue-oriented small screen productions. Courtesy of Everett Collection

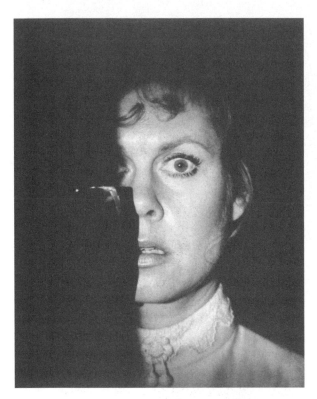

AN EYE-OPENING EXPERIENCE: Elizabeth's heralded performance as the real-life murderous Lizzie Borden in the 1975 TV-movie, *The Legend of Lizzie Borden*, earned her a second post-*Bewitched* Emmy nomination, but her father's disdain. Strangely, from the moment she played Borden, who was never convicted of the brutal killings of her father and stepmother, Elizabeth wanted to be referred to as "Lizzie." Courtesy of Everett Collection

THE MID-CAREER FRONTIER: Elizabeth received her third post-*Samantha* Emmy nomination for her portrayal *of Sayward Luckett Wheeler* in the elegantly filmed three-part TV mini-series, *The Awakening Land* in 1978. Her co-stars in the film included Hal Holbrook, a very young William H. Macy (in his first role), and Jane Seymour, who would go head to head with Elizabeth as the "Queen of TV-movies" in the 1980s and early 1990s, before she would take the lead in her own female pioneer TV role as *Dr. Quinn, Medicine Woman*. Courtesy of Everett Collection

A "STARR" IS BORN: Elizabeth once more appears in a strong female character of the West in the 1980 television film, *Belle Starr*, one of her better TV-movies from every perspective (writing, directing, cinematography, and performance). Courtesy of Everett Collection

LIFE IMITATES ART: Elizabeth as the visually-impaired *Alaxandra McKay* with her seeing-eye best friend *Emma* in a scene from *Second Sight: A Love Story*, which aired on March 13, 1984. The two bonded so closely off-screen that Elizabeth ended up adopting Emma in real life. Sadly, Emma died shortly thereafter. Courtesy of Everett Collection

MURDER, SHE WROTE IN MIAMI: Elizabeth is seen here in a publicity shot from her first appearance as real-life *Miami Herald* crime reporter *Edna Buchanan* in *The Corpse Had a Familiar Face*, which originally aired on CBS, March 27, 1994. Lizzie would later return to the role in 1995's *Deadline for Murder*, which became her final on-screen performance. She and CBS had intended to continue with a series of Buchanan films. Courtesy of Everett Collection

A STAR COME RAIN OR SHINE: Elizabeth finally received her much-deserved star, if posthumously, on the Hollywood Walk of Fame, January 4, 2008, during a thunderstorm that proved no match for the love and devotion of hundreds of her loyal fans who ignored the downpour and focused on honoring their favorite star. Lizzie's family and friends said she would have laughed at the fact that it was raining. Michael Germana— Globe Photos

PART IV

Reconciled

"My darling, charming Elizabeth . . . she has a touch of immortality. *Bewitched* is her light-hearted gift to the world, whatever shadows she battled."

—Sally Kemp, 2012

Nineteen

Spirits and Angels

"You almost got the feeling that she was
a little girl playing a grown-up."

—Doug Tibbles, *Bewitched* writer, assessing Elizabeth's personality

In character or in reality, Lizzie employed a carefree spirit and wit even in the most challenging of situations. Whether she was playing *Samantha* who frequently defended her mortal marriage before her mother *Endora,* or whether she was playing herself in real life fighting for independence from the troubled Gig Young as well as from her father Robert Montgomery. In each scenario, scripted or nonscripted, Lizzie was *playing*. She maintained a strong sense of decorum, while not losing her stable sense of humor. She was beloved by viewers at home who were bewitched by her charm on screen, and the people she met off camera were just as bedazzled by her presence in person.

In the early 1990s, former restaurant manager/hostess DD Howard used to work at the tony Le Dome restaurant on Sunset Boulevard in Beverly Hills. At the time, Le Dome (which has since closed its doors) was the hot spot for the Hollywood elite to meet, eat, and mingle. Celebrities as diverse as Goldie Hawn and Kurt Russell, the Kirk Douglases, even Ronald and Nancy Reagan among many others, walked through its fashionable doors.

As Howard recalls, Lizzie and Bob Foxworth were frequent patrons of the establishment, and both were cherished by Le Dome's staff for their unaffected and unassuming ways:

> After managing restaurants for over ten years, you really come to recognize personalities for who they are really when they come into a restaurant. You know who the nice people are and you know who the not-so-nice people are. You can see it right away. The essence of who they are is right there in front of you.
>
> Well, not only were Elizabeth and Bob two of the nicest people who ever came through our doors, but they were two of the nicest people I have ever met in my entire life. They definitely made my top ten list. They were a charming, sweet, beautiful couple. And she was always laughing and smiling.
>
> Many times she would come in with [her manager] Barry Krost, who she had a great banter with, or groups of friends. Whenever she arrived, you knew a party was gonna happen. The staff certainly always looked forward to seeing her. She was just always so interested in everyone, and who they were as a person, whether it was someone she and Bob were dining with, or whether it was one of the waiters or busboys. It was almost like she diverted attention from herself back to you.
>
> When she'd walk in the door, I would say, "You look so fabulous!" And then she'd turn it around and say, "And '*you*' look gorgeous!" We'd then go on to have a regular conversation about what *I* was doing that day, or what was going on in *my* life.
>
> She was just so sincerely interested in other people. She was curious and interested in everyone and everything. And that really represented just how endearing she was.
>
> She was simply a shining star if there ever was one. The place just lit up when she walked in the room. She was an angel.

According to Tom McCartney, Lizzie discussed her sunny side of life in 1993 with journalist Bart Mills, who interviewed her, strangely enough, about her quite unsunny performance in the TV-movie, *Black Widow Murders: The Blanche Taylor Moore Story*. Portraying Blanche was by far her darkest characterization since her appearance in 1975's *The Legend of Lizzie Borden* (both films were also based on true-life tales). But Lizzie read between the lines and found laughter between the tears. In speaking with

Mills, she recalled the day the *Widow Murders* cast met for its first pre-production read-through of the script. Many of writer/co-executive producer Judith Paige Mitchell's lines drew laughs, and Mitchell said to the cast, "But I didn't know this script was funny."

But as far as Elizabeth was concerned, and as she expressed to Mills, "Life is funny even when it's upsetting. The more human a story is, the more real and the more true it is, the more likely you are to find subconscious humor in it. You may not see it on the page, but when you say it out loud, you have to laugh."

Lizzie also "just had to laugh" about *I Dream of Jeannie's* attempts to duplicate *Bewitched's* success in the 1960s, as well as when the *Tabitha* series tried to do the same in the 1970s, and when TV audiences actually laughed, at least to some extent, at various magic-based, female-oriented shows or characters that tried to replicate the guffaws Lizzie created as *Samantha* on *Bewitched*. While the *Tabitha* series may not have fared so well, *Jeannie* certainly found a resounding success, as did other "re*sorce*ful" women on the small screen:

Sabrina, the Teenage Witch (with Melissa Hart, ABC, 1996–2003) skyrocketed in the ratings, as did *Charmed* (1998–2006, CW; Alyssa Milano, Shannon Doherty, Holly Marie Combs, Rose McGowan). Before those good-smitten witches came along, *Angelique/Cassandra Collins* (played by Lara Parker) did her best on the gothic daytime soap *Dark Shadows* (ABC, 1966–1971), right beside *Witchiepoo* (Billie Hayes, on ABC's Saturday morning's *H.R. Pufnstuf* from1969–1970; who also played a storybook witch on *Bewitched*), and Juliet Mills was *Phoebe* on *Nanny and the Professor* (ABC, 1970–1971, which also starred a very young Kim Richards, before her quite different performances on today's *Real Housewives of Beverly Hills*). Even ABC Family's recent *Secret Circle* drama features a young band of sorceresses.

But in the fall of 1989, ABC's main network tried to more directly recapture the magic of *Bewitched* with a new "witch-uation comedy" called *Free Spirit*. It starred Corinne Bohrer (a kind of pre-*Friends* Lisa Kudrow) as *Winnie Goodwinn* who was reluctantly sent to Earth as a housekeeper/baby-sitter for the *Harper* family led by Franc Luz as *T. J. Harper*, the father. The children included *Jesse Harper*, as played by *How I Met Your Mother's* Alyson Hannigan (who would later portray the witch *Willow Rosenberg* in *Buffy*, *the Vampire Slayer*, not to mention a character named *Samantha* in the short-lived 1993 series *Almost Home*, created by a writer named Lynn Montgomery, no relation).

Free Spirit was a noble attempt, but it failed to appropriately reimagine the magic of *Bewitched* on several levels, not the least of which was the poorly funded cinematic quality. The show was videotaped in front of a live audience (allegedly), which meant it already had two strikes against it. Supernatural sitcoms should neither be videotaped nor presented in front of a live anything. The on-camera tricks and effects need to be properly executed and filmed. Imagine the tediousness of waiting in the studio seats while the crew sets up the magic for the home audience? Needless to say, *Free Spirit* was gone by the following January, with the ghost of *Bewitched's* stellar past lingering in its wake.

Meanwhile, "free spirit," the phrase, remains to this day the best way to describe Lizzie's personality. Throughout her life, good, bad, or indifferent, she took everything in stride, with an occasional grain of salt over old wounds. Her core relationships always proved challenging, but she dealt with them head-on, although at times moving on too fast. Not one to offer second chances, she subscribed to the old adage, "Fool me once, shame on you; fool me twice, shame on me." Lizzie tended not to let things fester, even when she learned that she had cancer. At first she was angry, but then came to immediate terms with her tragic reality in 1995.

According to her commentary from 1989, Elizabeth responded to less serious and complicated circumstances in simple terms, whether discussing the possibility of a *Bewitched* reunion ("Forget it!") or hearing about those who sought to do such a movie without her ("Anybody can do whatever they like. I don't care!"). Her amassed fortune from *Bewitched* coupled with her family's cache of cash allowed her the freedom to do as she pleased. She worked by choice, and from her work she gave choice performances, even if that work was only recognized with Emmy nominations and not a single victory.

Politically minded and theatrically gifted, she never ignored her ability to communicate, but always made certain to share a laugh amidst the probable pangs of losing Emmys to her peers, pangs she may have hidden with a Pagliacci smile. Whether engaged in a game of darts on *The Mike Douglas*

Show or a home tennis match with Bill Asher or Bob Foxworth, her true victory was never spoiled.

Whether riding colts on her family's sprawling properties stateside or in the English countryside, or rushing to play the mares at the Santa Anita or Hollywood Park Race Track, for Lizzie it was never about winning the horse race; it was about the human race to live, work, and play.

The essence of that playful spirit was thoughtfully reiterated by family members and friends on January 4, 2008 at the Hollywood Walk of Fame ceremony that cemented her star.

Liz "Dizzie" Sheridan approached the podium. She described the first day she met Lizzie through a mutual friend (writer William Blast, *The Legend of Lizzie Borden*), shortly after moving to Los Angeles, how they played croquet, and became fast friends.

The next day Lizzie called Dizzie and wondered what kind of shampoo she used and if she'd like to go the race track, all in the same breath. Lizzie also insisted that Dizzie stay in her guesthouse, which Sheridan proceeded to do until she found a place of her own. At which time Lizzie lent Dizzie the required down payment. A few weeks later Sheridan paid her back on their way to the race track . . . in Elizabeth's chauffeur-driven limousine. Upon seeing the cash, Lizzie screamed and playfully tossed the money all over the car, the chauffer, Sheridan, everything. From there, they journeyed on to the track and proceeded to spend the extra loot.

As it turned out, Dizzie was one of the few people who ever paid Lizzie back for her generosity, a true and loyal friend indeed. Elizabeth could not have cared less if Sheridan ever paid her back, but the fact that she did earned Dizzie high marks in Lizzie's highly selective realm of friendship.

Actor David Knell played Elizabeth's son, *Ed Reed*, when she took the lead in the 1980 TV-movie Western, *Belle Starr*. This film was the second professional acting job Knell had won upon moving to Los Angeles only a short time before. The first production he appeared in was for a segment of *Great Performances*, called "Life on the Mississippi" in which he played Mark Twain. Two weeks into the performance Knell broke his arm and his role had to be recast, all of which somehow later led to his being cast in the ground-breaking (and ironically titled) 1979 feature film *Breaking Away*.

At the time, Knell was only in his late teens, and because he was just starting out in the business, had little free cash to spread around. He didn't even own a car, only a bicycle, which he'd ride to various auditions, location shoots, and/or rehearsals.

One day, shortly before *Belle Starr* began filming, Lizzie hosted a first read-through of the script at her home in Beverly Hills, which Knell defined as "interesting." It had dialogue that he defines today as "very stylized and not modern at all." At any rate, those present at the reading were the film's entire main cast and crew, including the movie's director John Alonzo, as well as Robert Foxworth, whom Knell remembers as "a nice guy."

Knell, who lived in Laurel Canyon at the time, says he took the "longest route possible" to Elizabeth's home. "It was very scenic and wonderful." But when he arrived at Lizzie's door, it was very comedic and hilarious, for it was at this point that he was introduced to her trademark sense of humor. "She was very playful!" he says.

Indeed, upon first seeing Knell at her door, alongside his bike, Lizzie mused, "What time *yesterday* did you leave?"

Knell laughed, and from that moment on, enjoyed working on *Starr* with Lizzie, whom he called "great," particularly when it came to mounting horses during filming. "She rode very well," he recalls. Little wonder, of course, because Lizzie had been riding since she was three.

The exterior scenes for *Starr* added to the movie's realism. It was filmed on location in Agoura Hills, California, which is now a modern, developed area. But in 1980, the cast was in awe of its then-wilderness. Having just completed filming for "Life on the Mississippi," another production filmed on location in a hinterland setting, Knell in particular was "very much into authenticity" when it came to acting. So much so that when he was cast to play Lizzie's son *Ed* of the Old West in *Starr*, he decided not to wash his hair because "nobody did back then, and it seemed like it would be weird if I did." Instead, while filming one *Starr* moment, it became "weird" for Lizzie that he did not.

The scene was in *Ed's* bedroom on the farm he shared with *Belle,* shortly before a great fire in the barn, which is ignited by vigilantes who seek to rid the county of *Belle* and her band. Knell as *Ed* is sitting on the bed and the script calls for Lizzie as *Belle* to run her hands through his hair. Upon noticing that his locks were somewhat hygienically challenged, Knell muses, "Lizzie let out a big *'Yick!'*" As to just how "authentic" Lizzie's hair was during the shoot, Knell sustains, "I think she probably washed hers and just made it look dirty."

In all, Knell says his time with Lizzie on *Starr* was well-spent. "It was just a joy working with her. I think the one particular scene that I remember the most [is the one] where I almost got to kiss her, which was great, but they changed the script and we never got to do it." Just as well the kissing scene never took place. Having such a moment between *Belle* and her son, no matter how troubled they were, would likely have been too ambiguous an endeavor for the network censors. However, as Knell concludes, "It definitely would have added an additional layer to [their] already complicated relationship."

While network officials continued to censor scenes from Lizzie's fictional films, she, of course, was no stranger to complicated relationships in real life. Yet, again, her playful nature, like a good portion of her very real character, was inspired by her grandmother Becca.

As Elizabeth expressed to *TV Radio Mirror* in April 1970, Becca . . .

> . . . made games of everything. You asked the meaning of a word, she'd say, "What do you think it means?" And, when you came up with your child-ish' explanation: "That's marvelous, Elizabeth; now let's look it up and see what the people say it means." In short, the dictionary. And often [after] we found out, she'd say, "But I like your definition much better."

As Bob Foxworth had expressed on A&E's *Biography*, it was Becca who had also inspired Elizabeth's obsession with the race track. In fact, one day in her dressing room while filming *Bewitched*, she was sprawled out on the floor with a copy of the racing form.

As was explained in *TV Radio Mirror*, November 1969, a publicist walked in on her and howled in protest. Lizzie looked up from her scratch-sheet, pencil-clenched in teeth, and wondered what was wrong. "If you ever want to ruin your image," said the publicist, "this sort of thing will do it."

Elizabeth didn't give it a thought and continued on in her carefree way. It was an effervescence that today might be described as "emotional intelligence." But she had developed that part of her being years before science came up with a name for it, particularly when she was a young lass playing on the Montgomery family compound in Patterson, New York, with her cousin Panda and friend Sally Kemp. "Of course we all enjoyed playing together as children," Kemp recalls, "and Panda had the same little exquisite face as Elizabeth. But Elizabeth had that *intellectual curiosity*; her intelligence, her interest in being alive in the moment. I don't think she had any aspirations about being a classical actress."

Whereas Sally, on the other hand, is still eager to act in, for example, a live stage production of *Trojan Women*, the Greek tragedy by playwright Euripides (that was once made into a 1971 feature film starring Katharine Hepburn). She wants to play *Hephzibah*, and she wants do it in an amphitheater "in Greece somewhere," and she doesn't care if "anyone ever sees it."

Conversely, she believes Elizabeth "never gave a hoot about any of that. Life was fun for her and she wanted it to be that way."

As reporter Rose Perlberg assessed in *TV Picture Life*, October 1965, "*Fun* was the word that cropped up most constantly in our conversation with Liz. To her, work is fun . . . the idea of having . . . babies is fun, and being married seems to be the most fun of all."

Lizzie herself admitted as much to *Modern Screen* magazine in May 1965. "I'm not riddled with ambition," she said. "Acting is something I've done because it's fun and hard work. I enjoy hard work. But a career with me is about as close to last as second can get. First is my life: love, children, and a home."

In January that year, she added in *TV Radio Mirror*:

When women choose a life of competition with men in the marketplace, it is usually due to circumstances beyond their control . . . like sickness in the family or some inner drive for success that's caused by a childhood frustration. Most women try to walk the tightrope between home and office, and some of them manage to do surprisingly well at it. In my case, the problem is much the same for both *Samantha* and me. For the sake of home and husband, she'd like to kick the witchcraft habit, but finds it too hard to do. I'd like to concentrate all my heart and soul on my private life, but I find it impossible to forsake acting. I grew up in the actor's world of make-believe, and it's become part of my living tissue. My great hope is that, like *Saman-tha*, when I pursue my special brand of witchery, it will not offend my husband but make me more intriguing to him.

Of course, none of that was easy in 1965 when *Bewitched* was a massive hit and she was married to Bill Asher. It was difficult before she worked on the show, and remained a challenge after she ended the series. Lizzie may have pursed acting, but she never pined after economic success. She was born into that. However, she hungered for other forms of success, in romance, friendship, and family. She never gave up on love in any of its forms, even if she sometimes found too much of it, too soon.

At twenty, she married socialite Fred Cammann, and divorced him one year later. At twenty-three, she wed actor Gig Young and after six years, divorced him, too. Shortly after that, she fell in love with Bill Asher and their honeymoon lasted approximately eleven years. It was her twenty-year romance with Bob Foxworth, whom she finally married approximately twenty-eight months before she died, that was her lengthiest relationship.

Over the years, she endured personal disappointments throughout the long, grueling professional hours, beginning with *Robert Montgomery Pres-ents*, and followed by numerous TV guest star appearances, feature films, *Bewitched,* and then later, her TV-movies. She survived the heartache of her personal life with the backbone she sustained by way of her strict upbring-ing. She viewed herself as a Hollywood product, and she was okay with that. She pegged the glamour and glitz for what it was worth, well-aware of the countless actresses who looked to their careers for happiness because they lacked inner peace within themselves. For Lizzie, acting was a normal, natural thing.

Her parents had talent and performing was something she did. It was "fun" to do. It was not something for which she compromised her life. And she knew that from the onset of *Bewitched's* popularity, and most proba-bly before, as she relayed to *Modern Screen* in 1965:

It's wonderful and gratifying to know that people are enjoying the idea that you enjoy . . . bringing them something that gives pleasure. But if you're lucky enough to have success with a series, it's something that you really can't think of as being your own. You should be grateful, of course, and you have a responsibility to the people who are watching, but success itself is something just loaned to you. Once it's gone, if you felt you'd lost something then the other part of your life, your basic personal life, would not be completed. That's not right! I've always felt that way.

In 2004, New Path Press published *The Seesaw Girl and Me: A Memoir* by Dick York, who appreciated Lizzie's playful spirit. As is explained in this very honest book, there were moments in *Bewitched* when he and Lizzie:

> . . . really did develop a close personal relationship above and beyond the characters, but necessary to the characters (of *Darrin* and *Samantha*). I mean, we did play games. Liz was a game player and a crossword puzzle fan, and we invented all kinds of guessing games and word games . . .

Her TV-movie co-star, veteran actor Ronny Cox, agrees with that.

Cox is best known in classic TV history for his short-lived role as the father on *Apple's Way*, created by Earl Hamner as a contemporary take on his mega-hit family period piece, *The Waltons* (which was set in the Depression). The liberal-minded Cox is also known for iconic feature films like 1972's *Deliverance*, in which he co-starred with Burt Reynolds, Ned Beatty, and Jon Voight (father to Angelina Jolie).

Farrah Fawcett, in one of her first pre-*Charlie's Angels* TV roles, made a guest appearance on *Apple's Way*, and would later star in NBC's acclaimed 1984 TV-movie, *The Burning Bed*—a film that shared many similarities with the network's 1974 TV-movie, *A Case of Rape*, in which Cox had co-starred with Lizzie (both movies featured iconic blonde stars who played characters that were physically assaulted and mentally abused). Cox also worked with Lizzie in her 1992 TV-movie, *With Murder in Mind*. But it was on *Rape* where they met and bonded, mostly due to her approachable personality, their shared political ideals, and because they both enjoying playing games. Real games. Not head games. Cox explains:

> I grew up poor in New Mexico, really poor. All we had was a radio and a deck of cards and dominoes. So I knew every card game known to man

and I played those kinds of games my whole life. Plus, those were the kinds of things that you could do that didn't cost money.

Like Cox, Lizzie enjoyed such everyday games, he thinks, because she craved a certain amount of normalcy in her life. "She came from a world of acting and the theatre," he says, where there's such "vicious competition. And I don't discount for a second Lizzie's competitiveness."

But Lizzie's love for games, be it Gin, Scrabble, Charades, or Backgammon, the last which was all the rage when Lizzie and Cox met, were outlets for her "competitive nature," says Cox, who classifies himself as a "real competitor." So much so, he used to have a tennis court on his property and on every day that he didn't work (which was rare, because he's not stopped working since *A Case of Rape*), he enjoyed playing tennis. And if it came down to who wanted to win more, he or Lizzie, Cox says,

> . . . it would be me. Most people I know of who are as fiercely competitive are also not the best losers in the world. But whether I win or lose, I don't lord it over people. And I think that's a rare thing, and that was also Lizzie's quality. And the thing about Lizzie is that she was never a prima donna in any sense of the word. Working on [*A Case of Rape*] was one of the smoothest sets I've ever been on, and that was mostly because of her. We connected more on a personal level. It was not that I was knocked out by her stardom or [that] she was knocked out by me. We just immediately hit it off.

Time and again, Lizzie earned the veneration of her peers, at least in word, if not always in deed. According to Kasey Rogers, who replaced Irene Vernon as *Louise Tate* on *Bewitched*, she was "a very gifted actress. She excelled at whatever she did, be it drama or comedy. And when she appeared on *Bewitched*, she played *Samantha* with the same sensitivity and love that she possessed in real life."

Rarely, however, did such praise transfer to actual public acknowledgement in any formal award, at least when it came to television. For example, she was recognized on several occasions for her theatrical craft on the New York stage, as when she received the "Daniel Blum Theatre World Award for Most Promising Newcomer"—for *Late Love* in 1953–1954 (which was also Cliff Robertson's debut). Past recipients of the award included James Dean, Eva Marie Saint, and director Leo Penn (Sean's father).

The television world, however, was a whole other ballgame. Although she received a total of nine Emmy nominations, five of which were for *Bewitched*, Elizabeth never won. Her non-*Samantha* nominations were for non-*Samantha* performances: The self-centered *Rusty Heller* on *The Untouchables* ("The Rusty Heller Story," ABC, October 13, 1960); the abused housewife *Ellen Harrod* in *A Case of Rape* (NBC, February 20, 1974); the vile ax murderess in *The Legend of Lizzie Borden* (ABC, February 10, 1975); the pioneer woman *Sayward Luckett* in *The Awakening Land* (NBC, February 19, 20, 21, 1978).

Still, an Emmy victory eluded her—"a bridesmaid, but never a bride." Why?

According to what Richard Michaels said in 1988:

> That's just the way this town is. They [the Academy of Television Arts and Sciences] just didn't want to give it to her. And I think she was a little hurt. But she was also an adult. Even though the Emmy is a major form of acknowledgement, it's not the only form of acknowledgement in the world. Audiences adore her today, just as much as they did in the 1960s. No one will ever forget her or the show. When people find out that I directed the show, especially little kids, who by the way, weren't even born when the show initially aired, the first question I hear is, "What is Elizabeth Montgomery really like?" or "How did she twitch her nose?" That, more than anything, proves her mainstay in television history . . . In the motion picture and television industries, personalities are involved in the awards, and you have to consider winners and losers in the context of their times. Elizabeth was a very private person, and she was never a socialite. She'd never go to a Hollywood party just to be seen. Maybe if she [had] rubbed more elbows, she would have won. But that wasn't her style.

Some years before Lizzie and *Bewitched* were Emmy contenders, the Television Academy had awarded another female TV icon the accolade, not once, but twice. Lucille Ball had won for her various *Lucy* personas over the years and embraced the attention. But when she returned to weekly TV in 1986 with ABC's short-lived *Life with Lucy*, she failed to win points with her peers, her fans, and the critics, and she was devastated by the lack of support on all fronts. But as Michaels also pointed out, shortly before Ball died in 1989 (of a heart ailment), droves of fans lined up around the hospital in which she spent her final days. "She couldn't believe it. She was amazed. And just thank God she found out [how much she was loved] before she died. But I'm not so sure Elizabeth was as lucky."

Before he won an Emmy for his work on *Bewitched*, Bill Asher, Michaels' mentor, received the coveted accolade for helming episodes of Ball's first comedy, *I Love Lucy*. When Ball later switched formats to *The Lucy Show*, during *Bewitched's* rein, Lizzie lost the Emmy twice to the red-headed phenomenon, and Asher was not at all pleased. At the press conference following the 1966 awards ceremony that included his own *Bewitched* victory as a director, he refused to speak with the press unless Lizzie's contributions to *Bewitched* were acknowledged.

Notwithstanding, Asher, like Michaels, thought Lizzie remained unfettered by failing to win over her peers with an Emmy. "It just didn't matter to her," he said in 1988. Yet consider this: Don Knotts was nominated and won the Emmy five times for his beloved interpretation of the shaky gun-shy *Deputy Barney Fife* on *The Andy Griffith Show* (CBS, 1961–1968). It is the stuff of Hollywood legends how much Knotts enjoyed his life off-screen, but one would not exactly define the actor as a heavy socialite. Lizzie, on the other hand, most probably never won an Emmy, at least for *Bewitched*, because her performance as twitch-witch *Samantha* was under-rated and natural. "It didn't seem like she was acting," says film scholar Rob Ray, "But it was actually great acting. She made it look too easy."

Fellow media archivist Tom McCartney adds:

> From what I understand, apparently only a dozen people vote for the Emmys from the nominations cast by everyone in a category; unlike the Oscars where all actors vote for the Best Actor or Actress, etc.; and with all members of the Motion Picture Academy voting for Best Picture for example. With the Emmys, it's always been a small group of cronies who did the voting, and it's still controlled by a small group of people. Maybe (the animated) *Lucy* was right (in *A Charlie Brown Christmas*) . . . maybe it *is* also all controlled by a syndicate back East.

McCartney muses about something that may hold more than a measure of truth. According to *The Emmys* (Perigee, Third Edition, 2000), author Thomas O'Neil reveals what can only be classified as shocking information about how the awards were allegedly distributed, at least by that time. For example, one year, *The Mary Tyler Moore Show* garnered Emmy wins for nearly its entire cast, excluding the star herself. As a result, *Moore* co-star Ed Asner, who won that year (and other seasons) for playing *Lou Grant*, was none-too-pleased and gave it good to the Emmy board, claiming his lead actress (and off-screen boss, Moore's MTM Productions produced the series) was "robbed"; he called the voting process "thoroughly inconsistent." "Thankfully," Asner says, today, "Mary did win, and much deservedly so."

Apparently, the Emmy committee that voted on the nominees consisted of a very select group of business suits from Beverly Hills. For many years, the Emmys were nothing but a battleground between the West and East Coasts, with the East boasting the sophistication and style of New York and Washington, D.C., news programs and variety entertainment, and the West glorifying modern technology and celebrity appeal.

While this select and affluent sector would allegedly be some sort of avant-garde, they were also products of the confines of L.A.'s cloistered television industry, periodically falling victim to their own sequestered arrogance. Consequently, they may have dubbed *Bewitched* and its like as unworthy, most likely because they never objectively watched the programs in the first place, thus dispelling any potentially sincere winners or losers. However, none of that mattered to Lizzie. She failed to win the Emmy for female comedy series lead three more times, losing twice to Hope Lange for *The Ghost and Mrs. Muir* (NBC, 1968–1970) and once to Mary Tyler Moore for *The Dick Van Dyke Show.*

"I think it's funny," she said in 1989 about her frequent losses. She then proceeded to compare herself to Susan Lucci, another legendary multi-nominated actress who never won, at least not until ten years later. Fortunately for the soap star, she finally garnered the amulet for playing the iconic *Erica Kane* on *All My Children* (ABC, 1970–2011). "Maybe the two of us should work together," Lizzie laughed, "do something really brilliant, and then both lose. That would be extremely comical."

But seriously, Lizzie "always knew" that she wouldn't win. "There are a lot of people voting," she said before going on to praise the work of fellow Emmy-nominee Lange who won the Best Actress in a Comedy in 1968 for playing *Mrs. Muir* opposite Edward Mulhare as *The Ghost*. "I thought she was very good, actually. I liked that series," she said of the show that was spawned from the 1947 feature film starring Gene Tierney and Rex Harrison. "You know," she added, "I saw that movie for the first time about three months ago (approximately March 1989). What an amazing movie!"

As it turned out, Robert Montgomery was also never recognized with an award from his peers. As Elizabeth recalled to Ronald Haver in 1991:

"There are times when I think that perhaps he was a bit underrated. And that might be because of the fact that he never really fell into any kind of niche . . . But I just feel he was versatile. He'd try different things. I think that certainly he was appreciated for *Night Must Fall*, because he got an Academy Award nomination for that one."

Released in 1937, directed by Richard Thorpe, and co-starring Rosalind Russell and Dame May Whitty, *Night Must Fall* was based on the play by Emlyn Williams with a screenplay by John Van Druten:

> *Mrs. Bramson* (Whitty) is a wealthy but crotchety matriarch who rules over a sequestered estate for which [she] hires *Danny* (Montgomery) a proficient handyman, whom her niece/companion *Olivia Grayne* (Russell) does not thoroughly trust.

As Lizzie told Haver, her father was excited about the possibility of winning an Oscar for the role, and her mother had already picked out a dress for the event. But Robert Montgomery didn't stand a chance. "It was kind of sad," Lizzie intoned. Approximately two days before the dinner ceremony, an annual event that Elizabeth said was once tastefully presented (as opposed to today's "big hoopla stuff"), the Montgomery household received a call from MGM, the film's studio. "Don't even bother to show up. (Spencer) Tracy's going to get it."

On February 28, 2012, *The Hollywood Reporter* published the article, "The Artist's James Cromwell Slams Academy Awards, Proposes Solution for Flawed Voting Process." Using one of Lizzie's words, Cromwell said the Oscars have become:

> . . . a lot [of] hoopla, which is not really what we do as actors and as artists. We like to do the work, and the work stands for itself, and then the industry takes over. The Academy Awards were basically created by the industry to

promote pictures. They weren't really to acknowledge the performances. Then it became sort of this great popularity contest and now, it's an incredible show and it's seen all over the world. But the strain on us to put ourselves up against other people to think that it's some sort of a contest, and it isn't a contest . . . we're all in this together.

Cromwell then recalled his own experience as a nominee and what then-Academy president Arthur Hiller told him in 1995: "Listen, the Academy Award is just a crapshoot. To be nominated, for your peers to tell you that your film or your performance is one of the five best, that's the Academy Award."

A random *Letter to the Editor* in *The Hollywood Reporter*, dated February 13, 1990, may have best defended Elizabeth's particular talent in the small to big picture scheme of things. In response to the trade magazine's unappreciative review January 24, 1990 of her performance in that year's premiere of her CBS TV-movie, *Face to Face*, Gary Bennett, of West Hollywood, wrote:

> I hope Elizabeth Montgomery didn't read your review of her telefilm *Face to Face*. While your reviewer's lazy critique was generally flattering, his comment that she made the Emmys " 'look bad' " by garnering five nominations for her " 'junky' " *Bewitched* work was downright insulting, not to mention inaccurate. In its prime, *Bewitched* was an enchanting show, and it is to Montgomery's credit that she was nominated so often. As for his statement that she *now* shows "considerable talent," she proved that fifteen years ago with the telefilm *A Case of Rape*.

In 1975, three years after Elizabeth decided to end *Bewitched*, Harry Ackerman, the show's executive producer, took his young son Peter to visit her on the set of *The Legend of Lizzie Borden*, which like *A Case of Rape* was a stark departure from her previous comedic work.

For Peter, *Borden*, *Rape* and other of Lizzie's non-*Bewitched* TV-movies, such as *The Victim* (ABC, 1972) and *Act of Violence* (NBC, 1979, which like *Borden* was directed by Paul Wendkos) were too jarring to watch. He explains:

> During the time she made those movies, I was not an actor, beyond school plays, anyway. So, the creative choices that she made did not reach me. I

was kind of grossed-out by the idea of the *Rape* movie, and to this day I have never watched it, or believe this or not, any of her other post-*Bewitched* work. I think I so loved the Liz I knew, which is just like *Samantha*, I just never wanted to watch her not being *her*. TV-movies like *A Case of Rape* were a new trend back in the day so it was hard for me as a pre-teen or young teen to grasp the subject matter, unlike [it is for] the youth of today.

It was, however, still riveting and "fun" for Peter to meet Lizzie on the *Borden* set:

> My Dad was working at Paramount and took me to see her. I had not seen her since the end of *Bewitched* and in fact never saw her again after that. But she was the same *Liz* to me, and I do not recall any tension between her and my Dad who had remained loyal to Bill Asher after their divorce. In fact, upon hearing that I was taking tap lessons, Liz asked me to show her my steps. And I did!

Besides that challenging day when the wives of a few crew members visited the *Bewitched* set and called Lizzie "fat," she was usually cool when kids or adults visited a set. According to Montgomery curator Thomas McCartney, the cast and crew who worked with her from her 1985 CBS TV-movie *Amos* were impressed with her informal persona: "She was around the set a lot and liked to watch everyone work. She was always very sweet, and many specifically remembered her eyes and the way they smiled at whoever she was talking to. In fact, they sparkled and smiled. She was a little bashful, but kind, considerate, and very much a down-to-earth."

Apparently, there was one particular crew member on *Amos* who had more directly experienced Lizzie's kind heart. He had recently lost his wife and infant son in childbirth and fortunately had a honey-eyed four-year-old daughter to help soothe his grief. For a time, however, he was unable to find a regular babysitter and a few makeup girls from the set volunteered. But when shooting fell behind schedule, the makeup team was unable to pinch-hit, and the little girl's father went into panic mode. Who would babysit his daughter now? Of course, the answer was none other than Lizzie Montgomery.

According to McCartney, Lizzie actually volunteered for the job. "And the little girl's father was just astonished," McCartney declares. "He couldn't comprehend that Elizabeth Montgomery was actually babysitting his child. It was all pretty humorous."

Equally charming and surprising was how Lizzie responded to a reference to her age, a topic of which she was quite protective and sensitive. At one point during this adventure in babysitting, she and the little girl were playing a game. "And they looked really cute together," McCartney explains. So cute, that someone on the set turned to Lizzie and said, "Oh, how sweet. She looks like she could be your daughter."

To which Lizzie laughed and replied, with her acerbic humor intact, "You mean my *granddaughter*. I'm a little long in the tooth to have a four-year-old."

McCartney deciphers:

> She was just an incredibly modest lady, and treated that little girl with such respect. Some mornings, the little girl would come in looking all disheveled and Elizabeth would just shake her head, and try to make the child presentable, but in a non-obstructive way. She'd laugh and say to the little girl, "Your father dressed you this morning, didn't he, kiddo?" But she would also tell everyone how polite she was, and how refreshing it was to encounter such a well-mannered child. She constantly complimented the girl, and her father, on her manners. She would play games with the child like hopscotch. She even got on the floor in her nurse's white (costume) to teach her how to play jacks, and apparently, that was quite a sight.

Lizzie even grew concerned whenever the little girl's father made not-so-wise moves. One day the child fell asleep on the set and curled up in a fetal ball. She immediately covered her with a blanket or towel of some sort, then approached the father and politely explained: "When children *curl up*, they're usually cold and too tired to do or say anything." According to McCartney, the father looked at Lizzie as if she was Moses giving a sermon from Mount Sinai. "I doubt he forgot whatever it is she told him that day."

Similarly, it's not likely that Sally Kemp and Rebecca Asher will ever forget what happened the day Kemp's little grandson apparently had an encounter with Elizabeth's playful, carefree spirit, literally. Elizabeth once professed to *TV Photo Story* magazine that she had seen a ghost in England. Billy Clift, her former hairstylist, talked extensively about his encounters with her spirit in his fascinating book, *Everything Is Going to Be Just Fine: The Ramblings of a Mad Hairdresser*. And now, Lizzie "transparently" materialized to Kemp's youngest relative. Sally explains:

> Elizabeth's daughter, Rebecca Asher, came to visit with friends of ours. And my grandson, I think he was three or four, asked Rebecca how her mother was, and [said] that she (Elizabeth) had *visited* him. Rebecca and all of us were surprised, but couldn't get any more out of him. He was busy playing with his trains. Small children can very often see spirits and accept them. I guess Elizabeth just decided to *pop in* to see us since Rebecca was visiting too. Good timing on Elizabeth's part since she had never met my grandson and my daughter, who I was staying with in L.A. when this happened. Pity it couldn't have happened in life. But it didn't surprise me. It's something Elizabeth *would* do.

Twenty

Humanities

"I hope to continue to live my life so that [my children] will be proud of me. I don't mean as an actress, but as a mother, and as a human being."

—Elizabeth Montgomery, *Screen Stars Magazine*, August 1967

In many of her post-*Samantha* interviews, Lizzie frequently related working on *Bewitched* to taking an eight-year college course in the entertainment industry.

However, as do many from all walks of life, she attempted to learn something from *every* experience. She was an intelligent, open-minded individual, ever-willing to consider perspectives and opinions on any topic. She was shy, but that just made her a good listener. She was a dedicated worker, daughter, and wife, even when her father and a few of her husbands weren't all that supportive or encouraging. She was a loyal friend to many in her close circle who loved her dearly and, as far as her children were concerned, Elizabeth was an outstanding parent who cared a great deal about not only her immediate family, but the family of humanity. As Billy Asher, Jr. relayed on MSNBC's *Headliners & Legends* in 2001, she was "a great influence and . . . role model."

Despite being raised in the self-absorbed community of Hollywood, West or East Coast divisions, Elizabeth always had a solid grasp on priorities. She appreciated diversity and possessed integrity. Although reserved, she would speak her mind when discussing the importance and power that accompanies ignoring differences among peoples and nations, and instead concentrating on what makes everyone the same. As she explained in 1989:

> I've never liked the exclusivity of other people because they are of another race, another religion, another whatever. If you don't like somebody, don't come to me and say, "I don't like that person because he's black"; that's not an excuse; or "I don't like that person because he's Italian"; that doesn't make any sense to me. But if you say, "I don't like that person because he's rude and kicks dogs," well, then, I'd say, "You're probably right."

Lizzie's common human charm contributed to an across-the-board allure that remains today. She appeals to a variety of people for different reasons in a multitude of roles, on screen and off. She was the kind of person you could approach at parties. And according to the June 1965 issue of *TV Radio Mirror*, that's exactly what happened at one festive first-season gathering on the set of *Bewitched*. A gentleman advanced toward her and said, "Miss Montgomery . . . you not only play the part of a witch to perfection, you *are* that witch."

Whereupon she responded, "Why, isn't everybody?"

Not really. Liz Sheridan believed the role of *Samantha* fit Lizzie like a glove. As Sheridan expressed to MSNBC's *Headliners & Legends*, "She *was* that person. She was so much like that lady that I guess it was not like acting to her. She [had the] chance to be herself."

Ironically, it was advice from Robert Montgomery that helped his daughter "be" *Samantha*. In doing so, she became more popular with this one character on TV than he ever was with several roles he portrayed in various mediums. As was explained in *Cosmopolitan Magazine*, July 1954, he once reminded Elizabeth that every time she walked onto to a stage, she must bring something of herself with her. She couldn't just depend on scenery and lines. He had instructed her to bring the audience some special essence of herself, no matter how small; something that wasn't there before she stepped out from behind the curtain. He didn't care whether it was sadness or "an air of being afraid of somebody or a feeling of slapstick comedy," just something that would make the audience "sit up and notice" her. "All good actors do that," he added, thinking Elizabeth had that quality.

"She enters a scene with an air of authority, making a strong, positive contribution."

As Lizzie told Ronald Haver in 1991, "It's every actor's dream to bring originality and part of what you are to every part you play, if you can, or else delve deeply into all sorts of research." In more directly connecting the dots between playing *Samantha*, the sensitive issue of age, and maintaining a balance of priorities between home and career, Elizabeth offered a unique perspective to *TV Radio Mirror* in June 1965:

> "I'm very much like *Samantha* in some respects," she said, but in one particular way, "I can never be like her. *Samantha*, being a witch, can remain young, beautiful and charming, indefinitely. I'm only a woman and can hold on to my attractions for a limited period of time. Nothing is sadder to me than to see a woman who rolled along on her sex appeal when she was in her twenties suddenly wake up to the fact that she has reached forty. The beauty and cuteness that were once thought so attractive have gone, and it is a revolting sight to see a fortyish female trying to be a sex kitten. This is why I am trying to base my own life on more substantial and longer-lasting qualities; a home, a loving husband, fine children, longer-lasting things. A happy home is as valuable to you at fifty as it was in your twenties. And to be loved and admired by a husband and children, whom you love and admire in return, grows better as time wears on. It's a much better investment in happiness than playing the social butterfly . . ."

She didn't define herself as an ambitious career woman. She thoroughly enjoyed acting, but not to the degree where it became a compulsion that dominated her life. She didn't have to work to be content, but if she found a part that fascinated her, one that she perceived as entertaining or significant, then she was happy going to work. This was reportedly one of the reasons why she never signed a long-term contract before agreeing to do *Bewitched*; she envisioned playing *Samantha* as a challenge and signed on in a heartbeat.

She didn't always agree with her agents, who often urged her to take large roles that she classified in June 1965 as too "showy." Such parts were rejected if she sensed "something false to myself in them." At which point, she'd agree to take on more modest characterizations.

By the time she settled in as *Samantha*, Elizabeth sought to at least temporarily distance herself from nonconformist characters. "I'm not comfortable in such parts. But give me a normal young woman to do, and I'll play it for all I'm worth."

Strangely, the twitch-witch *Samantha* was one of her most "normal" roles. Others, like the prostitute *Rusty Heller* from *The Untouchables* or axmurderess *Lizzie Borden* certainly cannot be classified as normal, at least not within the "likability" mode of America's mainstream. But somehow, as she did with *Samantha*, Lizzie's talent so captivated her audience that she allowed them to identify with even the most unlikable characters, mostly because her *performance* was likable.

When she played characters like the compassionate, but stubborn paleontologist *Dr. Diana Firestone* in 1990's *Face to Face*, as with *Samantha*, both the character and the performance were likable. In such instances, as with the plight of wildlife, Lizzie somehow utilized that combination for a good cause, off-screen, just as she had allowed *Samantha's* struggle for acceptance in the mortal world to represent the quest for equality among all people in the real world.

On January 24, 1990, Lizzie appeared on *CBS This Morning* to promote Hallmark Hall of Fame's *Face to Face* TV-movie. At first, *Morning* host Kathleen Kennedy asked her to talk about the movie, which was shot on location in Kenya, Africa. When Kennedy then wondered if Lizzie learned anything while working on the movie, Elizabeth went on to speak in support of wildlife conservation on the resplendent African continent. She had always wanted to travel to Africa, performing in *Face to Face* provided the ideal opportunity for her to do so, and she was happy to get paid for it in the process. She also expressed how pleased she was to be working for Hallmark, how the entire journey to Africa was a "great wonderful" educational experience.

However, she added, "Not to be morbid, but we better get pretty interested very fast in the conditions there about the poaching. It has gotten so outrageously out of hand. And it's scary to think that if it keeps up, Africa just may not be there as we know it. It is Eden is what it is, and it should be left that way."

Or as she concluded in 1989, in general, "There are certainly a lot more important things to care about in the world besides acting."

According to Sally Kemp, her childhood friend and former classmate at the New York American Academy of Dramatic Arts, "Elizabeth really wasn't that driven to act. I may be wrong and she may have just played it cool, but she was more interested in living. She wanted to be alive. She cared about things."

As previously discussed, Lizzie's involvement with the 1984 CBS-TV movie, *Second Sight: A Love Story*, proved to be an emotionally draining experience for her, mostly because, in real life, she adopted the seeing-eye dog used in the film. A closer inspection of *Second* uncovers further insight into Lizzie own life-affirming perspective:

> The visually impaired *Alaxandra* (Lizzie) discovers life's boundless possibilities with the assistance of *Emma*, her seeing-eye dog. After she's assaulted by a burglar and realizes she can't rely just on herself anymore, *Alaxandra* reluctantly teams with *Emma* and, for the first time since being blinded as a teen, comes to trust another soul, this time, an animal; although in more time, she accepts the love of a good man (portrayed by Barry Newman).

For Lizzie, it was a happy ending to a project she had wrestled with for two years. "We went through three writers before getting it right," she told *TV Week* magazine at the time. What concerned her most was that *Alaxandra* needed to be authentic:

The tendency in movies was to make the visually impaired "so saintly and adorable that you could hardly stand it," Lizzie said. She objected to the way the character was initially written in the first few drafts of the script, but was later pleased when the writers gave *Alaxandra* flaws. "Now she has a real edge and is quite imperfect," Elizabeth decided.

By the time *Second Sight* aired, she was a veteran of countless stage and screen performances, but copped to the challenges of playing a visually impaired character. She couldn't work out the *non-focusing* since she had "a tendency to look at people a lot." Even when she was a child, her mom scolded her for staring at other people, which reconfirms her parents' sometimes stern insistence on proper social graces.

However, her research and preparation in playing *Alaxandra* was extraordinary. She blindfolded herself at home and conferred with sightless people and their instructors. When she was "in the dark," she became frustrated and disoriented even when certain of her territory. "To tell the truth," she admitted, "I had this enormous desire to peek out from the blindfolds."

Emily Wickham, a teacher of the blind, served as consultant on *Sight* and instructed Lizzie on the proper use of a cane. "You just don't tap anywhere and get by," Lizzie revealed at the time. "You always have to have a border. A person can't just go freewheeling down the street like in a swashbuckling movie."

In further research for the film, she discovered that the majority of those who are visually impaired desire more independence and less assistance from others. She found that many such individuals are self-sufficient and able to cope. They have everything laid out at home and labeled. They know where their clothing is; their colors are even categorized. They know what is in the refrigerator and in their closets, and the location of the furniture.

From her perspective, the visually impaired had already conquered their handicaps, but the moment someone with the best of intentions even offers assistance, they lose ground. "To a blind person," she said, "this is the most annoying thing possible. The last thing they want to feel is helpless."

According to Christian Beltram, a life-long fan of Lizzie's who is visually impaired, a decade or so after she completed work on *Sight*, she donated her time to Learning Ally (formerly named the Recording for the Blind and Dyslexic Foundation or RFB&D), a nonprofit organization which records educational books on audio for the disabled. This association in particular "deeply mourned her passing," as she had volunteered throughout the last year of her life, recording a book of children's verse, *When We Were Very Young*, along with several radio and television public service announcements. One televised public service announcement even involved her reprisal of the famous nose wriggle, which she had not performed on camera since appearing in a series of Japanese TV commercials that were only broadcast in Japan, and certainly not since filming her final *Bewitched* episode in the spring of 1972.

Her efforts generated a great deal of excitement and national interest for Learning Ally, which led her to enthusiastically agree to be the honorary chairperson for the organization's third annual *Record-A-Thon*, which transpired on June 3, 1995 in Los Angeles. "She generously lent her name to all of our letters of appeal for the event and was planning to be one of our celebrity readers for the days," said Don Haderlein, who then served as studio director and media coordinator for Learning Ally's Los Angeles branch. "Tragically, a month later she was diagnosed with the cancer that took her life."

With the modern-day onset of the Internet and social networking, and as with many retro pop culture icons, Lizzie's online fan base has increased significantly, documenting just how popular she remains.

New Yorker Kathy Perillo has been blind since birth. She has also been a huge fan of Lizzie's and *Bewitched* since the show's debut. She was just ten years old when she first heard Elizabeth in 1964. "I just loved her voice and her acting ability," Perillo says, ". . . the way she spoke to *Darrin* and in different scenes with her mother (*Endora*)."

Perillo's mother and relatives read her magazine articles about Elizabeth. "And I got to find out more about her life," she recalls. "I just loved her personality and the way she would talk and say, "*Well!*" I [had] never heard such a beautiful voice. Then I came to understand that she was so beautiful and attractive. She also had a great personality. Very charming."

And Perillo should know. She met Elizabeth a few times in person over the years. She explains the events leading up to what became very special moments in her life:

> My family and I were planning a trip to California, around 1969. And I said to my Mom, "You know, I'd really love to meet Elizabeth Montgomery, if it's possible." So we found out that her father was then the President of Lincoln Center, here in New York. So we said, "Let's start locally." So we called Lincoln Center. We got to speak to his secretary and we told her the situation, that I was a blind fan of his daughter and we were planning a trip and could we possibly meet her in July. She said, "Okay, I'll send a letter off to her secretary's office and we'll see if we could arrange it."
>
> On May 12, we then received a letter from Elizabeth Montgomery's secretary saying it wouldn't be possible [to meet her] because she was having

a baby, and that she'd be away somewhere resting. So I was disappointed. Anyway, we [arrived in California] in July, and me being the persistent person that I was, I said to my Dad, "C'mon, can't we please rent a car and go there? We have her address and just drive up and see if anyone's there? If anyone can give us any information?"

So we arrived there, went right up to her house, and rang her bell. They didn't have any security or anything. She had like twenty steps, I believe. And her governess came out, with Elizabeth's two little sons and said, "She's not home, but let me get Mr. Asher for you."

So, shortly thereafter, the governess returned to the door with Bill Asher alongside her. He said it was so nice to meet us, and that he would try and arrange a meeting for us the next day if we would tell him our hotel and he would call us that evening.

So we were staying at the Ambassador Hotel at the time on Wilshire Blvd. And he said, "I'll call you around 6:30 tonight and tell you what time to call tomorrow." It got to be after 6:30. It was like 7:15 and I said, "Oh, no . . . maybe he didn't want to make us feel bad. Maybe she wasn't able to meet us!"

All of a sudden, the phone rang. I almost died. And I remember all of this, every detail like it was yesterday, when in fact it was over forty years ago.

Anyway, my Mom answered and spoke to him and he said for us to come by, 1:30 the next day, and we did.

We finally met her, on July 16, 1969, the day the astronauts took off for the moon. She talked about how she had gotten up early that morning to see the take-off and she was so cordial and friendly. And Bill was there again, too. He was on his way to a meeting, and they allowed us to take pictures of them and us together. Liz gave me a straw handbag, which had a three-dimensional horse on the front of it that I could feel. It's something I'll always treasure. She then went on to talk about how she loved horses and how she always went to the race track; how she enjoyed horseback riding. She talked about her dogs and cats.

I had also given her a scrapbook of some articles that I put together, and she appreciated that. But she said they always got her age wrong, that she was born in 1936 and not 1933.

Right before we left she gave us her phone number and I did call her that year to wish her a Merry Christmas. Bill Asher answered the phone, and then put her on the line. She was very sweet and wished me and my parents a happy holiday.

Then later in 1989, when Lizzie did *Love Letters* on Broadway with Robert Foxworth in New York, my parents went backstage to meet her and she hugged us all, me, and my friends Linda and Paulette.

Paulette had a guide dog and Elizabeth bent down and hugged the dog and said that she had the dog from *Second Sight*. She raised it after the movie, and kept it as her own.

I said, "Remember me? I met you when I was fourteen!"

"Oh, yes! I wish we were 'all' fourteen!" she said. She had beautiful perfume on. I remember that and when she hugged me and everything, but he [Foxworth] didn't come to the door. I don't think he would have been as gracious. We really never met him. But Mr. Asher certainly was gracious.

I met him again in 2008, when I attended the *Bewitched* Fan Club at one of the conventions in Burbank. They had a tribute to Bill Asher and they asked me to speak and pose [for photographs] and then I got to sit next to him, and he had his arm around me and he kissed my hand. He was still gracious then, you know, even though he was in a wheelchair and everything.

I thanked him and said, "You made my dream come true. If it wasn't for you, I never would have been able to meet Elizabeth!"

Vince Staskel, born with cerebral palsy, is another of Lizzie's fans. Today, he is the principal and executive producer of VPS MediAbility Productions in Poughkeepsie, New York, which is currently producing radio shows for Able Pathways (formally Disabled Radio). He is also promoting a stable of six authors with disabilities and assisting in the development of the "This Is Life" radio show on KFWB in Los Angeles.

Vince also serves on the board of directors for The Classic TV Preservation Society, a nonprofit organization that seeks to close the gap between popular culture and education.

A television fan his entire life, Vince grew up in Shenandoah, Pennsylvania, during the 1950s and 1960s, when the small screen was his companion and playmate. He walked with crutches as a child and found it difficult to participate in many outdoor activities due to limited mobility. Classic TV shows granted him not only the opportunity to watch but actually participate in the on-screen action.

As he recalls, "Television was a big part of my life. I would dance [with] *American Bandstand*, wear my coonskin cap during *Davy Crockett*, fire my toy rifle with *The Rifleman*, and clown around with *The Three Stooges*. These shows became my friends and playmates."

Bewitched, in particular, was also one of his favorite programs, and Lizzie one of the TV stars who most inspired him, both as a human being and to work in the entertainment industry. As a youngster, he followed her career and was "thrilled to see her starring in her own sitcom. Of course her beauty is only one of the first things that caught your eye. But in addition to that, it was her acting versatility. I loved watching her. She had such a wonderful way to draw you into her character. You knew right from the start that she was a good witch who only wanted to do positive things for people. *Samantha* has a great deal of power but only used it sparingly for only good purposes."

"To me, spiritually," he concludes, "it showed the existence of true love in the world. I followed her career and saw the full range of her acting ability. Yes, Ms. Montgomery could also play bad, excellently. As her fan base grew, so did she as an actor. I was captivated by her. *Bewitched* was and still is a major part of my life experience."

Lizzie clearly hit a chord with the disabled community, the down-trodden, the under-privileged, the put-upon, the physically, mentally, visually, and vocally impaired, and minorities of every kind. The late gifted author Lauri E. Klobas was a loyal advocate of the challenged community, she was also as a big fan of Lizzie's. In her book, *Disability Drama in Television and Film* (McFarland, 1988), Klobas included a review and analysis of Lizzie's renown TV-film, *Second Sight: A Love Story*, about a blind woman's relationship with her seeing-eye dog and the new man in her life. The year her book was published, Klobas offered an explanation of Lizzie's diverse popularity, touching on closed captioning for television programming, which is widely available now (and which Lizzie had unsuccessfully once rallied for on *Bewitched*):

> Before closed captioning was available on TV, people who were deaf tuned into action shows where the story line could be followed without dialogue. I remember asking deaf friends in the pre-captioning days what they liked

to watch and *Bewitched* was at the top of their list. It was Montgomery's expressive face and "speech-readable" mouth that attracted them. Of course, the graphic manifestations of magic needed no dialogue to be enjoyed by any member of the audience.

Emmy-winning TV producer Dan Weaver has worked on acclaimed talk shows such as *The Phil Donahue Show* and *Hour Magazine*. In 1996, Weaver, who is hearing-impaired, was the guiding creative force behind a tribute to Elizabeth on *Entertainment Tonight*. He had the wonderful fortune of meeting Elizabeth twice. First, in 1986, when he produced a special for *Donahue* called "AIDS: Face to Face." Weaver recalls:

> Phil had wanted to do a show on people battling AIDS in their final stages. It was a powerful experience, and the program was nominated for two Emmys, and received an Alliance for Gay and Lesbian Artists (AGLA) Award. These awards predated the Gay and Lesbian Alliance Against Defamation, (GLAAD) Awards, which also celebrate the most outstanding images of the LGBT community in the media.

On behalf of the show, Weaver, who is gay, proudly accepted the award. "It was a magical night," he says, including a surprise meeting before the program with Lizzie and Robert Foxworth. Before showtime, Weaver couldn't resist the chance to introduce himself and his life partner, Lee. "Thinking back," Weaver intones, "Elizabeth and Robert were early allies in the LGBT equality movement in Hollywood. That was during the time when many people believed that you could *catch* AIDS and that it was *God's punishment of gays*. Yet there they were, and she was as gracious and beautiful as I'd imagined."

During their brief conversation, Weaver said he also "felt her incredible sensitivity." In a nervous attempt to make small talk, he mentioned that a friend of his was being considered to do some publicity work for her. Upon hearing this, Lizzie's expression changed and she became "defensive," Weaver recalls, "saying that [it] wasn't true," and proceeded to ask Weaver if that's the line his friend was telling everyone. "I felt the panic in her voice."

In hindsight, Weaver believes his innocent remark was probably inappropriate, since he was a stranger to her. Also, too, his friend may have been exaggerating his prospective employment as her publicist. "I regretted that I had said anything," Weaver goes on to explain, "yet it made me drawn to her even more . . . her feelings, her vulnerability, and her fragility. I think these qualities motivated her to help the underdogs, others that may have those feelings sometimes, too, like [those in] the LGBT community and the disabled."

One of Weaver's favorite autographs is a beautiful note he received from Lizzie, thanks to a mutual producer friend who met her at a PBS fundraiser. Weaver's friend told Elizabeth of his incredible fascination with her which, Weaver admits, "I have gotten teased about over the years."

No matter. Both he and Lizzie kept a sense of humor about it all. Her note to Weaver said, "You may be demented, but you obviously have impeccable taste."

"I loved her humor," Weaver adds.

His other meeting with Elizabeth transpired at a "looping session," where an audio track is recorded after either a movie or TV show is filmed. As a surprise, Weaver's partner Lee had arranged this "second chance" for me. Weaver explains:

> I walked in and there she was in the sound booth, speaking Swahili for her TV movie, *Face to Face*. When she came out for a break, I practically pounced on her. Luckily she hadn't remembered our first encounter, but this one became equally uncomfortable for me. This was finally a chance to connect with her. But I overwhelmed her on what amounted to a short work break. I did what many fans do. I couldn't stop talking and did a soliloquy on why she was important to me. Ugh! She was flattered at first and then became uncomfortable. Thinking back, if I were in her shoes, I would have felt the same way.

Years later, in 1996, he was producing the tribute to Elizabeth for *Entertainment Tonight*, where he met "her wonderful daughter Rebecca," who smiled upon hearing how he met her mother. I am sorry I never got to convey this in the right way to Elizabeth, but it meant a lot to be able to share my thoughts with Rebecca. I'm just someone who truly felt a connection with Elizabeth, someone who sensed her shyness and her goodness. I felt her compassion even as a child. There was a universal appeal of *Bewitched* that made people from many diverse groups feel welcomed each Thursday night at 8:00 PM [when the show originally aired on ABC]. Echoing Lauri Klobas' thoughts, Weaver recalls:

> I remember it being one of the first shows I watched with special effects, and for a hearing-impaired person where there weren't subtitles back then, I am sure it was a fun show to watch. Her real-life passion for social causes, witnessed in some *Bewitched* episodes, came through.
>
> The show found innovative ways to work in messages (with episodes like "*Samantha* Twitches for UNICEF," and "Sisters at Heart," the latter of which dealt with bigotry). In those days, dealing with such a real issue like racism was rare on TV; and for a supernatural sitcom to take it on was very courageous and creative. Elizabeth and Bill Asher were pioneers in social cause storytelling.
>
> I learn best through storytelling and visualization, perhaps another reason I was drawn to this series that was so visually interesting
>
> As a video storyteller some four decades later, the show had a huge impact on my career, and using TV as a creative tool in educating others on social issues that impact us all. . . . Elizabeth's beauty both externally and internally, had a truly magical ability to take such a supernatural and *out-there* concept and give it so much grounding and reality.
>
> I always sensed a bit of insecurity with her, one that I have known well throughout my own life. When I would watch her on the screen I had strong feelings about what Elizabeth, the actress, was going through personally. I've learned over time that she so wanted to please her dad, and I felt that. She was a tremendously gifted woman, but I imagine a very sensitive person who, like all of us, had her demons. But I totally also got that she was a very loving person who cared deeply about people, and never saw herself as a celebrity.
>
> I think she struggled with being a celebrity. In a way, she was probably similar to *Samantha*, just wanting to live the simple life, one where people didn't see her any differently than themselves. I think she accomplished this by never forgetting the underserved in this world, and the power in changing lives by taking on personal actions, like doing narration of audio books for the blind. She was a terrific actress and funny. But there was a depth in her that showed much sensitivity and vulnerability. She played *Samantha* as simply someone who was trying to fit in, to have her family accept her husband's world. There was always love for both sides, but it was a challenge. And *Samantha* always had respect for everyone's point of view. It was

not easy for her to be in a minority in a mortal world, but she so wanted to embrace it and share those simple and universal family values.

That one word answer she gave (prejudice, in defining *Bewitched's* central theme) really crystallized why the show was so real to me and why I have loved it on one level; I could sit and be entertained yet on another level really consider a much heavier philosophical perspective.

Today, Weaver is a partner and Senior Vice President of Talent Development for Diversity Works LLC (www.diversityworksllc.com), a marketing and communications agency whose clients include lesbian, gay, bisexual, and transgender (LGBT) certified businesses, nonprofit organizations, and corporate allies. Their tagline is: Turning Pride into Profit.

"We work with companies to help build their strategic relationships in the LGBT Marketplace," he explains, "which is an $800 billion dollar industry. As a minority group, the LGBT market is third only to the African-American and Hispanic populations, and actually exceeds the Asian-American buying power."

What's more, Diversity Works supports all groups, but has particular interests in LGBT seniors, LGBT people with disabilities, and the transgender community. "We believe these groups have some of the most significant unmet needs and face the most discrimination."

According to Weaver, one quarter of all gay seniors fear revealing their sexuality even to their own doctors, while an estimated 40 to 60 percent of the transgendered population is unemployed due to workplace discrimination. So for him, "It's been interesting finding out about Elizabeth's compassion for diversity and disability groups. She was a special soul put here, who used her time well, and is on to her next mission. Her work, whether on screen, at home, or with her charitable causes, lives on like a beautiful tale in a storybook."

Twenty-one

Political Science

"My parents never tried to force their opinions on me, politically, religiously, or any other way."

—Elizabeth Montgomery, *Modern Screen Magazine* (July 1970)

Lizzie frequently employed her widespread image for the benefit of others, remaining civic-minded throughout her life and career, in spite or despite conservative views expressed by her mother and father. As she explained to Ronald Haver in 1991, broaching politics with her father was like talking to a brick wall.

For one, her stand on Vietnam was not a popular topic with him. As she put it, "He just figured, 'Well, there's no sense of even getting into this with someone like that!' " She felt it was more productive that they were on different coasts; she on the West (*the left*); he on the East (*the right*). "And it was just as well that we weren't in each other's company a lot because it would have been unpleasant . . . for a whole mess of people."

Despite such political friction with her father, Lizzie went on to protest the Vietnam war, and lent her name, along with a great deal of personal time, money, and energy to a wide variety of charitable and political causes, including supporting human equality and the Peace movement; helping to further AIDS research, and reaching out to the disabled community. However, she modestly defined her social involvement as adequate. "There are times when I know I could still be doing more," she said in 1989.

According to Ronny Cox, Lizzie's liberal-minded co-star from the issue-driven TV-movies *A Case of Rape* and *With Murder in Mind*, their shared political views were at the core of their friendship:

> Elizabeth was very left-wing, not as left-wing as me, but very left-wing. And it was refreshing for each of us to run into someone whose politics were sort of as vociferous as the other person's . . . someone who we could each blow off steam with, especially at that time.

While *Bewitched* was on the air through the 1960s and early 1970s, Ronny was "there in '68 . . . working in the streets with the kids" during the upheaval surrounding Martin Luther King, Jr.'s assassination and the subsequent riots.

At the time, the Civil Rights Movement was in full swing. There was massive resistance to, among other things, desegregation of public restrooms, buses, restaurants, and schools. The anti–Vietnam war movement was commencing. Michael Harrington's book, *The Other America* (Scribner, 1997) would later document the gaps between America's rich and the poor; the haves and the have-nots. Cesar Chavez was challenging America in the Grape Boycott; music was alive with revolution, from the likes (and dislikes) of The Beatles to The Smothers Brothers. It was the day of *The March on Washington* (from the Washington Monument to the Lincoln Memorial) for jobs, to halt discrimination against African-Americans, and equality for all. *Everyday people* of every race, creed, and color were there, in numbers 250,000 or more, walking arm-in-arm down Constitution Avenue, alongside celebrities such as sports legend Jackie Robinson (who had shattered the color barrier in Major League Baseball).

By the time *A Case of Rape* aired in 1974, Ronny says influential people like the Harvard educated poet Robert Lowell refused to visit the White House due to the U.S. involvement in the Vietnam war. In Ronny's view, Lowell (born in 1917) in particular, played an important role in the revolution of the 1960s.

But from any perspective, Lowell's writings are significant, especially his early works, including *Land of Unlikeness* (1944) and *Lord Weary's Castle*, the latter for which he received the Pulitzer Prize for Poetry in 1947 at the age

of thirty. Both books were influenced by his conversion from Episcopalian-
ism to Catholicism, and explored the dark side of America's Puritan legacy.
Before Vietnam, he also actively objected to World War II, became a conscientious objector, and was subsequently imprisoned.

According to Cox, it was only after Lowell began questioning mainstream artistic choices that issue-oriented films like *Rape* (which helped to
push forward nationwide landmark legislation that changed the rights of
rape victims) could be produced and introduced to TV home viewers.
Before then, Cox says:

> It was either frothy comedy or some sort of made-up drama. We were a
> nation still going through the throes of the Southerners disagreeing with
> the Civil Rights Act and us coming out of Vietnam. Everyone was vilifying
> the hippie movement. People were still having trouble voting. We were
> not that far removed from '65–66. And just look around at the world today!
> We still have inequalities!

Back in 1974, Cox had serious arguments with those in the artistic community who questioned the association between politics and the arts.
"Because in those days," he says, "there was this total segregated idea, that
entertainment was *here* and the real world was *there*. So I think in some ways
(*A Case of Rape*) probably made some people squirm a little bit."

The same could also be said for his 1972 big screen film *Deliverance*,
which hit theatres slightly before *Rape* premiered on TV. This movie also
made an integral artistic contribution to the era, for it too dealt with the
issue of sexual assault, but this time a man was violated. Cox shares his
memories of working on the film in his new book, *Dueling Banjos: The
Deliverance of Drew* (Decent Hill, 2012). He says *Deliverance* was ground-
breaking if only for the healthy social dialogue it created:

> This was the first time men had had to deal with the whole concept of rape.
> For the first time people were realizing that rape isn't [just] a sexual crime.
> It's violent and out of control. I'm not even sure there's hardly any sexual
> component to it. It's an act of humiliation . . . the *me-dominating-you* aspect.

In comparative analysis of *Case* and *Deliverance*, he believes both films
"changed a lot of people's psyches. Because now for the first time, men had

to deal with the kind of thing that women had to deal with for years." Before *Case* in particular, he says, once a woman was raped, her sex life was open to extreme scrutiny. "If she just dated someone, the deck was stacked against her. And you couldn't say anything if a man had prior arrests. He was completely off limits."

Yet it was Lizzie's caring and compelling drive to serve others that made her so accessible to Cox on the set of *Case*. He was impressed with her unaffected demeanor, considering her father's conservative stance and her prestigious upbringing, as well as with her obvious decision to shun arrogance, and retain an open-minded and keen understanding of priorities:

> You have to admire Lizzie. She could very easily have just been one of the *haves*. And that's what sets her apart; that sensibility of saying, "No! I don't agree with the right wing paradigm." To them, it's the *zero sum game* . . . getting a lot of money or getting a lot of power or getting [a] lot of stuff doesn't mean anything (unless the *Left* loses). They want this trickle-down-stuff, and if they would just be historians and realize that when the least of us—especially the middle class—does the best that's when everybody else does the best. The paradigm for this country is to make sure that [the] vast middle is doing well and then you'll pull the poor up from the bottom and the rich still do well. And Elizabeth realized that.

Although he's enjoyed his share of stardom, Cox admits to not experiencing Lizzie's level of success. He did not know her father, nor did they have discussions about her father. "I can only talk from my own sense of it," he says, "but I think she looked around and saw those right wing guys, the soullessness of them, not caring for the other people," and decided from there.

However, he remains particularly puzzled as to how Lizzie became part of an artistic community like Hollywood, filled with celebrities of all shapes, sizes, and success levels, some of who may be defined as arrogant and self-centered:

> Who knows? In some ways it sounds paradoxical. In some ways it's as though our religions almost mitigate against us ever getting together . . . in lots of ways. If you take what I call *the right-wing extreme religions of the world . . . the right wing elements of the religions of the world . . . right wing Christian*

*fundamentalists, right wing Muslims, right wing Jewish, right wing Buddhists . . .
those ultra-right wings . . .* they always mitigate. . . . . they always propagate an
us-against-them mentality. But that's the way of these guys having their
power! I grew up in a small town of fundamentalist right-wing religion
bigots of the worst order. I was overwhelmed with what I observed as deep
hypocrisy and disregard for humanity. So, I vowed at a very early age to
choose a more productive path. In some ways, I'm sort of prejudiced against
organized religion because of that. Because I saw such hatred, such bigotry
coming from those kinds of places, no caring for humanity at large, no
caring for our fellow man. That turned me off.

Ronny Cox doesn't know for certain, but he'd "like to think that Lizzie
saw the same things from the *excessives* . . . the same lack of caring from *her*
side of the tracks."

If Lizzie was the most down-to-earth actress in Hollywood, then her male
counterpart, beyond Robert Foxworth in that community, would have to be
none other than Emmy-winning actor Ed Asner. Asner is best known for
playing the tough-as-nails-but-gentle-of-heart *Lou Grant* on *The Mary Tyler
Moore Show,* and its sequel *Lou Grant.* The *Grant* role, a supporting role on a
half-hour situation comedy, was the first in TV history to be spun-off into a
one-hour dramatic series. He made TV history again when he recently
reprised his role as wealthy art collector and smuggler *August March* on updated
edition of *Hawaii Five-O.* He first played *March* on the original *Five-O,* starring
Jack Lord, a frequent co-star of Lizzie's. According to the article, "Ed Asner
Visits Hawaii," published in *The Los Angeles Times,* on March 19, 2012, the
day the new *Five-O* segment aired, it was the first time a guest performer
played the same character on separate versions of the same series.

But Asner is also well-known for heralded performances in countless
other television programs and feature films, everything from programs in
which Lizzie also appeared (*Armstrong Circle Theatre, Alfred Hitchcock Presents,
The Untouchables*), to mini-series like *Roots* and *Rich Man, Poor Man,* TV-
movies like *The Gathering,* to big screen family films like *Elf* and *Up!*

Like Lizzie, Asner's success never went to his head, even at the super
height of his popularity during the *Mary Tyler Moore Show* days. Although

he could well have afforded a Mercedes or BMW like many of his Holly-wood peers, Asner pulled into various studio parking lots of the day in a 1977 Oldsmobile Cutlass. He explains how and why that happened, and more:

I came from a middle class Jewish Orthodox family. My father couldn't read or write English. He had morals and standards. I was afraid of him because the four older kids made me afraid of him. And yet he never laid a glove on me. I was a mama's boy. Up until the beginning of second grade we lived in a railroad apartment which we owned, which was above my father's junkyard. My classmates were Mexican. The junkyard was across from a farmer's packing house. So I certainly had humble beginnings in terms of ostentation.

We moved to what I regarded as a white bread village. So I made friends in the class. I went through public school and high school and being the youngest, I was more sheltered than the rest of my siblings, who before long were all away and I was on my own. I encountered whatever I had to encounter on my own.

I became a success in high school but in my sophomore year, all my friends were invited into fraternities and I wasn't. And I saw which way the wind blew for me. I said, "Okay, I had been the class clown up to that point. I can't look to friendship to be surrounding me, I've got to excel, so I started excelling and achieved."

My greatest regret was joining a fraternity in my senior year! It was totally unnecessary, but my buddies were in it, so I thought I'd join and I betrayed my standards by doing so. I went to college, the University of Chicago. I was there a year and a half. I got involved in acting, which was extracurricular, became open to acting, dropping out of college.

I then took on a series of jobs, all of them blue collar and I suppose the fact that I held onto the Cutlass signifies two things: That I was tight and that I identified and I'd always be identified as a common middle class working stiff!

Both of my sisters were social workers in their post-college years. Maybe some of that rubbed off on me. I know in certain cases it did. They certainly had their liberal ideals.

And [World War II] was on at the time. And we were Jews. We had some idea of what befell Jews, not only in Europe but the anti-Semitism that was certainly rife in America at that time!

I was willing to join a fraternity that my friends were in at one time and after I went to three meetings they voted on you. And I found out that two people blackballed me: A guy from the next block and a football player I knew and was friendly with. But my friend who was in the fraternity told me about it and I said, "Was it because I was Jewish?" He said, "Yeah." I was greatly relieved! "Oh," I thought, "it wasn't because it was me!" How goddamned stupid can you get?!

Anyway, I went on and joined the other fraternity to my regret.

So, being a Jew in Kansas City, Kansas, discrimination was of that mild a nature, but it was enough to make me realize I was one of the *others* but being an *other* I think makes you tend to identify with the character of others who are *others*.

I think that primarily dictated, having been a working stiff and a union man, [that] finally it was natural that I should pursue whatever causes I spoke for, because I was always a loudmouth, a clown. How do you say it? *A loudmouth goon clown.*

Asner later combined his voice, refreshing self-deprecating humor, compassion for his fellow man, and keen sense of priorities to do good work. And although he and Lizzie clearly came from very different backgrounds, they attained an equally successful footing in Hollywood, while retaining the same strong sense of integrity, if not always aware that they were on the same side.

Asner, a liberal and political advocate like Lizzie, had appeared alongside her at many charity functions, while also playing opposite her on game shows like *Password*. Oddly enough, Asner had no idea that Elizabeth was a liberal; he thought she may have followed in the footsteps of her conservative-minded father. He explains:

The fact that she was the daughter of *Mr. Republican* was intimidating to me. He was the tuxedo-and-top-hat-and-tie type. I was never offended by anything he said or did that I can recall, but in those days he represented the *other side*. I never approached politics with her. I never got familiar with her other than as Bob Foxworth's wife. The fact that she was married to Bob had to indicate something. He certainly was a liberal, but we never really exchanged familiarities. I certainly enjoyed her (performances) and was terribly depressed at her demise. Heartbreaking! And I thought she was a fine upstanding woman. But I did not identify the liberal (in her), although she certainly didn't get in the way of her liberal husband. From what I've now learned about her, I deeply regret not having been able to exchange some warmth with her, now knowing exactly who she was (as a human being). But she was not forthcoming.

Lizzie's shy behavior struck again, but her heart, as usual, was in the right place. Knowing Lizzie, she may have been just as intimidated by Asner as he was of her. But certainly she must have respected his integrity and the sacrifices he made in his life and career due to his liberal beliefs, specifically when his political views once cost him his job. Asner explains further:

There were times when I spoke up for causes. I was lucky that some of those times I hadn't done sufficient background (research) but I was still correct in my positions. When I came to New York, being a member of both SAG and AFTRA, I had signed the Stockholm Peace Pledge. And I wondered . . . I had heard of people being denied because of signing.

When I had to fill out my Loyalty Oath for clearance with the networks and I only filled out one, evidently that applied across the board. I wondered if they'd catch me up on signing this Stockholm Peace Pledge. That's how fearful I was. It didn't reflect on me. Most of those years until I came out to speak up on Central America, El Salvador, I kept my mouth shut, not willing to be identified, not willing to be tagged.

And when I spoke out on El Salvador—speaking out on what I consider to be a humanist position, not liberal, it produced a maelstrom of opposition that led to the cancellation of *Lou Grant*. And when I did speak out, we went to Washington to announce the initial contribution of aid to El Salvador. There was a large press conference and the second questioner at the table, and he said, "Are you for free elections in El Salvador? What if those elections turn out a Communist Government?" It's like a freight train hit me in the face. And I gave some wimpy answer and I went on to the third questioner, but I was troubled with what I had answered. I gave some cockamamie answer and I went back to the second questioner.

In my mind, I'm saying, "I've come all this way for this, all this distance? And I'm gonna waffle?" Not here! And I said I wasn't satisfied with my initial answers: "All I can say to you is if it's the Government the people of El Salvador choose . . . then let them have it!" And with that, I felt I was signing the end of my career. I felt that it would rebound. There was rebounding but it wasn't over that specific answer, but I'm sure it was the provocation that led to all the attacks. I was labeled a *commie* and this and that and the *Lou Grant* series got cancelled!

Although it's been nearly three decades since Grant's cancellation, Asner has never stopped working or fighting the good fight. Lizzie would have been proud.

Had it not been for the loyal original following of Trekkers and Trekkies, the original *Star Trek* series, broadcast on NBC from 1966 to 1969 (and one of Lizzie's favorite shows), may not have made it past its first season. One particular episode, "Plato's Stepchildren," involved the virile *Captain Kirk*, as played by Caucasian William Shatner, under alien mind control, forced to kiss *Lt. Uhura*, portrayed by African-American Nichelle Nichols. It was the first time a scripted TV series presented an interracial intimate moment between characters, however contrived within a sci-fi/fantasy storyline. Even more significant was that the segment was broadcast November 22, 1968—the fifth anniversary of President Kennedy's assassination, which was also the anniversary of the day rehearsals began for the *Bewitched* pilot.

In 1977, Lizzie starred in *A Killing Affair*, a CBS TV-movie co-starring African-American athlete turned actor turned controversial public figure O. J. Simpson. They were big city detectives who were partners on the street and at home, locked in a heated romance that included one water-downed bedroom scene with Simpson stationed just above her, to one side.

According to the article, "TV Breaks Old Taboos with New Morality," published in *Jet Magazine*, a progressively mainstream African-American publication, December 1, 1977, Lizzie rallied for additional scenes in the bedroom, but CBS censors rejected her suggestions. So, she had to settle for what she could get or the scenes, and potentially the entire film, would have been shelved. But even the subtle sequence that did manage to make the cut was considered cutting edge television. As *Jet* worded it, "Black skin lovingly pressed against white skin on television screens is a delicacy rarely seen."

It took *A Killing Affair* to pull back the covers on this sensitive and usually avoided interracial material, which was then one of TV's most inflexible taboos. But the audience was not repelled. Instead, the film was embraced by its viewers. Broadcast on Wednesday, September 21, 1977 it garnered a 29 percent Nielson rating share. Although it ranked behind the popular and quite tame *Charlie's Angels* on ABC, *Killing* toppled *The Oregon Trail* on NBC by four points.

David Gerber, the movie's producer, explained to *Jet*: "The story started off with a white couple, but we wanted to do something different with the script and turned it around to an interracial couple. CBS had the guts to show it and I think they handled it right."

Considering the uneasy nature of *Killing's* racially mixed romance, reaction to the movie was generally mild. Neither Lizzie nor Simpson received any significant letters of protest. However, as *Jet* perceived it, America didn't completely sit on its anger. A Chicago television station and newspaper received a few crank calls and letters, and far more seriously, one southern station received a bomb threat convincing enough that the building was momentarily evacuated.

"We all expected such response as an inevitable result," CBS censor Van Gordon Sauter told the magazine. "The movie featured the kind of relationship many viewers feel uncomfortable with. If there were a proliferation of such programs (depicting interracial relationships) there would probably be a considerable degree of indignation expressed."

According to a September 1977 edition of *The Abilene Reporter-News* in Texas, Lizzie was at the time visiting a Renaissance Faire in the San Fernando Valley in California when a middle-aged female *Bewitched* fan approached her and asked what she was working on. "I'm doing a television movie with O. J. Simpson," she replied. "It's a love story between two police detectives."

The woman's face went blank and she said, "You. O. J. Simpson. A love story? Well!" She then went back into the crowd.

"Oh, I'm sure I'll be getting hate mail and I don't care," Lizzie told *The Abilene*. "Both O. J. and I realized we would get a strong reaction from the show, but we went ahead and did it. I think it's a good show, though I hate the title."

According to further reports in *Jet*, and just as *A Killing Affair* aired, a flood of hate mail was credited with destroying the then on-screen love affair between white actor Richard Guthrie's character and his on-screen African-American girlfriend played by Tina Andrews on NBC's daytime serial *Days of Our Lives*. Guthrie had argued that the show's producers "got cold feet on the budding romance" because the story line was unpopular. "The studio had been getting a lot of hate mail from people threatening to stop watching the show," huffed Andrews at the time, "when they get enough of those letters they respond. One letter said, 'I hope you're not going to let that (n-word) marry that white boy.' Apparently they are not. I was canned."

Why would an America that for the most part tacitly accepted the O. J./ Lizzie flame turn against the fledgling Guthrie-Andrews lovelight?

Harvard psychiatrist Dr. Alvin Poussaint took his analysis a bit further. "During the day television is watched mostly by white women," he observed, who might have then have viewed Tina Andrews' performance as a threat. Whereas in the 9:00 or 10:00 PM time slot of that era you may find a significantly different audience that might observe this: an African-American (like O. J. Simpson who was not at that time the controversial figure he would later become in 1994) having an affair with a white woman, which would fit the stereotype that successful black men desire white women, via what Poussaint called the "guess who's coming to dinner" scenario (in reference to the 1967 Sidney Poitier film of the same name that was remade in 2005 with Will Smith).

Poussaint added:

> Plus *A Killing Affair* was a one-shot thing. We don't know what protests might have come if the movie were a continuing series. Soap operas are ongoing and they reflect a slice of real life. The viewer usually lives a fantasy through the characters, which is why Tina Andrews' character may have run into trouble. Then too, TV is still uncomfortable with interracial romances. For *A Killing Affair* they picked a superstar like O. J. Simpson and that may have been why there weren't more protests. Simpson represents a big, virile, handsome cat who seems gentle and non-threatening.

At least that was the perception at the time. Today, the film is almost unwatchable. Not because of the interracial romance between Lizzie's and Simpson's characters, but because of the questions and incriminating cir-cumstances that have since surrounded and assassinated Simpson's real life character (the murder trial after the death of his wife Nicole Simpson, attractive and fair-haired like Lizzie; while the movie's ironic title doesn't much help its case).

Beyond the racial, political, and particular controversies that surrounded the lives of certain performers, Lizzie's involvement with *A Killing Affair* further proved her attempts to push the creative envelope and ultimately allowed television—by way of her career choices—to become an educational platform for narrative mainstream entertainment outside the realm of PBS.

Unlike *Samantha's* singular marriage to two *Darrins* on *Bewitched*, Lizzie was married four times to different men, ultimately to Bob Foxworth. When Lizzie and Foxworth appeared on *The Dennis Miller Show* in 1992, Miller looked at Foxworth and asked, "Which *Darrin* are *you?*"

Foxworth played along with the gag, and replied, "The third one!"

Six years later, and thirty-six months after Lizzie died, Foxworth wed Stacey Thomas, and they remain married today. Before he met Lizzie on the set of *Mrs. Sundance* in 1973, he was with Marilyn McCormick, whom he was married to from 1964 to 1974—nearly the same time Lizzie was married to Bill Asher. Lizzie and Bill divorced in 1974. So did Bob and Marilyn, though not before they had two children, Bo and Kristyn Foxworth (both actors), who later became step-siblings to Lizzie's three children (with Bill Asher), Rebecca, Robert, and Billy Asher, Jr.

When Lizzie and Bob moved in together, it was like *The Brady Bunch*, combining families from two different marriages, and that kind of fit. Lizzie had attended the New York Academy of Dramatic Arts with *Brady* star Florence Henderson, while Foxworth's curly brown locks and piercing blue eyes resembled *Mr. Brady* actor Robert Reed.

All five children were lights in Lizzie's life, although she was never satisfied with her maternal performance. As she expressed in 1992 to John Tesh on *One on One*, "I will never win any Mother of the Year awards," but she also believed "parents and kids have to grow up together."

When asked if it was tough being Robert Montgomery's liberal daughter, she replied:

> Yeah, absolutely . . . There were people who didn't like him and, as a result, they were people who decided they didn't like me. And those are things you just kinda have to cope with and that's a little tough, but you get used to it. I guess.

She never got used to it. Her father's political views were not always welcome in Hollywood which, in 1989, she described as "a town that claims to be so damned liberal all the time, but isn't." It was outspoken opinions like that which probably didn't help her case in winning the majority Emmy vote amongst her peers.

Fortunately, she was adored by millions of fans, while her political advocacy and love and respect for Foxworth quenched her slight desire to pontificate. They were a glamorous humanitarian team, superheroes of the Hollywood set, battling for world peace, the disadvantaged, the downtrodden, and those suffering from the pain and discrimination of AIDS, and for the rights of those in the lesbian, gay, bisexual, and transgender (LGBT) community.

Although it was Foxworth who usually voiced their collective concerns in the court of public opinion, at various forums Lizzie would stand beside him, firmly, silently, with that famous closed-lipped smile which became one of her many facial trademarks. While that periodically perky smirk may have represented her apprehension to speak, she believed in exactly whatever Foxworth professed which, according to *The Los Angeles Times* in 1986 was the following:

> Before I am an actor and a famous face, I am a human being and a (parent) and a citizen of this nation and of the world. I think I have a right, as well as a responsibility, to speak to the [nuclear arms] issue as well as any other issue.

It was a speech he gave at a rally for The Great Peace March for Global Nuclear Disarmament of 1986, which was undermanned, plagued by insurance problems, heckled by protesters, and attacked by bureaucrats. Nevertheless, Lizzie and Foxworth, along with numerous other celebrities, showed their support as approximately 1,400 marchers struck out across 3,235 miles of American desert, mountains, plains, and cities, bent on mass persuasion against the perceived evils of nuclear arms.

The march was the brainchild of David Mixner, then twenty-nine years old and a longtime activist in several liberal causes, specifically in regard to LGBT issues. His credentials include the 1968 presidential campaign of Senator Eugene McCarthy, directing Los Angeles Mayor Tom Bradley's 1977 mayoral campaign, co-chairing Senator Gary Hart's 1984 presidential quest, and the Vietnam Moratorium. Mixner was also one of the prominent LGBT fundraisers for Bill Clinton during his 1992 campaign but famously broke with the President over the "don't ask, don't tell" policy implemented in 1993, and was ultimately arrested at a protest in front of the White House. At such events, Lizzie was usually a figurative if not oratorical voice.

Mixner says today:

> Elizabeth was one of the first Hollywood celebrities to step forward to fight for LGBT rights. At the time, everyone in Hollywood was keeping a respectful distance from the issue, but not Elizabeth. She attended events, helped raise money and often dined at Mark's, a famous gay restaurant in West Hollywood. Never wanting to receive accolades for her work, since in conversation with me she just kept saying, "It is the right thing to do." She was a person who made us feel we had value by her presence in those dark and difficult years.

Lizzie's presence certainly gave value to Dick Sargent's life.

In 1991, her former *Bewitched* co-star announced his homosexuality, and requested her presence as Co-Grand Marshall for the 1992 Gay Rights Parade in Los Angeles. "You wouldn't see her at parties," Sargent's former publicist Howard Bragman told *People Magazine* in 1995, "but you would always see her at benefits."

Shortly before Sargent died in 1994 of prostate cancer (and *not* AIDS, which has been falsely reported over the years), he gave an interview to writer Owen Keehnen for *Chicago Outlines* magazine, "the voice of the gay and lesbian community," which was later published in Keehnen's book, *We're Here, We're Queer* (Prairie Avenue Productions, 2011), during which he commented on Lizzie's support. She knew of his sexuality, Sargent said, because his "lover was alive when we did *Bewitched*." He and his partner, Albert Williams, a screenwriter, would attend parties and play tennis with Lizzie and Bill Asher. "She really loved my lover very much," Sargent said of the man who in 1979 dropped dead of a cerebral hemorrhage at the home they shared in the Hollywood Hills. He said Lizzie respected "the hell out of me for doing this [coming out]. She thinks it's marvelous and has nothing but encouraging words."

In 1991, *The Star* magazine decided to out Sargent and as he told Keehnen, "they quoted everyone like they talked to them." Sargent called Lizzie and read what the tabloid had quoted her as saying: "Well, if that's his lifestyle, I just hope it makes him happy."

"Oh, shit," Lizzie mused to Sargent over the fabricated line. "They gave me the only cliché in the article."

"I love her," Sargent concluded. "She's a very bright and caring lady."

In 1992, Elizabeth touched on the subject of Sargent's once-secret sexuality for an interview with *The Advocate*, a national gay magazine. In Robert Pela's article, "The Legend of Lizzie," she said the topic never came up. She simply decided his sexuality was none of her business and that such discretion at times was the very definition of friendship.

In the same article, she also addressed the long-circulated gay rumors surrounding another *Bewitched* co-star: Agnes Moorehead, who died of cancer at sixty-seven in 1974, ten years after the show debuted and two years after it was cancelled. Again, the topic of sexuality, this time with Moorehead, as before with Sargent's, was just not something that arose.

Elizabeth then further explained how some members of the *Bewitched* cast and crew considered the series a metaphor for the social and cultural issues confronting those individuals outside the mainstream. *Samantha* was forced to conceal her supernatural heritage, and pretended to be mortal ("normal?"), like some gay men and women were forced to pretend they were straight. As far as Elizabeth was concerned, *Bewitched* was about repression and the subsequent frustrations that follow. She felt it was a positive message to relay in a clandestine manner, while she admitted that being raised in Hollywood exposed her to alternate lifestyles since her youth.

The Advocate then made note of her support of Sargent and the LGBT community in general and wondered if she felt she might be perceived as gay herself. But none of that phased Elizabeth; she had more important things with which to concern herself. For one, she appeared in the Gay Pride Parade in support of Sargent.

But she was considering playing a lesbian in a TV-movie that never went into production. It wasn't anything specific, but she thought portraying such a role might have proved intriguing.

Then again, she had already, years before, played a similarly-repressed character . . . in the guise of *Samantha Stephens* on *Bewitched*.

On April 15, 1989, Lizzie's fifty-sixth birthday, she and Bob Foxworth served as honorary co-chairs and hosts of the National Gay Rights Advocates Eleventh Anniversary Celebration, which was held at the Museum of Contemporary Art in Los Angeles, and whose honorees included Lizzie's devoted manager Barry Krost.

More than anything, the caring couple was heavily involved with amfAR, the American Foundation for AIDS Research, and APLA, AIDS Project Los Angeles.

In 1989, they attended "The Magic of Bob Mackie," a fashion presentation celebrating the designer's countless years in the business. Known for his work with Elizabeth's good friend Carol Burnett on *The Carol Burnett Show,* Mackie's event was held at the Century Plaza Hotel in Los Angeles, and also attended by Burnett, Cher, Jackie Collins, Joan Rivers, and Cheryl Ladd, all proceeds for which supported APLA's service to people with AIDS and AIDS-related complex (including mental health counseling, dental care, and in-home health care).

In 1987, Lizzie and Foxworth helped to raise more than $15,000 at a benefit performance of the stage play, *Tamara,* in honor of the Twenty-seventh Anniversary of Amnesty International.

She also joined him at the preview party of the eight-part PBS mini-series *Television,* which was given at the KCET-TV headquarters in L.A. According to a press packet for the program, this series documented the "evolution and the astonishing global power and impact of the world's most powerful communication medium."

The Los Angeles Times called Lizzie radiant in a gown bedazzled by her grandmother Rebecca Allen's diamond and emerald brooch. Foxworth wore Western accessories including a unique bolo tie, trimmed with silver feathers, and a diamond stud in his left ear. The latter, a gift from Lizzie, who once more worked that celebrated silent smile, as Foxworth explained how the stud symbolized his "freedom from *Falcon Crest.*"

Shortly before he left the series, however, Lizzie was invited to join the show for an arc of episodes, but she declined. Instead, another media sorceress, Kim Novak, who played a witch in the 1958 feature film, *Bell, Book, and Candle,* stepped into the part.

Lizzie had more important fish to fry, as when the opportunity to express and expand her political arena arrived in 1988. It was then she narrated *Cover Up: Behind the Iran-Contra Affair*, the feature film documentary that was critical of Reagan-Bush policies in Central America. She would later lend her voice to the follow-up film, *The Panama Deception*, which won the Oscar in 1992 for Best Feature Length Documentary.

Lizzie was dedicated to both films, but her work ethic was always sound. As she said in 1989: "Work takes a certain amount of concentration and energy, even though it always looks like I'm having fun (for example) when I'm looping. Luckily, I'm pretty good at it" (as Dan Weaver experienced in 1990 during Lizzie's looping session for *Face to Face*).

One day, Barbara Trent, director of both *Cover Up* and *The Panama Deception*, had asked Lizzie to loop a few lines of narration under slightly challenging working conditions. As Trent later told *People* magazine in 1995 after Lizzie's death: "We were too embarrassed to [ever] ask her to come back into our little Santa Monica studio, where the temperatures sometimes went up to 80 degrees."

But none of that mattered to Lizzie. She was hot for the topic. The message she was sending was in direct opposition to the Reagan administration and the man himself, who had long been a friend to her parents. But when it came time to vote for Reagan (in 1980 and again in 1984), her mother Elizabeth Allen refused to debate the issue. As Lizzie recalled in 1989, the conversation went something like this:

"Well, you and Daddy knew him."

"But your father must have talked about him to you, didn't he?"

"Are you kidding?" (Lizzie knew her father was wise enough not to debate such topics with her, but that didn't stop her from telling her mother exactly what she thought of Reagan.)

"If you asked him what time it was, he would tell you how to take a watch apart and put it back together again, but you'd never find out the time; never. Nothing's changed, except he's probably not smart enough to take apart a watch and put it back together."

"Oh, Elizabeth!" her mother protested (in much the same way Agnes Moorehead would at times object to Lizzie's forthright opinions on the set of *Bewitched*).

336

"Okay, sorry," Lizzie concluded to her Mom. "No more politics. Promise. Never mind."

"I just wouldn't get into it with her," she said in 1989. "But the man is loathsome." David White listened to Lizzie's Reagan rant and agreed.

He had worked with the former president on an episode of TV's *G. E. True Theatre* (aka *General Electric True Theatre*)—an anthology series Reagan hosted from 1953 to 1962. As David recalled, Marc Daniels (Bill Asher's precursor on *I Love Lucy*) directed the episode and, at one point between filming, various conversations transpired, periodically turning to the subject of politics, a hot topic between Reagan and White in particular:

"You know, David, what's good for General Electric is good for America."

"No, no, Ronny boy . . . *what's good for General Electric* is what's good for *Ronny Reagan* . . . and the stockholders. And besides . . . we always have Westinghouse."

Upon hearing David relay this interchange in 1989, Lizzie laughed and said, "I never met (Reagan), and I probably would have hated him . . . I *hope* I would have hated him."

"He's just shallow and incompetent," continued White, who was angry with Reagan and the first George Bush on an entirely different level. His son, Jonathan White, after whom *Larry Tate's* son was named on *Bewitched*, died in the Pan Am Flight 103 incident over Lockerbie, Scotland in December 1988. It was Pan American World Airways' third daily scheduled transatlantic flight from London Heathrow Airport to New York's John F. Kennedy International Airport. On Wednesday, December 21, 1988, the aircraft flying this route—a Boeing 747-121 registered N739PA and named "Clipper Maid of the Seas"—was destroyed by a bomb, killing all 243 passengers and sixteen crew members. Eleven people in Lockerbie were also killed as large sections of the plane fell in the town and destroyed several houses, bringing total fatalities to 270. As a result, the event is also known as the "Lockerbie Bombing." During the 2011 Libyan civil war a former government official claimed that Muammar Gaddafi had personally ordered the attack. (According to *The Los Angeles Times*, Abdel Bassett Ali Megrahi, the Libyan intelligence officer convicted in the bombing, who denied any role in the plot, died in Tripoli, Libya, May 20, 2012.)

For David, it was a personal attack of another nature and a tragedy from which he never recovered. As he told Lizzie in 1989, only a short time after the incident, he received a letter of sympathy from the White House, specifically, from Reagan's successor, George H. W. Bush:

> It arrived on my birthday, about four or five days after the parents of the victims of Pan Am 103 went down and met him. And by then I'm sure he thought *I better get my ass in gear*. *"A kinder gentler nation" is what I said we were going to have repeatedly.*

But when David opened the letter, he was unimpressed. In fact, he laughed. Or as he put it, "I cracked up." He was indignantly amused by the cardboard backing that was placed behind the letter in order for it not to wrinkle. "So I can hang it up in my den," David assumed. "They thought I should think it's a big deal. And I don't think it's a big deal."

"That's incredible," added Lizzie who expressed her own fury about the Pan Am incident. "I was angry when it happened. And when I realized that Jonathan was on the plane, I just couldn't believe it. When I called *Mouse* (*Bewitched* producer Marvin Miller), I said, 'Are you sure?' He said, 'Yeah . . . I talked to David at the gym.'"

But now David was right in front of her, in near tears. As he went on to assess, "In October of 1988, they [international officials] knew there were bombs (on the plane) that they put in cassettes. I have an article from *Newsweek* [that states this]. They were warned a couple of times, not just for Helsinki."

According to the Report of the President's Commission on Aviation Security and Terrorism, on December 5, 1988 (sixteen days prior to the Pan Am attack), the Federal Aviation Administration (FAA) issued a security bulletin saying that on that day a man with an Arabic accent had telephoned the U.S. Embassy in Helsinki, Finland, and had told them that a Pan Am flight from Frankfurt to the United States would be blown up within the next two weeks by someone associated with the Abu Nidal Organization. He said a Finnish woman would carry the bomb on board as an unwitting courier.

David concluded with a heavy heart and even heavier words, that he missed his son immensely, and was clearly not pleased with those he thought were responsible for his death:

Bless his heart. I wanted him to be his own person. [But] I say you don't need an enemy when you have a government like ours. I have no faith in this country at all. Individual people, I like, but [not the] people who run the government.

Then, in a swift shift to help lighten the mood, David turned to Elizabeth and asked:

"So how many children do you have now?"

"The same three," she replied. "Bob [Foxworth] and I finally went, '*Uh, no, I don't think so*' [with regard to the possibility of them having more children when they first got together in 1974]. He has two, and I have three, and they're all grown. They're wonderful. We've got five between us, and that's more than enough."

"You don't want to raise children any more, do you?" White continued in jest.

"Every time we get tempted," Lizzie answered, "this friend of mine, who's a costume designer, Frances Hays, one of my best friends, says, 'Call B.A.' And I said, 'What's that?' And she said, 'Babies Anonymous.'"

While Lizzie was working on *Bewitched* in 1960s, Ronald Reagan hosted another anthology series, this one a western syndicated show called *Death Valley Days*. She was more than familiar with his work and his persona, and subsequently reveled in performing one particular scene from her 1985 NBC TV-movie, *Between the Darkness and the Dawn* when her character *Abigail Foster* made a sarcastic reference to Reagan in a dinner-table scene. *Abigail* had been in an epileptic coma for twenty years. Upon awakening in 1985, she learned of America's new leader, and was shocked. "Ronald Reagan is president?!" she said incredulously, in response to the election of a former actor as the world's most powerful decision-maker.

Twenty-two

~

Final Exams

"I keep thinking about how I might have cancer."

—*Blanche Taylor Moore*, as played by Elizabeth in *Black Widow*
Murders: The Blanche Taylor Moore Story (1993)

One of Lizzie's favorite *Bewitched* guest stars was Christopher George, who
played the lead in the first season episode, "George the Warlock":

> *Endora* seizes an opportunity to dissolve *Samantha's* mortal marriage by
> enlisting the assistance of the supernaturally suave warlock named *George*
> (Christopher) to romance her daughter.

Like many of the show's guests in its first two years—Adam West (*Batman*), James Doohan (*Star Trek*), Billy Mumy (*Lost in Space*), and Bill Daily
(*I Dream of Jeannie*), Christopher George went on to star in a weekly series
of his own: *The Immortal*, a fanciful, if short-lived (only sixteen episodes)
take on *The Fugitive*, a wanted-man story with a positive twist:

> *Ben Richards* (George) is a test-car driver whose blood contains certain
> miraculous antibodies that allow him to live forever. In the interim, *Ben*
> searches for his long lost brother *Jason* (never seen), in the hope that he too
> may contain the same rare form of blood-type; while the wealthy senior
> *Arthur Maitland* (David Brian) who once rejected a blood transfusion from
> *Ben*, is now in hot pursuit to track him down.

340

Ben, like *George*, the warlock, was immortal, as were the entire band of charmers on *Bewitched*. None the least of which was *Samantha*, as played by Lizzie who leaves her own immortal legacy with a body of work that echoed and foreshadowed portions of her reality that warrants further examination.

In 1976, she appeared in the TV-movie *Dark Victory*, a remake of the classic 1939 feature film starring her friend Bette Davis.

> TV producer *Katherine Merrill* (Lizzie) is stricken with a brain tumor. Consumed with work, *Katherine* ignores her personal life and the symptoms of an impending physical disorder until finally collapsing at a cocktail party and tumbling down a flight of stairs. Once hospitalized, she falls in love with the attending physician, *Dr. Michael Grant* (Anthony Hopkins).

Here, Lizzie takes the viewer through the varied emotions connected with a devastating illness (surprise, frustration, anger), and the challenges of maintaining an intimate relationship through that period. In the end, and just as in the original Bette Davis movie, *Katherine* dies. But in the last few moments of Lizzie's edition, *Katherine* turns to *Dr. Grant*, smiles, and the camera freeze-frames on the love light in her eyes. It's a bittersweet ending to one of Lizzie's better post-*Bewitched* films.

Nine years later, in 1985, she starred in another TV-movie, *Between the Darkness and the Dawn*:

> *Abigail Foster* (Lizzie) awakens from a decades-long viral-induced epileptic coma. She finds her sister (Karen Grassle) has married her boyfriend (Michael Goodwin), and her mother (Dorothy McGuire) has become obsessed with being her caregiver. Fortunately, in time, *Abigail* manages to foster an alternate happiness with the new man in her life (James Naughton).

The ending for *Between the Darkness and the Dawn* is less bitter and more sweet than it is with *Dark Victory*, but a glaring discrepancy detracts from this movie's credibility beyond its far-reaching premise (although similar events have transpired). The story opens in 1965, when actress Lori Birdsong portrays a seventeen-year-old *Abigail* who is soon stricken into her catatonic state. The setting then swiftly shifts forward twenty years, and Lizzie is seen playing *Abigail*, who is now apparently thirty-seven years old.

Although Lizzie blurred the age of her documented birth, April 15, 1933, by the time this film aired, December 23, 1985, she was in reality fifty-two years old. Actors sometimes play younger characters. It's an unwritten Hollywood rule. But it's a bit of a stretch for Lizzie to have played a thirty-seven-year-old in the later period suggested in *Between the Darkness and the Dawn*.

However, she embraced the opportunity to change the face of time; as she had in 1992, when according to Tom McCartney, she registered as forty-nine years old for a medical examination during filming of the TV movie *The Black Widow Murders*. That meant she would have been born in 1943, and fifty-two years old when she died in 1995. But that didn't measure up either.

When Elizabeth died in 1995, writer Lynn Elber reported in *The Associated Press* that Lizzie was fifty-seven years old. That meant she would have been born in 1938 which, as previously documented, is simply not true.

Lizzie and younger brother Skip were in England in 1939 while their father Robert Montgomery worked on *The Earl of Chicago*. They were then shipped back to the States when he was called to service for World War II. They traveled on the S.S. Arandora Star, sailed from Southampton, England for New York on September 1, 1939 and arrived in New York City on September 12, 1939. According to the passenger list chart lines that were posted on www.harpiesbizzare.com, one of the top *Bewitched* websites, Lizzie was then six years old, and born in 1933, which was also her documented birth year in early studio biographies. All of which means that, in reality, she had just turned sixty-two on April 15, 1995, a month and three days before she passed away on May 18.

In August of 1975, Elizabeth broached the birthday subject with an interview for *TV-Movies Today* magazine, claiming she always told the truth about her age because of her third most influential relative: Rebecca Allen. As Lizzie explained it, when her grandmother was sixty, Becca told everyone she was sixty-five. "People always think you're older anyway," she said. "They therefore think I'm really seventy and are impressed with how youthful I appear.' "

When asked her age, Lizzie replied, "I was born on April 15, 1936, which has since become Income Tax Day and therefore is easy to remember." So that would mean she was fifty-nine when she died in 1995 which, again, is untrue.

More age-old tales were spun on the set of her 1985 CBS TV-movie *Amos* the premise for which dealt with, appropriately enough, the elderly residents at a nursing home. According to Montgomery archivist Thomas McCartney, Lizzie took a particular liking to Pat Morita, who co-starred in this film as one of the senior residents that was abused by Lizzie's maniacal nurse *Daisy Daws*. Morita had found fame late in life, first as *Arnold* on *Happy Days* (ABC, 1974–1984) and then with *The Karate Kid* movies of the 1980s. On the *Amos* set, Morita, who was born in 1932 and died in 2005, realized he and Lizzie were approximately the same age, and while he portrayed the elderly *Tanaka*, she played a middle-aged *Daisy*.

Morita laughed off the same-age reference, claiming it must have been the water in Japan that helped him retain his youth. Lizzie blushed and made every attempt to downplay the somewhat awkward assumption. "She'd get real embarrassed about the age comparison," McCartney explains, claiming that makeup had contributed to her youthful appearance and Morita's older look. "But no one was buying it. She had a naturally young, blithe spirit," he says.

She also had a way with numbers. Upon further early influence from her beloved grandmother Becca, Lizzie frequented the race track and loved to gamble, which is really what her life became. And although *Dark Victory* and *Between the Darkness and the Dawn* had comparatively uneven endings, both films foreshadowed what would later become Lizzie's darkest hours.

In the final analysis, it was never Lizzie's performance as *Samantha* or any of her characterizations or unique talents that were in question. It was her *choices* for certain roles, before and particularly beyond *Bewitched* that proved to be intriguing, if not downright mind-boggling. But her friend and TV-movie co-star Ronny Cox wouldn't have had it any other way. She was "an actress, and the fun is in playing the roles that stretch you," he says. In the decades since Cox was the affable dad on TV's *Apple's Way*, (CBS, 1974–1975), he's mostly played "bad guys," similar to Lizzie's choices in films like *The Legend of Lizzie Borden* and *The Black Widow Murders*. And although not evil in nature, her character in *A Case of Rape* was eons away from *Samantha* on *Bewitched*. "Hell!" Cox proclaims, such roles are "*twenty*

times more fun to play," because films like *Rape*, he says, give actors a chance
to showcase and expand their talents.

Case in point: When former *Charlie's Angels* star Farrah Fawcett
appeared in NBC's shocking TV-movie, *The Burning Bed*, directed by Robert Greenwald, this film was based on the book by Faith McNulty, with a
teleplay by Rose Leiman Goldemberg:

> *Francine Hughes* (Fawcett) is the loving mother of three children. But she is
> also the battered wife of *Mickey Hughes* (Paul Le Mat), who is both verbally
> and physically abusive. However, whenever *Francine* reaches out for help,
> she's turned away, and ultimately becomes incapable of bringing *Mickey* to
> justice. So, one terrifying night, after he rapes her, she sets their bed on fire
> with him still in it, asleep. As a result, *Francine* goes on trial for her life.

Just as in Lizzie's *Case*, Fawcett (who worked with Cox on *Apple's Way*)
played an abused woman who is forced to defend herself within a closed-
minded judicial system. Both actresses were allowed the opportunity to
utilize what Cox calls their theatrical "muscles" for what became physically
demanding and emotionally draining performances.

For some *Bewitched* fans, watching Lizzie—their once-cheerful witch-
with-a-twitch—get raped in *Case* may have been a traumatic experience.
But Cox believes that was the "essence of why she desperately needed" to
do such roles—so fans would "realize that this person on the screen" is only
a character played by an actor. Often times, actors are mostly identified with
one particular character, as it was and remains with Lizzie and *Samantha*.
But according to Cox, too many fans of actors mistake "brilliant acting for
the person."

In further defense of Lizzie's post-comedic *Bewitched* performances, Cox
poses:

> You can't play *Lizzie Borden*? You can't play an ax murderer? You can't play
> *King Lear* who goes crazy? I mean, that's what acting is! Lizzie didn't want
> to walk around for the rest of her life being *Samantha*! It's asking way too
> much to say, "No, no, no . . . don't be anything else! Just be *Samantha* for
> the rest of your life! I can't stand it if you do anything but being *Samantha*!"

"God, that's prison!" Cox bellows, figuratively, adding, "Slit your wrists!"

How would Cox compare Lizzie's childhood "play-acting" perform-ance as *Snow White* (for her grandmother Becca) to her portrayal of the *Wolf* in her Westlake School's French language production of *Little Red Riding Hood*?

"In playing *Snow White*," Cox deduces, "you still have all these people that love you and care for you and you're dealing with morality and things like that. At the end of the day you're still dealing with dwarfs and the wicked [queen], so you're dealing in fantasy."

Yet, he loves "the lightweight stuff, too," especially his friend's much later and more professional fanciful role as *Samantha*:

> Lizzie was brilliant on *Bewitched*, but that tapped like this much (gestures small space between index finger and thumb) of her talent. And I talked with her about this, too. She could play that character and phone it in. One of the things that Lizzie knew about acting [were] the tricks of the craft. She had that special spark . . . her personality sort of shone through in roles like *Samantha*. And in lots of ways she could just get by on that persona . . . that personality. But that wasn't all of her talent, only a measure of it.

Post-*Bewitched*, Elizabeth certainly leaned toward those edgier roles, more times than not, playing people with malevolent traits. Her manager Barry Krost explained in 2001 on MSNBC's *Headliners & Legends*: "If there was a wicked gene in a character, odds are, Lizzie would do it."

On A&E's *Biography* in 1999, Robert Foxworth said Lizzie was "thrilled" with the idea that she surprised her fans and detractors with Emmy-nominated performances as in *The Legend of Lizzie Borden*. To have viewers accept her in such a non-*Samantha* role and subsequently respect the theatrical diversity that she would bring to such a role as an accom-plished actress was "probably one of her great victories in life."

The Legend of Lizzie Borden was helmed by Paul Wendkos, a favorite director of Lizzie's, who also guided her in the 1958 "Bitter Heritage" episode of *Playhouse 90*, and the 1979 TV-movie, *Act of Violence*.

Director Boris Sagal was another of her favorite directors, guiding her and Ronny Cox through *A Case of Rape* in 1974. Before that, he directed her in the 1960 TV *Kraft Theatre* production of *The Spiral Staircase*, in 1978's

The Awakening Land, and in 1981's *When the Circus Came to Town*, the last which stood out from the rest, if only due to lighter content.

The actual driving force behind *Circus* was legendary producer Robert Halmi, who conceived of the story idea and was responsible for casting not only Lizzie, but acting legend Christopher Plummer, best known for his performance in the 1965 classic feature, *The Sound of Music*. By then, Halmi had produced more than 140 feature and TV films (and went on to produce countless more), and was considered one of the industry's busiest and most respected producers. As he revealed to *The Toronto Star* in 1981, Halmi viewed working with the former-*Bewitched* star as "a wonderful opportunity for Liz to do what she does best. She's fantastic. She makes you laugh, she makes you cry. She's physical. She's sexy."

While Halmi's words could have just as easily described what Lizzie brought to playing *Samantha* on a weekly basis, her *Circus* co-star Christopher Plummer would never as willingly embrace a regular TV role. "It's bad news, I think, for someone like me," he told *The Toronto Star*. "You get so terribly identified with one role you can't be taken serious as an actor."

For years, Plummer was identified with the role of *Captain von Trapp* in *The Sound of Music*, just as Lizzie had been identified for so long with *Bewitched*. In 2011, he won the Academy Award for Best Supporting Actor for *Beginners*, in which he portrayed *Hal Fields*, a dying gay senior who comes out of the closet.

Four decades ago, both actors should have been pleased with the critical praise showered upon *When the Circus Came to Town*, which proved to be a nice addition to their already impressive resumes. In his 1981 review in *The Toronto Star*, critic Bill Kaufman said the film "convincingly manages to develop *Mary's* character and how she becomes involved with the raggle-taggle touring circus. Plummer plays *Duke Royal*, owner and ringmaster of the shabby big top, a flamboyant man who ultimately changes *Mary's* life with boy love and a guiding hand. The progression of *Mary's* involvement with circus life is skillfully fleshed out under the guidance of veteran director Boris Sagal."

In 1989, Lizzie said her performance in *Circus* was "tough work, physically, but so much fun to do." For many scenes, she was outfitted in a heavy headdress, and she wore fishnet stockings with runs and holes, in order to better authenticate the slight seediness of that particular circus portrayed in the movie. Prior to filming, she spent several weeks training with legendary stuntman Bob Yerkes and his son, Mark, who had trained actors, singers, etc. to participate in TV shows like *Circus of the Stars* (the era's answer to today's *Dancing with the Stars*). He's also worked on feature films like *Back to the Future*, *Star Wars: Return of the Jedi*, and *Hook* (and he currently hosts stunt training, on invitation only, at his Los Angeles home).

She always knew that certain productions would prove challenging. Actors are never sure of what lies ahead until the day of the shoot. Certainly, timing is imperative and performers must trust their colleagues on the set, behind and in front of the camera. In Lizzie's case, she was pleased that she would be allowed to do some of the stunts they had planned for her stand-in.

For example, she had donned a clown's garb for a few *Circus* scenes, but according to Thomas McCartney, she confessed at the time: "I have never been a clown person. Maybe I was scared badly by a clown when I was a child."

The "fear-factor" in that last sentence may have been some subconscious allusion to the intimating presence her father pervaded over her young life. It was a character flaw that Robert Montgomery may have developed by way of the tragic loss of his daughter, Martha Bryan, Lizzie's infant sister. Into this mix there were the other tragic losses in the early Montgomery lineage, namely with regard to Henry Montgomery, Lizzie's grandfather.

Author and genealogist James Pylant concludes:

[Henry's] suicide clearly had an impact on Robert Montgomery's life, and it would have extended into the relationship with his own children. Perhaps what is seen as his jealousy of Elizabeth's success as an actress was his resenting of her achieving fame too easily because she was Robert Montgomery's daughter. His father's early demise led Robert to toil as a railroad mechanic and an oil tanker deckhand before his big break in Hollywood, and maybe he felt Elizabeth hadn't earned her dues. And the death of his first child, Martha, may have made him more emotionally distant to Elizabeth.

Consequently, she may have attempted to earn those dues and her father's approval, while also igniting his fury by later fanning a bigger star than his via *Bewitched*, the lighter fare of which she then replaced with roles like *Lizzie Borden*.

Classic TV author, curator, and radio show host Ed Robertson offers these thoughts:

> Once *Bewitched* ended she was looking for projects that would allow her to grow as an actress, and further develop her dramatic skills, which she was not always able to do as *Samantha*, particularly in the last couple years of the show. I don't think she was necessarily trying to "shed" her image as *Samantha*, but I do believe she wanted to show audiences (and for that matter, casting directors and the like) that she could do much more than *Samantha*. That's why I think she did *A Case of Rape*, which had aired in the year 1974, and I think that's what may have attracted her to doing *The Legend of Lizzie Borden*. That, plus the project itself had a strong pedigree. Paul Wendkos had already established himself as an excellent director, plus Fritz Weaver (who played Borden's father), through his work on such shows as *The Twilight Zone*, was an accomplished, respected stage actor. I don't know whether Fritz worked with her father, but I imagine Elizabeth would have relished the opportunity to work with someone like him . . . The Lizzie Borden trial was, for its time, considered the *trial of the century*, as was the O. J. Simpson case more than a century later. Like Lizzie Borden, O. J. Simpson became a pariah, even though he was acquitted. And of course, a few years after doing Lizzie Borden, and about fifteen years before the Simpson murder trial, Elizabeth did a TV-movie with O. J. for CBS [*A Killing Affair*, 1977].

As to how all of this to relates to Elizabeth's performance on *Bewitched*, Robertson believes it's

> kind of an *apples and oranges* comparison. The subject matter of Lizzie Borden is much darker and more disturbing than anything she'd done on *Bewitched*. Which goes back to my earlier point: It appears she was looking for projects that would challenge her as an actress, as *The Legend of Lizzie Borden* certainly did. Given that the movie portrays Borden as having committed the murders [the case, though closer to closures, remains unsolved, even after all these years], it was Elizabeth's job to somehow make this cold, calculating, mercurial woman evoke sympathy from the viewers, even though she committed these heinous acts. To her credit, I think she did.

348

I'm sure some (of her fans) were shocked, especially those who may have been clinging to her wholesome image as *Samantha*. But I'm just as sure that those who loved her as an actress, taking into her account her body of work prior to and after *Bewitched*, were pleased and mesmerized by her performance.

When the Circus Came to Town at least offered a glimmer of the comedic sparkle Lizzie presented on *Bewitched*. The 1981 movie was made in association with her production company, Entheos Unlimited Productions. According to Roland L. Smith's book, *Sweethearts of '60s TV* (S.P.I. Books, 1993), Lizzie had signed a deal with CBS in 1979 that paid her $275,000 per film, an amount that would increase over the years. Add to that the shrewd investments and stellar profts from *Bewitched* (of which she and Bill Asher were part owners) and her annual income became substantial.

However, as Smith observed, retaining her integrity and remaining visible in pertinent television films wasn't always easy, "sometimes even the most determined efforts were in vain."

Plainly stated, it was challenging for Lizzie to find a good script. By 1981, she had one more movie left in the CBS deal, and she was considering several ideas, one of which was a comedy, but nothing was a lock. But then the *Circus Came to Town* which, as Tom McCartney says, Lizzie viewed as "a romantic comedy," the first such lighter concept she would consider since *Bewitched*.

The idea for *Circus* was generated by one sentence from Doug Chapin, who produced her previous film, *Belle Starr*. She was ready to drop the project altogether until writer Larry Grusin impressed her with his script, which McCartney says CBS executive William Self was initially apprehensive about sending her way. It was then her manager Barry Krost, Chapin's business partner, who then suggested she read it.

She did so, and subsequently hired director Boris Sagal, who besides guiding her through *A Case of Rape* and *The Awakening Land*, had also directed the 1980 TV-movie edition of *The Diary of Anne Frank* with Melissa Gilbert (of *Little House on the Prairie* fame), and would soon helm 1981's *Masada* mini-series (with Peter O'Toole and Peter Strauss, of *Rich Man, Poor Man*).

Krost had played an interconnecting role in Lizzie's post-*Bewitched* life

and career, protecting and guiding both her personal and professional decisions. She trusted him implicitly (it was in his apartment where Lizzie and
Bob Foxworth secretly tied the knot on January 28, 1993), and Krost had
enormous respect for her as a client and as a human being.

In 1999, author Michael Anketell published, *Heavenly Bodies: Remembering Hollywood and Fashion's Favorite AIDS Benefit* (Taylor, 1999). In the book,
producer Doug Chapin, Krost's business partner, explains how in 1986 Lizzie and actor Roddy McDowall (who died of lung cancer in 1998) were the
first two celebrities to lend their support to the initial Los Angeles fashion-
show (displaying the 1930s Hollywood designes of Adrian) to benefits HIV/
AIDS awareness. According to what Chapin told Anketell, Elizabeth
attended every one of their events up until the time of her death.

Other celebrities who attended the Adrian function, included Carol
Kane, Brenda Vaccaro, Bess Armstrong, JoBeth Williams, and Jackie Collins. Anketell writes:

> Had it not been for the valiant efforts of a few of Hollywood's favorite stars
> and their managers, Barry Krost and Doug Chapin, who encouraged them,
> neither Hollywood nor the fashion world would have taken any but passing
> notice of our efforts. Without stars, there would have been little press cov-
> erage and our message would not get out. But on the night of the Adrian
> show, the stars did come.

Anketell went on to explain how Lizzie was a stand-out participant:

> Possibly our most popular star that evening was Elizabeth Montgomery, the
> beloved *Samantha* of *Bewitched*. Elizabeth was the daughter of film star Rob-
> ert Montgomery and the wife of actors Gig Young and Robert Foxworth.
> She had starred in a couple of dozen TV movies in which she was often a
> victimized woman who would find her personal strength, though she also
> portrayed Western bandit Belle Starr and parent-hacker Lizzie Borden.

Krost then talked about Lizzie's personal involvement in bringing awareness
to AIDS and other causes:

> Elizabeth became very political and very caring and yet, at the same time,
> always was strangely shy for a lady who had all her life been around press
> and Hollywood. She protected her private life and she found the spotlight,
> at times, very uncomfortable, unless it was about a specific project—a

movie or a cause she believed in. She was one of the first public people to get involved in the very early days of the fight against HIV.

I think Elizabeth was on the side of anybody, any group of people that she thought was being treated inappropriately. But she was still shy. I remember when we arrived that first year at the Adrian event. There was a press line outside and she suggested we stop the car, get out and go in the side entrance. I said, "It sort of defeats the point of your being here." And she said, "Oh, yes, you're right," and she went in the front way, through the press.

In 1999, on *Bewitched: The E! True Hollywood Story*, Krost said: "If she was your friend she was there, good times, bad times. She was there. And if she was in your life, somehow you went to bed at night and the world was just a little bit safer. And very few people have that effect on you."

In 2001, on MSNBC's *Headliners & Legends*, he added: "When HIV came along, not only in a charitable sense, raising money and awareness . . . but also one-on-one with people; she spent an awful lot of time that way." She cherished her private life with, for example, her children of whom, as Krost explained, she cared a great deal. "It's a very delicate balance between being a star and what happened in the house. And I think she really protected that and felt very vulnerable."

Lizzie's son Billy Asher, Jr. relayed on the same show: "She felt a responsibility with her life and her career as being a celebrity . . . to use that at times to make other people aware of issues that she felt were important."

In all, there are those who are critical of celebrities, specifically, actors, intermingling their public personas with politics, believing that the twain should never meet. But during his appearance at the Los Angeles Festival of Books on April 22, 2012, Steven J. Ross, the author of *Hollywood Left and Right*, explained it this way:

I would say yes, you can have celebrities divorced from politics if you have business leaders divorced from politics, if you have all the CEOs in America divorced and if you have every other American divorced. They are citizens first. They are actors second. Why should we single out actors? And the reason why most people don't like it is nobody wants their dream factory burst. We all have our celebrity images. We all have our belief of who they are, and as early as 1918 you had people like Sid Grauman, who founded the famous Grauman's Chinese Theatre where we have all the handprints and the footprints, telling actors to keep your mouths shut when it comes to politics, because the moment you open your mouth you alienate half your audience.

Certainly, there was little sign of audience alienation when Lizzie's fans turned out by the droves when she, if posthumously, received her star at the Hollywood Walk of Fame ceremony, January 4, 2008. Her fans, co-workers, and family, including her three beloved children, were there to partake in the honor.

Today, Billy Asher, Jr. is the proprietor of a highly successful and respected music business (Asher Guitars). Rebecca Asher is a renowned TV script supervisor (*Raising Hope, Mad Men, Samantha Who?*), and Robert Asher is an artisan of many talents and crafts who at times works with his brother Billy (as does Bob Foxworth's son Bo). In one way or another, they each have followed in their parents' professional footsteps.

In looking back at the development of Lizzie's character, she evidently believed in at least some form of positive higher-consciousness that somehow guided her decision-making process with her life and career. It may not have always been a consistent belief, but it was a belief nonetheless. And although she may have enjoyed pulling Agnes Moorehead's religious leg during their *Bewitched* era, it was clear she was no slouch in the spiritual department, even in the most basic or sporadic way.

When she and her brother Skip were children, their grandmother Becca instructed them to pray when their parents were away. It was a solid, traditional way to handle a child's temporary, if intensely emotional feelings. But as Lizzie explained in the February 1970 edition of *TV Radio Mirror* magazine, she and Skip never said nightly prayers, nor did they attend church on a regular basis. "I suppose we believed in God," she acknowledged, but ". . . in our own way." She and Skip apparently did at least attend Sunday school and looked forward to going. But to her the Bible stories were more like fairytales. She didn't really take them seriously.

And by 1970, that seemed to fit. She was no longer a child of a star, but a star herself, many times over. She was also a mature adult, on her third marriage, with three children of her own. Her childhood days with Skip were long gone, and even though her child-like manner remained, she now faced adult decisions, and was responsible for leading the way for three little people who would one day become adults themselves.

By this time, she had become disillusioned with the way many parents of the day instilled the mortal fear of a condemning God who took pleasure in punishing bad children. "Using fright to teach religion seems to me to be very unhealthy," she said. "After all, if we can't base our beliefs in a Supreme Being on love, that how can any of us truly believe?" Lizzie also believed that many people turned to religion out of a deep need, and thought it was productive that they employed their faith to help deal with the turmoil of Vietnam and the race riots. Her three children, including Rebecca, just born in 1969, were then too young to ask about God. If they had wondered, Lizzie hadn't a clue as to how she would have replied. But she did want her kids to attend Sunday school like she and Skip had when they were young. "I feel that it is a good foundation for any child," she said. "After all, even as a piece of literature alone, there is so much that is fine and wonderful in the Bible."

"I think of God as the beauty in life," she concluded, ". . . it's loving and being loved. It's feeling good inside because you are living the life of a good person. Maybe it's a good idea to try new ways of looking at the subject."

It was a fresh perspective that helped to close an age-old generation gap between her and her conservative-minded parents. Years before, when she was only twenty, they had been pleased with her decision to at least be baptized if only shortly before her marriage to Fred Cammann, and even though that union ended in divorce.

In May of 1970, she addressed it all with reporter Nancy Winelander of *TV Picture Life* magazine. The conversation mixed religion, her marriages to Asher as well as Gig Young, and again, raising her children. The article described Lizzie as Episcopalian. Young was a Protestant; Asher, Jewish. As she intoned, both she and Asher "love our religion. Bill isn't the most religious man in the world. He doesn't go for a lot of the ritual, but he believes deeply in his Jewish religion and cultural heritage. I really haven't been a practicing anything for years. Still, I don't want to divorce myself from my heritage either."

Yet, she was surprised at how "meddlesome people can be," when it came to raising a family under one particular faith or the other. "After all," she added, "whose business is it how our children are raised?" But at the time, it was an issue, one that she had not confronted before. As Winelander explained, Lizzie had no children by the much older Young. If they had had kids, apparently, there would not have been any religious quandary with the Protestant Young. [Note: All Episcopalians are Protestants but not all Protestants are Episcopalians. Protestants include virtually all Christian sects outside of Roman Catholicism: Episcopalians, Baptists, Presbyterians, Methodists, Lutherans, etc.] Lizzie told Winelander:

> Gig wouldn't have cared anyway. He was very easy-going on matters like that. He had kind of a live-and-let-live philosophy. I think he would have left it pretty much up to me, no matter what he had been. Besides, our marital problems became so overwhelming the question of christening children just never had a chance to arise.

Former TV actor and present day Episcopalian priest Peter Ackerman is a happy anomaly with a unique perspective on Lizzie's persona, spiritual and otherwise. As the son of Screen Gems head and *Bewitched* executive producer Harry Ackerman and *Father Knows Best* actress, Elinor Donahue, Peter started acting on shows like *The New Gidget*, the 1980s syndicated reboot of his father's 1960s ABC/Sally Field sitcom (a few episodes of which were directed by Bill Asher). After a time, however, he became disinterested with acting on-screen (as did Lizzie, at least for a while), mostly because he found it more challenging to create and sustain a character on the stage. So after Peter married in the late 1980s, he began working in production for TV commercials, music videos, and in various other such capacities. This new career path culminated with him serving as a producer's assistant on the second and third seasons of TV's mega-hit, *Friends* (NBC, 1994–2004).

With *Friends*, Peter was happy at home (with his wife and now two children), but his vocational life was lacking. He subsequently embarked on a spiritual journey that lead him back to the Episcopal Church he grew up in, "where priests can be married and women." After an especially difficult day on the set of *Friends*, he made a dramatic and desperate plea to God: "I know I will like whatever You have in store. I am ready to do it. Just show me what YOU want. I am tired of trying to figure it out on my own."

So, today, he's not only an Episcopalian priest, but a married Episcopalian priest with a family; while in the 1960s, for him:

> *Bewitched* felt like family and was. After all, Bill Asher and Liz came over to the house a lot with their kids, Willie, Robert, and Rebecca, and they became the godparents to my youngest brother, Chris. There was really no difference that I saw growing up with *Samantha* on TV and Liz who came over our house. She was friendly, had a sense of humor and definitely had that fun/wicked 'pixie' sense about her.

Quite young at the time, Peter did not have a sense of Lizzie's eminent heritage, but he was always impressed by her unaffected disposition. It was a trait he says she shared with her brother Skip, with whom one day, Peter, his father, Lizzie and others had shared a limo, "probably all going to a Rams game," he says. As Peter recalls, Skip "was a relatively quiet, thoughtful, and serious man, but not aloof or anything. To me, a kid, he was just a guy."

Peter has a theory as to how the Montgomery siblings absorbed the same approachable demeanor:

> Social scientists will one day figure this all out, but remember back in those days there were no paparazzi hunters. My mom (Elinor Donahue) and I would go grocery shopping or to get an ice cream and people would ask her, "Aren't you . . . ?" and sometimes ask for an autograph. But it was no big deal. As people began playing the *game* of Hollywood, and making themselves less accessible, that's when the mess happened that we have today with celebrity. Suffice it to say, I assume Liz, like my parents, never played "the game."

Former child star and *Bewitched* guest actor Eric Scott has a contrasting take on Lizzie's affability. Best known as *Ben Walton* on *The Waltons* (CBS's long-running and critically acclaimed family series; 1972–1981), Eric appeared on the *Samantha* episode, "Out of the Mouths of Babes," which aired in 1971. This was right around the same time he was cast in the CBS

TV-movie *The Homecoming,* which ultimately was the backdoor *Waltons* pilot that led to his weekly stint as *Ben.* In "Babe," on *Bewitched,* he played *Herbie,* a basketball-loving neighborhood boy who befriends a shrunken and pre-teen *Darrin* who is made so by one of *Endora's* manipulative spells. Eric had several scenes with Lizzie in this episode, and remembers her fine balance of humility and sophistication on the set:

> I thought she was one of the most beautiful ladies I had ever seen. I had worked with people like Elke Sommer and other actresses that were just gorgeous. But there was something about Elizabeth that was just *wow.* And at the end of the production, when I asked everyone for their autograph, she wrote hers like a movie star. And she carried herself so very regally.

Like Lizzie, Eric retained a strong sense of normalcy amidst the glitter of Hollywood. After *The Waltons* ended its original CBS run in 1979 (only to return as various CBS and NBC TV reunion movies until 1997), acting roles were few and far between. Forced to explore alternative sources of income, he began work for Chase Messenger Service in Los Angeles. Today, some forty years after his first scenes as *Ben Walton* and *Herbie* on *Bewitched,* he is now the proprietor of Chase, and acts periodically. He found TV stardom as a child and business success as an adult, while remaining cordial and unassuming in every decade—a demeanor he credits to his parents, who raised him within a solid moral structure. His family was not wealthy like the Montgomerys, and his mother (who served as his manager) and father (a hairstylist) struggled to make ends meet. But ultimately, the Scott brood triumphed, most assuredly because they worked as a team. He knows why he survived Hollywood unscathed, but is amazed as to how Lizzie managed so well to retain her firm grip on priorities.

> I don't know how she did it. I really don't. Someone was looking out for her. And hopefully it was her parents. I know that's what did it for me. As a parent of three children myself, I've realized it's the environment that we create for our kids that dictates how they're going to end up. If you give them a lot of love and give them a lot of structure, they thrive. If you have them vacillating and trying to figure out too much, they falter. My eldest is in college. My middle one is in grade school. And my youngest Jeremy is just seven, the same age I was when I started acting. In fact, he's a mini-me.

He reminds me so much of myself. He's a Cub Scout and I'm a Cub Scout leader. He plays guitar, is taking up drums, and will soon start to play the keyboard.

Jeremy also plays baseball and basketball, just like Eric's character *Herbie* did on *Bewitched*. "It's funny," Eric goes on to say, "Jeremy has been in baseball for the last two years, and our family became close friends with the coach's family. And I had recently attended a *Waltons* reunion in Virginia, so my wife Cindy explained to the coach's wife that we'd be out of town for a while for the reunion. And they were like, 'Why?'"

"Because," Mrs. Scott replied, "Eric was on the show," a fact about which the coach's wife had not a clue. Since that time, and upon learning of Eric's childhood fame, other parents of kids on the team have approached him in awe and said, "I just heard."

"I live in a small town and the word got out," he says with a laugh. "And the recognition is actually very sweet, but I would never want my kids to live in that shadow. So, I don't know how Elizabeth's parents did it . . . how she grew up so well . . . without being in *that* shadow . . . or even if that shadow was attainable."

Twenty-three

~

Graduation

"I remember telling everybody that I was her best friend.
But then I realized that everybody in the theatre, and there were
hundreds of people there, could probably say the same thing.
She made you feel important."

—Liz Sheridan, reflecting on Elizabeth's memorial service,
MSNBC's *Headliners & Legends* (2001)

From the moment she graduated from the American Academy of Dramatic
Arts, at only twenty-one, Lizzie was working, non-stop, so much so she
lost her diploma at an NBC rehearsal hall the day after she received it. Such
a loss, however, did not diminish her ambition or her career. As detailed
elsewhere within these pages, Elizabeth went on to make over 200 guest-
appearances on various TV shows of the era, and then came *Samantha*.

Beyond *Bewitched*, Lizzie never again played a regular character in a
weekly series. She had *been there, done that* with the twitch-witch for eight
years, which she viewed as a college extension course in entertainment and
adult education. She was tired of the grind, plain and simple. She wanted
to have a life, to live the scripts of life, rather than star in one every week.

After she stayed the course as *Sam*, she wanted to spend more time with
her children, and still be able work periodically, which she did with her
various TV-movies. Today, actors can star on weekly shows, make TV-
movies, feature films, even appear in live stage plays. In Lizzie's day, there

were contract confinements and it wasn't as easy to cross over and/or in between different media. Today, with the blur of television, features, DVD, movies on demand, streaming videos, YouTube, new online networks, it's a different world.

Upon completing *Bewitched*, Lizzie was many times approached about starring in a new weekly series. But she kept rejecting them, along with a few TV-movies she felt were not the right fit.

In 1976, George Schaefer directed the television film, *Amelia Earhart*, about the famed female pilot. Lizzie was offered the lead, but turned it down, and the part went to Susan Clark.

In 1979, CBS wanted to transform Lizzie's hit TV-movie, *Jennifer: A Woman's Story*, about a wealthy widow who takes over her husband's company, into a series. But she declined the offer.

In 1981, ABC approached her about playing *Krystle Carrington* on *Dynasty*. She said no, and the role went to Linda Evans, whose career was rejuvenated because she said yes. Evans had not been seen on TV in any regular capacity since her *Big Valley* days (1965–1969) on ABC. Before that, she appeared in *Beach Blanket Bingo*, directed by William Asher. Two decades later, she ended up playing *Krystle* until 1989. That could have been Lizzie, but for her, a nighttime soap was unappealing.

And as previously mentioned, in 1986, Elizabeth even deflected a chance to work alongside Bob Foxworth in CBS' *Falcon Crest*. Instead, the part went to Kim Novak (who years before had also played a witch, in *Bell, Book and Candle*, the 1958 feature that was said to have inspired *Bewitched*).

In 1987, Lizzie was asked to portray *Poker Alice* in the CBS TV-movie of the same name. *Alice* had an incurable penchant for gambling, and Lizzie loved to gamble. But maybe that plot hit too close to home, or maybe she declined because this movie was a back-door pilot for a weekly series. Either way, it was no dice. The part went to another Elizabeth . . . Elizabeth Taylor, who at one point called Lizzie and asked, "Are you *sure* you don't want to do this role?" For whatever reason, Lizzie was sure.

Then, in 1994, she agreed to star in the CBS TV-movie *The Corpse Had a Familiar Face*, based on the career of murder mystery investigative journalist Edna Buchanan. Lizzie loved doing the movie. According to what Liz Sheridan told MSNBC's *Headliners & Legends* in 2001, she was fascinated with Edna's courage, and subsequently wanted to appear in an entire series of Buchanan films. When the *Familiar* ratings proved substantial, CBS complied with Lizzie's wishes.

The following year, she starred in a sequel: *Deadline for Murder: From the Files of Edna Buchanan*, for which *Variety's* Adam Sandler gave a scathing review, May 8, 1995:

The explanation in the opening credits of the telefilm *suggested by the life and career of Edna Buchanan* should warn viewers that the two-hour spec is likely to have little resemblance to the Pulitzer Prize-winning Miami Herald crime reporter's novels or life, both of which make for far more interesting fare than this dubious offering.

The first confirmation comes with show's use of Santa Monica to double for Fort Lauderdale, and MacArthur Park as downtown Miami, serving as the backdrop for the travails of *Buchanan* (Elizabeth Montgomery).

Her days are spent responding to the call of the wild, writing about the town's gruesome murders and shady characters, while solving crimes the cops seem incapable of closing.

In Buchanan's Miami, drug lords rule and the town is populated by mafia kingpins, ponytailed bodyguards, and marble-floored estates.

When a local mobster is murdered along with his mistress and a tow truck driver who came to the couple's aid on a dark, rainy night, ace reporter Buchanan and a local tabloid show reporter, *Joe Flanigan* (Scott Cameron), race to discover the identity of the killer and a motive.

In the process, story's subtext has Buchanan solving a pair of crimes unrelated to the main murder, resulting in the clearing of one man and the conviction of another.

But writers Les Carter and Susan Sisko create a script that lacks the staccato tempo or vivid articulations of the real-life Buchanan's novels, such as *Suitable for Framing*, which chronicles the exploits of her fictional alter-ego, police beat reporter *Britt Montero*.

Show's dialogue frequently is lame, lacking any punch even in the most crucial of circumstances and delivered by cardboard characters who fail to connect with viewers or each other.

Montgomery's *Buchanan* is a rumpled but efficient sort, who sleeps with a gun under her pillow and argues frequently with her mom (Audra Lindley), who is temporarily sharing *Buchanan's* home while the exterminator is debugging mom's pad.

A relationship with police detective *Marty Talbot* (Yaphet Kotto) is equally strained, as they frequently butt heads on investigations led by *Talbot* and written about, and ultimately solved, by *Buchanan.*

But *Buchanan* presumably can relate only to the town's new coroner, *Aaron Bliss* (Dean Stockwell), and the pair strike up an instant friendship.

Though attempts to advance the relationship often are interrupted by the call to service—hers a ringing cellular phone; his a pager—the pair try in earnest nonetheless.

The movie suffers from a lack of credibility on other fronts: Viewers may have difficulty believing Montgomery as the hard-bitten scribe, toiling endlessly without regard for the clock. Her acting style makes its hard to tell whether a joke or a dramatic line meant for serious cogitation was just delivered.

The only bright spot in this laborious offering is the tow truck driver's widow *Rosinha*, played convincingly by Saundra Santiago, who viewers may recall as *Gina*, a detective in the popular *Miami Vice* series.

Santiago delivers show's best dramatic perf, rising above the din of her co-stars. But it comes too late.

Joyce Chopra's direction is perfunctory at best, and takes no risks in telling this mostly vapid tale.

However dismissive that review may have been for *Murder*, like *The Corpse Had a Familiar Face* before it, was a ratings bonanza. In fact, it became the highest-rated TV-movie of 1995. Consequently, Elizabeth had intended to play *Buchanan* in two or three movies a year, as Peter Falk had reprised his *Columbo* character for new ABC-TV movies in the 1990s based on his popular *NBC Mystery Movie* series of the 1970s. (At one point, Lizzie had even been interested in playing *Mrs. Columbo* in a semi-sequel to Falk's seminal show. But the lead for that series, which failed, went to Kate Mulgrew, who later starred as *Captain Janeway* on *Star Trek: Voyager.*)

Meanwhile, *Deadline* co-star Saundra Santiago's memories of working with Lizzie are "nothing but pleasant":

> She was a gem of person to work with . . . very giving in her scenes with actors, particularly with my scenes. My character [*Rosinha*] had a lot of emotional moments and she was very attentive to those moments. She was one of the most gracious women I've ever worked with, and I really had a lot of fun with her. She was very open and forthcoming in our conversations. I remember clearly how she was so completely available to me as an

actress at all times. She was not one of those actors who stayed in their trailers and only came out when they had their scenes. That was not her at all. She talked about her children. She loved them very much. It was clear that she had a loving relationship with them, and she was proud of the job she did with them as a mother.

Mirroring Cliff Robertson's recollections of Lizzie in their youth, Santiago goes on to say how "grounded" Lizzie was as a person. "She knew how to keep herself *real* [in Hollywood]. She was the most unassuming actor I've ever worked with . . . very humble and very sweet. She was a real pro . . . a very lovely woman."

A fan of *Bewitched*, Santiago was initially apprehensive about talking with Lizzie about her most famous role:

> I didn't want to mention *Bewitched* when we first started working together, because I figured everyone did that with her, and I wanted to keep things on a professional level. And I certainly didn't want to ask her if she would wiggle her nose. But after a while, I felt safe enough to at least bring up the show. I expressed to her what an iconic role I thought *Samantha* was . . . how I loved all the characters on the show, and how I used to run home from school just so I could watch it [in reruns]. And she seemed proud of that. She looked at *Samantha* as a fond memory. She spoke of *Bewitched* very well . . . almost . . . wistfully.
>
> But, you know, when you're sick, you start to appreciate *everything*. I couldn't imagine that she didn't know she was sick. She might not have wanted to say anything because of the insurance. They [the studios, networks] make actors get physicals. I remember Kathy Bates [who battled cancer] once talking about how she hid her [chemotherapy] treatments because she was afraid of not getting any work. And Elizabeth very much wanted to work. She enjoyed [doing the Buchanan films], and *Edna* was a good role for her.

And since *Murder, She Wrote* was on its way out at CBS, the network was looking to fill that older-female-mystery demographic. But fate had other plans.

"No one ever knew she had cancer," Santiago says of Lizzie. "And then when she died, it was shocking to me . . . to work so closely with someone like that . . . and then only to have them pass away such a short time afterward. It was just so sad."

Upon working with Lizzie, Saundra was not aware that her father was Robert Montgomery, who in 1981 had succumbed to cancer, which, as it turns out, had also taken the life of Saundra's father. "It's not a discriminating disease," she says. "It'll grab onto whoever it can."

And as much as she wants to remember the happy experience of working with Elizabeth, Saundra can't help but recall a few other developments that transpired on the *Deadline* set that she calls "eerie and kind of weird." She explains:

> At one point during filming, Elizabeth's appearance was very *ashy*, and someone on the set said, "Give her some color." But she didn't make a big deal of it. The makeup man just came over and touched her up a little bit. She took it all in stride. I also noticed that she was very thin, but everybody in L.A. is thin, and you just don't think anything of it. She still looked beautiful, and she never complained about anything . . . or being tired or any of that.
>
> And then after we completed the movie, I wanted to get a picture with her. But I didn't have my camera. So I asked one of the crew to take our picture, and these were the days before digital cameras, and all he had was a Polaroid [instant camera with film that immediately develops]. So he took the picture, and we had to wait for it to dry. But it didn't come out clear. It was all blurry. And I remember thinking to myself, "Geez . . . why didn't that picture come out?"

Santiago had become apprehensive of taking pictures ever since a trip to Santorini Island in Greece, which she calls "a very superstitious place. It's a volcanic island, with all kinds of 'spirits.' And I took a few pictures there, and they all came out like the Polaroid picture that crew member took of me and Elizabeth. There were a lot of ghost-like images all over the place. It came out very strange."

Away from the set of *Deadline for Murder*, Lizzie was busy nursing Robert Foxworth, who had recently undergone hip-replacement surgery. As the actor told *People* magazine on June 5, 1995, Lizzie was strong and confident, whereas he was apprehensive. "She was there for me when I first tried getting up on crutches."

Foxworth "was quite devoted to her," says actress Bonnie Bartlett, who had known Lizzie from New York in the 1950s and when they both appeared in 1975's *The Legend of Lizzie Borden*. Like Saundra Santiago had lost her father to cancer, Bartlett lost her father, mother, and brother to colon cancer, the same form of the disease that did not spare Lizzie's life. "If my father would have had the proper exam, he would have pulled through," Bartlett says. Just like Lizzie, "he didn't have to die. And as I recall, she was never tested for colon cancer, and neither was my Dad."

According to *People* magazine, Foxworth, Bill Asher, and Lizzie's children each tried to get Lizzie to see a doctor. But she refused, even after her daughter Rebecca noticed how thin she had become on the set of *Murder*. Still, Lizzie disregarded the notion, and ultimately ignored what were in effect warning signs that something was wrong . . . deadly wrong.

But as Saundra Santiago has revealed, and as Liz Sheridan once explained on A&E's *Biography* in 1999, that's how Lizzie was; she kept things to herself. There was "no dwelling." She was secretive and preferred that people didn't know if she was upset or worried or in pain, in anguish of any kind; she toughed things out. As Sheridan later expressed to MSNBC's *Headliners & Legends* in 2001, Lizzie never really wanted to face anything that was "bad or ugly." She was in a "huge state of denial."

Such denial, however, still did not betray her loyalty. Lizzie instructed the powers-that-be to cast Sheridan in *Deadline for Murder* so the two could visit. As Sheridan later revealed at Lizzie's Hollywood Walk of Fame ceremony, January 4, 2008, "She was getting ill and I didn't know it. She didn't let on."

Then, in mid May 1995, the phone rang at Sheridan's home. She picked up the receiver, and heard Lizzie's voice with a simple, "Hi."

In attempt to break through the tears with a smile, Sheridan asked, "So, what's new?"

"Oh, a little of this and a little of that," Lizzie replied, bravely. Then she giggled, Sheridan followed suit, and in between those little laughs were the last words they spoke.

By then, Lizzie had finally checked into Cedars-Sinai Medical Center in Los Angeles. As *People* magazine reported, exploratory surgery had brought the tragic diagnosis: colon cancer. Bill Asher said Lizzie's mood was upbeat but nervous. First she was shocked. Then she was angry.

By the time her doctors performed additional surgery to remove the cancer's growth, she was too weak for radiation therapy, and the disease had progressed. At that point, and as Bob Foxworth explained in 2006 on *Entertainment Tonight*, she wanted "to go home." He knew then, he said, that *she* knew she was going to die. And that she wanted to die at home.

As Billy Clift, Lizzie's hairdresser and good friend, relayed in his compelling book *Everything Is Going to Be Just Fine: Ramblings of a Mad Hairdresser* (Everything Is Going to Be Just Fine Society, 1998), Bob Foxworth had explained to him the events of Lizzie's last night of life. She had experienced a great deal of pain, made dire sounds, and her breathing was highly erratic. They were Foxworth's most challenging hours at her side. He made every valiant effort to remain awake, but by 6 AM, he needed some sleep. Then, two hours later, Elizabeth's nurse awakened him. There were new developments. Lizzie had become restful, tranquil, and then she passed away . . . at approximately 8:23 AM, May 18, 1995.

In the end, at least Lizzie was surrounded by the family she loved and held dear: Foxworth, Bill Asher and her three children with Asher, Billy Jr., Robert, and Rebecca in particular, who was most often at her mother's bedside, soothing her throughout interrupted bouts of sleep.

Foxworth told *People* those last days with Lizzie were "loving and intense," a fitting description for one who lived a life filled with many contradictions, some delightful, others confounding. One moment, she joked about wanting pina coladas poured into her IV. At another, she felt energetic enough to cheer on the New York Knicks during a televised basketball game—one of the simple pleasures which she embraced. But as Asher also told *People*, Lizzie knew she was "losing the battle."

It was a fight for her life that ended in the early morning hours of May 18, 1995, when she was alone in her bedroom at home, taking her last breaths, with her loved ones waiting quietly in the living room, as she had requested. "She didn't want anyone to see her that way," Asher said. Then she slipped away.

According to what Billy Asher, Jr. relayed to MSNBC's *Headliners & Legends*, his mother's physicians were surprised that she was still hanging on in those final days. She wasn't going to take-off during the dark of night, young Asher told them. When she's ready to go, he thought, it'll be in the morning with the light and the sun, "and that's kind of what happened."

As it had been for Lucille Ball—shortly before she died of a ruptured aorta on April 26, 1989 at Cedar-Sinai Hospital—countless cards, letters, gifts, and calls arrived at Lizzie's room at the same hospital and at her home in Beverly Hills before she passed away in 1995.

Lizzie, like Lucy, felt an overwhelming outpouring of adoration. Most of the senders were viewers who considered themselves family members and friends, people whom she had only met through the magic of television, and then others with whom she actually worked in television, like her friends Cliff Robertson and Sally Kemp.

But unlike Liz Sheridan, who at least had a chance to speak with Lizzie on the phone before she died, Cliff and Sally would not be granted that opportunity. Shortly before his "Lizbel" passed away, Robertson shared a random in-studio TV interview with Robert Foxworth after which he said, "Bob invited me to drop by the house . . . for a visit."

"I'm sure Elizabeth would love to see you," Foxworth said.

"I was looking forward to it," Robertson recalled in 2011, "because I had not seen her in a long time."

So, that spring day, sometime in mid-May 1995, Robertson followed Foxworth to the home he shared with Lizzie in Beverly Hills. Upon arrival, they parked their separate cars and Foxworth went inside to tell Lizzie that her friend was waiting outside. Only a few moments later, he emerged to tell Robertson that she was too ill for visitors. "And she died shortly thereafter," Robertson lamented. "I never got to see her. She just didn't want to see anyone, and I didn't blame her. But to this day, I miss her . . . because we had such a rollicking good-pal relationship."

"I loved her dearly," says Sally Kemp. "You know . . . some people are a source of light in your life, and she was just a source of light in mine." And Sally was "deeply saddened" when she heard of Lizzie's passing because, like so many of her friends, Sally "hadn't known that she had been sick."

On June 18, 1995, a memorial service for Lizzie was held at the Canon Theatre in Beverly Hills. Herbie Hancock provided the music, and Dominick Dunne spoke about their days together in New York when they were both starting out in the business. Other speakers including Robert Foxworth, who read out loud sympathy cards from fans, her nurse, her brother, daughter, and stepson. Amanda McBroom sang, and the entire service ended with the lights going down. A beautiful shot of Lizzie on a video screen, flickered in the dark, and those in attendance rose and applauded. Lizzie had asked that any donations in her memory should be made to the William Holden Wildlife Association in Kenya or the Los Angeles Zoo.

Kemp, in New York at the time, was unable to attend the service, but a mutual acquaintance who was there said most of those present were "not old friends. They were people who were kind of new friends."

At the service, Sally and Lizzie's mutual acquaintance was approached by yet a third party, who asked, "Are you an old friend of Elizabeth's?"

To which the second party replied, "Yes—but I hadn't seen her for years and years. Are *you* an old friend?"

"Well," the third party responded in return, "I had only known her for about five years. But I think I was on my way out."

Says Kemp:

> So, that was like Elizabeth and not like Elizabeth, because she wouldn't make you feel like you were on your way out. You just were out. And I just wonder where that influence came from. I do know that her relationship with Bob Foxworth was a very challenging relationship. So, maybe it stemmed from that. She did seem to be attracted to troubled guys, and felt maybe that she could fix them, or that she felt comfortable with them.

In 1999, Liz Sheridan told A&E's *Biography* that Lizzie and Foxworth "became dear friends and lovers," and after that, it was difficult to keep them apart. They were two strong-willed people who "argued," but enjoyed reconciling, "making love and being happy and giggling."

Then, one day in 1993, Lizzie and Bob were sitting at their kitchen table, discussing some particularly important matter and he said, "You know—this situation would be so much easier if we were married."

Lizzie looked at him and asked, "Is that a proposal?"

He thought about that a half-a-second and said, "Okay."

To which she then added, "Yes."

So on January 28, 1993, they got married in a private ceremony in her manager Barry Krost's apartment in Los Angeles. About fifteen minutes later, Lizzie called her friend Sheridan to tell her the news. Sheridan said Lizzie was so "child-like and sweet."

According to Sally Kemp, Elizabeth was also "a multi-layered mystery, and I would love to one day know some of the answers, while I would also prefer to remember the young woman I knew."

Elizabeth had left an equally puzzling imprint on her friend, author and investigative journalist Dominick Dunne. As he observed in his book *The Way We Lived Then*, after *Bewitched* made her a star, he and his wife Lenny never saw her again "for reasons unknown." She disconnected from her friends and those she knew between divorcing Gig Young and just before marrying Bill Asher and subsequently playing *Samantha*. In fact, as Dunne explained, he and Lenny once passed Elizabeth on a sidewalk in Beverly Hills, but she refused to acknowledge them, a slight that cut deep, particularly for Lenny. But it would hurt Lizzie even more later on.

In 1991, she was interested in playing the lead role of *Pauline Mendelson* in the TV-movie, *An Inconvenient Woman*, based on Dunne's novel of the same name. But as explained in *The Way We Lived Then*, in a wrath of anger, he blackballed her, and the part went to Jill Eikenberry (*L.A. Law*). However, Dunne made allowances for Elaine Stritch, who was once engaged to Gig Young, to have a small role in the film.

Come 1995, however, things changed. Dunne had been covering the trial of O. J. Simpson, who had co-starred with Lizzie in the 1977 TV-movie, *A Killing Affair*. Upon learning of her cancerous death sentence, Dunne decided it was time for reconciliation. Whatever had divided their friendship now "faded into unimportance," he said. He could now only recall the happier times they once shared.

So, while she was still at Cedar-Sinai Hospital, and only two days before she passed away, Lizzie received a note from Dunne expressing just how wonderful it was to have been her friend. Bob Foxworth had read her the message, and she was happy to have heard it. Foxworth subsequently invited Dunne, who had known Lizzie from their early days of television—when he was a mere stage manager on *Robert Montgomery Presents* and on which she was a budding starlet—to deliver a eulogy at her funeral.

"You're the only one who knew her from that part of her life," Foxworth told him, which was not entirely true. Sally Kemp and Cliff Robertson both knew and worked with Lizzie on *Robert Montgomery Presents* and would have welcomed the chance to bid their dear friend a loving public farewell.

But Robertson never saw much of Lizzie after her divorce from Fred Cammann. Kemp never saw much of Lizzie after her marriage to Gig Young. And Robertson, Kemp, and Dunne never saw much of Lizzie after she married Bill Asher and *Bewitched* made her a star. But Dunne's ability to write paved the way, and cleared the air . . . for at least one final transmission that reconnected what turned out to be an unbroken if unspoken bond.

But she had that kind of effect on everyone in her life, certainly Foxworth who told *Entertainment Tonight* in 2006, "To some extent, a part of her lives in me. And it's not so much about a thought. That's just the way it is."

On MSNBC's *Headliners & Legends* he added, she was "completely gracious and giving and kind, and easy-going and unaffected and unpretentious. And as we hung out together and played together and had dinner together I was more and more seduced and . . . bewitched . . . if you will, by this wonderful woman."

On that same show, Billy Asher, Jr. explained how his mom "lives in a lot of people's homes and in their hearts," and that her "greatest legacy is her ability to give young girls growing up the idea of how strong a woman could be."

One of those young women is assuredly Billy's sister, Rebecca Asher, who in also appearing on *Headliners & Legends*, said she more than anything misses hearing her mother's lyrical sounds. "She had a beautiful voice."

Today, Rebecca, who is just as private as her mother was, went on to describe Lizzie as "almost child-like . . . She loved surprises, and art, and being creative at Christmas . . . she loved all of that. . . . She just had this kind of magical persona."

Billy, Jr. delivered a near identical description of his mother on *Legends*: "She had this mystical child-like quality about her."

Throughout Lizzie's life, however, her child-like ways played both in her favor and at times against her better judgment. It was productive when she transferred that real-life charming aspect of herself onto the screen as *Samantha Stephens*, which became one of the most popular and likable characters in TV history. It played against her in the immature way she established and then disavowed friendships.

As Sally Kemp and Dominick Dunne discovered, if Elizabeth felt affronted by or uncomfortable with something a friend said or did, intentional or not, even in the slightest way, that was it: the friendship was over. There were no second chances. However, like so much of her true-to-life character development, this character flaw can be traced back to her childhood relationship with Robert Montgomery. As she explained to Ronald Haver in 1991:

> It took me awhile to understand maybe why people either at school or other friends kids that I knew didn't pay any attention to me and then all of a sudden they did . . . It's like I'd get all tickled about, "Oh, somebody wants to come to my birthday." And then they'd come to my birthday, and I'd be hoping to see them again, and then I'd never see them again until like my next birthday . . . It didn't occur to me right away that there were some people who really only wanted to come to see (my father) . . . That was kind of hard sometimes . . . to think that you'd found a new friend and then realize that that wasn't it at all.

On New Year's Eve, 1967, in the prime of Lizzie's magical turn as *Samantha* on *Bewitched*, she had a friend in famed sportscaster Vin Scully, with whom she co-hosted ABC's *Tournament of Roses Parade*. In 2011, Yahoo! Sports reporter Dave Brown interviewed Scully for a segment he called *Answer Man*. Brown mentioned having screened Lizzie's promo for that classic *Tournament* broadcast and asked Scully what it was like to work with her during what was the peak of *Bewitched's* success. Scully replied:

> All I can tell you is that she was a sweet, unaffected superstar. In those days, forty years ago, she was queen of television. I was in awe of her presence. After being with her for a little while, I realized she was so down-to-earth. She was a mother, she was a wife; she was not theatrically inclined at all. I didn't realize until the day of the parade, but we had to go up a tower. It wasn't literally a tower, it was a platform of six or seven steps. And she couldn't go up it. She was scared to death. She had a phobia about heights. She put her face in my back and put her arms around me and I took her up the six steps and got her seated and she was fine. The most important thing for me about that is to tell anyone, including you, that she was the nicest girl. It was really an honor.

A *witch's honor* . . . as when on *Bewitched*, with either her left or right hand, but preferably her left, Lizzie's *Samantha* occasionally made a particular gesture to (either) *Darrin* that signified that she was revealing the absolute truth about a given situation, much like the Boy Scout's Honor, but not. Here's how it worked: she'd place the index and middle fingers of her hand on either side of her nose with her fingertips pointing toward her eyes. While giving the sign, she'd intone, "Witches' honor," which in many ways was an omen of things to come.

At the close of 2011, actress Donna Douglas, who played *Elly May Clampett* on *The Beverly Hillbillies* in the 1960s, settled a lawsuit over a Barbie doll that used her character's name and likeness. According to *The Associated Press*, Douglas had originally sought $75,000, but the details of her actual settlement were confidential.

On September 22, 1994, *The Toronto Star* reported a similar suit, although on a much larger scale in which Lizzie claimed Sony (by way of Screen Gems/Columbia) owed her $5 million in *Bewitched* licensing dues. A short time before she passed away in May of 1995, the suit was settled and, as with the Douglas case, the amount was confidential. But Lizzie was clearly looking out for her fortune, and ultimately did not want to have her children go through that legal battle without her.

On September 10, 1995, less than four months after she died, television's top executives, producers, agents and actors turned out to honor her at the *Women in Film's Second Annual Lucy Awards*. The award, named for Lucille Ball, had also been bestowed upon *Bewitched* guest star Imogene Coca (*Your Show of Shows*), Brianne Murphy, Fred Silverman and Tracey Ullman, and it is given for innovation in television. During the three-hour ceremony, which was held at the Beverly Hills Hotel, Robert Foxworth delivered a touching tribute to Lizzie, while afterward her daughter Rebecca Asher accepted the award.

On April 19, 1998, the Duet Nightclub in Los Angeles hosted a birthday celebration/wardrobe sale/auction in Lizzie's name. Donations of her belongings collected by her children and Robert Foxworth were auctioned to benefit the AIDS Healthcare Foundation (which was established in 1987). According to www.bewitched.net, the benefit raised approximately $15,000 to $20,000.

On June 12 and 13, 1999, Lizzie's family—led by daughter Rebecca—

held an estate sale of her belongings at her Benedict Canyon Drive home in Beverly Hills. As documented by www.bewitched.net, some of the items sold included her 1977 Bentley (with the license plate, BENTLIZ), which fetched $15,000; a 1970 Oldsmobile Cutless in sound condition (which sold for $4000.00); and some African jewelry that Lizzie and Bob Foxworth had brought back from their on-location-in-Kenya shoot for their 1990 Hallmark Hall of Fame TV-movie, *Face to Face*.

Approximately six years later, on June 15, 2005, the network executives at TV Land announced plans to erect a nine-foot bronze statue of her likeness as *Samantha* in Salem, Massachusetts, which *TV Guide* had years before labeled "America's Number 1 witch city."

While *Bewitched* was still in production and at the onset of its seventh season (1970–1971), Lizzie and the cast and crew traveled to Salem for what became the show's only main on-location shooting for an arc-storyline involving *Samantha's* trip to a witches' convention. As Lizzie said in 1989, "The crowds were crazy in Salem. It was really spooky. I mean it was terrific because it meant they felt (we) were terrific." Lizzie's co-star Dick Sargent also said in 1989, "It was the first time I felt like one of The Beatles."

Decades later, the scene was not all that different in Salem at the induction of Lizzie's *Samantha* statue. According to *The Boston Globe*, the *Bewitched* minions were still present in droves, as nearly 2,000 people gravitated toward the city's Lappin Park at the corner of Washington and Essex Streets to unveil Lizzie's larger-than-life likeness:

She sits on a broom. In the background, a crescent moon rests atop a cloud on a pedestal. She's dressed as she mostly appeared on *Bewitched*: as an average housewife of the 1960s in a typical housedress. She's smiling, with her left arm turned up at the elbow, and legs crossed at the ankles; the perfect lady; the perfect woman . . . at least of the era.

On stage partaking in the commemoration: Bill Asher, *Bewitched* performers Bernard Fox (*Dr. Bombay*), Erin Murphy (*Tabitha*), and Kasey Rogers (*Louise Tate*, 1966–1972), Salem's Mayor Stanley J. Usovicz, Jr., and Larry W. Jones, President of TV Land and Nick at Nite, who explained:

Bewitched was and still remains a magical and beloved series. The series has been enchanting audiences for over forty years, and it is filled with heart and humor. Because several episodes were filmed in Salem, it is truly fitting that we would celebrate it with a statue here.

Added Mayor Usovicz:

We are pleased to welcome the statue of Elizabeth Montgomery as *Samantha Stephens*, to Salem. Our connection to this beautiful piece of contemporary art goes beyond the episodes filmed here. *Samantha* saw the magic in every-day life, and so do we.

The sculpture represented the network's fifth effort to honor people, places, and moments from America's small screen heritage by recognizing the *Sam* site as a "TV Land Landmark." The network's first salute—a bronze statue of *Ralph Kramden* of *The Honeymooners*—was unveiled in 2000 and now adorns the entrance to New York City's Port Authority Bus Terminal. In May 2002, a bronze statue of Mary Tyler Moore from *The Mary Tyler Moore Show* was uncovered and now stands on Nicollet Mall in downtown Minneapolis, MN. An *Andy Griffith Show* statue, which depicts Griffith and a young Ron Howard as *Sheriff Andy Taylor* and his son *Opie* walking, hand-in-hand (as in the opening credit sequence of that classic series), is located in Raleigh's Pullen Park and was unveiled in October, 2003. In July of 2004, TV Land honored yet another of television's most enduring icons, Bob Newhart, with a life-sized bronze sculpture commemorating his role as *Dr. Robert Hartley* on *The Bob Newhart Show* in Chicago.

Thomas Hill, Vice President and Creative Director for TV Land, explains how Lizzie's *Samantha* likeness joined their statuesque legacy:

One of the very first statues we did was Mary Tyler Moore—and the original concept was to find some way to have her tossed-hat be floating forever above her outstretched hand (as in the opening credits sequence of *The Mary Tyler Moore Show*). But the laws of physics and the limitations of forced air/magnets/tricks with mirrors forced us to capture the moment just before her hat actually left her hand. In those same conversations, we quickly generated other ideas for dozens of beloved TV characters—and we wanted *Samantha* to fly! Since *The Flying Nun* didn't have quite the pop culture staying power of *Bewitched*.

Creating a TV Land Landmark required extensive preparation and conversation between the various stakeholders. "Finding just the right location was never easy," Hill acknowledges. He once even suggested placing Dick Van Dyke's *Rob Petrie* on an endless commute between his *Alan Brady Show's* writer office in New York City and the New Rochelle home he shared with Moore's *Laura Petrie* and Larry Mathew's little *Richie*, "but train seats are hard to book permanently."

As to Lizzie's potential *Samantha* statue landing, Connecticut was once considered as an option, but as Hill recalls, "the civic leaders in Salem seemed more open to embracing the connection."

Into this mix, Studio EIS, a three-dimensional design and sculpture studio in New York founded by brothers Ivan and Elliot Schwartz, created Lizzie's life-sized bronze sculpture, as well as the Griffith and Newhart sculptures. The Schwartz brothers also created statutes of the Founding Fathers—which are located in the National Constitution Center in Philadelphia, and commemorative objects for museums, including the Smithsonian. The week Lizzie's statue was erected, Studio EIS was filled with more than a dozen life-like military figures, part of a project for the Marines.

All EIS's statues were initially received without pause or controversy, that is, except for Lizzie's *Samantha*, due to its placement in the middle of Salem, a town best known for its historic hanging of nineteen citizens accused of witchcraft. It all transpired in 1692 but remained a hot topic centuries later in 2005. As was discussed in the article, "*Bewitched* Statue Bothers Some in Salem," by David Segal, and published in *The Washington Post* (May 10, 2005), capitalizing on that history with a statue of a broom-gliding media witch rubbed a few locals the wrong way. "It's like TV Land going to Auschwitz and proposing to erect a statue of Colonel Klink," said John Carr, a former member of the Salem Historic District Commission. "Putting this statue in the park near the church where this all happened, it trivializes the execution of nineteen people."

But that night on June 15, 2005, the statue's mold and fate had already been cast, shaped, and determined by a vote of the Salem Redevelopment Authority, which owns Lappin Park, where Lizzie's likeness was placed. Mayor Usovicz liked Carr's odds. No disrespect intended, he said. The town takes its dark past seriously and deals with it reverently in museums, but that doesn't mean it should have declined to showcase a pop culture icon.

"Will this statue redefine Salem? Absolutely not," he explained. "Will it add to the experience of coming here? Definitely."

On *Bewitched*, *Samantha* and company may have lived in Westport, Connecticut. (In fact, as Screen Gems executive Harry Ackerman explained in *The Bewitched Book* [and elsewhere], he had drafted an original "eight- or nine-page treatment" for a show he called *The Witch of Westport*.) But as to those few seventh year episodes shot in Salem for the witches' convention, it made the city a logical place for TV Land to erect its statue, especially when they visited the town during Halloween and found that thousands of revelers had descended upon the area.

"What we saw was a huge Halloween party," said Robert Pellizzi, a TV Land senior vice president. "So we thought, it certainly makes sense to ask." They sought advice about where to place the statue and they made a generous offer. Not only would the town get the bronze for free, but TV Land also offered to renovate Lappin Park and to pay for upkeep of the statue, too. In return, of course, TV Land hoped for public relations points, including some good photo opportunities when the statue was unveiled.

"If I were one of the people who had a house on the beautiful common there, would I hate it?" asked Ivan Schwartz, partaking in a conference from June 15, 2005 that addressed the issue. "Yes, probably. But it seems like [Salem] was going down that path long before this TV Land thing ever surfaced."

"That path" was the path of cashing in on Salem's witch backstory, something the town has been doing for a while (that is, police officers have a witch and broom stitched into their uniform emblems; at Halloween, various costume shops and haunted-houses open, etc.). Yet, for residents such as John Carr, the camp was getting a little out of hand. "God bless the mayor, but he thinks that statue is contemporary art," Carr said at the time. "The whole idea is bad taste beyond belief." Either way all these years later, the controversy has subsided, and Lizzie's stilted bronzed presence remains.

"Unfortunately," Thomas Hill was unable to attend the statue's dedication, so he has "little recollection of the imbroglio," but he's sympathetic with the historians who "didn't want this dark chapter in Early American history to be treated frivolously. But, naturally, I see America's pop culture history as a valid inspiration for public art."

However, Hill does recall TV Land's President Larry Jones partaking in a TV news discussion program during which he defended the statue against someone representing the historically minded. "But the show had also booked a third guest, representing the modern day *Wicca* perspective—pro-witch, I suppose?"

Hill concludes, this particular Wiccan's presence "made the entire debate appear rather absurd." Consequently, despite even her physical absence, Lizzie's name—and likeness—remained infused with political conflict and social issues—and she would have loved it.

On January 4, 2008, at yet another ceremony, this time presided over by honorary mayor Johnny Grant in Hollywood, California, Lizzie finally received her star on the Hollywood Walk of Fame. In attendance at the rain-drenched ceremony were a multitude of her fans, including radio host and journalist Jone Devlin, who recounts her experience of that day:

> It was a cold, blustery, day, very rainy. Yet in spite of the awful weather, there was a good sized crowd there—and most of us arrived literally hours early just to be ensured of a *good spot*. Everyone in the group was happy and excited, sharing their memories of *Bewitched* and Elizabeth Montgomery and happily greeting people that they'd only ever *met* on *Bewitched* websites. The presentation was wonderful, touching and heartfelt, but what I remember the most is how everyone stayed for the entire thing . . . even when it was pouring down icy rain, even when people's umbrellas gave out, drenching them and everyone around them, even when a small brook began to form beneath our feet as the drainage system lost its race with the driving downpour. To me that, above everything else was a testimony to how much Elizabeth Montgomery meant to her fans and friends; and it is a moment I'll never forget.

Devlin and her fellow *Bewitched* fans then heard special memories shared from Lizzie's children Rebecca and Billy Asher, friend Liz Sheridan and Robert Foxworth. Each of those who spoke mentioned how delighted Lizzie would have been with the ceremony. The downpour of rain, which all speakers believed she would have found amusing, could not compete with the outpour[ing] of respect from the loved ones and fans who attended the event despite the cloudburst. "It is *so* awesome that it is raining," Rebecca said at the ceremony. "I can't even really express it. She [Lizzie] is so happy right now."

According to Devlin, Rebecca went on to explain how there are not many things more gratifying than seeing "someone you care about" being recognized for their work, especially if that individual happens to be a parent. Rebecca then described her mother as "an incredible human being . . . full of grace and wit and beauty and brilliance." How every day, Lizzie brought a sense of wonder to everything she did, and gave a unique perspective to everything she rested her eyes upon. In short, Rebecca enthused, "She was incredible!"

Rebecca then expressed how she and her brothers Billy, Jr. and Robert appreciated how they directly experienced their mother's influence on the lives of others. They saw it that day at the ceremony, and continue to see it every day in the eyes of those who find out that they're Lizzie's children. Rebecca said her mother worked hard and always challenged herself and her audience with the characters she chose to play. Rebecca expressed how much she and her brothers always loved their mom and still do; how proud they remain of her; how honored they were to have been present at the ceremony on their mother's behalf. Rebecca then thanked the crowd for their loyalty to Lizzie, and left the podium.

At which point, Bob Foxworth approached the podium, and delivered an equally heart-felt and revealing sentiment. He began by defining Lizzie as shy, a quality of her character and personality that he said benefitted her life and career. He said her shy demeanor added a special sparkle to every character she portrayed because in the process of discovering who the character was she would "dig into herself and reveal someone that maybe she didn't even know she was."

Consequently, to each of her roles Lizzie brought a special quality, whether it's with what Foxworth called "women of the west," as in TV films like *Belle Star* or *The Awakening Land*, the latter of which he described as a "beautiful and historical film," or *The Legend of Lizzie Borden*, which he called "a classic for television." Each time, he said, she revealed more of herself—"it was like the peeling of an onion."

Foxworth was certain that the crowd was well aware of her comedic talents by way of *Bewitched*. But what they might not have known, he said, was that Lizzie was "hysterically funny" in her private life as well. He explained how she was not "terribly enamored with the glitz and glitter of Hollywood," how she would much rather dirty her fingers in the garden than get "all gussied up" and attend some "fancy function," and even though she loved doing that, too, it wasn't her favorite thing in the world.

Foxworth then concluded his speech as he had started it, saying, "She was a very private person and that sense of privacy came from her shyness."

But when it came to advocating for young minds or human rights, the ill or disadvantaged, Lizzie's personal objectives took a backseat to compassion and concern for others . . . for better or for worse. More times than not, "she had a lot of problems with her self-confidence," Bill Asher said in 2001 on *Headliners & Legends*. So, she stayed home a great deal. She could at times be considered a Hollywood recluse. Other times, not so much, because she enjoyed parties, especially if they were charity events.

In keeping with her indeterminate style, she kept everyone guessing, while one thing was certain: Elizabeth had little desire to age.

Ginger Blymer is a retired movie hairdresser whose famous clientele included the likes of Natalie Wood, Sean Connery, Tom Cruise, Tom Hanks, Meg Ryan, and more. She worked with Lizzie on *The Awakening Land* and *Belle Starr*, both of which Foxworth had defined as classic films about "women of the west."

In 2002, Blymer authored *Hairdresser to the Stars: A Hollywood Memoir* (Infinity Publishing), in which she remembers how much Lizzie loved horses, the racetrack, games, and any sort of mental competition; how Elizabeth's home was filled with "wonderful things," like a merry-go-round-horse in the bar, and a hundred pillows on her bed. At Christmas, Blymer wrote, there were amazing decorations throughout Lizzie's home. "The staircase with pine wound up the bannister. It smelled great."

Blymer also recalled how Lizzie once called Foxworth "the love of her life"; how Blymer talked with him shortly after Elizabeth passed away; how he told her that Lizzie never wanted to get old.

"So, she didn't."

☆

Award-winning actress, comedienne, talk show host, writer, political blogger, social advocate, and comedienne Lydia Cornell is a loyal fan of both Elizabeth's and *Bewitched*.

Best known as *Sara Rush*, the "virginal blonde bombshell" on the classic sitcom, *Too Close for Comfort*, Cornell became one of the most popular blonde female sex symbols of the 1980s, as was Elizabeth in the 1960s. On *Comfort*, Cornell was the happy-go-lucky TV daughter of the Emmy-winning Ted Knight, who had found fame playing the egotistical anchorman *Ted Baxter* on *The Mary Tyler Moore Show* in the 1970s. Off *Comfort*, Cornell was struggling with an addiction to alcohol and drugs.

Beginning with the discovery of her young brother's body after he died of a drug overdose, Cornell has endured one shattering personal tragedy after the other. At one point, she says, "I had three boys and two dogs, including my husband, and they were all going through puberty at the same time." Her stepson, whom she raised since the age of four, suffers from brittle bone disease. "He's amazing," she adds.

Cornell's pretty amazing, too. In 1994, she halted her substance abuse during a "catastrophic spiritual awakening." Today, she is a grateful recovering alcoholic, who mentors teens and is a motivational speaker for recovery groups across the country. "Every bad thing I've ever been through has turned out to be something good or something hilarious. I have turned it all into comedy, somehow. I am grateful for every 'wrong turn.'"

Lydia's poignant stories of transformation are laced with an innate sense of humor and comic timing, some of which was inspired by Lizzie. She explains:

> *Bewitched* was my favorite show growing up. What a beautiful, wonderful soul Elizabeth Montgomery was! I looked up to her as a role model. She had this mysterious secret intelligence behind the eyes, which gave me hope as a woman in a man's world in Hollywood. There was nothing vacuous, shallow or *bimbo* about her.

As to any personal struggles that Elizabeth may or may not have had with substance abuse, Cornell says:

My heart goes out to her. As an artist who struggled with alcoholism, I know full-well the darkness that clouds the joys. At seventeen years sober, I have found that nothing in the material world, no drink, drug, marriage, lover or career success can fill that hole in our heart with a permanent peace until we seek a spiritual solution. I only wish she could have found the peace she was seeking while she was alive. Like Steve Jobs, I believe our secret lives and the resentments or bad thoughts we harbor about ourselves and others often fuel our *diseases* which show up as a reflection of our deeply engrained mindset.

A mindset Ed Asner (who co-starred with Cornell's TV dad Ted Knight on *The Mary Tyler Moore Show*) believes may have been instilled into Elizabeth by her father Robert Montgomery. "Maybe that's where the cancer came from?" Asner suggests. Or maybe it stemmed from a combination of a number of sources?

Whether an actor, singer, dancer, writer, or director, be it for the big screen, TV, or the stage, there are many prevalent and destructive patterns that develop for those within every section of the entertainment industry. The fame, the money, the perks: it all becomes intoxicating and self-destructive, in more ways than one.

For one, Whitney Houston's tragic death from a toxic mix of drugs, drowning, and alcohol on the eve of the Grammy Awards in 2012 shocked the world. Consequently, on March 8, 2012, *The Los Angeles Times* published an informative article about the rampant substance abuse issue pervading the music industry in particular. *The Day the Music Died* was written by Randy Lewis, who wondered, "If celebrities who have access to every resource available can't get help, what hope is there for the majority of people who haven't even experienced the smallest fraction of their success?"

Or as Harold Owens, senior vice president of MusiCares/Musicians Assistance Program (MAP) Fund told the *Los Angeles Times*, "You can't reach an addict when he's not ready." Owens should know. He's been counseling others in substance abuse since he became sober approximately twenty-five years ago. "I've been through the struggle," he said. "To an alcoholic, I like to think it's a self-diagnosed disease: Nobody can tell you you're an alcoholic until you tell yourself."

Suffice it to say, Lizzie may have joked about drinking in interviews with John Tesh and Ronald Haver, and may have even joked about wanting pina coladas poured into her IV on her deathbed (as was explained in *People Magazine*, June 5, 1995). She may have inherited a drinking problem from her mother and her paternal grandfather Henry Montgomery, Sr. Her father Robert Montgomery may have driven her to drink. Her relationship with the father-figure alcoholic Gig Young may have increased that drinking. The social drinking era of the 1960s may have camouflaged her drinking issues. Her drinking issues may even have compromised her relationships with her peers, thus cutting her chances for any Emmy victories, and on and on.

Either way, if she had any real issues with alcohol, Lizzie never acknowledged them, at least not publically. She may have admitted it to herself, or to her family and maybe a few close friends. but not to the world, and no medical documentation or statement was ever made to suggest it.

Maybe that's all because, as Liz Sheridan had expressed on MSNBC's *Headliners & Legends* in 2001, Elizabeth never wanted to face anything that was "bad or ugly." Upon learning that Lizzie had cancer, or even when she was started to lose weight, Sheridan believed her friend was in that "huge state of denial."

In essence, Lizzie may have been inadvertently "protected" from the truth, because admitting the truth in such instances of substance abuse or even potential substance abuse, usually hurts. However, nothing hurts more than death.

Studies have shown that alcoholism contributes to and exacerbates colon cancer, which is what killed Lizzie. Her weight also seemed to fluctuate over the years, if ever so subtly. And research has proven that weight fluctuation also contributes to colon cancer.

The bottom line is this: Whatever adversities Lizzie may have failed to conquer, that doesn't tarnish her memory, or make her a *bad* person. Her losses, just as much as her victories, merely make her a human person. She was someone who cared for others, but somehow neglected her own well-being. She may have needed help in certain areas, but didn't know how to seek it, and then ultimately never received it, for whatever reason. Either way, she's not any less wondrous a being who brought countless hours of magic to the world. And her death may not have been in vain.

As Harold Owens went on to tell the *Los Angeles Times*, "There's a harsh saying, 'Some must die so that others can live.' I think the impact that the deaths of Freddie Mercury and Rock Hudson had on the public perception of AIDS are a good analogy to the situation we have now."

Randy Lewis of the *Times* also interviewed Recording Academy President Neil Portnow, who has worked in the music industry since the 1970s as a record producer, music supervisor, and record company executive. Portnow said:

> We need to have a clear-cut understanding of (substance abuse) as a disease, the things that lie behind it and the things that are necessary to treat it. Given the breadth and scope of who this affects in our culture, a more healthy perspective would be very welcome.

Or as Lewis himself deduced, "If (Whitney) Houston's death contributes to a broader understanding of addiction and substance abuse, her legacy might include more than the million-selling recordings she left behind."

In like manner, if Lizzie's demise contributes to the same, on supposition alone, her legacy might include so much more than *Bewitched*, her TV-movies, and even her charitable work while she was alive.

AFTERWORD

Elizabeth Montgomery may have placed too much emphasis on age, and she may or may not have made the best choices with regard to her health, consciously or subconsciously. Either way, she died much too young and long before her time.

Instead of expiring at a ripe old age, following the climactic incidents of what, by most accounts (wealth, fame, good looks) was a happy (public and private) life, Elizabeth swiftly withered away, taking with her extraordinary occurrences, circumstances, and situation comedies and dramas. Instead of her death momentously culminating with a massive celebrity funeral that could have easily been monitored by a widespread audience as a spectacular turn of events, she protected with great dignity a personal agony from becoming a three-ring circus (that she would never have invited *to town*).

She gave herself little credit for artistic accomplishments that also failed to win the formal acceptance of her peers. Her life had been full, exciting, difficult, short, and then she died, without the usual large-scale Hollywood horns and whistles services that have become popular in recent years.

Sometime before or after that, Lizzie's body was cremated, and she departed into a timeless realm, a world of the ageless.

Beyond the unbreakable bond with her devoted children, Lizzie's most intimate relationships with husbands and friends were not always the lengthiest. Her link with her parents, particularly her father, wasn't always the healthiest. Although she never won the coveted TV Emmy amulet and once deemed herself unworthy of any "Mother-of-the-Year" award, the lives of everyone she touched—be they family members, co-workers, peers, recipients of her altruism, once-close friends, or all-too-distant fans—were indelibly changed forever, and for the better.

For the ever-shy Lizzie, such illumination, by way of her celebrated birth in the limelight to later carving out her own celebrity status, came with a lofty price. The public perception of the fanciful *Samantha*, coupled with the high expectations of her father and her lack of confidence, was overwhelming, even for someone who was used to the glimmer and clutter of Hollywood. Robert Montgomery, her most influential relative, may have been her severest critic. Rebecca Allen, her most beloved grandmother, may have been her most loving influence. But Lizzie herself was her own worst enemy.

She lacked certain career ambitions, but still pushed herself too hard. She was raised in a chic environment, but her surroundings were under-pinned with a weak foundation. She craved the *average* life, clamored for it away from what often becomes the false glitter of Hollywood. As an adult, she rejoiced in the simplest of pleasures, whether seeing a movie or sharing a pizza (as she would sometimes do with the crew on any one of her TV sets). Such everyday experiences were foreign and nonexistent in her pro-tected and privileged youth.

But as she matured, she retained a youthful spirit. She abhorred haughti-ness, but at times could be perceived as much too proud. She welcomed routine conversation, but entertained power-lunch types. She reveled in the spectacle of everyday living, but like most TV and film personalities, felt the periodic anguish that was magnified by celebrity status—a status that was placed upon her extremely likable persona. As Bill Asher said on 1999's *Bewitched: The E! True Hollywood Story*, it was "hard not to" like Elizabeth.

Asher met the criteria of the father-figure type that frequently caught her eye, an appeal also evident in her second marriage to Gig Young, whom she wed after divorcing her first husband Fred Cammann, who was her contemporary in age (she was twenty-one, he was twenty-four).

Her fourth husband Bob Foxworth was eight years her junior and fell outside the confines of the father-figure scenario, although his first name matched that of her dad's. They had met on the set of *Mrs. Sundance* in 1973, two years after the original network demise of *Bewitched*, not one episode of which Foxworth had ever seen and a creative staple that Lizzie wanted to leave behind. She was immediately enchanted with Foxworth who in turn fell expediently under her still potent spell.

Had she and Cammann met at a later time and place, their marriage may have stood the test of time. Instead they wed too young amidst the sophomoric pretense of high society that left them ill-prepared to meet the responsibilities required to make a mature marriage work.

Lizzie was a sophisticated and cultured descendent of American royalty, a royalty that may have had a skeleton or two in its closets, but royalty nonetheless. Throughout it all, she was still imbued with a delightful candor and near naiveté that some in even the most economically challenged families may never grasp. Although not metaphysical like *Samantha*, she was just as heavenly in her appeal. She may have lacked the magical capabilities of her most celebrated role, but that only meant she was a mere mortal like the rest of us, flaws and all. We're all human. We all make mistakes. To quote the title of Doug Tibbles' third-season opening *Bewitched* episode—the show's first color segment, and one in which we learn that *Sam* and *Darrin's* little daughter *Tabitha* has supernatural powers just like her mom—"Nobody's Perfect."

Although Lizzie lived a colorful life, textured with various hues, she did not have super powers like *Samantha* or even *Tabitha,* but she retained a super spirit. Even in her darkest hour, she shined her bright light, and we all basked in her glow.

With or without conscious clarity of her mission, she accomplished extraordinary levels of charitable work, via the fame by which she felt sometimes burdened. For her it was the worst of times, the best of times. The fun, enchanting woman that bewitched us all was periodically bothered and bewildered by an era that she helped create. She seemed much too ready and only strong enough to "pop out" one last time, possessing until the end a complex inner glow and beauty that was coupled with an insecurity that at times was publicly perceived as unassuming poise, and yet a legitimate poise, refined in the finishing school of life.

Overwrought by an underlining thread of sorrow that seeped into, was expressed by, and heralded in her later dramatic TV films, her psyche may have been drained. Pummeled by colorectal cancer, her body had no chance of recovery. Overpowered and racked with emotion, she may not have lost the will to live, but merely succumbed to the difficult decision to die.

Yet before it was too late, prior to the unbearable pain, there was a break in the black cloud of her turmoil. Knowing Lizzie, she realized it was okay to be remembered and so dearly loved by so many people so many years after she turned the world on with her twitch. She realized that, in the eyes of those who love truly, in the *big picture*, flaws and blemishes, physical or otherwise, are endearing, identifiable, and ultimately acceptable, leading to growth of the soul.

From this perspective, and in the eyes of millions, she remains a *supernatural* presence in the fondest way. Her physical being is no longer here, but her metaphysical spirit remains with countless performances: recorded on television, in film, online, in audio, in print, in word, and in deed.

Although not especially religious, she was a spiritual person. For as she once said, rather profoundly, in reflecting on the true priorities of her life and career, "I think of God as the beauty of life. It's loving and being loved."

For family members, friends, colleagues, and countless fans, she was and remains both loving and loved. Elizabeth Montgomery may be gone from this world, but Lizzie is nowhere near forgotten by this world. She lives on in her work and in the cherished memories of those who knew her personally and in what has come to be known in certain esoteric circles as the collective subconscious.

Along this mystical, magical stream of thought, some believe our journey is mostly a spiritual one, with our final destination likened to a rocket soaring into space. The pieces of us that we don't need, namely, all the negative stuff, melt away as we move closer to what some call the "Light," until all that is left is the little capsule that holds our soul.

If true, and why not believe it so, then Lizzie's capsule is missing her father's critical voice, her own self-doubt, the failed relationships, the dark performances, the Emmy losses, the political divide, her missteps, and any and all disease.

All that's left are the positive, productive thoughts—the happy horseback rides, the victories, all of the hugs and kisses she gave and received, her carefree spirit, the countless hours of laughter she instilled by way of her more joyful performances, the generous acts of loving-kindness that she displayed and experienced, and the indelible spark of intelligence that gleamed in her pretty green eyes—all bundled together, magnified, and multiplied somewhere *above*. It is her good deeds, fine work, and noble heart, mind, and soul which have become her immeasurable, priceless, and immortal legacy on Earth.

As her friend Bud Baker wrote nearly fifty years ago, using one of her favorite words, "Bad tomorrows don't exist for her," from here on in, "they're all going to be good for her. That's the great rudder in the turbulent waters of show business, this sense of balance. There is always going to be a dawn and green grass and sun, kids to play with and footballs to kick. . . . She's having *fun*."

In this sense, Elizabeth's . . . Lizzie's . . . Lizbel's ethereal essence is somewhere beautiful, nose-wriggling the light fantastic, leaving Hollywood to wonder if it will ever again emanate a more luminary . . . twitch upon a star.

"We are quicksilver, a fleeting shadow, a distant sound.
Our home has no boundaries beyond which we cannot pass.
We live in music, a flash of color.
We live on the wind and in the sparkle of a star."

—The *Bewitched* witches' anthem

APPENDIX

LIVE ON STAGE

Brigadoon (summer stock, circa 1952)

Biography (summer stock, Luise Rainer Company, circa 1952)

Late Love (National Theatre and the Booth Theatre, Broadway, 1953)
Opened: 10-13-53 Closed: 1-2-54 Performances: 95

The Loud Red Patrick (Ambassador Theatre, Broadway, 1956)
Opened: 10-3-56 Closed: 12-22-56 Performances: 93

Romanoff and Juliet (summer stock, Plymouth Theatre, 1956)
Opened: 10-10-56 Closed: unknown Performances: 389

Cat on a Hot Tin Roof (Bell Theatre, Los Angeles, 1978)
Opened: 3-5-78 Closed: 3-11-78 Performances: approximately 9

Love Letters (1989, The Promenade, Off-Broadway/Edison Theatre on Broadway)
Opened: 10-31-89 Closed: 1-21-90 Performances: 96

TV GUEST STAR ROLES

Robert Montgomery Presents (NBC, 1950–57, 60 minutes, twenty-eight episodes):
"Top Secret" (12-3-51), "The Half-Millionaire a.k.a. The Vise" (7-6-53), "Two of
a Kind" (7-13-53), "A Summer Love" (7-20-53), "Anne's Story" (7-27-53),
"Duet for Two Hands" (8-3-53), "Red Robin Rides Again" (8-10-53), "Pierce
3098" a.k.a. "Whom Death Has Joined Together" (8-27-53), "Grass Roots"
(8-24-53), "Our Hearts Were Young and Gay" (2-15-54), "Once Upon a
Time" (5-31-54), "In His Hands" (6-28-54), "The Expert" a.k.a. "The Mar-
riage Expert" (7-5-54), "Story on Eleventh Street" (7-12-54), "It Happened in
Paris" (7-19-54), "Patricia" (7-26-54), "Home Town" (8-2-54), "About Sara
Caine" (8-9-54), "Personal Story" (8-23-54), "A Matter of Luck" (8-30-54),

"The People You Meet" (9-6-54), "Ten Minute Alibi" (9-13-54), "The Bao-bab Tree" (4-23-56), "Dream No More" (7-21-56), "Catch a Falling Star" (7-23-56), "Southern Exposure" (7-30-56), "The Company Wife" (8-27-56), "Mr. Parker's Rhubarb" (9-3-56)

Armstrong Circle Theatre (NBC/CBS, 1950–63, 30/60 minutes, two episodes): "The Right Approach" (6-2-53), "The Millstone" (1-19-54)

Kraft Television Theatre (NBC, 1947–58, 60 minutes, six episodes): "The Light is Cold" (9-22-54), "Patterns" (1-12-55, 2-9-55), "The Diamond as Big as the Ritz" (9-28-55), "The Last Showdown" (4-11-56), "The Long Arm" (7-11-56), "The Duel" (3-6-57)

Studio One in Hollywood (CBS, 1948–58, 60 minutes, three episodes): "Summer Pavilion" (5-2-55), "The Drop of A Hat" (5-7-56), "A Dead Ringer" (3-10-58)

Appointment with Adventure (CBS, 1955–56, 60 minutes, two episodes): "Relative Stranger" (11-20-55), "All Through the Night" (2-5-56)

Warner Brothers Presents (ABC, 1955–56, 60 minutes): "Siege" (2-14-56)

Climax! (CBS, 1954–58, 60 minutes): "The Shadow of Evil" (5-24-56)

Playhouse 90 (CBS, 1956–60, 90 minutes): "Bitter Heritage" (8-7-58)

Suspicion (NBC, 1957–59, 60 minutes): "The Velvet Vault" (5-19-58)

The DuPont Show of the Month (CBS, 1957–61, 90 minutes): "Harvey" (9-22-58)

Cimarron City (NBC, 1958–60, 60 minutes): "Hired Hand" (11-15-58)

Alfred Hitchcock Presents (CBS, 1955–62, 30 minutes): "Man with a Problem" (11-16-58)

The Loretta Young Show (NBC, 1953–61, 30 minutes): "Marriage Crisis" (2-15-59)

The Third Man (BBC, syndicated in U.S., 1959–65, 30 minutes): "A Man Takes a Trip" (4-15-59)

Riverboat (NBC, 1959–61, 60 minutes): "The Barrier" (9-20-59)

Johnny Staccato (NBC/ABC, 1959–60, 60 minutes): *Tempted* (11-19-59)

Wagon Train (NBC, 1957–65, 60 minutes): "The Vittorio Bottecelli Story" (12-16-59)

The Tab Hunter Show (NBC, 1960–61, 30 minutes): "For Money or Love" (9-25-60)

Alcoa Presents: One Step Beyond (ABC, 1959–61, 30 minutes): "The Death Waltz" (10-4-60).

The Untouchables (ABC, 1959–63, 60 minutes): "The Rusty Heller Story" (10-13-60)

The Twilight Zone (CBS, 1959–64, 30/60 minutes): "Two" (9-15-61)

Thriller (NBC, 1960–62, 60 minutes): "Masquerade" (10-30-61)

Frontier Circus (CBS, 1961–62, 60 minutes): "Karina" (11-9-61)

Checkmate (CBS, 1960–62, 60 minutes): "The Star System" (1-10-62)

Alcoa Premiere (ABC, 1961–63, 60/30 minutes): "Mr. Lucifer" (11-1-62)

Saints and Sinners (NBC, 1962–63, 60 minutes): "The Home-Coming Bit" (1-7-63)

Boston Terrier (6-11-63, 30 minutes, ABC): "Salem Witch Hunt"

Burke's Law (ABC, 1963–66, 60 minutes, two episodes): "Who Killed Mr. X?" (9-27-63), "Who Killed His Royal Highness?" (2-21-64)

Rawhide (CBS, 1959–66, 60 minutes): "Incident at El Crucero" (10-10-63)

77 Sunset Strip (ABC, 1958–64, 60 minutes): "White Lie" (10-25-63)

The Eleventh Hour (NBC, 1962–64, 60 minutes): "The Bronze Locust" (11-6-63)

Bewitched (ABC, 1964–72)

Season One (1964–65)

1) "I *Darrin*, Take This Witch, *Samantha*"; 2) "Be It Ever So Mortgaged"; 3) "Mother, Meet What's His Name?"; 4) "It Shouldn't Happen to a Dog"; 5) "Help, Help, Don't Save Me"; 6) "Little Pitchers Have Big Fears"; 7) "The Witches Are Out"; 8) "The Girl Reporter"; 9) "Witch or Wife"; 10) "Just One Happy Family"; 11) "It Takes One to Know One"; 12) ". . . And Something Makes Three"; 13) "Love is Blind"; 14) "*Samantha* Meets the Folks"; 15) "A Vision of Sugar Plums"; 16) "It's Magic"; 17) "A is for Aardvark"; 18) "The Cat's Meow"; 19) "A Nice Little Dinner Party"; 20) "Your Witch is Showing"; 21) "Ling Ling"; 22) "Eye of the Beholder"; 23) "Red Light, Green Light"; 24) "Which Witch is Which?"; 25) "Pleasure O'Riley"; 26) "Driving is the Only Way to Fly"; 27) "There's No Witch Like an Old Witch"; 28) "Open the Door, Witchcraft"; 29) "Abner Kadabra"; 30) "George the Warlock"; 31) "That Was My Wife"; 32) "Illegal Separation"; 33) "A Change of Face"; 34) "Remember the Main"; 35) "Eat at Mario's"; 36) "*Cousin Edgar*"

Season Two (1965–66)

37) "Alias *Darrin Stephens*"; 38) "A Very Special Delivery"; 39) "We're in for a Bad Spell"; 40) "My Grandson, the Warlock"; 41) "The Joker is a Card"; 42) "Take Two Aspirins and Half a Pint of Porpoise Milk"; 43) "Trick or Treat"; 44) "The Very Informal Dress"; 45) "And Then I Wrote"; 46) "Junior Executive"; 47) "*Aunt Clara's* Old Flame"; 48) "A Strange Little Visitor"; 49) "My Boss the Teddy Bear"; 50) "Speak the Truth"; 51) "A Vision of Sugarplums"; 52) "The Magic Cabin"; 53) "Maid to Order"; 54) "And Then There Were Three"; 55)

"My Baby the Tycoon"; 56) "*Samantha* Meets the Folks"; 57) "Fastest Gun on Madison Avenue"; 58) "The Dancing Bear"; 59) "Double Tate"; 60) "*Samantha* the Dressmaker"; 61) "The Horse's Mouth"; 62) "Baby's First Paragraph"; 63) "The Leprechaun"; 64) "Double Split"; 65) "Disappearing *Samantha*"; 66) "Follow that Witch (Part One)"; 67) "Follow that Witch (Part Two)"; 68) "A Bum Raps"; 69) "Divided He Falls"; 70) "Man's Best Friend"; 71) "The Catnapper"; 72) "What Every Young Man Should Know"; 73) "The Girl with the Golden Nose"; 74) "Prodigy"

Season Three *(1966–67)*

75) "Nobody's Perfect"; 76) "The Moment of Truth"; 77) "Witches and Warlocks Are My Favorite Things"; 78) "Accidental Twins"; 79) "A Most Unusual Wood Nymph"; 80) "*Endora* Moves in for a Spell"; 81) "Twitch or Treat"; 82) "Dangerous Diaper Dan"; 83) "The Short Happy Circuit of *Aunt Clara*"; 84) "I'd Rather Twitch Than Fight"; 85) "Oedipus Hex"; 86) "*Sam's* Spooky Chair"; 87) "My Friend Ben (Part One)"; 88) "*Samantha* for the Defense (Part Two)"; 89) "A Gazebo Never Forgets"; 90) "Soap Box Derby"; 91) "*Sam* in the Moon"; 92) "Ho Ho the Clown"; 93) "Super Car"; 94) "The Corn is as High as a Guernsey's Eye"; 95) "The Trial and Error of *Aunt Clara*"; 96) "Three Wishes"; 97) "I Remember You . . . Sometimes"; 98) "Art for *Sam's* Sake"; 99) "Charlie Harper, Winner"; 100) "*Aunt Clara's* Victoria Victory"; 101) "The Crone of Cawdor"; 102) "No More Mr. Nice Guy"; 103) "It's Wishcraft"; 104) "How to Fail in Business with All Kinds of Help"; 105) "Bewitched, Bothered and Infuriated"; 106) "Nobody But a Frog Knows How to Live"; 107) "There's Gold in Them There Pills"

Season Four *(1967–68)*

108) "Long Live the Queen"; 109) "Toys in Babeland"; 110) "Business, Italian Style"; 111) "Double, Double Toil and Trouble"; 112) "Cheap, Cheap"; 113) "No Zip in My Zap"; 114) "Birdies, Bogeys and Baxter"; 115) "The Safe and Sane Halloween"; 116) "Out of Synch, Out of Mind"; 117) "That Was No Chick, That Was My Wife"; 118) "Allergic to Ancient Macedonian Dodo Birds"; 119) "*Samantha's* Thanksgiving to Remember"; 120) "Solid Gold Mother-in-Law"; 121) "My, What Big Ears You Have"; 122) "I Get Your Nanny, You Get My Goat"; 123) "Humbug Not Spoken Here"; 124) "*Samantha's* Da Vinci Dilemma"; 125) "Once in a Vial"; 126) "Snob in the Grass"; 127)" If They Never Met"; 128) "Hippie, Hippie, Hooray"; 129) "A Prince of

a Guy"; 130) "McTavish"; 131) "How Green Was My Grass"; 132) "To Twitch Or Not To Twitch"; 133) "Playmates"; 134) *"Tabitha's* Cranky Spell"; 135) "I Confess"; 136) "A Majority of Two"; 137) *"Samantha's* Secret Saucer"; 138) "The No-Harm Charm"; 139) "Man of the Year"; 140) "Splitsville"

Season Five (1968–69)

141) *"Samantha's* Wedding Present"; 142) *"Samantha* Goes South for a Spell"; 143) *"Samantha* on the Keyboard"; 144) *"Darrin* Gone and Forgotten"; 145) "It's So Nice to Have a Spouse Around the House"; 146) "Mirror, Mirror on the Wall"; 147) *"Samantha's* French Pastry"; 148) "Is it Magic or Imagination?"; 149) *"Samantha* Fights City Hall"; 150) *"Samantha* Loses Her Voice"; 151) "I Don't Want to Be a Toad"; 152) "Weep No More, My Willow"; 153) "Instant Courtesy"; 154) *"Samantha's* Super Maid"; 155) *"Cousin Serena* Strikes Again (Part One)"; 156) *"Cousin Serena* Strikes Again (Part Two)"; 157) "One Touch of Midas"; 158): *"Samantha* the Bard"; 159) *"Samantha* the Sculptress"; 160) *"Mrs. Stephens,* Where Are You?"; 161) "Marriage, Witches' Style; 162) "Going Ape"; 163) *"Tabitha's* Weekend"; 164) "The Battle of Burning Oak"; 165) *"Samantha's* Power Failure"; 166) *"Samantha* Twitches for UNICEF"; 167) "Daddy Does His Thing"; 168) *"Samantha's* Good News"; 169) *"Samantha's* Shopping Spree"; 170) *"Samantha* and *Darrin* in Mexico City"

Season Six (1969–70)

171) *"Samantha* and the Beanstalk"; 172) *"Samantha's* Yoo-Hoo Maid"; 173) *"Samantha's* Caesar Salad"; 174) *"Samantha's* Curious Cravings"; 175) "And Something Makes Four"; 176) "Naming *Samantha's* New Baby"; 177) "To Trick or Treat or Not to Trick or Treat"; 178) "A Bunny for *Tabitha*"; 179) *"Samantha's* Secret Spell"; 180) "Daddy Comes for a Visit (Part One)"; 181) *"Darrin* the Warlock (Part Two)", 182) *"Samantha's* Double Mother Trouble"; 183) "You're So Agreeable"; 184) "Santa Comes to Visit and Stays and Stays"; 185) *"Samantha's* Better Halves"; 186) *"Samantha's* Lost Weekend"; 187) "The Phrase Is Familiar"; 188) *"Samantha's* Secret Is Discovered"; 189) *"Tabitha's* Very Own *Samantha*"; 190) "Super Arthur"; 191) "What Makes *Darrin* Run"; 192) *"Serena* Stops the Show"; 193) "Just a Kid Again"; 194) "The Generation Zap"; 195) "Okay, Who's the Wise Witch?"; 196) "A Chance on Love"; 197) "If the Shoe Pinches"; 198) "Mona *Sammy*"; 199) "Turn on the Old Charm"; 200) "Make Love, Not Hate"

Season Seven (1970–71)

201) "To Go or Not to Go, That is the Question (Part One)"; 202): "Salem, Here We Come (Part Two)"; 203) "The Salem Saga (Part One)"; 204) "*Samantha's* Hot Bed Warmer (Part Two)"; 205) "*Darrin* on a Pedestal"; 206) "Paul Revere Rides Again"; 207) "*Samantha's* Bad Day in Salem"; 208) "*Samantha's* Old Salem Trip"; 209): "*Samantha's* Pet Warlock"; 210) "*Samantha's* Old Man"; 211) "The Corsican Cousins"; 212) "*Samantha's* Magic Potion"; 213) "Sisters at Heart"; 214) "Mother-in-Law of the Year"; 215) "Mary, the Good Fairy (Part One)"; 216) "The Good Fairy Strikes Again (Part Two)"; 217) "Return of *Darrin* the Bold"; 218): "The House That *Uncle Arthur* Built"; 219) "*Samantha* and the Troll"; 220) "This Little Piggie"; 221) "Mixed Doubles"; 222) "*Darrin* Goes Ape"; 223) "Money Happy Returns"; 224) "Out of the Mouths of Babes"; 225) "*Sam's* Psychic Slip"; 226) "*Samantha's* Magic Mirror"; 227) "Laugh, Clown, Laugh"; 228) "*Samantha* and the Antique Doll"

Season Eight (1971–72)

229) "How Not to Lose Your Head to King Henry VIII (Part One)"; 230) "How Not to Lose Your Head to King Henry VIII (Part Two)"; 231) "*Samantha* and the Loch Ness Monster"; 232) "*Samantha's* Not-So-Leaning Tower of Pisa"; 233) "Bewitched, Bothered, and Baldoni"; 234) "Paris, Witches' Style"; 235) "The Ghost Who Made a Spectre of Himself"; 236) "TV or Not TV"; 237) "A Plague on Maurice and *Samantha*"; 238) "Hansel and Gretel in *Samantha*-land"; 239) "The Warlock in the Gray Flannel Suit"; 240) "The Eight-Year Witch"; 241) "Three Men and a Witch on a Horse"; 242) "Adam, Warlock or Washout"; 243) "*Samantha's* Magic Sitter"; 244) "*Samantha* is Earthbound"; 245) "*Serena's* Richcraft"; 246) "*Samantha* on Thin Ice"; 247) "*Serena's* Youth Pill"; 248) "*Tabitha's* First Day at School"; 249) "George Washington Zapped Here (Part One)"; 250) "George Washington Zapped Here (Part Two)"; 251) "School Days, School Daze"; 252) "A Good Turn Never Goes Unpunished"; 253) "*Sam's* Witchcraft Blows a Fuse"; 254) "The Truth, Nothing But the Truth, So Help Me, *Sam*"

BEWITCHED-RELATED PERSONAL APPEARANCES

"Chevrolet's *Bewitched* Bonanza Commercial" (9-27-64)
"Lux Beauty Soap Commercial" (broadcast in Canada, 1965)

"ABC Fall Preview Special" (August 1965)
"Jan & Dean" (unsold series pilot, 1966)

General Personal Appearances

Igor Cassini "Movie Revival Ball" (1953–54) Segment: 11-1-53

Here's Hollywood (NBC, 1960–62, 30 minutes) Segment: 6-15-61

The Mike Douglas Show (syndicated, 1963–82, 90/60 minutes) Segment: 11-4-66

The Hollywood Palace (ABC, 1964–70, 60 minutes) Segment: 10-1-66

The Tournament of Roses Parade (1-2-67, ABC)

The Joey Bishop Show (ABC, 1967–69, 90 minutes) Segment 12-22-67

Password (CBS, 1961– 67/ABC, 1971–75, 30 minutes) Segments: December 12–16, 1966; May 15–19, 1967; May 5–9, 1971; September 13–17, 1971; November 29–December 3, 1971; February 7–11, 1972; July 17–21, 1972; October 2–6, 1972; December 4–8, 1972; April 9–13, 1973; June 11–15, 1973; November 19–23, 1973; January 7–11, 1974; April 22–26, 1974; July 15–19, 1974; July 29–August 2, 1974; March 24–28, 1975

Password Plus (NBC, 1979–82, 30 minutes) Segments: January 8–12, 1979; February 26–March 2, 1979; July 30–August 3,1979

The Hollywood Squares (NBC, 1966–81, 30 minutes) Segments: November 9–13, 1970; May 1–5, 1972; June 19–23, 1972; November 10–14, 1975; January 19–23, 1976

The Merv Griffin Show (syndicated, 1962–86, 90/60 minutes) Segment: 12-21-70

The 28th Annual Tony Awards (NBC, 4- 21-74, 120 minutes)

"Japanese Cook" commercials (eight in total, 1980–83)

Entertainment Tonight (syndicated, 1981– present, 30 minutes/60 minutes) Segments: 12-21-85, 2-18-91, 3-25-94

CBS Morning Show (1987–99, 120 minutes) Segments: 1-24-90, 5-12-92

KCBS News (Los Angeles CBS affiliate) Segment: 2-19-91

One on One with John Tesh (NBC, 1991–92, 30 minutes) Segment: 5-12-92

The Dennis Miller Show (syndicated, 1992–2004, 60 minutes) Segment: 5-8-92

The Los Angeles Gay and Lesbian Pride Parade (6-28-92)

TV-Movies

The Spiral Staircase (NBC, 10-4-61, 60 minutes)

The Victim (ABC/Universal, 11-14-72, 90 minutes)

Mrs. Sundance (ABC/20th Century Fox Television, 1-15-74, 90 minutes)

A Case of Rape (NBC/Universal, 2-20-74, 100 minutes)

The Legend of Lizzie Borden (ABC/Paramount Television, 2-10-75, 100 minutes)

Dark Victory (NBC/Universal, 2-5-76, 150 minutes)

A Killing Affair (CBS/Columbia, 9-21-77, 100 minutes)

The Awakening Land (NBC/Warner Bros., 420 minutes, three-part mini-series):
"The Trees" (2-19-78), "The Fields" (2-20-78), "The Town" (2-21-78)

Jennifer: A Woman's Story (NBC/Marble Arch, 3-5-79, 120 minutes)

Act of Violence (CBS/Paramount Studios, 4-10-79, 100 minutes)

Belle Starr (CBS/Hanna-Barbera, 4-20-80, 97 minutes)

When the Circus Came to Town (CBS/Entheos Prods/Meteor Films, 1-20-81, 90 minutes)

The Rules of Marriage (CBS, 5-10/5-11-82, two-part film, 240 minutes)

Missing Pieces (CBS/Entheos Unlimited, 5-14-83, 96 minutes)

Second Sight: A Love Story (CBS, 3-13-84, 100 minutes)

Amos (CBS, 9-25-85, 100 minutes)

Betweeen the Darkness and the Dawn (NBC, 12-23-85, 100 minutes)

Hallmark Hall of Fame: Face to Face (CBS, 1-24-90, 93 minutes)

Sins of the Mother (CBS, 2-19-91, 93 minutes)

With Murder in Mind (CBS/Bob Banner Associates, 5-12-92, 100 minutes)

The Black Widow Murders: The Blanche Taylor Moore Story (CBS, 5-3-93, 92 minutes)

The Corpse Had a Familiar Face (CBS, 3-27-94, 120 minutes)

Deadline for Murder: From the Files of Edna Buchanan (CBS, 5-9-95, 92 minutes)

FEATURE FILMS

Your Witness (a.k.a. *Eye Witness*) (U.K./released in U.S. 8-26-50)

The Court-Martial of Billy Mitchell (Warner Bros., 12-31-55, 100 minutes)

Bells are Ringing (MGM, 6-23-60, 126 minutes)

Johnny Cool (United Artists/Chrislaw Productions, 10-2-63, 103 minutes)

Who's Been Sleeping in My Bed? (Paramount/Amro-Claude-Mea, 12-26-63, 103 minutes)

How to Stuff a Wild Bikini (MGM, 7-14-65, 93 minutes)

Bewitched (Sony/Columbia, 2005, 90 minutes)

VOICEOVERS

On the Radio

Craven Street (five-part radio play, 1993)

Appendix

For Audio Books

Beauty's Punishment and *Beauty's Release* (Publisher, 1994, each 180 minutes)
When We Were Very Young (Penguin Audio, 5-12-1995)

In Movies

Bikini Beach (American International Pictures, release date: 7-22-64, 99 minutes)
Cover Up: Behind the Iran Contra Affair (Empowerment Project Studios, 7-13-88, 72 minutes)
The Panama Deception (Empowerment Project Studios, 7-31-92, 91 minutes)

On Laserdisc

Here Comes Mr. Jordan *(Columbia, 1991, Laser Disc Audio Track, 88 minutes)*

On Televison

The Flintstones (ABC, 1960–66, 30 minutes): episode: *"Samantha"* (10-22-65)
Batman: The Animated Series (Warner Bros., syndicated, 1992–95, 22 minutes): episode: "Showdown" (9-12-95)

AWARDS AND ACCOLADES

The Daniel Blum Theater World Award

1953: Most Promising Newcomer (*Late Love*)

Emmy Nominations

1961: Outstanding Single Performance by an Actress in a Leading Role (*The Untouchables*)
1966: Outstanding Lead Actress, Comedy Series (*Bewitched*)
1967: Outstanding Lead Actress, Comedy Series (*Bewitched*)
1968: Outstanding Lead Actress, Comedy Series (*Bewitched*)
1969: Outstanding Lead Actress, Comedy Series (*Bewitched*)
1970: Outstanding Lead Actress, Comedy Series (*Bewitched*)
1974: Outstanding Lead Actress, Drama Series (*A Case of Rape*)
1975: Outstanding Lead Actress in a Special Program, Drama/Comedy (*The Legend of Lizzie Borden*)
1978: Outstanding Lead Actress in a Limited Series (*The Awakening Land*)

Golden Globe Nominations

1965: Golden Globe Award Best TV Star, Female (*Bewitched*)
1966: Golden Globe Award Best TV Star, Female (*Bewitched*)
1969: Golden Globe Award Best TV Star, Female (*Bewitched*)
1971: Golden Globe Best TV Actress, Musical/Comedy (*Bewitched*)

Other Awards

Laurel Awards Nomination
1964: Golden Laurel Top Female, New Face (Fourth Place)

The Women in Film Crystal + Lucy Awards
In recognition of excellence and innovation in creative works that have enhanced the perception of women through the medium of television.
In 1995, The Lucy Award went to Elizabeth Montgomery, accepted by Rebecca Asher

TV Land
Superlatively Supernatural Series
2004: Winner: *Bewitched*

Favorite Dual-Role Character
2003: Nominated: *Samantha/Serena, Bewitched*

2005: Honorary Statue
Elizabeth Montgomery as *Samantha Stephens*, Salem, MA

Star on Hollywood Walk of Fame
2008: Hollywood, CA
Accepted by Rebecca Asher and William Asher, Jr.

"Elizabeth Montgomery was an inspired choice to play a witch, because her natural affect was such a perfect counterpoise to the traditional Halloween witch. Fit and beautiful, with a bright and sunny disposition, she was one of those rare beauties who somehow remain accessible, oblivious to their own powerful allure."

—Thomas Hill, Vice President, TV Land (2012)

"Elizabeth Montgomery was TV's version of Grace Kelly . . . a legend . . . so wonderful at playing comedy, drama, and romance. She was one of a kind and is sorely missed."

—Monika Cottrill, television historian (2012)

"Thank you."

—Elizabeth Montgomery, on *The Dennis Miller Show*, responding to enthusiastic audience members voicing their adoration: "I love you" and "We all do"! (May 12, 1992)

SOURCES

Many organizations, publishers, books and publications, documents, and online sources proved invaluable to the writing of this book, beginning with:

Jon Mulvaney of The Criterion Collection, who granted generous permission to quote excerpts from Ronald Haver's interviews with Elizabeth Montgomery that are heard on the 1991 audio commentary from the fiftieth anniversary laserdisc release of the Robert Montgomery film, *Here Comes Mr. Jordan*; Eileen Spangler of *TV Guide* magazine; Steve R. Biller at *Palm Springs Life* magazine; Gwen Feldman from Silman-James Press; Claudia Kuehl and Joan "Joey" York for the excerpts from *The Seesaw Girl and Me: A Memoir* by Dick York; James Pylant and his online article, "The Bewitching Family Tree of Elizabeth Montgomery," from www.genealogymagazine.com; Rene Reyes, Martin Gostanian, and Gary Browning at The Paley Center for Media in Beverly Hills, California, where, on February 27, 2012, and March 2, 2012, I was graciously allowed access via Console 11 in the Scholars' Room to view the following programs: *Appointment with Adventure*: "Relative Stranger" (original airdate: CBS, 11-20-55), *The Spiral Staircase* (original airdate: NBC, 10-4-61), *Kraft Television Theatre*: *Patterns* (original airdate: NBC, 1-12-55), *Mr. Lucifer* (original airdate: NBC, 11-1-62), *Kraft Television Theatre*: *The Diamond as Big as the Ritz* (original airdate: NBC, 9-28-55); Jim Pollock at MSNBC; and Kevin Burns at Prometheus Entertainment.

Additional sources that were referenced for this book include *The Complete Directory to Prime Time Network and Cable TV Shows* by Tim Brooks and Earle Marsh; *Total Television* by Alex McNeil; www.bobsbewitching daughter.com; www.earlofhollywood.com; www.harpiesbizarre.com; www .bewitched.net; and www.imdb.com.

Portions of chapter 8, "Spirits and Demons," were drawn from *Final Gig: The Man Behind the Murder* by George Eells (Houghton Mifflin, 1991).

Portions of chapter 10, "Lizmet," were drawn from *Please Don't Shoot My Dog: The Autobiography of Jackie Cooper* (William Morrow, 1981).

Additional book sources include: *Heavenly Bodies: Remembering Hollywood and Fashion's Favorite AIDS Benefit* by Michael Anketell (Taylor Publishing Company, 1999); *Sweethearts of '60s TV: The Women of Action, Dream Wives, Girls Next Door, Comic Cuties, and Fantasy Figures from Your Favorite Shows* by Ronald L. Smith (S.P.I. Books, 1993); *Straight Shooting* by Robert Stack (Berkley Books, 1981); *Everything Is Going to Be Just Fine: The Ramblings of a Mad Hairdresser* by Billy Clift (Everything Is Going To Be Just Fine Society, 1998), among others.

Various commentary and references from articles from *TV Guide* appear throughout this book, and all such commentary and references appear courtesy of *TV Guide Magazine*, LLC. (See full list on in Periodicals section of Bibliography.)

In all, new quotes and commentaries that appear in this book were culled from exclusive interviews with Elizabeth Montgomery and selected individuals; conversations that took place directly with the author in person, via telephone in 1988 and 1989, or in person or via telephone in 2011 and 2012. Additional quotes and commentaries were resourced from various magazine, newspaper, or TV interviews and/or documentaries relating to or about Elizabeth Montgomery, and dated from 1933 to 1995. TV and movie character quotes were culled from various fictional TV show or films associated with the roles performed by Elizabeth Montgomery and her co-stars in scripted performances from 1953 to 1995.

The television program and film character quotations and actor commentaries from the various nonfiction and fiction TV shows or movies are reproduced within this book for educational purposes and/or in the spirit of publicity for those particular productions, be they scripted or unscripted in nature.

In each case, every effort was made to acknowledge specific credits whenever and wherever possible, and we apologize in advance for any omissions, and will undertake every effort to make any appropriate changes in future editions of this book if necessary.

BIBLIOGRAPHY

BOOKS

Anketell, Michael. *Heavenly Bodies: Remembering Hollywood and Fashion's Favorite AIDS Benefit*. Dallas. Taylor Publishing Company. 1999.

Arce, Hector. *Gary Cooper: An Intimate Biography*. New York. Bantam Books. 1980.

Barney, William Clifford. Preston, Eugene Dimon. Editors. *Genealogy of the Barney Family in America* (Springfield, Virginia: Barney Family Historical Association, reprinted 1990), entry 3251.

Blymyer, Ginger. *Hairdresser to the Stars: A Hollywood Memoir*. Infinity Publishing. PA. 2002.

Brooks, Tim. Marsh, Earle. *The Complete Directory to Prime Time Network and Cable TV Shows (1946–Present)*. Ninth Edition. New York. Ballantine Books. 2007.

Boyer, G. Bruce. Cooper Janis, Maria. Lauren, Ralph. Ansel, Ruth. *Gary Cooper: Enduring Style*. PowerHouse Books. 2011.

Burnett, Carol. *This Time Together: Laughter and Reflection*. New York. Harmony Books. 2010.

Carpozi, George. *The Gary Cooper Story*. New Rochelle, New York. Arlington House. 1970.

Clift, Billy. *Everything Is Going to Be Just Fine: Ramblings of a Mad Hairdresser*. Everything Is Going to Be Just Fine Society. 1998.

Cooper, Jackie. *Please Don't Shoot My Dog: The Autobiography of Jackie Cooper*. New York. William Morrow & Company. 1981.

Cooper Janis, Maria. Hanks, Tom. *Gary Cooper Off Camera: A Daughter Remembers*. Harry N. Abrams. 1999.

Dunne, Dominick. *The Way We Lived Then: Recollections of a Well-Known Name Dropper*. Crown. September 1999.

Eells, George. *Final Gig: The Man Behind the Murder*. Harcourt Brace Jovanovich. 1991.

Esposito, Joe. *Remember Elvis.* TCB JOE Enterprises. 2006.

Grams, Jr., Martin. *The Twilight Zone: Unlocking the Door to a Television Classic.* OTR Publishing. Maryland. 2008.

Jordan, Rene. *Gary Cooper.* Utica, New York. Pyramid. 1974.

Karol, Michael. *The ABC Movie of the Week Companion.* September 1977. (*The Abilene Reporter-News*; Texas).

Lamparski, Richard. *Whatever Became Of . . . ?* Volume III. New York. Ace Books. 1970.

McClure, Rhonda R. *Finding Your Famous (& Infamous) Ancestors.* Cincinnati. Betterway Books. 2003.

McNeil, Alex. *Total Television: A Comprehensive Guide to Programming from 1948 to the Present.* New York. Penguin. 1991.

Parrish, James Robert. Pitts, Michael R. *The Great Western Pictures.* Scarecrow Press. 1976.

Pilato, Herbie J *Bewitched Forever.* Texas. Tapestry Press. 2004.

Pilato, Herbie J *The Bewitched Book.* New York. Dell. 1992.

Podell, Janet. Editor. *The Annual Obituary.* St. Martin's Press. 1982.

Russo, J. Anthony. *Creativity or Madness: The Passion of a Hollywood Bit Player.* BookSurge Publishing. 2005.

Wayne, Jane Ellen. *Cooper's Women.* Prentice Hall Press. 1988.

Smith, Ronald L. *Sweethearts of '60s TV.* S.P.I. Books. March 1993.

Stack, Robert (with Mark Evans). *Straight Shooting.* New York. Macmillan. 1980.

Stetler, Susan L. *Biography Almanac. Volume 1.* Detroit. Gale Research Company. 1987.

Thompson, Gary. *Gary Cooper (Great Stars).* Faber & Faber. 2010.

Wayne, Jane Ellen. *Cooper's Women.* New York. Prentice Hall Press. 1988.

Wright, John W. (a passage from). *History of Switzerland County, Indiana. From their Earliest Settlement.* Chicago. Weakley, Harriman & Co. Publishers. 1885.

York, Dick. *The Seesaw Girl and Me: A Memoir.* New Jersey. New Path Press. 2004.

Zicree, Mark Scott. *The Twilight Zone Companion.* Second Edition. Los Angeles. Silman James Press. 1992.

PERIODICALS

Anderson, Nancy. "Liz Montgomery's Mother Role." Online. *Ladies' Circle.* July 1970. Downloaded January 7, 2012.

Ardmore, Jane. "An Old Beau Tells All about Liz Montgomery's Past." Online. *TV Radio Mirror.* September 1967. Downloaded January 7, 2012.

Ardmore, Jane. "Elizabeth Montgomery: My Two Husbands Are Expecting." Online. *Silver Screen*. September 1965. Downloaded January 7, 2012.

Ardmore, Jane. "How Would You Like to Try My Sourdough Bread?" Online. *TV Radio Mirror*. September 1966. Downloaded January 7, 2012.

Armstrong, Lois. Cortina, Betty. Gliatto, Tom. "That Magic Feeling." *People*. June 5, 1995. pp. 42–47.

Asher, William. "The Love Letter that Made Liz Montgomery Weep." Online. *TV Radio Mirror*. *July 1967*. Downloaded January 7, 2012.

Barbee, Pat. "Featuring Elizabeth Montgomery and Robert Foxworth at Home." *Beverly Hills 213*. February 5, 1992.

Bell, Joseph N. Bell. "TV's Witch to Watch." Online. *Pageant*. April 1965. Downloaded March 7, 2012.

Bostick, Jim. "Salem's *Bewitched* Statue." *Gather Entertainment*. June 19, 2006. Online. December 12, 2006. Downloaded March 26, 2012.

Brandt, Lily. "Liz Montgomery Says: I Hope This Spell Lasts." Online. *Inside Movie*. October 1966. Downloaded January 7, 2012.

Braxton, Greg. "Ed Asner Revisits Hawaii." *Los Angeles Times*. March 19, 2012.

Burroughs, K.V. "Elizabeth Montgomery Divorcing." Online. *Movieland and TV Time*. September 1972. Downloaded January 7, 2012.

Butterfield, Alan. "*Bewitched* Star's Brave Last Days." *National Enquirer*. May 30, 1995.

Chance, Tabitha. "From *Bewitched* to Besieged." *TV Guide*. November 10, 1979. pp. 14–16.

Cook, B.W. "William Asher: The Man Who Invented the Sitcom." *Palm Springs Life*. December 1999.

Deane, Ellen. "Liz Montgomery Says: Too Much Happiness is a Bad Thing." Online. *TV Circle*. August 1970. Downloaded January 7, 2012.

Del Valle, David. "Getting Lizzie with It." Camp David. May 18, 2010.

Dozier, William. "The Man Who Helped Deliver a $9000 Baby Tells How It Happened." *TV Guide*. January 27, 1968. pp. 15–18.

Efron, Edith. "He's Almost Invisible in the Glare of Success." *TV Guide*. May 29, 1965.

Elber, Lynn. "*Bewitched* Star Dies from Cancer." *Fort Worth Star-Telegram*. May 19, 1995.

Fischer, Paul. "Interview: Nicole Kidman." Online. www.darkhorizons.com. Downloaded June 6, 2005.

Fleishman, Jeffrey, and Johnson, Glen. "Pan Am 103 Bomber Dies in Tripoli." *The Los Angeles Times*. May 21, 2012.

Francis, Terry. "One of These Babies is a Witch: Only Samantha Knows Its Real Life Secret." Online. *TV Radio Mirror*. 1966. Downloaded January 7, 2012.

George, Lewis. "Now Liz is a Shooting Star!" *Globe*. 1980.

Hano, Arnold. "Rough, Tough and Delightful: The Ashers Agree on What They Want, Including Who's the Boss." *TV Guide*. May 13, 1967. pp. 19–22.

Hesse, Earle. "Liz Montgomery Confesses: Those TV Ratings Give Me the Willies (Yes, Even When I'm on Top of Them)." Online. www.harpiesbizarre.com. *Screen Stars*. August 1965. Downloaded March 22, 2012.

Holland, Jack. "What Makes Samantha Run?" Online. *TV Mirror*. March 1968. Downloaded January 7, 2012.

Hubbard, Ben. "Lockerbie Bomber in Coma, Near Death, Brother Says." Online. *Associated Press*. Downloaded August 29, 2011.

Jacques, Steve. "A Case of Rape: Liz and the Secret Fear All Women Face." 1974.

Jason, Jackie. "Elizabeth Montgomery's Baby Book." Online. *TV Photo Story*. April 1966. Downloaded January 7, 2012.

Kaufman, Bill. "Plummer Joins the Circus to Romance Former Witch." *The Toronto Star*. January 20, 1981 (Newsday).

Kessner, Jane. "*Bewitched*'s Liz Montgomery: My Husband Pushes Me Around (And I Love It!)." Online. *Motion Picture*. September 1966. Downloaded January 7, 2012.

Kessner, Jane. "Her Past Catches Up with Liz Montgomery." Online. *TV Radio Mirror*. April 1970. Downloaded January 7, 2012.

Landy, Jane. "Liz Montgomery's Real-Life Miracle." Online. *Modern Screen*. July 1970. Downloaded January 7, 2012.

Lewis, Richard Warren. "Double, Double, Toil and Trouble." *TV Guide*. November 28, 1964. pp. 20–23.

Lim, Dennis. "That Special Cassavetes Touch." *The Los Angeles Times*. May 27, 2012.

Massarella, Linda. "*Bewitched* Star Dies of Cancer." *The New York Post*. May 19, 1995

Mayher, Jane. "Sisters at Heart: A Very Special *Bewitched*." Online. *TV Picture Life*. December 1971. Downloaded January 7, 2012.

McCabe, Kathy. "*Bewitched* Statue Charms Salem Fans." Online. *The Boston Globe*. June 16, 2005. Downloaded January 7, 2012.

McCartney, Anthony. "Drowning Killed Houston but Drugs Took High Toll." Online. *Associated Press*. Downloaded March 23, 2012.

McConnaughey, Janet. "Settlement in *Elly Mae Clampett* Barbie Doll Suit." Online. *Associated Press*. Downloaded December 12, 2011.

Perlberg, Rose. "Natural Childbirth: What Liz Montgomery Says." Online. *TV Picture Life*. October 1965. Downloaded January 7, 2012.

Post, Kathleen. "A Second Baby, A Special Problem." Online. *TV Radio Mirror*. November 1966. Downloaded January 7, 2012.

Post, Kathleen. "To Hex With Sex: How Liz Montgomery Found Something Even Better." Online. *TV Radio Mirror*. June 1965. Downloaded January 7, 2012.

Pylant, James. "The Bewitching Family Tree of Elizabeth Montgomery." Online. www.genealogymagazine.com. Downloaded. February 8, 2012.

Rand, Flora. "Pregnant Liz Montgomery Tells Why: My Next Baby Will Be Born on TV!" Online. *TV Radio Mirror*. August 1965. Downloaded January 7, 2012.

Resnick, Sylvia. "The Day Liz Montgomery Drew Closer to God." Online. *TV Radio Mirror*. February 1970. Downloaded January 7, 2012.

Sanders, Lynn. "Elizabeth Montgomery Sounds Off on Parents, Protesters and the Problems of the Generation Gap." Online. *Silver Screen*. October 1970. Downloaded January 7, 2012.

Searle, Ronald. "Wherein a Dastardly Plot is Uncovered by Our Artist, Ronald Searle." *TV Guide*. June 18, 1966. pp. 15–18.

Segal, David. "*Bewitched* Statue Bothers Some in Salem." Online. *Washington Post*. May 10, 2005. Downloaded January 7, 2012.

Stang, Joanne. "The Bewitching Miss Montgomery Hollywood." Online. *New York Times*. November 22, 1964. Downloaded January 7, 2012.

Starr, Jacqueline. "Liz Montgomery Worries: Are My Babies in Danger?" Online. *Screen Stars*. August 1967. Downloaded January 7, 2012.

Wilkie, Jane. "Two Babies in One Year: 11 Babies in Five Years." Online. *TV Radio Mirror*. November 1969. Downloaded January 7, 2012.

Windeler, Robert. "TV's Top Series Add Ingredients." Special to *New York Times*. Hollywood. July 20, 1967.

Winelander, Nancy. "Liz Montgomery Tells: How Her New Baby Made Her More of a Mother." Online. *TV Picture Life*. May 1970. Downloaded January 7, 2012.

Winelander, Nancy. "This is the Baby Liz Montgomery Thought She Could Never Love!" Online. *TV Picture Life*. October, 1969. Downloaded March 17, 2012.

"Cheers & Jeers." *TV Guide*. July 16, 1994. p. 6.

"Dressing Up for Parties." *TV Guide*. October 30, 1953. p. 22.

"Like Dad, Like Daughter." *TV Guide*. July 24, 1953. pp. 8–9.

"More Montgomery Magic." Online. *TV-Movies Today*. August 1975. Downloaded January 7, 2012.

"Salem's Samantha Statue." *New England Travels*. Online. October 30, 2007. Downloaded March 26, 2012.

"Samantha Goes Home." *TV Guide*. September 5, 1970. pp. 6–7.

"Samantha/Jeannie: The Debate Continues." *TV Guide*. August 27, 1994. p. 29.

"10 Actresses Pick Hollywood's Greatest Lovers." Online. *Photoplay*. February 1965. Downloaded January 7, 2012.

"The Tide Has Turned for Elizabeth Montgomery." *TV Guide*. August 19, 1961. pp. 8–10 (also titled on p. 8 as "Along Came the Untouchables").

"TV Breaks Old Taboos with New Morality." *Jet*. December 1, 1977.

"TV Land Landmark Immortalizes Samantha Stephens of *Bewitched* in Salem." Online. *PR Newswire*. June 15, 2005. Downloaded March 27, 2012.

ADDITIONAL SOURCES

Bewitched: The E! True Hollywood Story. August 22, 1999. Recorded on videotape.

Biography. A&E. February 15, 1999.

CBS This Morning. January 24, 1990. Recorded on videotape.

CBS This Morning. May 12, 1992. Recorded on videotape.

Cheers & Jeers. TV Guide. July 16, 1994. p. 6.

The Earl of Hollywood: The Life and Career of Robert Montgomery (www.earl ofhollywood.com).

"Elizabeth Makes Bell Ring." *Minneapolis Star-Tribune*. March 30, 1980.

"Elizabeth Montgomery Reveals Surprising Truth Behind Squeaky-Clean '60s Sitcom." *National Enquirer*. August 4, 1992.

Internet Movie Database (www.imdb.com).

Lawrence Witte Static. *Denton Journal*. Denton, Maryland. November 20, 1964.

The Mike Douglas Show. November 4, 1966.

"More Montgomery Magic." Online. *TV-Movies Today*. August 1975. Downloaded January 7, 2012.

MSNBC's *Headliners & Legends*. August 1, 2001. Recorded on videotape.

One on One with John Tesh. May 12, 1992. Recorded on videotape.

Salem's Samantha Statue. New England Travels. Online. October 30, 2007. Downloaded March 26, 2012.

Samantha Goes Home. TV Guide. September 5, 1970. pp. 6–7.

Samantha/Jeannie: The Debate Continues. TV Guide. August 27, 1994. p. 29.

Social Security Death Index, Online.

10 Actresses Pick Hollywood's Greatest Lovers. Online. Photoplay Magazine. February 1965. Downloaded January 7, 2012.

Thomas Crane Library. "Lee Remick, Quincy Star of TV and Movies Bride of William A. Colleran in New York City." St. Vincent Ferrer Church. August 3, 1957.

The Tide Has Turned for Elizabeth Montgomery. TV Guide. August 19, 1961. pps. 8-10 (Also titled on p. 8 as *Along Came the Untouchables.*)

"TV Breaks Old Taboos with New Morality." *Jet.* December 1, 1977.

William Asher's 2003 interview with father and daughter team Terry and Tiffany DuFoe, today of www.cultradioagogo.com.

TV Land Landmarks Immortalizes Samantha Stephens of Bewitched in Salem. Online. PR Newswire. June 15, 2005. Downloaded March 27, 2012.

www.emmytvlegends.org/interviews/people/william-froug

www.hw.com

www.spenceschool.org

1870 U.S. Census U.S. Census of Kings County, New York, population schedule, Brooklyn, 6th ward. Dwelling 643, family 1017; National Archives microfilm M593-948.

1900 U.S. Census of Dutchess County, New York, population schedule, town of Fishkill, ED 8, SD 3, sheet 15, p. 148A, dwelling 271, family 331; National Archives microfilm T623-1022.

1900 U.S. Census of Kings County, New York, population schedule, Brooklyn, ED 356, SD 2, sheet 7. National Archives microfilm T623-1022.

1920 U.S. Census of Dutchess County, New York, population schedule, Beacon, enumeration district (ED) 6, supervisor's district (SD) 7, sheet 11B, p. 216, dwelling 217, family 217, National Archives microfilm T625-0197.

1930 U.S. Census of Los Angeles County, California, Los Angeles. ED 19-68. 2815-24-25.

ACKNOWLEDGMENTS

Twitch Upon a Star is a result of the support, talent, diligence, and general enthusiastic assistance from several individuals, not the least of which was Elizabeth Montgomery. Who could have known that the unpublished excess of our original *Bewitched* interviews would later be incorporated into this new biography on her entire life and career? She generously offered her time, memories, and boundless energy, and this book simply and clearly would not have been possible without the unique imprint of her remarkable personality, wit, words, and wisdom.

I appreciate everyone who granted interviews for this book, each of whom delivered intimate recollections, professional perspective, and insight into Elizabeth's illustrious life and career in either, 2009, 2011, and 2012 via telephone, email, or in-person: Peter Ackerman, Ed Asner, Bonnie Bartlett, Christian Beltram, Ray Caspio, Lydia Cornell, Ronny Cox, William Daniels, Jone Devlin, Kenneth Gehrig, Florence Henderson, Thomas Hill, DD Howard, Kenneth Johnson, Sally Kemp, David Knell, June Lockhart, David Mixner, Kathy Perillo, David Pierce, James Pylant, Rob Ray, Cliff Robertson, Ed Robertson, Saundra Santiago, Eric Scott, Randy Skretvedt, Doug Tibbles, Charles Tranberg, Lin Bolin Wendkos, Dan Weaver, David White, and Vince Staskel.

Into this mix, entertainment historian Thomas McCartney and his unending efforts, knowledge, and extensive research into the archives of Elizabeth Montgomery and all media proved to be an invaluable resource. Tom is worth his weight in gold and is the best in the business. There is no way this book would have become what it is without him.

I would also like to thank the professional and courteous team at Taylor Trade Publishing, including although not limited to editorial director Rick

Rinehart, acquisitions editor Flannery Scott, senior production editor Alden Perkins, copyeditor Jocquan Mooney, and Kalen Landow, director of marketing and publicity, all of whom trusted, believed in, and supported my vision for this book. They are a testament to integrity and patience in the world of publishing.

An especially grateful acknowledgement is extended to my representative Roger J. Kaplan who worked exhaustively in seeing this project through long before we had a publisher.

Although the following individuals did not grant interviews directly for his book, they provided substantial memories from my previous interviews (from 1988 through 1990) and/or conversations (from 2001 to 2006) that were incorporated into this book: Harry Ackerman, Billy Asher, Jr., Rebecca Asher, Richard Bare, Frederic G. Cammann, John L. Greene, Art Metrano, Richard Michaels, Kasey Rogers, Sol Saks, Dick Sargent, Dick York, Irene Vernon, and especially William Asher, Sr. If it hadn't been for Bill (who passed away shortly before this book went to print), I would never have met Elizabeth. No matter how many times he was married before or after he was with Elizabeth, it was always abundantly clear that she remained the love of his life. And now they're together again . . . forever.

Further appreciation to the following for inspiration in a variety of ways that contributed to this book in one way or the other over a twenty-year span: Meredith Asher, Robert Asher, Abigail Borwick, Carol Burnett, Elinor Donahue, Michael Dambers, Dominick Dunne, Brian Feinblum, Bernard Fox, Robert Foxworth, William Froug, Alice Ghostley, Sandra Gould, Michael Greenwald, Angie Horejsi, David Lawrence, Greg Lawrence, Dewey Mee, Diane Murphy, Erin Murphy, Ben Ohmart, Wendy Ogren, Melanie Parker, Alice Pearce, Scott Penney, Steve Randisi, Brendan Slattery, Ed Spielman, John Scheinfeld, Charles Sherman, Tom Stevenson, Steve Thompson, Fredrick Tucker, Dan Wingate, and Karen L. Herman, Director, Archive of American Television, Academy of Television Arts and Sciences Foundation.

Additional gratitude is expressed to many dear friends for their unfailing support in countless ways: Chris Alberghini, Sam Amato, Rudy Anderson, Matt Asner, George Barrett III, Lex Blaackman, Thomas Centron, Matthew

Acknowledgments

Cook, Jim Cutaia, Giovanna Curatalo, Danny Gold, Kathe Finucane, Lawrence Finucane, Tamara A. Fowler, Cindy Heiden, Jim Heil, Martha Hinds, Ann Hodges, Roger Hyman, David Keil, Mark Langlois, Jeff Lindgren, Monica Lindgren, Andrea (Whitcomb) May, Marty McClintock, Gwen Patrick, Marypat Pena, John Perevich, Rene Piacentini, Louis Tomassetti, Peter Tomassetti, Frank Torchio, Thomas Warfield, Lele Winkley, and Carol Zazzaro.

The stamina required to complete this book could not have been sustained without the unconditional love and guidance provided by my sister Pamela R. Mastrosimone, brother-in-law Sam Mastrosimone; nephew Sammy Mastrosimone; my cousins Marie Burgos, Nicolas Burgos, Noreen D'Agostino, Eva Easton-Leaf, David Leaf, Mary Sue Wiengard, Susie Arioli, Gerald Maranca, my aunt Susan Borelli, and my uncle Vincent Tacci.

A special note of thanks to the kind and encouraging loved ones and friends who are no longer here, but who offered a great deal of support through the years: Mary Turri, Elva and Carl Easton, Tony and Anna Fort, Rita (Turri) Tacci, Rita Valerie, Val and Amelia Valerie, Angelo and Alice Schiano, Jerry and Fay Maranca, Frank and Alice Arioli, Anthony Pilato, Ludwig Pilato, Sonny Turri, Pat Borrelli, Donny Arioli, Linda and Mario Bosio, Doris Prince, and my beautiful dog, Boo Boo.

Continued gratitude to Love-Is-God who I believe not only lives in the *Light,* but *is* the Light—an awe-inspiring source that constantly offers instructions as to how we are to best lead our lives for the highest good of all those concerned. All we have to do is listen . . . the instructions are sometimes delivered through whispers and dreams; other messages are loud and clear (Thank God!).

A particularly personal note of deep appreciation to my parents who have passed into spirit: Herbert Pompeii and Frances Turri Pilato or, as they are now known in the Light, *Saint Pompeii* and *Saint Frances of Turri.* When I think of them, I think of life itself, and a great spiritual instruction that directly contributed to this book:

Honor Thy Mother and Father not only commands us to respect our parents while they are alive, but directs us to live fully the life we've been granted by way of them after they're gone.

Elizabeth Montgomery did that. She lived fully the life she was given via her mother Elizabeth Allen and father Robert Montgomery, as well as through her maternal grandmother Rebecca Allen, all of whom, for better or worse, were core figures in the development of her refined character.

By completing this story of Elizabeth's life and career, which is a reflection on the past, I have finished a chapter in my own journal, and will continue to embrace my life and vocation to the best of my ability.

In doing so, I honor my mother and father . . . as well as the great mother and father of us all.

SUGGESTED READING

BOOKS

Bewitched Forever: The Immortal Companion to Television's Most Magical Supernatural Situation Comedy (Special 40th Anniversary Edition) by Herbie J Pilato (Tapestry, 2004)

The Bewitched Book: The Cosmic Companion to TV's Most Magical Supernatural Situation Comedy by Herbie J Pilato (Dell, 1992)

I Love the Illusion: The Life and Career of Agnes Moorehead (BearManor Media, 2009)

The Bewitched History Book: The Omni-Directional Three-Dimensional Vectoring Paper Printed Omnibus for Bewitched Analysis by David Pierce (BearManor Media, 2012)

Everything Is Going to Be Just Fine: The Ramblings of a Mad Hairdresser by Billy Clift (Everything Is Going to Be Just Fine Society, 1998)

Dizzie and Jimmy: My Life with James Dean: A Love Story by Liz Sheridan (Regan Books, 2000)

Hollywood Left and Right: How Movie Stars Shaped American Politics by Steven J. Ross (Oxford University Press, 2011)

WEBSITES

www.harpiesbizarre.com

www.bewitched.net

www.bobsbewitchingdaughter.com

http://earlofhollywood.com/

http://montgomeryin-moviesondvd.blogspot.com/

http://bewitchedcollector.tripod.com/

http://vicmas.tripod.com/sight.html/

www.mischahof.com/bewitched

www.1164.com

www.asherguitars.com
www.elvispresleynews.com
www.emmytvlegends.org
www.jeanniebottles.com
www.tvconfidential.net
http://stusshow.com/
www.queervoices.org
www.stonecoyotes.com
www.classictvps.blogspot.com

INDEX

Page numbers in *italic* indicate illustrations. Numbers preceded by *C* indicate color inserts; numbers followed by lower-case letters indicate black-and-white inserts following those respective pages.

ABOUT THE AUTHOR

As the author of *Bewitched Forever* (Tapestry, 2004) and *The Bewitched Book* (Dell, 1992) writer/actor/producer **Herbie J Pilato** has researched, studied, and chronicled the life and career of Elizabeth Montgomery, and the history of *Bewitched*, its content, and development, for countless TV shows, magazines, newspapers, and websites. He has appeared on hundreds of radio shows around the world and has served as a consultant and commentator for A&E's *Biography* of Elizabeth Montgomery; *Bewitched: The E! True Hollywood Story*, *Entertainment Tonight's* tribute to Elizabeth Montgomery; *Entertainment Tonight's* weekend special on *Bewitched*; Nora Ephron's *Bewitched* feature film of 2005; Sony's DVD release of the original *Bewitched* series; and Sony Signature's licensing of *Bewitched* merchandise.

Pilato is also the author of *NBC & ME: My Life As A Page In A Book* (BearManor Media, 2010); *Life Story: The Book of Life Goes On* (BearManor Media, 2008); *The Bionic Book* (BearManor Media, 2007); *The Kung Fu Book of Wisdom* (Tuttle, 1995); and *The Kung Fu Book of Caine* (Tuttle, 1993). He has worked as a producer, consultant, and commentator for the TV Guide Channel's five-part series, *TV's 100 Most Memorable Moments*; TLC's *Behind the Fame* specials on *The Mary Tyler Moore Show*, *The Bob Newhart Show*, *L.A. Law*, and *Hill Street Blues*; Bravo's five-part series, *The 100 Greatest TV Characters*; as well as for the DVD releases of *Kung Fu* and *CHiPs*.

Pilato has also been published in magazines such as *Sci-Fi Entertainment*, *Sci-Fi Universe*, *Starlog*, *Classic TV*, *Cinema Retro*, *Retro Vision*, and *Electronic House*.

As an actor, Pilato has appeared on daytime serials *General Hospital* and *The Bold and the Beautiful*, and classic TV shows like *Highway to Heaven* and *The Golden Girls*. As a public relations representative for NBC in the 1980s,

Pilato worked on *The Tonight Show* starring Johnny Carson, the Bob Hope Specials, *An All-Star Salute to President Ronald "Dutch" Reagan*, and the *1984 Democratic Debates*, among countless other TV shows and specials.

Pilato presently writes the heralded *Classic TV Corner* blog for Jack Myers' renowned mediabizbloggers.com, and is the president and creative director for Pop-Culture Consultants, an entertainment consulting firm. He lives in Cerritos, California, where he founded *The Classic TV Preservation Society*, a nonprofit organization that seeks to close the gap between popular culture and education.